# A Psychoanalysis for a Reemergent Humanity

SUNY series, Insinuations: Philosophy, Psychoanalysis, Literature
———————
Charles Shepherdson, editor

# A Psychoanalysis for a Reemergent Humanity

## The Metapsychology of Willy Apollon

Edited by

LUCIE CANTIN, JEFFREY S. LIBRETT,
and TRACY MCNULTY

EU GPSR Authorised Representative:
Logos Europe, 9 rue Nicolas Poussin, 17000, La Rochelle, France
contact@logoseurope.eu

For information, contact State University of New York Press, Albany, NY
www.sunypress.edu

**Library of Congress Cataloging-in-Publication Data**

Names: Cantin, Lucie, editor. | Librett, Jeffrey S., editor. | McNulty, Tracy, editor.
Title: A psychoanalysis for a reemergent humanity : the metapsychology of Willy Apollon / edited by Lucie Cantin, Jeffrey S. Librett, and Tracy McNulty.
Description: Albany : State University of New York Press, [2025]. | Series: SUNY series, insinuations: philosophy, psychoanalysis, literature | Includes bibliographical references and index.
Identifiers: LCCN 2025020607 | ISBN 9798855804881 (hardcover : alk. paper) | ISBN 9798855804904 (ebook) | ISBN 9798855804898 (pbk. : alk. paper)
Subjects: LCSH: Apollon, Willy. | Psychoanalysis. | Psychology and philosophy.
Classification: LCC BF175.4.P45 P65 2025
LC record available at https://lccn.loc.gov/2025020607

# Contents

## Clinical Concepts and Their Application

# Introduction

## Willy Apollon's Revision of the Metapsychology: Departures from Freud and Lacan

Jeffrey S. Librett

### At the Limits of Civilizations, the Human Includes the Strange(r)

The following programmatic collection of essays presents a new version of the psychoanalytic metapsychology: a renewal and displacement of Freudian and Lacanian psychoanalysis for today and tomorrow. The historical epoch of "today" (we can't, of course, know tomorrow) is understood here as the age of "mondialisation," translatable loosely as "cultural globalization," or more literally as "worlding" or "world-formation." As used here, the term "mondialisation" refers to a global cultural and civilizational crisis of meanings, values, and behavioral orientations, something like the nihilism Nietzsche experienced in a less advanced form, and tried to find terms for, in the late nineteenth century. Only now it's much more drastic, as it involves the virtual twilight of all *particular* civilizational forms, a twilight conditioned by recent financial and technological globalization (which however is neither its essence nor its cause). The idea—spelled out in several of the chapters below—is that subsequent to the high moment of financial globalization, and running counter to certain aspects of the latter, "mondialisation" (again, "cultural globalization," or more literally "world-formation") arose: an epoch of cultural and civilizational conflict (including conflict over conceptions of "man" and "woman," "gender," etc.), which throws individual subjects into disarray (but also opens up new possibilities) as it suspends norms, prohibitions, ideals, and beliefs of all sorts.

Civilizations are here understood as broad systems of belief (each englobing multiple cultures "rooted" in turn in particular languages), whose principal function is to provide "foundations" for the credibility of the norms, prohibitions, rules of behavior, and meaning-constitution that define these cultures in turn. On this view, each civilization tends to promote a view of "the human," as against the views of other, competing civilizations. Each thinks it possesses the proper definition of the human (and excludes all others).

In our age, however, humanity itself is reaching a new phase in its development. The question of what happens at the end of the relatively separate existence of particular civilizations (or at least those we know)—which are currently de facto placing each other in question by virtue of their immediate and ubiquitous copresence—surges up with a hitherto unimaginable force (even as discourses like that of "civilizational states" and right-wing populism deny the inevitability and actuality of this question).[1] This is a historical situation that neither Freud nor Lacan lived to experience in its current, rather extreme manifestation. The situation of "mondialisation" requires of psychoanalysis that it innovate to accommodate new subjective experiences for which the possibility of a secure context of clear belief systems (however oppressive these may have been) is no longer accessible. This represents a positive challenge and opportunity for psychoanalysis to move finally beyond the confines of its Western civilizational orientation.

But for psychoanalysis to address subjectivity in the entirety of the age in which we currently live, it must consider *the entire range of subjective structures* inhabited by the people of this age. For various reasons, psychoanalysis has traditionally focused its clinical attention on neurosis, and generally made neurosis the central model of its theoretical articulation of the human subject as such. In stark contrast, the metapsychology as presented in this volume attempts to account for all subjective structures—not just neurosis, but also *perversion* and *psychosis*—with equal adequacy, respect, acceptance, and affirmation. Notably, it includes a new conceptualization of *transference*, whose development was necessitated by the fact that traditional Freudian and Lacanian concepts of transference tend toward the conclusion that the psychotic, who will not develop this sort of (imaginary) transference, cannot be analyzed.

The creation of a psychoanalysis that includes both perversion and psychosis while distinguishing between both of these subjective structures and mental illness per se should be of particular interest at this historical juncture. With respect to psychosis, the grave limitations of the deinstitutionalization movement, as it was carried out, and of the promise of antipsychotics, both since the mid-twentieth century, can no longer be ignored or denied. And with respect to perversion, the manifest epistemic inadequacy of an ahistorical and simple tug-of-war between moral-political condemnation and social normalization (or assimilation to neurosis) should be clear to anyone serious about psychoanalytic thought. The recognition and reflection upon the full range of subjective structures becomes, moreover, all the more pressing in an age when, because of erosion and multiplication of the symbolic orders, these structures themselves may be shifting.

Further, these two separate points of reference for a rethinking of the metapsychology I've introduced thus far—non-neurotic subjective structures (perversion and psychosis), on the one hand, and the age of cultural globalization, on the other—are linked together in an important way. Both phenomena place in question, and edge out beyond, the limits of civilization, the first on the level of the individual, the second on the level of the world-system. The psychotic departs from their civilization, and mondialisation questions all civilizations and makes them increasingly unavailable for adoption as home bases of belief. And so together, both the treatment of psychosis in particular, and the extension of psychoanalysis into an age in which all particular civilizations and cultures are beginning to founder in the process of their interpenetration, require of psychoanalysis that it rethink a whole array of its fundamental concepts outside any particular civilizational context, but in an anthropologically informed perspective. These concepts include, for example, the imaginary, symbolic, and real, the unconscious, the masculine and feminine, the question of sexuality and the cultural constructions of man and woman, the status of culture and civilization themselves, the role and sense of puberty and adolescence in human development, desire and its object, and the position of analysis with respect to the aesthetic and the ethical dimensions. The chapters that follow articulate and explore from various angles the rethinking of these concepts that has been carried out by Willy

Apollon in his revision and displacement of Lacanian metapsychology in Quebec, Canada.

Apollon, a Haitian psychoanalyst who attended Lacan's seminars while completing his PhD in philosophy at the Sorbonne in the 1970s, founded forty years ago with colleagues in Quebec City the "Groupe interdisciplinaire freudien de recherches et d'interventions cliniques et culturelles" (Gifric), or "Interdisciplinary Freudian Group for Clinical and Cultural Research and Interventions." Apollon's work combines a rigorous philosophical dimension with an unwavering clinical commitment, and augments these with an anthropological interest, as well as a specific ethico-political engagement. This engagement involves a lifelong devotion of his work to those often held to be strangers within our societies (and even within psychoanalysis)—especially the "madman"—in psychoanalytic terms, the "psychotic"—but also the "pervert," and on a larger scale, those who belong to cultures situated outside the Occidental civilizations.[2]

In the practical clinical application of these priorities and interests, taking the work of the late-career Lacan (the Lacan who focused particular attention on the register of the "real" and the notion of *jouissance*) as point of departure, Gifric has launched, developed, and maintained under Apollon's leadership a number of major concrete projects over the last decades. These include a Center for the Psychoanalytic Treatment of Young Psychotic Adults (also known by its street address as the "388"), created in 1982 and still thriving today (with extraordinary results) as a state-supported outpatient/inpatient clinic for the treatment of psychosis; two psychoanalytic family clinics (one in Quebec City and one in Montreal); the Freudian School of Quebec (*École freudienne du Québec*); a publication series (*Savoir*); and annual clinically oriented training seminars in (post-)Lacanian psychoanalysis that are offered in both French and English.

The task of the present volume is to present in a coherent overview the provisional results of Apollon's work in concert especially with the other senior analysts of the École freudienne du Québec (EFQ), Danielle Bergeron and Lucie Cantin. The relentless focus and illuminating clinical and conceptual contributions of Bergeron and Cantin, moreover, as principal longtime collaborators of Apollon, and as devoted and rigorous analysts both within and without the "388" Center, should be recognized here. In addition to Apollon, Bergeron, and Cantin, the other contributors to this volume are psychoanalysts, analysts in training at the EFQ, and scholars of humanities with extensive experience in the Gifric approach.

This is the second major collection of essays in English representing the work of the Quebec group. The first such collection—*After Lacan: Clinical Practice and the Subject of the Unconscious*—containing essays by Apollon, Bergeron, and Cantin and edited by Robert Hughes and Kareen Ror Malone, was published by State University of New York Press twenty years ago in 2002. In the intervening two decades, not only has the reputation and influence of the Quebec group grown on an international level, and especially in the United States, but the group has continued to develop both metapsychological theory and the understanding of our situation in history, as Apollon has evolved his particular notion of *mondialisation* in lecture series and publications since 2007. A new book-length presentation of the perspective of the Quebec School in English is therefore overdue.

In the remainder of this introduction, I situate Apollon's metapsychology in some of its main continuities with, and differences from, the metapsychologies of both Freud and Lacan. To do so, I first recall the primary aims and structural or paradigmatic elements of *Freud's metapsychology*, above all insofar as it concerns the individual psyche or subject. And I offer an interpretation of the functioning of these elements in Freud's theoretical framework. I then consider how these main elements reappear, differently, in *Lacan's metapsychology*. These reconstructive indications enable us to discern *Apollon's displacements* of the Lacanian and Freudian versions of the main *synchronic* metapsychological elements. I go on to consider two main aspects of the *diachronic* dimension in Apollon's metapsychology—adolescence and the categories of man, woman, masculine, and feminine (viewed within a development of the subject through which it is taken to diverge radically from the biology with which it nonetheless maintains its connection)—in relation to Freudian and Lacanian conceptions. I then characterize his approach to the notions of desire and its object, concluding with a quick sketch of the volume's trajectory.

## What is Metapsychology? Identity and Difference of the Psyche in Freud's Three Models

Freud introduces the term "metapsychology" into his published writings in *The Psychopathology of Everyday Life* (1901).[3] In context, he is arguing that "a large part of the mythological view of the world, which extends a long way into the most modern religions, is nothing but psychology projected into the external world" (258). In these formations, one constructs a "supernatural reality" (259) by projecting an image of one's dimly perceived inner states ("psychical factors and relations in the unconscious") into the outer, supernatural world, the world beyond the world.[4] For early Freud, given his self-identification as scientist, this otherworldly world is "destined to be changed back once more by science into the *psychology of the unconscious*" (259). Thus he aspires to "transform *metaphysics* into *metapsychology*" (259).[5] The project is initially in line, therefore, in a broad sense with Enlightenment-style rationality, and in a narrower sense (at least in its point of departure), as is well-known, with a positivist physicalism working specifically with the thermodynamics of Helmholtz, in an institutional-discursive context determined by the Berlin Physics Society (Berliner Physikalische Gesellschaft), founded in 1845, with its anti-Romantic (ultimately anti-Schellingian), anti-vitalist orientation.[6] But while Freud certainly persists throughout his career in carrying out the project of the reduction of superstition through metapsychology, he starts out tentative and ends up even more clear about the complexity and difficulty of this problem. For example, he first uses the term "metapsychology" again fourteen years after the *Psychopathology of Everyday Life*, and when he does so he grants that "in the present state of our knowledge there are only a few points at which we shall succeed in providing a metapsychological presentation of a psychic process" ("The Unconscious" [1915]).[7] Depending on one's calculation, further, it seems we only have about five of Freud's planned twelve essays on the metapsychology, so his progress in this project was at any rate halting, despite Freud's prolific productivity in general.[8]

Even more strikingly, by the end of his career, in "Analysis Terminable and Interminable" (whose German title, "Die endliche und die unendliche Analyse," more literally means "Finite and Infinite Analysis" [1937]), Freud's scientistic optimism with respect to the overcoming of metaphysics by means of metapsychology has become somewhat chastened (as is also in evidence with the development from "The Future of an Illusion" [1927] to "Civilization and Its Discontents" [1930]). "Of all the erroneous and superstitious beliefs of mankind that have supposedly been surmounted there is not one whose residues do not live on among us to-day in the lower strata of civilized peoples or even in the highest strata of cultural society. What has once come to life clings tenaciously to its existence. One feels inclined to doubt sometimes whether the dragons of primaeval days are really extinct" (SE, XXIII, 229).[9] The world is apparently not so easily "enlightened."

But not only does metaphysics, or "supernatural reality," resist reduction to metapsychology; the belief in metapsychology itself here takes on the status of a superstitious and needy belief, or poetic fantasy. It is inscribed in what it is to overcome. More specifically, metapsychology itself takes on self-ironically the image of a dangerous and magic-wielding female figure on whom we depend in order to resist death or impotence. Freud is considering the question of how the ego is to be enabled by psychoanalysis to "tame" the drives (and so arrive at the end of an analysis), and more specifically how the drive is to be "brought completely into the harmony of the ego," when he writes:

> If we are asked by what methods and means this result is achieved, it is not easy to find an answer. We can only say: "So muss denn doch die Hexe dran!" ["We must call the Witch to our aid after all!"]—the Witch Metapsychology. Without metapsychological speculation and theorizing—I had almost said "phantasying"—we shall not take another step forward [keinen Schritt weiter]. Unfortunately, here as elsewhere, what our Witch reveals is neither very clear nor very detailed. (XI, 366; XXIII, 225)

In Goethe's *Faust*, the text Freud is quoting here, the Witch is supposed to make Faust young again so he can seduce the young maid Margarethe. Metapsychology as the Witch whose brew is theoretical Viagra?[10] But whom does Freud need to seduce? And as if this were not skeptical or complicating enough, Freud quotes the satirical playwright Johann Nestroy a few pages later as saying "Every step forward [Fortschritt] is only half as big as it looks at first" (369, 228). Without following this discussion further—in which Freud tries to clarify the "quantitative" (i.e., "economic") factor, noting that he has given it insufficient attention thus far in his career—I wish here simply to underline the point that, while Freud maintains his investment in the metapsychology to the end, the complex *self-irony* with which he surrounds it in this late text indicates that he is feeling some uncertainty as to whether it can achieve, in its current (incomplete) form, the tasks to which it has been assigned.

Why is it, then, that Freud's metapsychology can never quite accomplish its original aims? The reasons for this are complex, no doubt, but they certainly concern both what he was attacking and the weapon of attack. 1) The reduction and "overcoming" of "metaphysics," given the pervasiveness and elusiveness of its limits, is a more complex and difficult task than Freud initially imagined, as Martin Heidegger, Jacques Derrida, and many others have continued to explore. 2) Freud's scientism, and especially his materialist and determinist physicalism concerning the organic and psychic dimensions, were, on the one hand, insufficiently self-examined in terms of epistemology and the philosophy of science, as ongoing work in neurophenomenology, neuropsychoanalysis, philosophy of mind, and philosophy of science indicates, precisely in the open-endedness of the fundamental discussions even today. And on the other hand, Freud himself shifted the ground of the Enlightenment and positivist legacies beneath his feet by means of his own studies of the unconscious. This unsettled and altered the epistemic foundations of a possible science of the psyche, as well as the status of something like "superstition" (see, again, the developments from "The Future of an Illusion" [1927] to "Civilization and its Discontents" [1930]).[11] The attack was changing the weapon throughout his trajectory, but the weapon was also resisting this change. Moreover, as Apollon argues, the Western scientific discourse is marked not just by Western metaphysics but more broadly by Western civilization in general, and this Western scientific discourse is tending today (albeit not without various forms of resistance) to become the new religion of the West as extended across the globe. From this vantage point, it appears that Freud's scientism, especially in its narrowly positivist, physicalist, materialist, and determinist form (not that his thought did not exceed this form also), remained limited to his civilizational point of view, as one *Weltanschauung* among others.[12]

In Apollon, by contrast, if his metapsychology is still directed against a "superstition," that "superstition" would now be primarily the unfounded belief in any particular civilization's superiority over the others in the determination of the human. And of the three Lacanian subjective structures (i.e., neurosis, perversion, and psychosis), from this perspective, psychosis—despite its delusional and hallucinatory symptomatology—would ultimately be the least "superstitious," whereas neurosis would be the most. This is because the neurotic tends to internalize sociocultural norms and civilizational beliefs and promises, whereas the psychotic, not so much. This rather different determination of the target of metapsychology's "demystifying" potential requires, of course, significant shifts in its conceptual makeup (as also in the sense of a term like "demystification"). Before we get to these, however, we need to consider not just the aims of Freud's metapsychology, but also its central conceptual composition and the problems it faced, and more briefly, Lacan's response to these problems.

What are the main terms of the metapsychology? And what tasks are they to perform in providing the coherent basis of a reduction of supernaturalist illusions to the realities of the psyche? Let us return to Freud's use of the term in "The Unconscious" (1915):

> It will not be unreasonable to give a special name to this whole way of regarding our subject-matter, for it is the consummation of psycho-analytic research. I propose that when we have succeeded in describing a psychical process in its dynamic, topographical and economic aspects, we should speak of it as a metapsychological presentation. We must say at once that in the present state of our knowledge there are only a few points at which we shall succeed in this. (SE, XIV, 181)

So what function do these three models—dynamic, topographical, and economic—fulfill in the grounding of a theory of the psyche or subject in Freud? Certainly, they aim to put into place the energetics of the psychic apparatus that Freud derives from his scientific education, including his work with Breuer. Their function is to provide the theoretical underpinnings of the metaphorical or phenomenological, purely psychic energetics, cut off from the neurophysiological foundations in literal, physical energies he was still trying to provide in the *Project for a Scientific Psychology* of 1895. But the articulation of this now purely psychic energetics as a model for the functioning of the psychic apparatus poses specific problems for the determination of the internally cohesive structure of the subject within which the energies are supposed to flow. To approach these problems, it helps to consider the following.

One of the main aspects of Freud's conceptualization of the unconscious that makes this entity, the unconscious, particularly difficult to understand, along with the figures of the conscious and the preconscious that accompany it, is that all three of these terms combine *separateness* as distinct entities, on the one hand, with a *togetherness* or constitutive structural interconnectedness, on the other hand. That is, neither unconscious nor conscious nor preconscious can strictly be situated in just one spot with clearly defined borders, and yet each of them is not equally everywhere in the psyche either, to the degree that they are imagined as either spatial containers or extended things. The unconscious, conscious, and preconscious are *inseparably* connected and interpenetrating, and yet *separate*. How to understand this *unity* and multiplicity inhabiting the psyche, or its self-*identity* and its self-*difference?* My interpretive proposal is this: Freud's three models of, or "points of view" on, "psychic processes" try precisely to resolve this paradoxical tension. Their primary task is to account for the multiplicity, the unity, and the mediation between the multiplicity and the unity of the main elements in the Freudian psyche.

In "The Unconscious," under the heading of "the topographical point of view," Freud starts out by distinguishing "psychic acts" that are conscious (cs) from those that are unconscious (ucs), and further distinguishing the *descriptively* unconscious from what he here calls the *systemically* unconscious, dividing *latent* acts that are susceptible of being rendered conscious from *repressed* acts that are not. The repressed is what he will also call the "dynamic" unconscious in "The Ego and the Id." The topography that results from these distinctions is one that places the preconscious (pcs) on the border between the unconscious and the conscious. The main function of the *topographical* model is therefore to conceptualize these different statuses of psychic acts as distinctly *separate* from one another, that is, to do justice to their separateness, or multiplicity.[13] The governing metaphors of this model are both spatial (topical) and graphic, as Freud very explicitly and repeatedly uses the word "writing down"—*Niederschrift*—for the fixation of traces onto the surfaces of these distinct regions or places of cs, pcs, and ucs (SA, III, 132–34; SE XIV, 174–76).

By virtue of its very structure, however, the topographical model already keeps unsettling itself, involving Freud in questions of how to understand the *relations* between the ucs and the cs, as these relations are mediated by or through the pcs (at their border, which—as Jacques Derrida taught us to observe, is always self-displacing). Questions about whether this borderland or frontier territory, the pcs, belongs actually to the ucs, or alternatively to the cs, and questions about whether the censorship is to be situated between the ucs and the pcs, between the pcs and the cs, or both—all of these questions that plague Freud are forms of the question as to how we can conceive of the *interrelatedness* of ucs and cs once we have *separated* them topographically with the pcs as borderland or borderline.[14]

Because these separate elements or aspects of the psychic (or psychic acts), as conceived initially in topographical terms, maintain certain interrelationships, Freud rightly feels the need to supplement the topographical model with something more interrelational (not of course in the sense of the term used by "relational therapies" today), or even fusional. What keeps the different "places" in the psyche together, as it then turns out, is their common existence as "force"—as a play of forces with and against each other, ultimately the pure *Drang* or *Drängen*—the impulsion—of the drive.[15] This existence of the psyche as the play of driving forces is also what gives it a kind of "reality" qua "effectivity." Freud thus writes in "Einige Bemerkungen über den Begriff des Unbewußten in der Psychoanalyse" (Some Remarks on the Concept of the Unconscious in Psychoanalysis, 1912) that from a "*dynamic* point of view" [dynamischen *Auffassung*] the idea becomes "wirksam" ("effective" or "effectual")—it "pushes toward the act," as Apollon will say. In German, "reality" is "Wirklichkeit," so this "effectivity" says precisely that the "dynamic" perspective is that of the "reality" of the unconscious, a point to which we return with Lacan. The unity of the psyche seems to consist in its existence as the real play of forces. Hence, Freud speaks here—under the heading of the *dynamic* model—of the possibility that the passage from one status to another in the psyche is not a matter of a change of place—which requires a disunity of places—but of a "change of state (in the same place, with the same material)" ([*Zustandsänderung . . . welche sich an dem nämlichen Material und an derselben Lokalität vollzieht*] 133, 174). That is, the idea of a "functional change of state [*Zustandsänderung* (134)]" seems to provide an account of the unity of cs, pcs, and ucs—their interrelational inseparability—by avoiding or overcoming the spatial differentiation of the topographical model. The forces that define this state always return to the same place, or rather they never leave it, even as they act as forces upon the surrounding forces, since their difference has now been placed along a temporal axis and thereby effaced, in order to preserve the sense of an essential unity and continuity (the same thing, just altered in its *Zustand*—its condition or state). And it is interesting and not by chance that Freud says, at the end of the second section of "The Unconscious," that he can't *decide* between these two models—for the decision cannot be made.

The undecidability of *topography* and *dynamics*—again, of the spatial, material differentiation and the temporally shape-shifting fundamental unity (as forces in play) of the metapsychological elements (cs, pcs, and ucs)—prompts Freud to supplement these points of view or models with the *economic* point of view. This latter point of view explains the dynamics—changes of state—in terms of cathexes, decathexes, and countercathexes—investments and de- and counter-investments of representations—with libidinal energy, and these investments are described at the same time in terms of topographical language, moving from place to place. That is, the economic model includes within itself the topographical and the dynamic models from which it is supposed to be distinct but whose copresence it is called upon to mediate. This is indeed why Freud says in "the Unconscious," when he introduces the "economic" point of view, that "We observe, how we have *gradually* [allmählich] come to the point, in the presentation of psychic phenomena, of bringing to bear a third point of view, aside from the dynamic and the topographical, the economic one, which strives to follow the fates of the quantities of excitation and to gain at least a relative measure (approximation) of them" (my italics, S.140). The *gradualness* of this introduction is not just expositional here, but pertains to the logic of the interrelations between the models, for the economic model is supposed to integrate the other two with itself and to mediate between them, providing a sense of the identity of the identity and difference of the psyche.[16] But at the same time, this makes the distinctions between them less than perfectly clear. At any rate, the German for cathexis—*Besetzung*—which also refers to acts of military occupation—is apt to its purpose in Freud's economic theory. For he mobilizes this language to tie together the *separation* of territories with their *transformations* into each other, or the slide from a topography to a dynamics of *Zustand*-alteration. And what could be more useful for this purpose than the language of military occupations and taking possession (*Besitz*)? The "vicissitudes of quantities of excitation" (*Schicksale der Erregungsgrößen*) are the troops conscripted and employed here. And the military metaphors are used also for the very struggles between models themselves, by displacement or contagion: theory is itself not just a matter of the conscious ego but also a libidinally invested matter. For example, Freud writes at one point that "The functional assumption has . . . easily defeated the topographical one" or more literally "has pushed it off the field of battle" (*die topische mit leichter Mühe aus dem Felde geschlagen*) (180, 139). At the end of this development, however, Freud stresses the provisional necessity of all three points of view for the description of any given psychic process.

But to take one step further (while recalling Freud's warning taken from Johann Nestroy): as is not generally noted, the models for the psyche that view the psyche as differentiated, unified, and something-in-between are not simply unrelated to the elemental aspects of the psyche whose interrelationships or lack thereof these models are meant to account for. Rather, each model or viewpoint has affinities with, and even perhaps represents the characteristic viewpoint of, one of these elemental aspects. More specifically and concretely, the differentiating attitude of the *topographical* model is akin to that of *consciousness*: for example, consciousness recognizes the principle of non-contradiction, and knows about negation, and so it traffics in differentiations. It breaks up the world into its pieces. The viewpoint of the *dynamic* model—tracking changes of state in the unchanging—has a fundamental affinity with the *unconscious*, which is supposed to be oblivious to contradiction, and to know nothing of negation, and so this model itself is like a faculty of the undifferentiated. Like the dynamic viewpoint, the unconscious does not, so to speak, distinguish between conscious and unconscious. The *economic* point of view, finally, is like the point of view of the *preconscious*, defining the point of (non)passage between topos and dynamis, between differentiated and undifferentiated, as the preconscious defines the point of (non)passage between conscious and unconscious.

If this is this case, moreover, one can take a further step and say in schematic terms that, given the sense in which the second topography (ego, id, and superego) displaces and redoubles the first topography (conscious, unconscious, and preconscious), the topographic, dynamic, and economic models or points of view represent the general perspectives of the ego, the id, and the superego, respectively, insofar as the latter are aligned with the principles of differentiation, fusion, and the mediation between these two. The superego, for example, is the unconscious part of the ego, and it tries to reconcile drive with reality (ultimately, as the space of extension). Indeed, if Freud was not able to complete the metapsychology, perhaps it was because these de facto homologies made it impossible for the models for the understanding of the psyche to master the psyche from without. This is not surprising, for in principle the psyche can never be mastered from without, since it perfuses itself through any psychic activity that would master it.[17]

## Metapsychology in Lacan: Identity and Difference in the Imaginary, the Real, and the Symbolic

What happens when we move to Lacan? Consider the three registers—the imaginary, the real, and the symbolic—which represent a crucial, perhaps *the* crucial, expansion of the conceptuality of psychoanalysis in Lacan's work.[18] The imaginary (re)defines the status of the ego as a narcissistic enclosure, differentiating itself in an originary alienation—the "mirror stage"—from what is around it (and from its own internal disarticulation) by identifying with an external mirror image, upon which the parental smile rests. Selfsameness of the ego arises here only as marked by a difference between itself and the image it takes for itself, thereby introducing an intrinsic aggressivity in the tendency to reappropriate the external image.[19] The separate coherence of the psyche, or the subject, and of its parts, is always an imaginary one. And the imaginary espies separate entity-egos everywhere it looks. In short, the notion of the imaginary replaces or translates topography (as well as conscious and ego) as a principle for the constitution of separate, animated topoi.[20]

In contrast, the real is a nonrepresentable X (which would mean it cannot be identified in its difference from other entities surrounding it) that "always returns to the same place,"[21] because it never left that place, which is nowhere (or everywhere) in the space of the extended or of any supposed purely intellectual plane. It only morphs in time, not in space, as the changes of state in the "same place, with the same material." The real is the dynamic dimension of the psyche, conceptualized by Freud as the "effective" play of forces, but also as libidinal energy, and by Lacan as the dimension of jouissance, a fluid "substance" that exceeds the differentation between excess and absence (as he puts it in the ambiguous phrase "le plus-de-jouir").[22]

Finally, the Lacanian symbolic order is defined by reference to language—which is how Freud defines the preconscious, namely as what language enables (or, for all intents and purposes, is)—and the symbolic order mediates between the imaginary and the real, that is, between discrete differences and nondifferentiation. Language—which provides an economy, as the signifier is the universal medium of exchange like money—mediates between the real of the subject and the imaginary of the ego in the social network.[23] It is, as Saussure said, a system of differences, that is, a unity of multiplicity, or a multiplicity of unity—and so connects its elements while holding them apart. Syntax, or metonymy—the world of topoi—comes together with semantics, or metaphor—the world of self-selecting, qualitative energy flows—mediating the dimensions of desire and symptom.[24] So the symbolic order is the Lacanian "equivalent" (*mutatis mutandis*) of the viewpoint of the economic model in Freud, along with the associative connections of this model with the preconscious and the superego by way of the common trait of mediation between unity and multiplicity.[25]

But how do the three models, or registers, *belong together* in Freud and Lacan? What enables their *synthesis*, assuming that the psyche, or the subject, should not remain dispersed at its roots? And if there is no synthesis, can the metapsychology still provide a rational account of the production of irrational effects within the psyche or subject? In Freud, as we have glimpsed, the ultimate interrelationship between the three models for the psyche was never quite formulated in a definitive version. Similarly, in Lacan the relationships of mutual (in)dependence between the imaginary, the symbolic, and the real were the focus of endless meditations and reformulation. In his later period, these efforts to formulate their unity were focused on the figure of the Borromean knot—a chain of three loops held together purely by the way they are intertwined, such that cutting any one of them will break the unity of the three—and ultimately on the notion that there is also a fourth ring, which he connects with a particular kind of symptom he calls the "sinthôme," an unusual sort of workable symptom that sometimes holds the other three together, detailed discussion of which exceeds the limits of this introduction.[26]

## Synchronic Metapsychology in Apollon: The Structure of the Subject

We are now in a position to situate Apollon's metapsychology in an initial way—which the chapters in this volume, beginning with Apollon's own, will expand in detail—in relation to the guiding metapsychological concepts of Freud and Lacan. The continuities are easy to indicate; the discontinuities, which the chapters below specify, take longer to unfold and appreciate in their theoretical and clinical implications. To begin with the most schematic overview: Apollon reinterprets the Lacanian imaginary as what he calls the "psyche"; he reinterprets the Lacanian real as what he calls "spirit"; and he reinterprets the Lacanian symbolic as "language" in a socio-pragmatic and post-structuralist sense. He understands language in its social function within an evolutionary framework (i.e., in terms of the evolution of homo sapiens) as expanding itself into culture and civilization. Within this context, he unfolds the specific role and significance of language for the subject both in general and today.

To start with "psyche": the position of the imaginary ego is taken up and transformed in Apollon's work into the "psyche," such that the "psyche" is now only a part or aspect of the human subject, notably as distinct from Freud where the "psychic apparatus" was a name for the whole of the subject. A "metapsychology" will now be clearly distinguished from a "psychology," at the very least insofar as a "metapsychology" must account for all dimensions of the subject-in-the-world, not just the psyche. Further, the psyche here displaces or departs from the Lacanian imaginary ego in a specific direction: the psyche is defined here as the human being insofar as it is an *organism*, a living being that attempts to maintain its homeostasis within a natural environment. The psyche is the consciousness, self-consciousness, and guidance system of the organism in nature and then (not without distortion and an endless struggle to maintain its equilibrium) in the "second nature" of culture, as a social-ego navigating its way through a social structure approached in pragmatic terms as an environment. But initially, in its "pure" state, the psyche is the organic mind of an organic being. In evolutionary-historical terms, Apollon places this development at around 7 million years ago, when our human ancestors diverged from their closest relatives. The psyche will be subject to two mutually counterposed disruptions, first that of the real—which Apollon characterizes in terms of a specific notion of spirit—and then that of language.

The first disruption of the psyche, in Apollon's thought both phylogenetically and ontogenetically, is the encounter with the *real*—what he calls "real castration" or castration (of the organic imaginary) by the real. Here, the Lacanian real is displaced in the direction of a certain notion of spirit, whose irruption within the natural space 200,000 to 300,000 years ago signals according to Apollon the arrival of homo sapiens, with its enormously inventive and creative development of culture and technology, beginning indeed prior to the invention of language. Phylogenetically beginning with the emergence of homo sapiens around 300,000 years ago, the organism's self-differentiation from (and belonging within) its environment by means of the maintenance of its internal homeostasis (i.e., the pleasure principle) is disrupted by the emergence of mental representations of things that do not exist, representations associated in some cases with a desire to create them, and at times followed by their actual realization. This divergence from empirical reality accounts for the extreme creativity and inventiveness of human beings, an intensity of activity (and receptivity) that however unsettles the human being's homeostasis. It introduces a "positive feedback" issuing from an inner exteriority, pushing the human being (qua organism) out of its natural comfort zone into a space beyond need, a space of the *unnecessary*, and in principle useless. For who *needs* a skyscraper or an airplane, or even beautifully decorated pottery or knives? This mysterious human tendency of driven creativity, which Apollon calls the *spirit*, constitutes his interpretation of the "beyond the pleasure principle" of Freud, aptly called a "death drive" principally because it takes us outside the realm of natural, organic life into that of culture, where we are free but also at one remove from instinctual guidance.[27] The spirit pushes for change but insists as the real, as what cannot be derived or denied, as "the same," the one essence of what (it) is, which is a way of saying that it pushes for its (impossible) expression, sharing, universalization. Spirit brings us, in Lacanian terms, the dimension of jouissance, not pleasure, and it continually unsettles the organism—the self-managing psyche—that we also are and continue—discontinuously—to (try to) be. The tension between spirit and psyche, which Apollon represents—based on clinical experience and not just on theoretical reflection—by means of the image of a "breaking in"—an "effraction"—of spirit into the psyche, creates an instability in the human, which in Lacanian terms would appear (mutatis mutandis) as a tension between the imaginary and the real. In disturbing or perturbing the organism, this tension constitutes the "body" in a psychoanalytic sense.

That is, Apollon revises the Freudian notion of the erotogenic body, placing it right at the junction—the collision—of spirit with psyche, *Geist* with *Seele* (both terms being defined anew here), or as the English romantics formulated something similar, of imagination with nature (here as the nature of the organic self). Spirit inscribes within the organism the traces of its traumatization of the psyche, and these traces are experienced as zones and spheres of influence within the body qua lived body, experienced in the form of feelings of pain and pleasure, longing, irritation, anxiety, jouissance, and so on, and linked with memories, phantasms and actual events, forming the point of departure for symptomatic formations. That Apollon uses the metaphor of "letter" to refer to these traces means at least two things: they are incisions (a writing) and they will enter into the articulation of linguistic meaning even as they themselves mean nothing, fly low enough to evade the radar of sense. The letter here inhabits the flesh of the organic systems it disrupts. How, then, do we get from the real of spirit and the organism (with the erotogenic body arising out of the sites of their collisions) to the question of language per se?

Even prior to conventional language, there is some kind of speech, expression verbal, gestural, and manual through which early modern humans will have tried to articulate their imaginings, impulses, ideas, intimate feelings (what Apollon calls the "ressenti" below). But when human communities saw themselves faced with the necessity to form larger groups for survival and advancement, the expression of such radically singular experiences had to be minimized for the purposes of large-scale cooperation, that is, homogenization. This necessity became the mother of the invention of language roughly 50,000 to 60,000 years ago. Language thus appeared on the phylogenetic scene long after the beginnings of the homo sapiens line, of which we have traces since more like 300,000 years ago; the function of language was to enable higher levels of human cooperation so that larger groups could be formed and work together.[28] This means that what language itself said and says is: "we want to hear from all of you, but not too much!—Don't get too weird!" *Language* is always opposed to the singular *speech* whose possibility it nonetheless promises to enable. That is, language—similar to what Lacan in his structuralist phase called the "symbolic order" (following Lévi-Strauss), or the order of the signifier, and what Freud thematized as the condition of the preconscious—functions to keep a large part of the creative singularity of the subject, his or her "madness"—the signified subject, in Lacanian terms—out of the social totality by requiring the use of a shared vocabulary with shared rules of syntax, and not just on the verbal level of "la langue." In the ontogenetic dimension, the language that defines the social link is communicated to babies and young children through families and caretakers, as representatives of the social order. But the letters of language do not precisely reflect the letters of the body—we're always dealing with two different alphabets, as it were—so language fails us in important ways. To express what the energy of mental representations does to our bodies we have to displace language, whether in creative activity or in symptoms or actings out, which can always get us into trouble with legal authorities or land us in the hands of therapeutic institutions.

With this notion of language, Apollon undertakes important displacements of the emphases in Lacan (but remains to some extent consistent with the last Lacan). Notably, Apollon is *not* suggesting that the "unconscious is structured like a language," a proposition to which Lacan committed himself—perhaps somewhat hastily—during the structuralist phase of the 1950s and revised around 1970.[29] Rather—in this respect, much closer to Freud—Apollon is arguing that the *conscious* is structured not just like but *by* language (qua determinant of and privileged synecdoche for the social link), and that the unconscious is "outside of language" (*hors langage*).

These then—psyche, spirit, and language—are the three main structural or synchronic elements of the formed human subject in Apollon's metapsychology, displacements of the functions of the conscious, the unconscious, and the preconscious, and also of the viewpoints of the topographical, the dynamic, and the economic models in the Freudian universe. Beyond these elements, we have considered also the "effraction"—the collision-like and inscription-like interaction between spirit and psyche—and the letter of the body—the *traces* of the effraction—that leans at once toward and away from becoming a language of words or social acts. The "unity" of the subject that emerges is at the very least a radically conflictual one, and one that exceeds the confines of the subject itself. Language as determinant of consciousness remains an internal exteriority; the nonmimetic mental representations of the spirit—and the never graspable but also inviolable intimacy of the "ressenti"—remain in excess of both language and the organism; and the organism can assimilate neither spirit nor language, nor can it be reconciled harmoniously with either. The situation is that of the undecidable identity and difference of the identity and difference of the subject (language remaining ultimately divided between its organic and spirited components, its imaginary and its real dimensions), whose absolute singularity can never be denied, but whose social and historical inscription in the becoming of humanity is equally essential.[30] Here is where Apollon's insistence on an ethics of responsibility becomes crucial, even as it remains difficult both conceptually and personally. For the assumption of responsibility for oneself involves both an affirmation of one's absolute singularity (and hence absolute separateness) and an affirmation of one's co-responsibility for the present and future of the humanity to which one belongs (and this in different senses on all three of the main metapsychological levels of one's being).

## Diachronic Metapsychology in Apollon: Puberty, Adolescence, and "Gender" Today

But what of the temporal and *developmental* concepts that, in Freud's and Lacan's theories of both the individual subject and humanity as a

whole, make up a crucial dimension in the field of conflict and conflu-
ence between biology and culture, precisely because what I've just called
the "structural or synchronic elements" of the subject are all understood
historically, that is, in terms of developmental or genetic narratives in a
time that retains but exceeds linearity? Since Apollon makes some very
important interventions in this diachronic dimension, it is necessary to
note a couple of them before concluding.

The first context of this diachronic dimension necessary to mention is that of the stages of childhood, which as several of the chapters
discuss, here comprise early (or first) childhood, middle (or second)
childhood, puberty, and adolescence. Each of these involves a different
experience of the unconscious in relation to the social surround, as the
chapters spell out. The main point to call to the reader's attention here
in advance, however, is the distinction Apollon introduces between
*puberty* and *adolescence*. The *novel approach to adolescence* that emerges
here is certainly *not* present in Freud *or* in Lacan. This new description
of adolescence furthermore not only underlines the crucial connections
between adolescence and the age in which we live, but also spells out
its particular importance for the contents and trajectory of an individual
analysis, hence also for the production of the analyst (i.e., the analyst's
training insofar as founded on his or her own analysis).

In Freud, the notion of a two-phased (*zwei-zeitig* is the term) sexual
development situates in puberty the rebirth of sexuality (following the
latency phase), and posits puberty as the beginning of a potential lifelong
struggle to fit oneself into the prescribed form of monogamy, within which
heterosexual, reproductive, genitally focused sexuality is the recognized
norm, albeit one whose artificiality and constraining character Freud
recognizes from the beginning.[31] No phase of adolescence distinct from
puberty gains expression in Freud's work.[32] With Lacan, the situation is
similar, except of course that the emphasis on a genital telos for sexuality
has been superseded by an ateleological, more resolutely polymorphic
notion, and that the idea of the "union" of the sexes, in which Freud
still to some extent believes, has been replaced by the "there is no
sexual relation," to which puberty/adolescence constitutes for Lacan an
introduction.[33] In Apollon, however, the experience of adolescence is
separate and radical (in the etymological sense, as going to the roots):
it constitutes the undoing of all that is imposed with particular force by
society on the pubescent girl and boy, for which Apollon sketches out
the general societal, cultural and civilizational dimensions.

To see what this means, we have to consider what was imposed on the pubescent, and why. Since puberty is the time of the physical maturation of the reproductive system, in the boy the primary manifestation of puberty in the organism comes in the form of the orgasm, while in the girl it takes the form of menstruation. These developments—which coincide with some increase in strength and cognitive abilities that makes them more dangerous to the social status quo—make possible sexual reproduction, which has the potential, in connection with action in the social domain, to transgress and undo the systems of kinship and class- and property-relations that the given culture imposes to ensure social harmony, and above all socioeconomic and cultural reproduction (as backed up by the larger civilizational belief systems). Puberty is therefore the time when the society needs to complete the inscription of the subject in the sociosexual dynamics in which it has been training the children since birth. Puberty is the period when, according to Apollon, what he calls the *"cultural montage of the sexual,"* the entire cultural system of sexuality and all that is related to it, is brought to bear on the young with renewed force—through media, schooling, parenting, therapeutic discourses, including mutual peer pressure and encouragement, and today social media interactions. For the sake of sociocultural reproduction, young women need to be made into proto-mothers, young men into proto-fathers and servants of the state (and/or market). And in both men and women, the feminine dimension—which Apollon defines as the tendency to give an aesthetic form to what comes from outside of language (i.e., the unconscious)—is to be censored, or at any rate contained within specifically delineated, circumscribed, and scrutinized discursive-institutional formations such as the culturally determined "arts." This imposition of the "cultural montage of the sexual" is what Apollon further terms—displacing and concretizing Lacan here—"symbolic castration." The montage adds a layer of cultural conventionality to the familial, school-, and media-based discourses of cultural norms whose imposition on the child prior to puberty Apollon calls "imaginary castration." While the latter—essentially as the parental condition of love and recognition—is linked to the mother tongue and the maternal figure, in whose presence the young child was still partially immersed, symbolic castration imposed by the montage of the sexual is understood as emanating more broadly from the society and culture at large.

In adolescence, however, which Apollon situates roughly between the ages of fifteen and twenty-five, he postulates that the individual—female or male—discovers within themselves a dimension that goes beyond all cultural and civilizational norms and values. This is what we commonly see as the existential or psychosocial crisis that often characterizes adolescence, and where the normative consciousness (e.g., the concerned parental consciousness) wonders: "what has gone wrong"? In fact, in this turbulence, something is going very *right*, that is, the young person is discovering an inner experience that has no relation to the parental discourses, or to the discourses of teachers, or even of the peers—the culturally and civilizationally inscribed others in general. The adolescent consequently discovers in a new way also the crucial importance of the address to another singular subject, and its difficulty, in the attempt to share the most intimate experiences, which as such exceed language. Such is the manifestation of the nonmimetic mental representations of the singular spirit, on which this individual will have to build a life, in assuming responsibility for their own most intimate experiences, inspirations, fears, horrors, delights, projects, and ideas.

This view of adolescence gives the entire question of adolescence a primary importance for an individual psychoanalysis that it has not had hitherto in the analytic tradition. This does not mean, of course, that early childhood and subsequent moments now lose their significance, especially since adolescence resonates particularly with early childhood experiences that exceed language. Beyond the clinical implications, however, Apollon also attempts to show that, in the age of *mondialisation*, given the conflict between civilizations, the adolescent experience is both exacerbated and confirmed in its apparent truth by the ways in which civilizations no longer feel self-evident to the degree that they used to: the conventions of credibility crumble away before our eyes. The tendency in our age toward a generalization of the adolescent experience poses everywhere complex new challenges, both within and without clinical psychoanalysis. These challenges include the necessity of combating the intensified attempt—an aspect of the general backlash against *mondialisation*—to reduce adolescence to puberty (taken most often ahistorically to be simply a natural manifestation of the organism's hormonal and neurophysiological development), and to reassert the privileges of particular cultural and civilizational modes of containment.

Apollon's second main intervention we need to consider concerning the diachronic dimension of metapsychological themes occurs in the area of what is currently called "gender" questions, which we have already touched upon, but which could use a bit more introductory elaboration here. Diachrony enters here both as history and as the future horizon for an aesthetically situated ethics. There are four levels on which what is generally discussed under the heading of "gender" figures in Apollon's recent writings and lectures. First, he situates the categories of "male" and "female" on a biological register, as outside the properly (or fully) human sphere, and within an evolutionary perspective. Second, he situates the notions of "man" and "woman" as constructs within cultural history and civilizational history, arguing that each culture "constructs the man and the woman it needs," that is, for its own sociocultural and civilizational reproduction. The given culture does this, of course, in concert with the rest of the cultural and civilizational language that, in any instance, is involved in the historical process of securing its own stability and continuation. This is where the "cultural montage of the sexual," which is culturally relative and historically variable, does its work. Third, there is the element of a person's "sex," which Apollon understands as the actual lived sexuality of the individual. He sees this "sex" as profoundly singular, within the context of a humanity so entirely heterogeneous that one can say that each person has *their own sex*. This "sex" thus exceeds by far any imaginary identifications a person may have with one or another image or concept of a sexual or gender identity or sexual orientation. Such images and concepts are always socially pre-given (even if in recently proposed forms) as conventional possibilities for identification; they can only concern the ego and from a relatively exterior point of view, having little to say about the individual subject's lived experience or unconscious feelings and representations ("ressenti"), which remain outside of language.[34] Fourth, there are the two categories of the "masculine" and "feminine," which Apollon develops in nonessentialist terms within an ahistorical horizon.

These two dimensions—the masculine and the feminine—are linked in their conceptual history to the notions of phallic and other jouissance in Lacan, but Apollon goes on to tie them explicitly with the dimensions of ethics and aesthetics, and on the aesthetic plane, with the sublime and the beautiful, respectively.[35] Here, the theme of sublimation which Freud introduced, and which has resonated throughout the psychoanalytic tradition (including in Lacan), receives renewed formulation.[36] And in this context, Apollon conceives the aesthetic sphere as opposed to violence—indeed, as the only alternative to violence. The beautiful and the sublime, the essential experiences of the aesthetic, are understood as ways in which the subject experiences, creatively and receptively, the transgressive, excessive character of spirit in the human with (and without) respect to civilizational beliefs and cultural norms. In the absence of arbitrary laws, the aesthetic steps in as a mode of self-(de)regulation that is open to the unconscious.[37] Moreover, the development and manifestation of *desire*, in Apollon's discourse, moves finally in the direction of the interplay between the experiences of beauty and sublimity, orienting the work of analysis toward an end in which the civilizational repudiation (or "censorship") of the feminine (in men, in women, and in those who find themselves between or elsewhere) is overcome by a sustained affirmation. The subject of the unconscious assumes responsibility for the consequences of this affirmation in the world, an affirmation that entails a movement beyond the symbolic order, with the attendant risks of this shift or drift. Given the interest in the creation of beauty for the sake of the other, on the one hand, and the desire for something that goes beyond individual existence (as discovered in the sublime), on the other hand, the *object* of desire takes on a transindividual dimension and comes to concern the future of the human as such. The metapsychology thus affirms a futural, and not just a past or present, dimension of diachronicity, under the conditions of human finitude, and in view of a possible universality based on universal singularity and radical difference. In this sense, Apollon displaces in an ethical direction Freud's and Lacan's formulations of both *desire* and its *object*, while elaborating further the "beyond" of the pleasure principle that both acknowledged.

To look back: I've sketched here the most central outlines of the Freudian and Lacanian metapsychologies, and placed against this backdrop a number of Apollon's fundamental metapsychological concepts both "synchronic" and "diachronic."[38] In the "synchronic" realm: we've considered the psyche as organism, the spirit, language, the effraction, and the letter of the body. In the "diachronic" dimension, I've sketched out the distinction between puberty and adolescence, the historical-anthropological account of the human (as moving from speech to language to culture and civilization both phylogenetically and ontogenetically), and the integration of this account into a psychoanalytic view of both the subject in general and the age of *mondialisation* in which we live. In addition, I've sketched quickly Apollon's multilayered approach to what people call "gender," an approach that distinguishes between various levels of historical development (biological, cultural-civilizational), singular experiences, and dimensions that can perhaps be viewed as trans-civilizational. All of the chapters that follow both turn around these concepts and turn them around, examine them in detail, and demonstrate their applicability to various aspects of psychoanalytic (and cultural) experience and practice.

## Foci of the Individual Chapters

Looking ahead: the collection begins, as indicated, with an overarching chapter by Willy Apollon, "The Human in Question," in which Apollon summarizes the main points of his conception of a psychoanalysis appropriate to the present age and emphatically oriented toward the future of humanity. The chapters in the rest of the volume are divided into three sections.

The *first section* contains two chapters that deal with the general theoretical questions of language, the out-of-language, and the aesthetic realm. Tracy McNulty outlines the concepts of language as determinant of individual consciousness, and of the unconscious as outside-of-language (*hors langage*), and she explains the relation of this outside-of-language to the act and to aesthetics, while tracing some of the key continuities and discontinuities between Apollon and Freud. Fernanda Negrete extends the analysis of the aesthetic and elucidates further its important role within the psychoanalysis that Apollon promotes, raising the question of the temporality of the aesthetic, and examining the theoretical affinities between Apollon and Gilles Deleuze and Felix Guattari, especially with reference to their work on Spinoza.

The *second section* goes into detail on the concepts of femininity and masculinity and related matters. Alexander Miller examines the notion of the "cultural montage of the sexual," which imposes symbolic castration during puberty, with references to Lacanian psychoanalysis and contemporary anthropology, as well as to public cultural and political arrangements and discourses. Daniel Wilson details the conceptions of woman, man, masculine, and feminine that emerge from Apollon's work, exploring illustrations from a range of contemporary cultural phenomena.

The *third section* contains three chapters that introduce and elaborate manifestly clinical notions (while including cultural-historical excurses and literary and cultural examples). Jeffrey Librett examines the Apollonian notions of the *address* to the Other and the *transference*, and places these in historical, clinical, and literary contexts, ending with a discussion of

Edgar Allan Poe's "MS Found in a Bottle." Danielle Bergeron unfolds the theory of the *symptom* as it takes its point of departure from the erotic body and considers its displacements across the trajectory of an analysis, using cultural figures and case vignettes as illustrations. Lucie Cantin then rearticulates the clinical implications of the four forms of the *fantasy*—originary fantasy, fantasies of seduction and castration, and fundamental fantasy—in terms of the synchronic and diachronic metapsychological notions and anthropological considerations advanced in Apollon's opening statement. These three chapters all further concern some of the successive stages in the logic of the unfolding of an analysis. An analysis begins with the transformation of the address into a transferential address; the symptom goes through a certain development in the course of an analysis; and the formulation and working through of the fantasies that underlie symptomization lead to the dispersion of symptoms and the end of an analysis.

The volume concludes with an interview between the contributors and Willy Apollon.[39]

## Notes

1. See *Telos* 201 (Winter 2022), Special Issue on "Civilizational States." On *mondialisation*, see Willy Apollon, "Citoyen du monde, . . . mais de quelle nationalité?"

2. Concerning the question of psychosis, one strand of inspiration comes from Gilles Deleuze, with whom Apollon studied while in Paris, and is visible in Apollon's writing, not to efface radical differences, ever since his dissertation on the culture of voodoo, published as *Le Vaudou: un espace pour les "voix."* See Willy Apollon, Danielle Bergeron, and Lucie Cantin, *La cure psychanalytique du psychotique: enjeux et stratégies.*

3. Sigmund Freud, *Standard Edition*, vol. VI.

4. We'll see in his opening essay that Apollon formulates these "psychical factors and relations in the unconscious" in terms (which recall phenomenology and Henri Bergson's vitalism) of the "lived" and then even more radically of the unconsciously felt (*ressenti*), which ultimately has to do with the very singularity of the creatively experiential spirit of the individual subject, beyond any possible accessibility through language.

5. Freud's gesture here is ambiguous, however, since on the one hand he speaks of a "psychology," and on the other of a "metapsychology." A scientific reduction of metaphysics—of "the myths of paradise and the fall of man, of

God, of good and evil, of immortality, and so on" (259)—appears to lead on the one hand to a "psychology" and on the other hand to a "metapsychology."

6. See Jessica Tran The et al., "The Epistemological Foundations of Freud's Energetics Model"; Jessica Tran The et al., "From the Principle of Inertia to the Death Drive: The Influence of the Second Law of Thermodynamics on the Freudian Theory of the Psychical Apparatus"; Jean Laplanche and J. B. Pontalis, *Vocabulaire de la psychanalyse*, 133–36; and for a much earlier, itself physicalist defense of Freud's applications of thermodynamics, Leon J. Saul, "Freud's Death Instinct and the Second Law of Thermodynamics."

7. In the "Metapsychological Supplement to the Theory of Dream," for example, published a couple of years after "The Unconscious," Freud reiterates this modesty concerning his metapsychology: "We are not, of course, intending to disguise or gloss over the uncertain and tentative character of these metapsychological discussions. Only deeper investigation can lead to the achievement of a certain degree of probability" (SE, XIV, 234).

8. See the Editorial Comments in the SE, XIV, 105–07 for the list of the texts we have and don't have, from the original project, and which other texts that were ultimately written address topics originally to have been addressed in the planned metapsychological writings.

9. In "The Uncanny" (1919, SE XVII), Freud had already shown, in reference to romantic and neoromantic literature, that the return of what has been historically overcome, such as superstitious beliefs, can induce a type of aesthetically pleasurable anxiety in certain situations, a modality of the persistence of the irrational to which he does not object there in an Enlightenment or scientistic modality, indeed all the less so as the figure of the physicist Spalanzani in ETA Hoffmann's tale himself functions as an exemplary source of the uncanny effect.

10. But of course Faust is—also for Freud, who frequently quotes Goethe, always with approval—a hero of the search for knowledge and experience beyond the confines of conventional sciences and morality, like Freud himself. And it is not only—even for Freud, no doubt—a mistake for him to be appealing to the "feminine" in the form of a "witch" to enable himself to come to terms through creative thinking with the dimension of the unconscious. After all, "Analysis Terminable and Interminable" ("Die endliche und die unendliche Analyse") ends with the discussion of the repudiation of the feminine as an obstacle to the concluding of any analysis. The function of the feminine in Apollon's thought, as represented in the chapters that follow, explicitly and emphatically shifts the feminine dimension in non-essentialist terms from the subordinate position it tends to have through Freud's works, and through much of the analytic tradition, into a central position, especially concerning the importance of the aesthetic dimension for all human existence.

11. One of Apollon's points of reference in his most recent lectures is contemporary work on consciousness on the part of quantum physicists, from Roger Penrose to Philippe Guillemant, who invoke a view of consciousness as exceeding calculation, and a model of science that is no longer materialist or determinist.

12. See Willy Apollon, "The Untreatable"; and "The Human in Question" below.

13. The emphasis of Jean Laplanche and J.-B. Pontalis (*Vocabulaire de la psychanalyse*, 484–89) on "différentiation" and "séparation" in their discussion of the function of the topographic model lends support to this view.

14. Perhaps indeed this over-arching question is what motivated Lacan to follow Kurt Lewin's example, assuming he knew of it, in extending his own quest into mathematical topology. See Lewin, *Principles of Topological Psychology*.

15. See Laplanche and Pontalis, 123–24.

16. It is not surprising that toward the end of his career, in 1937, some twenty two years later, Freud is giving himself a hard time for not having said enough about this "economic" dimension, unmasterable as it is, in principle, because the identity of identity and difference can never (pace Hegel) prevent itself from being haunted by the difference of identity and difference, and by the undecidability of its relation to that very difference.

17. The linguistically oriented way of putting this impossibility of completed self-reflection is the notion that there is no metalanguage, a position Lacan embraced from around 1960 on. See the article on "Metalanguage" in *Concept and Form: the Cahiers pour l'analyse and Contemporary French Thought*.

18. Paul Verhaege, "From Impossibility to Inability: Lacan's Theory of the Four Discourses," argues, to the contrary, that Lacan's four discourses (master, university, analyst, and hysteric) as articulated in and around Seminar XVII, *The Other Side of Psychoanalysis*, constitute his most important contribution, but even if this is the case, Lacan's theory of the registers is a necessary step toward the conceptualization of the discourses.

19. See Jacques Lacan, "Aggressivity in Psychoanalysis," in his *Écrits*, 101–24, an essay on the "imaginary" that tends to be skipped in favor of "The Mirror Stage," but in which the violent potential of the imaginary is made much more clear.

20. Cf. Freud's discussions of animism and the omnipotence of thoughts in the narcissistic formations, in *Totem and Tabu* and elsewhere, where Freud is already trying to reduce superstitions and religions to psychic processes and states, but also sees modern neurotic subjects as displaying "primitive" characteristics, which complicates the notions of the civilized and the primitive at once.

21. Lacan begins to use this formula for the real in Seminar XI, *Les quatre concepts fondamentaux de la psychanalyse*, "Le réel est içi ce qui revient toujours à la même place—à cette place où le sujet en tant qu'il cogite, où la res cogitans,

ne le rencontre pas" (49), thus also the place of a (traumatic) missed encounter. In the English: *The Four Fundamental Concepts of Psychoanalysis*, trans. Alan Sheridan (New York: W. W. Norton, 1977), "the real is that which always comes back to the same place—to the place where the subject in so far as he thinks, where the *res cogitans*, does not meet it" (49).

22. The notion of "plus-de-jouir," often translated as "surplus-jouissance," but only by effacing the sense of "no more enjoyment" that the expression also contains, was introduced by Lacan in Seminar XVI, *D'un Autre à l'autre*, from 1968–69. In Seminar XX, *Encore*, from 1972–73, in English as *On Feminine Sexuality: the Limits of Love and Knowledge*, 1972–73, trans. Bruce Fink (New York: Norton, 1998), Lacan speaks of "enjoying substance (*la substance jouissante*)" as "the substance of the body" but where the body "enjoys itself only by 'corporizing (*corporiser*) the body in a signifying way. That implies something other than the *partes extra partes* of extended substance" (French edition, 26; English, 23).

23. See the illuminating essays by Jean-Joseph Goux in his *Symbolic Economies*.

24. On metaphor and metonymy as figures particularly apt to the characterization of symptom and desire, see Jacques Lacan, "L'instance de la lettre dans l'inconscient, ou la raison depuis Freud" in *Écrits*, 493–530.

25. Of course, I am not suggesting that there are no displacements between these sets of "equivalent" terms from one of these major analytic thinkers to the next. Nor am I denying such displacements *within* the work of each of these thinkers. Needless to say, for example, Lacan's "return to Freud" brings with it the structuralist approach to language and culture, then mathematical logic, set theory, and topology, German philosophy from Kant to Heidegger, the tradition of surrealism, the French Jesuit syllabus, and so on, not to mention Lacan's own brilliance, boldness, and foibles. The point here is not to minimize the changes, but rather to reconstruct initial points of reference from the one metapsychology to the next.

26. Lacan's interest in topology develops from the topology of surfaces to the topology of knots. He begins to speak of the Borromean knot in Seminar XX, *Encore*, and of the "sinthome," a portmanteau word playing on the notion of a symptom, in Seminar XXIII, *Le Sinthome*, from 1975–6 (the third to last seminar year), devoted to the reading of James Joyce.

27. Immanuel Kant also formulated nicely this moment when the human being discovers the distance of humanity from nature: "He discovered in himself a faculty of choosing for himself a way of living and not being bound to a single way, as other animals are. Yet upon the momentary delight that this marked superiority might have awakened in him, anxiety and fright must have followed right away. . . . He stood, as it were, on the brink of an abyss," from "Mutmasslicher Anfang der Menschengeschichte," in Wilhelm Weischedel (ed.),

*Immanuel Kant Werkausgabe*, 88–89. English: "Conjectural Beginning of Human History," in Immanuel Kant, *Anthropology, History, and Education*, 166.

28. Cf. Michael Tomasello, *A Natural History of Human Thinking* and *Origins of Human Communication*, whose emphasis on the importance of the capacity to collaborate for human evolution and for the development of human language sheds some corroborative light on Apollon's views from the—differently oriented—standpoint of contemporary evolutionary anthropology.

29. In *Seminar XX, Encore*, Lacan says: "If I have said that language is what the unconscious is structured like, that is because language, first of all, doesn't exist. Language is what we try to know concerning the function of llanguage [*lalangue*]. . . . [T]he effects of llanguage [*lalangue*], already there qua knowledge, go well beyond anything the being who speaks is capable of enunciating [*susceptible d'énoncer*]" (138–39).

30. To situate this position in the history of appropriations of psychoanalysis, it may be useful to contrast it with that of André Breton, whose version of surrealism attempted to reconcile Freudianism with Hegelianism, which always posits the principle of the identity of identity and difference. For this Hegelianism, see Breton's "Surrealist Situation of the Object."

31. See for example, "The Transformations of Puberty," the third treatise in the *Three Essays on Sexuality* (SE, VII) from 1905, and "The Sexual Enlightenment of Children" from 1907 (SE, IX).

32. This absence is strikingly discernible, for example, in the discussion of Frank Wedekind's play about adolescents encountering a sexuality for which they lack language, *Frühlingserwachen* (*Spring Awakening*), by Freud and his colleagues on 13 Feb. 1907, the record of which we have in the *Minutes of the Vienna Psychoanalytic Society*.

33. See Lacan's note on Frank Wedekind's play, *Frühlingserwachen* (*Spring Awakening*), "L'eveil du printemps."

34. By elaborating in his seminar on the proposition "the address is sex," Apollon also situates sex within the gesture of intimate address to another, whereby one attempts to evoke experiences that go beyond words. Clinical Seminar, 26 Jan. 2021.

35. The associations of the sublime with the masculine and the beautiful with the feminine go back at least as far as Kant and Schiller, although they are formulated in the eighteenth century—needless to say—in rather different terms.

36. Lacan elaborates on sublimation, for example, in his Seminar VII, 105–96. For recent discussions of Lacan and the sublime, see Slavoj Zizek, *Sex and the Failed Absolute*; and Dany Nobus, *Critique of Psychoanalytic Reason*, 172–96.

37. Although she tended to stay far away from psychoanalysis, Hannah Arendt, *Lectures on Kant's Political Philosophy*, makes a similar point in her interpretation of Kant's "reflexive judgment" as a faculty of political orientation.

38. My choice of conceptual focus has been guided by a broad number of lectures, printed schemas, and writing from the last several years of Apollon's work, especially his schemas on "Les concepts fondamentaux de la métapsychologie" ("The Fundamental Concepts of Metapsychology") from 17 July 2020.

39. I wish to express here my gratitude to Nathan Gorelick, Tracy McNulty, and Daniel Wilson for their comments on an earlier draft of this introduction.

# Works Cited

Apollon, Willy. "Citoyen du monde, . . . mais de quelle nationalité?" *Mondialisation, défis pour l'human*, edited by Jean-Pierre Boisvert et al., GIFRIC, 2016, pp. 205–74.

———. *Le Vaudou: un espace pour les "voix."* Éditions Galilée, 1976.

———. Schemas on "Les concepts fondamentaux de la métapsychologie" ("The Fundamental Concepts of Metapsychology"). 17 July 2020.

———. "The Untreatable." Translated by Steven Miller, *Umbr(a): Incurable*, no. 1, 2006, pp. 23–39.

———. *Unpublished Clinical Seminar.* 26 Jan 2021.

Apollon, Willy, Danielle Bergeron, and Lucie Cantin. *La cure psychanalytique du psychotique: enjeux et strategies.* GIFRIC, 2008.

Arendt, Hannah. *Lectures on Kant's Political Philosophy.* Edited by Ronald Beiner, U of Chicago P, 1992.

Breton, André. "Surrealist Situation of the Object." *Manifestoes of Surrealism*, U of Michigan P, 1972, pp. 255–78.

*Concept and Form: The Cahiers pour l'analyse and Contemporary French Thought.* Accessed 13 Sept. 2023. http://cahiers.kingston.ac.uk/concepts/metalanguage.html.

Freud, Sigmund. *Studienausgabe (SA).* Edited by Alexander Mitscherlich et al., Fischer Verlag, 1975.

———. *Standard Edition of the Complete Psychological Works of Sigmund Freud (SE).* Translated and edited by James Strachey, Hogarth Press, 1957.

Goux, Jean-Joseph. *Symbolic Economies: After Marx and Freud.* Translated by Jennifer Curtiss Gage, Cornell UP, 1990.

Kant, Immanuel. "Mutmasslicher Anfang der Menschengeschichte." *Immanuel Kant Werkausgabe*, vol. 11, edited by Wilhelm Weischedel, Suhrkamp, 1982.

———. "Conjectural Beginning of Human History," *Anthropology, History, and Education*, edited by Günter Zöller and Robert Louden, Cambridge UP, 2007.

Lacan, Jacques. *Écrits.* Éditions du Seuil, 1966.

———. "L'eveil du printemps." *À propos du L'eveil du printemps de Frank Wedekind*, by François Regnault, Christian Bourgois, 1974, pp. 7–10.

————. *Le Séminaire, Livre VII: L'éthique de la psychanalyse (1959–60)*. Éditions du Seuil, 1986.

————. *Le Séminaire, Livre XI: Les quatre concepts fondamentaux de la psychanalyse (1964)*. Éditions du Seuil, 1973.

————. *Le Séminaire, Livre XVI: D'un Autre à l'autre (1968–9)*. Éditions du Seuil, 2006.

————. *Le Séminaire, Livre XVII: L'envers de la psychanalyse (1969–70)*. Éditions du Seuil, 1991.

————. *Le Séminaire, Livre XX: Encore (1972–3)*. Éditions du Seuil, 1975.

————. *Le Séminaire, Livre XXIII: The Sinthome (1975–6)*. Editions du Seuil, 2005.

Laplanche, Jean, and J. B. Pontalis. *Vocabulaire de la psychanalyse*. PUF, 1967.

Lewin, Kurt. *Principles of Topological Psychology*. Translated by Fritz Heider and Grace M. Heider, McGraw Hill, 1936.

Nobus, Dany. *Critique of Psychoanalytic Reason: Studies in Lacanian Theory and Practice*. Routledge, 2022.

Nunberg, Hermann, and Ernst Federn. *Minutes of the Vienna Psychoanalytic Society, Vol. 1: 1906–1908*. Translated and edited by M. Nunberg, International Universities Press, 1962.

Saul, Leon J. "Freud's Death Instinct and the Second Law of Thermodynamics." *International Journal of Psychoanalysis* 39 (January 1, 1958): 323–25.

*Telos*, no. 201, Winter 2022, Special Issue on "Civilizational States."

The, Jessica Tran, Pierre Magistretti, and François Ansermet. "The Epistemological Foundations of Freud's Energetics Model." *Frontiers in Psychology*, vol. 9, Oct. 2018, article 1861, pp. 1–10.

The, Jessica Tran, Jean-Philippe Ansermet, Pierre Magistretti, and François Ansermet. "From the Principle of Inertia to the Death Drive: the Influence of the Second Law of Thermodynamics on the Freudian Theory of the Psychical Apparatus." *Frontiers in Psychology*, vol. 11, Feb. 2020, article 325, pp. 1–8.

Tomasello, Michael. *A Natural History of Human Thinking*. Harvard UP, 2014.

————. *Origins of Human Communication*. MIT Press, 2008.

Verhaege, Paul. "From Impossibility to Inability: Lacan's Theory of the Four Discourses." *The Letter: Lacanian Perspectives on Psychoanalysis*, vol. 3, Spring 1995, pp. 91–108.

Zizek, Slavoj. *Sex and the Failed Absolute*. Bloomsbury, 2020.

# Opening

1

# The Human in Question

WILLY APOLLON

TRANSLATED BY ALEXANDER MILLER

Civilizations, despite appearances, do not really ask the question of the human; rather, each civilization posits itself, and imposes itself, as representing a concern for the best of the human. We might even say that this is the very definition of civilization. This is undoubtedly why we need to understand how this relationship between civilization and humanity is at the heart of the problematic of psychosis. Freud glimpsed the importance of this a hundred years ago in *Mass Psychology and the Analysis of the Ego*, but he didn't have the opportunity to confront it as we do today. As for the West, it clearly cannot ask itself this question, because it imposes itself on other civilizations—by all the means at its disposal, and in particular through its sciences, the new religion—as the very model of humanity. The West justifies its control [of everything] by claiming to represent the high point in the evolution of the human, the best of which it is capable. Any other civilization, from this occidental perspective, would therefore either need to join the West, or at least to think of itself within the framework of receivability that the West has established. Decolonization, from this perspective, would thus be little more than a dream that measures the deep slumber in which universities and research centers other than those of the West are kept, in those

35

countries where the historical stakes of civilization do not necessarily concur in recognizing or supporting the West's supremacy. It was within such a framework that Freud invented psychoanalysis by creating a space of speech for what his culture identified in women as hysteria, therefore breaking with the structure of address imposed by this culture. It is not clear that Lacan, in his indispensable contribution, ever thought of the return to Freud outside of this framework, in which Francophone Christian civilization still accredited the limits of an "unsayable" [*un impropre au dire*] that was borne by the signifier of the Name-of-the-Father.

Whatever the civilization and the cultural concerns it accredits, however, what Freud discovered and put at the heart of the psychoanalysis he invented by letting the hysteric speak is akin to what quantum physics has been confronting us with since the 1950s, 1960s and 1970s—the height of Lacan's call for a return to Freud. What scientific observation obtains, in the structure of the space-time in which we evolve, is merely the reaction of the observed object to the technical organization of observation. Indeed, the very structure of space-time, which radically conditions observation, is itself no more than the implementation of our reaction to an unobservable that haunts our consciousness of time, insofar as time is our lived experience. There is thus an unbridgeable gap between the feeling in relation to which the consciousness of lived experience is established and discourse—that is, the issue of an address to the Other, the object of which would pertain to the observable and which would claim to account for this feeling. Even more so when it comes to the lived experience that would bear witness to the consciousness of this feeling. As a result, the Other of the address has no access to the being's experience, even under the risky proposition of speech, and even less to what is felt, beyond any consciousness the being might have of it. This is how Freud discovered what he rightly called the unconscious, in the specific sense I wish to underscore here: something that is out-of-language, and thus excluded from the address, because it is fundamentally outside the subjective consciousness that defines lived experience.

For these reasons, the psychoanalysis Freud invented is first and foremost a subjective experience of the analysand, and cannot be conceived as or reduced to any action on the part of the psychoanalyst, who from the outset is in the position of that Other who has no access to the lived experience through which the being interprets what she feels. As for the speech that the psychoanalyst makes possible for the analysand, which we will come back to, it is a risk that the being is supposed to take with respect to what she feels, while also taking into account her expectation of the possible response of the Other in an improbable address. Psychoanalysis is not psychotherapy, and the analysand is not the psychoanalyst's patient. A psychoanalysis is a decision to embark on a risky journey, from which one cannot return unscathed, like a tourist, because of the effects produced in the body and in the being by the traversal of all the lands that have marked the subject's history. In a sense, psychoanalysis is a one-way ticket.

What fundamentally institutes this journey is that, under the guise or mask of traversing spaces that are defined by cultural requirements in which the concerns of civilization take precedence, such an undertaking is in fact aimed at a hypothetical restructuring of the lived experience of time in bygone eras. It is as if, by going back in time and reconsidering its effects, we can establish for ourselves a different position in the space of civilization that is culturally structured according to a certain relationship to the Other. The traveler always returns with the illusion that his position in the group is new: he experiences something in the journey through previously unexplored spaces that changes his relationship to the history structured by the beliefs and ambitions that, over time, the collective has established as normalcy. And at some level, the traveler is not wrong, even though he hardly perceives the extent to which the rules and norms of his culture, which manage the limits of the possible, have defined his position in the collective, or that the civilization that gives credibility to the limits of the receivable has overdetermined, in the so-called historical time of the collective, what has become unsayable for him. In such a manner, however, one does not truly travel, but is a tourist and thus returns.

The journey undertaken in psychoanalysis, by contrast, entails no such return. Success or failure—it does not matter—one does not come back, in any case not unscathed. Without knowing it, the analysand—and this is why I challenge her characterization as a patient—searches in vain for a refuge in her own space-time. An elsewhere, here and now! If Freud was not able to go further than such an exit from cultural space, it is because the concessions he had to make from the 1920s onward, to save psychoanalysis from the risks involved in refusing the receivable, did not allow the journey he was inventing to escape the cultural stakes of psychotherapy. And since then, things have not really changed—far from it. Lacan, for his part, having entered the field that was opened up for adolescence by Surrealism in the aftermath of World War I, perceived what was at stake in this quest that for the human transcends the receivable. But he did not have the opportunity to be confronted with the consequences of what, from 1990 to 2010, in the face of a burgeoning *mondialisation*, would turn civilization into a bronze statue with feet of clay. The intimate journey he took over from Freud is now being confronted by spaces that have become untethered from their historical reference points yet retain the concern—though not without unwittingly losing hope—that the West, particularly the iteration predominant in the historically Catholic countries whose languages derive from Latin, still offers the Human its best chance. Today, however, such a perspective fails to take into account the rupture introduced by an adolescence whose cultural ties have been severed by the confrontation of civilizations.

An intimate journey to the heart of what lived experience interprets and retains of what a being feels—there is no return from such is a journey, because it revisits all the stages at which a certain impasse ceaselessly haunted this lived experience, from childhood to adolescence. Such a journey aims to break certain links with the concerns of the collective by returning to puberty, when the formatting of the cultural montage of the sexual—which guarantees the collective's hold on a significant part of the young person's affectivity, or the interpretation of feeling—is put in place. It is a decisive confrontation that brings into play a symbolic castration in which the member pays with their jouissance for participation in the benefits offered by the collective. But it is also a key moment in the integration of a member, in which the collective wants to ensure that what the adolescent will discover, in the intimate feelings that mark their lived experience, will not result in the subversion of the rules that structure the space of the possible, in the social link and within the limits of believability defined by civilization.

What is at stake here repeats, at the level of the very structure that articulates the individual to the collective, or language as such, what the quantum physicist discovers while working with the structure of space his mathematics constructs: namely, that he has no verifiable access to what he calls time. The language in which a culture creates the rules and norms that define the social space of cooperation and coexistence will never be able to circumscribe the contours of the being's experience, in its consciousness of feeling, in order to silence mental representation to the point of subjecting this experience to the necessities of the social bond: at least not without a violence that is not sustainable in the medium term. This is what I have sought to capture with the concept of the "defect in language." In no way can language reduce lived experience to the perceptible; the subject's intimacy remains inaccessible to the Other and its power to control the social link. If psychoanalysis is to survive *mondialisation*, it will necessarily be with a metapsychology constructed for what *mondialisation* allows in the way of a staging of the human beyond cultural perspectives and civilizational concerns . . . there precisely where psychosis flourishes.

## A Metapsychology in the Time of *Mondialisation*

At a time when psychoanalysis must rethink itself, the function of metapsychology is tied to the fate of the human—beyond the colonization of certain cultural spaces, which *mondialisation* brings to light by confronting civilizations with the internal limits of beliefs and values in which they claim to define and thus enclose the human. As I noted in the early 2000s, financial globalization, which, thanks to the internationalization of capital, was supposed to break out of the old structures of colonization and give them a new dimension, was encountering a limit, namely, in the confrontation of civilizations that in the long or medium term was bound to blow up its Western foundations. I referred to this phenomenon by the very Francophone concept of *mondialisation*, emphasizing in 2004 that it heralded an insurmountable crisis, of which the financial dimension would only be the tip of the iceberg. Saying this, I meant to introduce the fact that civilizations, including and especially those of the West, were not yet at the stage of discovering that the human they all claim to be is in question. And yet this question is at the heart of adolescence, which is confused for good reason with puberty, the moment at which civilizations shape the new member of the collective to ends that psychoanalysis must interrogate if it is to make possible a space for this journey from which one does not return.

The recent pandemic confronts us with this question in a tragic manner. It forces us to face up to what mobilizes the forces at play in *mondialisation*: the fact that from now on we're going to have to deal, at a level that transcends any particular collective, with problems that concern all nations and that cannot be resolved by any one nation, however powerful it may be, or even a group of nations, but require the mobilization of all. These are problems whose solutions transcend what civilizations can promise, and which will at last open the space needed for this time in which what is at stake is the quest for something else, which subverts adolescence—the Human as such. Among these problems, violence against women, whatever form it may take, and which as such blocks access to femininity, is one that will subvert the cultural stakes of the montage of the sexual in all civilizations. In this context, psychoanalysis is for the moment the only experience that can support this concern for the human [*ce souci de l'humain*] that tears apart the adolescent's relationship to what has been imposed on him—and especially on her—as puberty, or as the cultural montage of the sexual, by way of a never-before-denounced censoring of the feminine. Psychoanalysis, thus conceived as the experience of a journey with no possibility of return, cannot survive without taking into account the absolutely new fact of the adolescent experience of the concern for the human. From now on, this question will be at the heart of the journey offered by the psychoanalytic experience, and the metapsychology required for such an experience must address the conditions that make this question inevitable at a time when the challenges of *mondialisation* are subverting the relationship of ethics to what a civilization renders believable or what it renders unsayable, in order to support and lend credibility to the rules and norms that define the limits of the receivable in a given culture.

I have thus wanted to approach this issue by putting into perspective the unbridgeable divide that separates the experience of the analysand, who takes the risk of transference, from what can be said about it to an Other, for whom such an experience is of the order of observation or experimentation. This perspective is even more important given that the analyst, whose unconscious subverts the structure of address by producing the transference, cannot put themself in the position of either observer or experimenter. Still less can the analyst put themself in the position of a therapist who knows how to bring back to the paths marked out by cultural norms and civilizational ideals someone who has been too far removed from them by circumstances said to be unfortunate, because they were beyond her control, or because of intuitions about a beyond of the limits of the receivable. The analysand must effectively decide what to do with the humanity that awaits its destiny in the vagaries of her life. She alone is responsible; for what adolescence has revealed to her is that what is at stake in this adventure is something greater than herself, something that exceeds her existence, something she has not chosen, something to which no other but herself has access.

## The Spirit

From this perspective on psychoanalysis in the context of *mondialisation*, the concept of the human, which transcends both cultural imperatives and civilizational concerns, is what decides what metapsychology must account for. If we must start from what scientists tell us, what we evoke with this concept appeared some one hundred to two hundred thousand years ago with homo sapiens. As for language, this human constructed it some fifty thousand years ago to survive in the conditions it likewise created, to cope with the circumstances and constraints of an environment in which humans were forced to organize their first collectives. When the human decided to create cultures and civilizations, to survive and to pursue its quest for the unknown objectives that guide its aspirations, it provided itself with the appropriate means to achieve these ends. And if today we interrogate humanity as an entity independent of the cultures and civilizations in which it manifests itself through its creations and works, we must try to grasp it as transcending the intermediaries it creates for its adventure and its survival. Today, for example, a handful of multi-billionaires are joining forces to fund leading scientists, including Nobel Prize winners, to set up laboratories with the aim of creating the means to vanquish death. A decisive moment in metapsychology consists in accounting for the *human quest* as an out-of-language that is manifested in subjective desire, under conditions that language creates by structuring the possible links between members of the collective.

To this end, the first, the essential, and the founding concept of this metapsychology is the concept of the spirit [*l'esprit*], which I retain from the philosophical tradition in which we find ourselves. For this concept, now overused outside this philosophical tradition, I want to retain a definition that, while being as simple as possible, can meet the rigorous demands of philosophical or scientific thought.

For the purposes of this metapsychology, then, we can put things as follows: *the spirit is the lived experience of a capacity to represent to oneself what does not exist, to want it, and, as required, to give oneself the means to create it.* This experience institutes the human as a three-dimensional subjective experience that creates a specifically human temporality, an experience distinct and independent from the time of the clock. Here, it is space that emerges as a fourth dimension, the structuring of which, with the creation of language, imposes itself as a survival requirement for humans much later, to follow again what scientists tell us.

So a three-dimensional definition: representation, desire, and the act of creating. This definition could be described as experimental and as instituting the spirit as the subjective experience of a time indissociable from an energy. No doubt even before birth, everyone has a very concrete, though not necessarily conscious, experience of this; we refer to this here as first childhood. The problem that psychoanalysis must take into account and deal with is that this experience *cannot* be conscious. This is not a theoretical issue per se, unless one wants to make it the subject of an intellectual debate, which immediately puts at stake the credibility of all involved, and therefore their relationship to a given civilization. Besides, it can only be a question here of the spirit as we experience it intimately, not as it would be objectively, independently of the experience that each of us has of it. We do not have the slightest idea of what this is outside of the representations each of us may make of it. The spirit as we live and experience it is certainly not the spirit in itself, because the experience we have of it cannot be separated from our consciousness of that experience, which does not include the spirit in itself. We obviously have no access to the Spirit as such, but this hardly prevents us from creating a representation of it—civilizations have never deprived themselves of doing so. But such a leap from time to space is not something to which humans can lay claim, even and especially in language. Indeed, this is what physics has been confronting us with since Einstein, and even more so with quantum physics. The time that gives consistency to our consciousness of the intimate experience that institutes us as human is not a reality that can be verified outside the act in which we affirm it. In this respect, agnosticism remains a philosophical position, perhaps the only one, internal to the interpretation of an experience that remains fundamentally outside language. We are only conscious at the very moment we experience that the representation we make of something that does not exist is a pure representation, as Kant tells us, inseparable from its temporal experience, and that as such it is not the representation of something that would be in the space-time structured by language. What we have here is a true experience—therefore a lived experience of which anyone can be conscious—which remains independent of the interpretation we make of it and which posits the human as such in the time of what is lived in this experience but outside the space that the collective structures with language.

We can recognize such experience in first childhood, just as we can in the adolescent or adult, the mathematician or quantum physicist. This first moment of thought, as pure representation, creates for us an intimate space that is distinct from the temporal experience of this same representation. This is a first articulation of space-time as a fundamental condition proper to the human in its capacity to create an intimate representation that has no relation to any object whatsoever. We need this intimate space to identify things that are represented but have no consistency other than their representation. We can refer to it as spiritual space, but its specific characteristic is to be an intimate experience, independent of and unconnected to the space of perception that will be overdetermined by the creation of language as the structure of the link between companions. This is, for example, the place of *number*, which we have created as an instrument for apprehending reality in a space-time framework in which we represent number with an act: the writing of the *numerical digit*. The mathematician needs this to give consistency, as it were, to what does not exist: to make it pass through writing into the space created by language, the digit, and thus to make it accessible to the Other in the social link. This is even more strongly the case for the quantum physicist, now aware that apart from the digit she knows nothing of what she still calls *time*. And what can we say of biologists? They must come to grips with this *thing* they are asked to manage but of which they can only grasp the effects, the consequences of which periodically subvert the proper functioning of the organism in the social link!

In the same movement, I propose that the object thus represented can be desired independently of its very existence. This second characteristic of the spirit, which experience reveals to us long before adolescence—even if it is in adolescence that it takes on its full dimension and autonomy—confronts us with a *quest*, of which we cannot say how far it will lead Sapiens, in relation to both those who preceded it in the history of evolution and those who are still for a time its contemporaries. It is as if the creation of language by Sapiens fifty thousand years ago heralded the disappearance of Neanderthal some twenty thousand years later. This *intimate quest for the unknown object* leads human beings to conceive of and then to desire that which does not exist; this is the consequence of the dimension of the spirit that instituted the human thousands of years ago, long before the creation of language, and even longer before the cultures and civilizations that followed.

Finally, the spirit that characterizes the human can, on occasion, invent whatever is necessary to bring into existence what is thus represented and desired despite its nonexistence. In other words, it can *create* that which did not previously exist, as we have seen more and more regularly for the last century and a half. This third characteristic of the spirit—which consists in creating what it wants or what it needs to gain access to what it wants—completes in a way this *spiritual space* that seems to be a *lived experience* specific to sapiens and that we cannot confuse with the psychic space that, according to science, we have inherited from evolution over the course of some 7 million years. Although it is realized in *subjective experience*, this third characteristic of the spirit introduces the being to the dimension of space as if by an effraction, in an exit from oneself that is not without risk for oneself or without consequences for one's companions. But what interests us here is not the debate on evolution as such, but *the human experience* that underpins the concept of spirit as an intimate lived experience. This spiritual space, with its three dimensions of thinking, desiring, and creating, appears with the human being and is part of an intimate experience that takes place in a *subjective time*. This subjective time is foreign to the psychic space that articulates the being to what is perceptible and observable in the collective and its environment and that has been perfected through evolution over millions of years. There is something specific in these dimensions that characterizes the spirit, and that makes sapiens radically different from other hominids who were once its contemporaries. From the outset, the human is distinguished by a lived experience of being conscious that it can transcend the limits of the psyche, which regulates the organism's relationship with the environment and the collective. From the outset, the human finds itself subjected *to a dimension of its own being* over which it has no power, and which can therefore subvert, for better or for worse, all the conditions of its existence, within the group as well as the environment. This is undoubtedly an experience that underpins the human's difference, but it is also one in which the anxiety that accompanies any departure from the immunological limits of pleasure is experienced, as is the jouissance that signs *the risk of wanting to live what cannot exist without it.*

## The Effraction of the Psyche and of the Limits of Pleasure

The concept of the effraction is intended to highlight the clinical consequences of this emergence of the spirit in the psyche inherited from evolution. In the first case, what is aimed for here concerns what Freud discovered and revealed in 1920 with *Beyond the Pleasure Principle.* To be retained from the concept of the death drive, first and foremost, is that it evokes an intimate lived experience, the object of which is the subject's experience of a dimension within herself that transcends her own existence and leads her to the gates of the sublime. It is to this intimate experience of transcending the limits of the psyche, signified in pleasure as an immunological marker, that I refer with the concept of the effraction of the limits of the psyche by the spirit. Pleasure is no longer the marker of success for the proper functioning of the psyche, or for any of the systems of the organism: something in the being wants more, is worth more, and goes beyond it—hence *jouissance*.

This *more* and this *beyond*—which have neither existence nor consistency of their own in the space where the psyche evolves within the limits defined by language in a given culture—thus put the immunity of the being at risk! They punctuate *the time of the being* in an intimacy that has no connection to what the psyche can refer to and control in space. From early childhood, *this more and this beyond* separate the being from what awaits it in the space where language defines the perceptible, the observable, and the receivable, thus cutting the being off from the Other. This *more and this beyond* to which it leads, which are inaccessible to the observation and the control of the Other and are at the heart of this metapsychology, evoke *the quest for the unknown object* that defines *the human*, whatever the culture or civilization in which it manifests itself.

Opponents of Freud's death drive understood this well, as did his first companion psychoanalysts, who constrained him to making concessions regarding the cultural consequences of such a clinical advance. This issue was at the heart of the return to Freud in which Lacan guided us. But the stakes of neurosis are also situated here, along with the limits of a psychoanalysis that sets itself the goal of helping people deal with this effraction of the limits of pleasure within a framework of cultural receivability and respect for what the beliefs and stakes of civilization make credible or unsayable for the maintenance of the structure of the social link. The stakes of perversion, and even more so those of psychosis, on the other hand, are to be found elsewhere and have thus long been left to the side. But there is another important dimension of the metapsychology that emerges with the effraction of the psyche, and thus of the limits of pleasure, by the spirit, and which has to be underlined in the context of *mondialisation*, which renders fragile the values of civilization by bringing cultural issues into conflict, and in which psychoanalysis must either evolve or become irrelevant: what is at stake in such a context is *the future of the human* as such, and not the *success of the individual within the cultural limits of a civilization* that offers itself as the model of what the human being should be.

Effraction can only be thought of in its aftermath. It is undoubtedly the action constitutive of the human, insofar as with this philosophical concept I mean to speak of both what science invites us to consider with the concept of Sapiens and what Freud introduces with his concept of the death drive. What I mean by this event of the effraction is the emergence of a dimension in Sapiens that transcends the limits of both the psyche and the functions of the organism, even at their best, that is, in the conquest of a space for the collective. What is experienced in the traversal of the limits of pleasure opens onto two paths: that of a violence that is uncontrollable within the limits of the social link that structures space-time, or that of the aesthetic that is invoked in this metapsychology, as what is experienced as possible beyond these limits. How can we describe, in the simplest manner, the lived experience of the sensibility constitutive of the temporality of the being, which is inaccessible to the Other but which transforms the space of the organism? The organism is the object to which the Other has access, in the space controlled by the collective; this sensibility, on the other hand, creates the *body* as the *time of subjectivity*, which is affirmed in *the consciousness of lived experience*. I thus describe this experience as the time of the aesthetic, a time that is foreign to the clock, and that comprises the feeling of or sensitivity to the beautiful—that which under no circumstances would the Other want to lose, and which the being lives as the best of its experience—and the feeling of the sublime, in which the being has the experience of something more important than its own existence. This is what often leads me to a somewhat radical formula, but one that captures what *mondialisation* is leading us toward: beyond the limits of the receivable, where civilization no longer lends credibility to cultural imperatives, it is either aesthetics or violence.


## The Aesthetic

This beyond-limits dimension of the Spirit, which founds the experience of *subjective time* that is constitutive of the human, introduces us to the field of the aesthetic: a dimension of the human necessarily associated with the concept of *femininity* in this metapsychology. The experience of leaving one's limits makes anxiety, as an anticipation of the end of oneself, what introduces the being to an awareness of a non-difference or non-gap between time and self. As a passenger of the instant, the being remains unwittingly captive to a future awaited by a past experience. This expectation of a future, rather than the past, overdetermines the present, the past being merely the obstacle to be removed. This experience is constitutive of the body, which ignores the limits where pleasure signals the immunity of the organism in conditions and spaces controlled by the collective through language and culture. This time, experienced as body, and in which the being makes its risky wager and plays its hand, remains a mystery, as quantum physics has taught us since the 1920s–30s, precisely as Freud was confronted with the death drive as a profound *discontent in civilization*. A below and a beyond of what culture prescribes or promises under the auspices of civilization thus brings into play what can only be referred to here as the human.

For the issues at stake in this metapsychology, we refer to a definition of the aesthetic to account for what the being is confronted with in this beyond-limits that engages it in the out-of-space of its lived experience. Inherited from Kant and Hegel, the most pragmatic dimension of this concept is here retained for psychoanalysis: the dimension that invokes a bodily experience, the feeling of the beautiful, and what it reveals to us of the humanity whose experience we either live or betray. What do we do that is beautiful? What do we do that subverts the structure of the address by mobilizing the feeling of the beautiful in the Other? We create *the aesthetic*. We dive into *this more and this beyond, this crossing of limits that creates the feminine in us*, opening our intimate being to spaces and to bodily experiences that were unknown to us until then, and that we would not renounce for anything in the world. We create music, painting, dance, sculpture, and erotism; we build temples and cathedrals and erect museums so as not to lose such creations. No matter the culture or the civilization from which they come, in no case would we want to forget these works that help us discover a dimension of ourselves that we did not know before—intimate places, experiences, and feelings—and that make us better and make us closer to all other human beings, beyond both space and time. Indeed, it is thus through feeling that we refer to the aesthetic in the psychoanalytic clinic; but what I refer to here as feeling is not the emotion that sends us back to the limits of the receivable, in those spaces controlled by culture and accredited by civilization. What I refer to here as feeling is more dangerous in a way. It initiates us into the aesthetic: the crossing of boundaries through which it arouses the feminine in the most intimate part of ourselves, in the temporality inseparable from bodily experience. It sustains the being where the beautiful carries it beyond the reach of culture and into those places where the sublime defies the values of civilization. Beyond what can be said and what language encloses in the structures of address, feeling bears witness to the paths of the human quest in the letter of the body. Aesthetic feeling opens us to the body that intimately identifies us, that singularizes us outside the space-time that culture controls, in a distance inaccessible to others, and whose letter, through its inscription, manifests the effraction of the organism in this subjectivation. I like to evoke the fact that the secret services of the large modern states know something about this, and can be identified in the search for, or protection from, the subject of the act in some imprint left by this letter of the body, whether vocal, tactile, ocular, gestural, auditory, or other.

## The Letter of the Body

There is nothing less obvious than an act. Indeed, what characterizes the act is that it has consequences in the Other that are not foreseeable; consequences that are not those anticipated by the subject from whom the act originates. From the point of view of this metapsychology, the act presupposes an effraction into the organism or the psyche that has been repeated and inscribed: a writing. This is why speech can be considered an act: it presupposes the letter of an inscription both in the subject's body and in the Other of an address. An act occurs because something has been inscribed, and this inscription has constituted a part of the body. This something was inscribed precisely because it could not be said, and then what was inscribed was repeated. In fact, I would say it is by dint of repetition that inscription occurs, and it is interesting for the clinic to know at what point something was inscribed by dint of repetition, by not having been able to be said. In a developing life, the various systems of the organism and their functions, tissues, and cells grow and develop according to their own rhythm and the needs of the captive ensemble of familial, environmental, and cultural contexts. What goes beyond and contradicts these contexts repeatedly disrupts the proper functioning of these systems and their operations and is inscribed as letters of the body in the lived experience of these effractions.

When I speak of the inscription of what cannot be said, I refer to the fact that the anxiety provoked by what cannot be said and the emotion that accompanies this anxiety make it such that a developing system must dysfunction in order to adapt. We cannot act as if, for us humans, there could be anxieties, emotions, and feelings in first childhood, second childhood, and puberty that would have no effect on the functioning of systems that must perform in a certain manner to promote the organism's development. To thus evoke the letter of the body is to take into account the effect on the organism of the anxiety created by what cannot be said, or what cannot pass through language. This effect is inscribed in a manner that institutes *lived bodily experience*, in its intimacy, as a dimension that differs from the space-time in which the organism operates, a dimension that concerns the lived temporal experience of the subjectivity to which the Other has no access.

## Childhood

In first childhood, what the mother sees, observes, and surrounds with her care is not the same as what the child lives or experiences in the intimacy of his being. Whether she is aware of it or not, an intimate part of the mother is very sensitive to this dimension of the child, often to the point of anxiety, but she has no access to it nonetheless. What she perceives is trapped by the mirror, and this perception is conditioned by science and culture. The child's intimate lived experience is elsewhere. The time that defines the child's bodily experience is not the time in which the mother lives her relation to the little being for whom she is responsible. The mother will refer to her own experience, will inquire with others, will speak to doctors, psychologists, and pediatricians about the child's experience . . . But what do they know? Scientists have produced the organism, and they speak of what they know on the basis of this creation. From the accumulated results of scientific research, childhood observation, and animal experimentation, they have produced the organism, and thus they guess at what is happening inside the child. But the effraction of the psyche by spirit that is constitutive of the human—at the level of the first mental productions, representations, and reactions of childhood—escapes them. There thus remains an insurmountable gap between scientific knowledge and the child's lived experience, and this gap already defines the space—inviolable because inaccessible—that is proper to the subject of the unconscious. This space is rejected from the address but returns, subverting the maternal function in creations that surprise and delight the mother beyond what was expected in the address. Such drawings of a child, or the surprising skills they may demonstrate in music, dance, and other creative activities, by subverting the function of the Other, are already an initiation into the experience of the aesthetic, out-of-language, and thus unconscious. But like everyone in front of the mirror, the child, without knowing or understanding anything about what is happening, gradually becomes aware of the gap between the way adults look at him, what they say about him, and his own lived experience. Already here something important is repeated, something that cannot be said, that can only be inscribed in the developing organism and in its functioning.

But there is something even more serious and more important that occurs in this period of first childhood. From birth to five or six years old, the child is in a constant relation with the body of the mother, but the organism of this woman who is called the mother is not the same things as the mother's body. Indeed, it is only in adolescence—and this needs to be accounted for—that the youngster, whether boy or girl, will be able to discover that his or her mother is in fact a woman. Nonetheless, the child in the mother's arms is in an intimate relation, unbeknownst to each of them, with something in the body of this woman that is of the order of a lost jouissance—even a jouissance that this woman has never experienced, because it has been censored by the culture. The woman that culture positions as mother is not just a female organism, as civilizations would have it, but a woman in whose body an essential dimension has been culturally censored. And from infancy onward, the young human grapples, unknowingly and without being able to say anything about it, with this censored thing in the body of the mother. This woman who is said to be the child's mother, meanwhile, is not herself without an intimate relation to this dimension of her own being, with the censorship that was implemented long before puberty, and which is a constitutive letter of her body as a woman in the culture in which she evolves.

The question thus arises: Is the child there as a substitute for this censored jouissance? In the representation of the child the woman makes for herself—beyond the culturally conditioned perception she has of the child—what place does she give to this child's subjectivity? Without knowing it, the infant is already grappling with this question, which links its most intimate lived experience to that censored thing in the mother's body that cannot pass through language. This thing in the mother's body conditions many acts with regard to the child, acts to which the child in turn reacts without ever knowing anything about it. This woman has no direct access to what this situation may give rise to in terms of mental representations and reactions that go against or in support of the development of the child's organism; science has even less. The child's subjective universe thus remains outside the language that would make it possible to become conscious of it. The result is a specific dimension of the unconscious that touches on the historical dimension of the censoring of a part of the human in the being, which will profoundly mark the body of the child, whether boy or girl. For the purposes of this metapsychology, this historical dimension is understood in terms of a censoring of femininity, no matter the culture in which it takes place.

Here begins, for every human, the structure of address: the relation to the Other that is controlled by the culture through language, but is also overdetermined by the letter that institutes the body as the site for the collection of what cannot be said and by what remains unsayable in the structure of companionship, thus having no other path than the act that transgresses the conditions of the address. What, then, is at the heart of a woman's address to a child? Could it be what could not be said and what was not possible, concerning the dimension of her being as a woman that was censored, between this woman and a man? Does the child bear the letter of something unsayable, the letter of a failed address between a man and this woman? It is in this way that we can think of the dimension outside space-time that characterizes the letters that constitute the body, as each being goes through experiences for which there are no words in the language that structures the social link. We can also see here the extent to which the space-time that seems to structure the address is produced by language, in which culture, with its rules, norms, and conditions of receivability, defines the limits of the address.

In this first childhood, then, it is the adult who addresses the child, setting the limits of the child's possible address in an initiation to language that ensures the necessary link between child and adult. Then, in second childhood—when education takes precedence, through the transmission from one generation to the next of a cultural formatting supposed to guarantee the ideological survival of the collective—what is expected of the child is that he or she should address the Other. But at this precise moment in the child's development as a subject, what he would have to say is in fact unaddressable precisely because of the transmission of the values and norms that define the identity of a member of the collective. Simply put, what the child is grappling with at the most intimate level of his being is not part of what is expected of him. The child may even represent parents other than those who present themselves in this role. What the child represents as its origin has little to do with what he has to deal with in the address to which he is summoned by language. At stake in second childhood is the entry into the language that structures the social link, the relations of companionship, in their culture. This organization of the social link puts to work a set of rules, norms, models, prohibitions, and cultural objects that define what is promoted, what is acceptable, and what is expected of a member of the collective. It is the very material of language that institutes the space-time within which meaning is defined for the member of the collective.

In this singular place of language, in which the collective recognizes itself and which conditions the structure of the address, the meaning of what can be said is thus assured by the welcome of the Other. And the only way for the child to measure this welcome, which alone guarantees the meaning of what he says, is in the satisfaction of the Other. It is expected that what the child puts on stage in the address to the Other, or in response to the Other's address, will conform to a cultural expectation that is signaled by the Other's satisfaction. Henceforth captive of this satisfaction, the child is nonetheless subject to the human capacity to represent what does not exist, to desire it, and then, possibly, to create it. A conflict is thus installed between what, at the most intimate level of the child's being, will be sustained by what cannot be the object of any address, which will develop outside the space-time whose language structures the social link, and the need to enter the social link by submitting to the rule of the Other's satisfaction, which conditions the success of participation in companionship.

What loss, then, will the child have to endure in this second stage, when entry into language is overdetermined by the stakes of the address that is controlled by the Other? If the child goes off track here, he will become the object of the specialist—the doctor, psychologist, child psychiatrist, etc.—who will have the task of determining the point of failure to be rectified in order to reintegrate the child into meaning as a member of the collective. But the act, in which what the child cannot say escapes him, can displace the comfort of the Other in its function as guardian of what can be said and what makes sense in the address. Thus destabilizing the function of the Other, this act can also precipitate a rejection, in which the child will grasp himself as rejected in an aesthetics of the worst [*une ésthetique du pire*]. Through these dynamics, the satisfaction of the Other takes on such a dimension that the subject must submit to the loss of intimate lived experiences or unaddressable representations, in order to think of itself in the position of the object of the Other's satisfaction—imaginary castration. And this is where the child finds himself confronted with a maternal demand, which it would seem that neither the father nor the child can satisfy, or even should. Indeed, how could another human being be empowered to restore to this woman who is the mother what she has been deprived of as a fact of culture, irrespective of the civilization that lends credibility to this censoring of femininity? So, in addition to the losses involved in entering the structure of address, second childhood will leave its mark on the boy by bringing him face to face with an object in the demand of a woman that is unsayable, which subverts the mother's discourse, as well as a certain number of her attitudes, actions, and reactions; as for the girl, for whom the gift of the doll has already instituted the address to her mother as a mirror, she gradually finds herself in a space where, whatever the loss she may have assumed in her self-representation to satisfy the cultural norm, the troubling feeling, bordering on the unbearable, that there is something her mother is hiding from her persists and calls into question the validity of the mirror.

Second childhood thus marks a second stage in the establishment of the unconscious. It is the time of repression, of what the Other must never know, even though it is the essential. It is a question here, in the concrete lived experience of the being, of what has no place in language, of what no signifier can carry in the structure of the address, and which, thus unaddressable, will only have its chance in the act, where it leads the subject, necessarily but not without consequences, into a transgression of the limits of the receivable. What cannot pass through language, and has instead been inscribed as body, subtracts a part of the energies from the proper functioning of the organism, so as to make its way in the act, outside the receivable, for better or worse. The consequences of this transgressive nature of the act, for others and for the subject, require that the being manage its aftermath; indeed, such management becoming a condition of survival in the social link, and if it is lacking, the question will emerge as to how one might disappear from the gaze of the Other, to not have to bear condemnation or reprobation. The act drains what cannot be said, but its effect in the Other can subvert the structure of the address in which the Other has the function of guardian of the receivable. The consequences deriving from the effect of the act can thus introduce the child to an aesthetic dimension beyond the limits of which the Other serves as guardian.

It is at this point that psychic structures become more precise, as modalities of managing the passages-to-the-act in which what remains out-of-language subverts the limits that a culture imposes on the psyche in the structure of the address in which it defines meaning. These psychic structures regulate the impossible relation between an out-of-language—the unconscious—that insists and that inscribes itself in the letter that detaches the body's quests from the proper functioning of the organism and what culture will uphold as repression, what is to be rejected from the structure of address in order to articulate and undertake the concerns and objectives of the collective and to submit this out-of-language to the rules of companionship. Second childhood is the true entry into the conflict that requires what psychoanalysis will conceive as an *ethics: a management of the consequences of the act in its choices in the social link.*

# Puberty

In the context of *mondialisation*, in which the concern for the human is becoming a decisive priority in relation to cultural objectives and civilizational concerns, the metapsychology of psychoanalysis must be resolutely clinical and must distinguish puberty from adolescence without ambiguity. The erasure of such a distinction is part of the formatting strategy needed to maintain the concerns and objectives of the collective in the cultural construction of members' identities. Extreme right-wing groups—whether religious, cultural, or political—are united on this point, and are not prepared to make concessions that would be experienced as betrayals. The fear of disappearing remains an unsayable for some groups in the face of certain civilizational issues. And in the context of the clash of civilizations provoked by *mondialisation*, puberty becomes a strategic moment in the formation of new generations. Culture, which defines the characteristics of the identity of a member of the collective within the social link supported by the structure of address, thus takes on decisive importance and signification for clinical metapsychology.

At puberty, when the neurophysiological maturation of reproductive capacities occurs, the youngster becomes a sure and determining value for the survival and the development of the fundamental values and concerns of the collective. The cultural function of formatting new members of the collective thus takes on an importance that no society can risk renouncing—even and especially in the context of *mondialisation*, which threatens the future and even the end of civilizations. It is a fact of history that civilizations disappear, and with them the cultures to which they give credibility. Puberty is the strategic moment when *the Other* in *the structure of the address* is strengthened in its function as guardian of the receivable, and thus comes to support, in its response and expectations, the rules, norms, prohibitions, and values that define cultural identity and belonging. Here, culture assumes its function of formatting the identity of membership within the structure of companionship defined by language and given credibility by a whole range of civilizational issues.

For the clinical metapsychology that interests us here, the action of this formatting of the group member's identity is articulated primarily in the *cultural montage of the sexual*, which lies at the heart of the structure of the address. Culture produces the sexual during the time of puberty, according to its objectives and in light of the stakes involved in controlling the structure of address. This production of the sexual, the stakes of which are the *control of the ideological reproduction of the collective*, is played out in the mechanism of the *censoring of the feminine* in the man. Each culture produces, as it were, the woman and the man that it needs, but this production is realized in the modalities through which femininity as such is censored in the cultural production of men at puberty.

Concretely, and from a clinical perspective, when a pubescent boy experiences the orgasm that his entourage, his school environment, and the cultural practices promoted in the media and social networks define as the specific experience of masculinity, he is very far from realizing the extent to which this represses his intimate experience and censors what could be the object of an address. A part of his being that is carried by unaddressable questions is repressed from the scene of the social link. At the same time, an expertise seems to be expected of him that has nothing to do with his intimate questioning of the unsatisfiable object of maternal demand or the unexplorable continent in which his mother seems to be evolving. Meanwhile, the boy has not failed to notice that, for the past year or two, he has been the object of an inexplicable rejection by girls in his entourage and at school. A dull uneasiness builds to the point of shattering the relationship he was struggling to maintain, on the verge of anxiety, with his mother. What runs through him and haunts him, inscribing itself in his body and eroticizing it, is in contradiction with the expectation of which he suddenly becomes the object as a result of the experience of orgasm, which opens a space, in the field of social relations, that he has difficulty integrating and that he was far from suspecting until now.

But what is most important, and what will be decisive for the child's psychic structure, is the anguishing worry surrounding a question that has never been addressed and that has remained unapproachable: What is the object of maternal demand? The experience of the physiological maturation of reproductive functions, far from providing any kind of answer, only complicates the matter, adding the question: What is it in the mother that corresponds to what the boy now experiences at puberty? Such a question is enough to cause the ground beneath the Other of the address to tremble. The discourses of his friends, who seem more informed, only add to the complexity and the anxiety that the letter of his body has generated with this unformable question. Very precisely, what seems to have changed in his mother's gaze and in her attitude toward him, since this event, has shattered the bond of complicity that until then served to put this questioning to rest. This rupture in turn repeats and is inscribed, deepening a delicious and intimate bodily wound that will never come into question, unless one day some symptom comes to prevent any possible encounter with this censored femininity, in himself or in the other. Even its evocation cannot be considered confidential. The silence this rupture in the mother-son relationship institutes bears already the seeds of a number of acts that will later be divided between subtle violence and an exquisite but unmanageable aesthetic in his relations with women.

The young psychotic, like those who will later be referred to as perverts, will not take long to identify the relationship called sexual by the culture—the relationship between a man and a woman—as an act of aggression against the woman. The young neurotic meanwhile cannot at first imagine, without anguish, such a relationship between his father and mother. In other words, no matter the psychic structure in which the pubescent tries to manage the acts that already begin to escape their control, as a result of the dimension now excluded from the address, such a relationship cannot be imagined as agreed upon between a man and a woman. Fundamentally, it is a question of losing what, since early childhood, has been experienced in the letter of the body as love, which led the child to accept many familial demands. In fact, the issue is that the pubescent boy did not know until then that his mother was a woman. Nor does he know what this term encloses of secret experience and things unspoken in culture. The young are in a universe, a space-time, in which the woman produced by culture in the structure of the social link is only a mother, having previously been a fiancée or future wife, or perhaps one who plays at being the pretty girl. They do not yet have the means to think of the opposite: that their mother could be a woman. The dimension of their mothers' being that makes them also—and firstly—a woman is precisely what culture censors in its montage of the sexual, which compromises the child's representation of love under the newly acquired concept of a certain desire. But what has been inscribed in the letter of their bodies concerning the insistence of an unsatisfiable object in maternal demand is already breaking through the cultural repression of the woman in the mother.

This censoring of the being, who is repressed under a function, is repeated in a whole set of formulas that will be confronted in "official" discourses that refer to the culturally established notion that what is at stake in the male orgasm has something to do with a certain status of women in the social link. This status determines the position of women in the structure of address by implying that they are the object of men's desire. This implication is maintained without any thought being given to what it effectively subtracts that is essential to the being of a woman, and even less to the fact that men would never be satisfied with the opposite. Psychoanalysis itself, since Freud, has kept the matter closed, not daring to cross the boundaries established by culture in the structure of address that manages the man-woman link in social relations. In this respect, it is most often content to be a psychotherapy whose aim is to find and consolidate the means that enable the neurotic to deal with this censorship of femininity in the man-woman relationship, while limiting the damage in terms of consequences on either side. Obviously, this has never worked for the pervert, let alone the psychotic. In the context of *mondialisation*, which confronts us in the same geographical space with an incoherence of cultural rules that breaks down the boundaries of collectives, and in which what is now at stake is therefore a concern for the human—whereas it used to be the success of the ego in the socio-cultural bond—a clinical psychoanalytic metapsychology must promote a time for this censored part of being, and cannot leave out-of-language, unspoken and thus denied, a dimension of the human that lies at the heart of the repression accredited by civilizational concerns.

As for the pubescent girl, with the experience of menstruation she discovers in her body, in the place of what she suspected in her mother's silence, something that seems to her to be a collective lie. The second half of her second childhood was marked by an equally unaddressable question that repeated itself, inscribing a muted worry in her body. What is it that Mom does not tell me? What happened to what everyone called love?

To whom can the girl address such anxieties? At the same time, however, the best thing that can happen to a prepubescent girl also occurs here. She has an experience that is decisive in a woman's life. She discovers, without understanding, what I like to call *"the guardian of jouissance"*—she discovers the father. This man's *gaze* cuts across what is happening with these changes, targeting a dimension of her being of which she was still unaware. The *object of this gaze* compensates, as it were, for the question of her mother's *silence*. Without answering her questions, this gaze soothes the anguish they cause in her body. For the pubescent girl grappling with the consequences of the organic maturation of her reproductive system, the father's gaze now takes on a whole new meaning. As a result of the events accompanying physiological maturation, she realizes, with deep trouble, the distance that separates her body from all that is said about it. She can now see in her father's gaze the expectation of a form of speech for which as of yet she has no words. *This gaze poetizes her*, making her suspect the existence of a dimension of her own being accessible only in the field of aesthetics, beyond the framework of the address. This gaze has nothing to do with those who evaluate the ongoing changes, said to be sexual, of her organism, just as they evaluate a new commodity. This gaze will mark the girl's body with an expectation the importance of which she is yet unaware, except for the fact that it transcends everything that culture seems to offer through what it promotes as sexual. With this gaze that transcends the cultural offer, she enters the aesthetic universe of erotism, without yet having the slightest notion of what this means, apart from the profound sense of disquiet that this new universe introduces into the letter of her body.

Managing this period of profound disturbance is not self-evident for the pubescent girl. Just as for the boy, the psychic structure now takes shape with a certain brutality that already worries those around her. Psychiatrists, psychologists, psychotherapists, even many who call themselves psychoanalysts have designated as perverse certain ways of managing the consequences of the cultural censoring of femininity, thus acting as good guardians, and even on occasion as the police, of cultural norms. Youngsters with a so-called perverse structure in fact revolt against the montage of the sexual, which reduces the jouissance they are beginning to discover to organ pleasure, namely, the orgasm of boys, thus ensuring that there is no room for a jouissance that would divert women from their status as objects at the service of the interests of the collective. They go to war against this cultural montage, which denies to the point of censoring it the question that haunts them. They cannot renounce their will to know what it is that is unaddressable and unsatisfiable in what constitutes the object of the demand of women. As long as this question remains unaddressable within the structure of the address, the cultural issue of the sexual will remain unreceivable for them: they experience it as something of the order of violence, which translates as an aggression against a dimension in the mother.

Boy or girl, the pubescent discovers here something that will remain a profound mystery of the address. They already glimpse a dimension of the veil of impossibility that will later cover over the stakes of a woman's desire, which is excluded from the address. The young neurotic senses, without yet being able to imagine its scope, what the young pervert already understands and sets out to resolve in fantasy scenarios. In the social space organized by the address, *jouissance* can only be thought of as *the intimate experience of leaving the subjective limits* in which culture defines what is receivable and *moving toward something unsayable* in the same space of the address. From this point forth, what agitates the being and keeps them, for the moment, in a position of refusing cultural injunctions is the fact of not knowing exactly what is censored in the mother by the cultural montage of the sexual in which she would be the object of a man's satisfaction. In effect, what has been inscribed in the body of what cannot be said, which is already tracing the paths of an eroticism the existence of which the child was unaware of, now pushes the pubescent to bend against the imperative of this montage of sexuality, which seems to censor the best of what one hopes to experience.

For the pubescent girl of a perverse structure, cultural censorship of a dimension of the life of a woman is a case of war. Under no circumstances can what develops naturally in her organism be used as a pretext to justify her being reduced to the status of an object that should satisfy one or another of her young companions, for whom, incidentally, she holds little esteem. She thus enters into a war against cultural receivability, a war in which, as far as she is concerned, there will be no room for compromise. But within the framework of the cultural montage of the sexual, such a position is unreceivable, and the enemy is hardly identifiable; it is anyone, including certain girlfriends. The girl has little in terms of a strategy for this struggle—which she intends to win, but which for the moment isolates her—and she will have to manage this undeclared war, however intense it may be, all while securing her place and recognition in the social link. In this struggle, she cannot imagine any concession that would not be a blow to her own existence. Indeed, without yet being able to justify such a position, what is mobilizing in her body gives her the feeling that what is culturally censored in this montage of the sexual is at the heart of what constitutes her as a woman. In this condition, she obviously does not see herself as the object of what the discourse of those around her designates as men's desire.

As for young psychotics, whether boy or girl, this montage of sexuality immediately appears as a violence against women, the means of ending which must be found. From second childhood already, young psychotics are affected by the injustice of having to renounce what can be built as a universe to live in, in order to submit to the need to satisfy the Other in the address and thus to have a place in the bond of companionship. The psychotic is already concerned about the power of the Other to reduce a part of experience to nothing, even though this Other has no access to the depths of one's being. This leads them already to put in question the structure of the address, seeing it as a trap in which the function of the Other is erected against the subject of speech. So, as they enter puberty and encounter the montage of the sexual, the psychotic sees an unnamed, unidentified violence that suppresses love and relations between beings, reducing one to the service of the other. The mental representation of an Other with unjustifiable power arises in opposition to the feelings that stem from what has been inscribed in the body. For the boy or young man, the consequences of this censorship of the feminine can go as far as the idea of cutting off his penis to avoid participating in what he perceives as unjustifiable violence against women. But without yet even thinking of taking action, the feeling that something is wrong with what society imposes, and that he should not participate in this wrong, is now inscribed in his body. At the heart of the source of evil that he discovers in the structure of address, he already hypothesizes a dimension hidden beyond culture, where such censorship must not exist. In the meantime, a sense of guilt may develop as the boy realizes that few others around him seem to share his feelings about this unidentifiable violence that all have at least the opportunity to perpetrate. Moments of this realization follow one another and become the subject of jokes, comments, and mockery that hurt him, increasing an inexplicable guilt and deepening the gap he experiences between an intimate experience felt in his body and the changes in his organism that seem to be the occasion of this violence.

The psychotic girl, during this period, goes through a profound drama from which she will want to help all women to escape, either by assuming responsibility for it or by inventing means that would enable such escape. She is confronted with her mother's silence on this dimension of her being that is censored by culture, which makes it that the object of her demand as a woman must remain outside the structure of address, and she grasps that this silence is not simply a lie on her mother's part but that the reasons for this silence come from something well beyond the cultural montage of the sexual. If she does not go to war against the culture that produces this montage, like the pubescent girl with a perverse structure will do, she does not submit to it either, like the young girl with a neurotic structure who imprudently takes such a risk to make a place for herself in the social link. Rather, the psychotic pubescent girl already glimpses, in what scientists will call her hallucinations and delusions—given the cultural framework in which they manifest themselves—exit strategies or radical corrections with which to attack the civilizational values and concerns that give credibility to this montage. The pubescent girl thus faces two basic problems: the violence of the Other created by the cultural montage of the sexual, which reduces her to the status of an object of satisfaction, and the censorship of a part of her being excluded from the structure of address. What becomes central to her experience, and the most important aspect for us to consider, is undoubtedly the latter: the censorship of a part of her being as a woman. This is the conclusion to which the situation of the psychotic pubescent girl leads us, since it is in this that the object of the hallucinations and mental representations that begin to disrupt her psychic universe finds its justification. From a metapsychological point of view, this situation and the strategies that the pubescent girl invents for managing it, regardless of her psychic structure, are a good indication of what pushes girls to confront the radical experience of adolescence long before boys.

## Adolescence

In the context of *mondialisation*, metapsychology must radically distinguish between puberty and adolescence—not merely as two different concepts, but as two distinct stages of life in which completely different, even contradictory subjective experiences are played out, thus marking two opposing periods in the life of any young person. The concrete experience of puberty is one of loss, something we identify as the content of a symbolic castration; this is a more substantial event than the repression to which the child was forced in second childhood, which I refer to as an imaginary castration. The Other in the structure of the address that organizes the social link has the power to define what is acceptable. Satisfying this Other becomes the rule that imposes itself from second childhood, and this rule founds and justifies the being's repression of a part of what was essential to it in order to have access to the Other that assures them a place in the social link. But this power of the Other in the structure of the address takes on its full importance at puberty, when, in addition to the self-imposed repression, *culture* adds the *censorship* of a dimension of being that *civilization*, in order to make the culture believable, will render unsayable. In the structure of the address, the being must therefore grapple with the fact that *the essential parts of their quest*—that which they would hold most dear if they could have access to it, and which is inscribed in the constitutive letter of the body, mobilizing a significant part of their energies—is, for all practical purposes, *unaddressable*.

This is the situation from which the experience of adolescence will extract the young person, confronting them with choices whose consequences, for better or worse, will shape the rest of their life, without them being able to take the measure of this at the time of these choices. In psychoanalysis, we thus need to have clear references for what the experience of adolescence has been for both the analysand and the analyst;

ultimately, on the side of the analyst, the *transference* depends on this, and the fate of the analysand's experience depends on the transference. To understand this, we must consider as closely as possible what is at stake in the experience of adolescence.

Every collective has an interest in ensuring the basic formation of each of its members during puberty, and certainly before the experience of adolescence. It is one thing to be qualified as an adult responsible for one's actions by a societal decision following the physiological changes that take place during puberty—this is what collectives generally refer to as adolescence—but it is quite another to assume responsibility for the consequences of a *lived experience* that takes a being out of *dependence on the Other* and leads to choices that are alien to the cultural requirements of puberty. In such an experience, there is a *solitude*, at once intoxicating and frightening and to which no Other has access, which is the challenge that lies the heart of a true experience constitutive of adolescence. Such an experience is like returning to square one, to the primitive situation of solitude and singular autonomy in which the being found itself in early childhood, with its capacity to represent and to desire its universe, but without yet having any means to create it.

What this metapsychology considers adolescence is in fact an experience that takes place in two stages. In the first, the being is *mobilized* by everything that has been inscribed in the body, at once constituting and fragmenting it on the basis of what is impossible to say, individual repressions, the effects of cultural censorship, and finally what is unsayable within the address. This stage marks a distance and an absolute solitude of the being in relation to all that the collective can expect or can prescribe through education. And this solitude marks a point of powerlessness of the Other, who has no access to what the being can henceforth think and want, thus constituting *an autonomous subjective space* experienced in the *bodily experience* of the feeling of being oneself [*le vécu corporel du sentiment d'être soi*]. This first stage opens the being to an inner space that, contrary to the puberty that has just been traversed, escapes all cultural influence. In the second stage of this experience, the being reconnects with that space within itself that, since first childhood on, *transcends the limits of the psyche*. This intimate space becomes the locus of a hitherto unknown jouissance that takes the being out of the cultural limits guaranteed by civilization. And it is this second phase, through its *dimension of essential transcendence of established limits*, that becomes decisive in the experience of adolescence and that will become a problem for the being. From a metapsychological point of view, it would be illogical to conceive of the history and future of human beings without accounting for such an experience, which distances each new generation from the collective. Where this will lead, in all it implies that is unpredictable and at times incompatible with what has already been achieved, depends on the capacities of the new generations, yet it is hard to imagine that civilizations would do nothing in the face of such a power for change being at the disposal of the least experienced members of a given collective.

Civilizations die and cultures disappear—it is a fact. What a culture creates lasts a few generations; what a civilization imposes and makes believable lasts the time necessary for the needs of the culture. Our great-grandchildren will not live by the cultural rules in which we remain enclosed, nor will they follow certain civilizational values to which we still attach great importance. There is necessarily *a dimension in the human individual that transcends* any *culture or civilization, and which is the object of the experience of adolescence.* The best and the worst of what we are engaged in today was an immanent but unsuspected possibility for those who preceded us two hundred years ago or more. These predecessors could not have imagined that we would create what we have created or that we would experience what we are experiencing with what they bequeathed us. Likewise, we cannot imagine what those who are now twenty to twenty-five years old will experience and what they in turn will have to create in the next forty years on the basis of their own experience of adolescence. This dimension that transcends culture and civilization mobilizes energies in the body that are useless in culture and civilization, because they are mobilized for *a quest whose unknown stakes* lie far beyond. Freud already spoke of these energies as a *death drive* that pushes beyond the immune limits of pleasure and that constitutes a *discontent in civilization,* carrying beings to want to create and experience things that culture and civilization do not yet have the means or the capacity to take on.

In this experience of adolescence, one discovers a dimension in their being that they could never have suspected, and which has nothing to do with what those around them consider their adolescence. The feeling that dominates in the time of this discovery is that what one can aspire to for oneself and for those for whom one cares goes far beyond what can be expected from the society in which one is constrained to live. A part of the being transcends, in its most intimate aspirations, the very limits that civilizational concerns and values make trustworthy, because they also concern human beings who are not part of this civilization. And in this age of *mondialisation*, which is already eliciting the future of the new generations, the experience of adolescence tends to make civilizations, which occasionally lend credibility to the worst in their culture, appear as an obstacle to the future of the human. The civilization that presents itself as the expression or even the model of the human being thus becomes in the experience of adolescence just a stage to be surpassed, if not an obstacle to be overcome, for anyone who effectively concerns themselves with what is best for the human [*se soucie effectivement du meilleur pour l'humain*].

In fact, beyond the active remnants in the body—the unaddressable and the impossible to say of first childhood, the repressions made necessary by the educational contexts of second childhood, the impasses in the address due to the effects of the cultural montage of the sexual at puberty—the experience of adolescence emerges as the discovery of an inner world that transcends all that culture has implemented under the guarantee of the credibility of civilizational values. This intimate dimension promotes an aspiration in the being: *a quest the object of which, though as yet unknown both as such and in the consequences it will have in the social link, subjects the being* in a relationship to the collective that leads it to subvert the structure of address. What henceforth inspires the being cannot be the object of an address to the Other without contesting the very function of this Other in the structure of address. *Desire*—this *intimate quest for something else*, which the being cannot renounce because it is the very stuff of subjectivity, and which ensures the unity of the body in the feelings that eroticize its fragmentation—is unaddressable in its emergence. Its object summons the being beyond what the address can sustain. In this way, it finally opens the adolescent to the true dimension of *love*, which makes the other the much-needed *companion of the quest and its consequences*. This desire evokes an intervention of adolescence, unsayable in the structure of the address and even out-of-language, which eroticizes the body and tears at consciousness with delight, without the adolescent yet knowing anything about it, except that it proves unreceivable in its consequences; it must still be discovered in the modalities of silent jouissance and in the consequences of the acts in which it expresses itself, which the adolescent must now already begin to manage. The concern for true friendship, which would survive the unpredictable surprises of love, is engaged in this delicate management. What cannot make its way into the address subverts the position of the Other via the act, where it summons feelings contrary to the Other's function. The aesthetic that emerges here is far from sufficient to control or even appease the consequences of acts that thus break with the structure of address.

From then on, the psychic structures—different modalities available to the being to deal with the consequences of this effraction of the structure of address—take on their full importance. The experience of adolescence will give psychosis and perversion their full dimension, namely, in the specificity of their refusal to accept the cultural issues associated with the montage of the sexual as what must define the structure of address. In the context of such an experience, it is clear how the montage of the sexual, through its central mechanism of censoring feminine jouissance, is the decisive means of controlling the consequences of adolescence, in which the survival of the collective is put at stake by this dimension of the being that transcends both cultural demands and civilizational values. Cultures and civilizations, through the army and religion respectively, make use of this dimension in the being that adolescence brings into play, both to ensure the survival of the collective, its objectives and interests, and to support a certain conception of the human being and its creations. History bears witness to the fact that this usage of the possibilities of adolescence by religion, by the science that tends to replace religion, or by the army to the benefit of civilizational issues or cultural objectives, has thus far not been possible without the censorship of the feminine. But, given the reservations and refusals of the psychotic, the struggle of the pervert against censorship in the montage of the sexual, and the context of globalization, which raises the prospect of a possible end to certain cultural concerns and civilizational values, this will be far from enough. Perversion and psychosis now find themselves in a context that reinforces their respective views. For the psychotic, it is clear that the perspectives of civilization need to be rebuilt, because the fate of the human is at stake. As for the pervert, they find themself at ease in this clash of civilizations, which is everywhere jeopardizing the validity of the cultural rules still underpinning the montage of the sexual that they contest. The neurotic, meanwhile, captive to the expectation of a possible solution to the montage of the sexual via personal success in the social link, finds themself at a crossroads with regard to the consequences of their choices, depending on whether they repress the experience of adolescence or take the risk of assuming it.

## The Human Quest,
## a Profound Desire for Something Else

A profound desire for something other than what culture can offer or civilization can promise results from the experience of adolescence, and this desire puts the individual at odds with everything the entourage expects and that the social link promotes. Whatever the psychic structure, over the next few years a multidimensional conflict takes root within the individual between what is repressed, promoted, or censored by culture from puberty onward and what adolescence makes them discover of intimate possibilities and aspirations that are unaddressable, unsayable, and unreceivable in social links. This dimension of *the unconscious* takes on decisive importance as everything that is mobilized by an unknown quest, and that *cannot pass through the structure of address in the social link*, will make its way directly into *acts* whose *consequences* for self and others will have to be managed by the adolescent. In their consequences, these acts open a space for an *aesthetics*, in which the erotism that haunts the letter of the body finds its full meaning. But these acts can also open a space of violence, in which their consequences for others engage the adolescent's responsibility. So desire, whose unconscious representation overdetermines the process of giving the quest a social form, becomes the source of an *ethics* that is rooted in the aesthetic to which adolescence gives access.

Within the problematic of this metapsychology, this link between ethics and aesthetics—even the dependence of the former on the latter—is fundamental. Unconscious desire gives form to what the experience of adolescence reveals as a dimension of being that, in its quest, transcends both cultural issues and civilizational values. Precisely, this desire is called unconscious because the "conscious" is what is defined in language by the conditions imposed by culture for access to the Other in the structure of address. Unconscious desire thus is not only out-of-language, subverting the structure of address by supporting a quest whose object transcends values; what this desire and its consequences bring into play opens, beyond good and evil, onto the jouissance of an aesthetics or of a violence, and must therefore be subject to ethical control. Unconscious desire acts outside of the space-time structured by law and morality for the social link, because its object lies beyond this space-time. The human that the adolescent experience reveals to be at stake in this desire exceeds the limits of this space-time, and the quest supported by unconscious desire necessarily concerns the becoming of the human in the individual as well as the collective. This becoming is played out at the very heart of the being *beyond good and evil*, beyond the cultural limits that civilization makes believable. The temporality of the subjective experience of this desire creates an intimate space specific to the being, which does not necessarily overlap with the space-time created by the structure of address in a given culture. Metapsychology must conceive of *ethics*, at the very heart of subjectivity and its capacity to transcend limits, as what is substituted for that *beyond the morality and the law* of the collective. From the experience of adolescence onward, the act, in which what cannot pass through language manifests itself, will bear in its consequences the best or the worst, for it no longer follows the beacons of good and evil that are defined by cultural receivability. Such an act knows no such cultural or civilizational markers because what it aims at is far beyond them and concerns the becoming of the human. The ethics that requires new beacons, beyond the limits of the receivable, thus cannot be conceived of without what, in this clinical metapsychology, must be considered as an *aesthetics*.

This latter concept thus takes on a particular significance and importance for us. It evokes a singular mobilization of the letter of the body in the implementation of the act. What is put in play in *the act* is precisely that which, from the unconscious, *cannot pass through language*, whose function of structuring the social link it would subvert. This is something unreceivable in a culture and inadmissible in a civilization, and this mobilization of the letter of the body manifests itself in a feeling—a bodily experience that signals a consciousness in the Other of an effect of the act of prior consent. The aesthetic thus reveals a kind of inversion, through the act, of the function of the Other in the structure of the address. In the structure of the address, the function of the Other is to decide on the fate of what the subject of speech expects or awaits. *The aesthetic*, on the other hand, concerns *the effect of the act in the Other and unbeknownst to the Other*. This brings us back, without defining it, to what constitutes the object of the censuring of femininity. Something unsayable, since it cannot be addressed to the Other, makes its way through the act, subverting the function of the Other by making either *the aesthetic* or *violence* emerge. The feeling of *the Beautiful* is thus the effect in the Other of an act by the subject of the unconscious. This places the subject of the act in a feminine position. The feeling of the Beautiful evokes the fact that in no case would the Other want to lose the consequences of the act, insofar as what such consequences make one discover is unknown, new, and enriching for oneself or for the collective. It is easy to see that violence would impose itself in cases where under no circumstances would the repetition of such consequences be desirable. This is what leads us to posit that the ethical rule for metapsychology, concerning the act that substitutes for the unaddressable or the unsayable, is that it is "either aesthetics or violence." Clinical metapsychology supports the importance of this dependence of ethics on the aesthetic as an essential point in the transference, the obsessional and the pervert providing the best examples.

The discovery of desire and of the body—as the subjective locus of *this quest that takes the being beyond good and evil*—allows the adolescent, whether girl or boy, to finally become aware of femininity as a censored dimension of being. The quest for something else, beyond the limits of the receivable and the unsayable, articulates the drive of desire with that dimension of the aesthetic that will, for a time, mark out the question par excellence of adolescence: *how far is too far?* This quest puts the fate of culture, even the future of civilization, in play; its censorship at the level of culture bears witness to a fear of disappearing that is fueled by the fact that the collective cannot control it. The stakes here are high for a psychoanalytic metapsychology overdetermined by the context of *mondialisation*: they concern the fate of *the human*, ever since cultures and civilizations were established by collectives for the sake of their survival some tens of thousands of years ago. Since these earliest collectives, women, from whom all members of the collective derive, have been a collective good and a supreme value, but also the source of deep-seated fear because of what the aesthetic experience of adolescence plunges them into. The experience of what is at stake in the concern of women to surpass all limits in search of an unknown object could not be envisaged and accepted without a profound fear of the consequences for the survival of collectives. And the experience of women creating an aesthetic universe that marks out for them and the group the limitlessness of this quest must have favored a particular fate for women in a certain number of collectives, if not all. In the strategies used to manage this quest, the status reserved for women by civilizations tells us a great deal about the fear aroused by the feminine dimension of women, which carries them away from the functions reserved for them by these same civilizations with a view to collective survival. Throughout the history of collectives, women have known every kind of status: goddess and witch, mother and whore, vestal virgin and lover, wife and mistress, beloved and madwoman, demon-possessed and hysteric, bitch, girlfriend, and shrew—and from these to whatever new forms the current disorganization of the cultural montage of the sexual may invent for the obscure violence of the censoring of femininity from puberty onward.

A clinical metapsychology must therefore take great account of the fact that this censoring of femininity concerns men first and foremost. It is in the pubescent boy that the aesthetic or violent effect of the act will begin to take shape—namely, the act that creates an erotic space for what in the woman cannot be the object of an address, and will therefore only find expression in such acts and their consequences. What is henceforth at stake is *masculinity*, or the phallus, which signs responsibility for the consequences of what is unsaid in the act. The human transcends cultural concerns and civilizational values: cultures pass, civilizations disappear, but the human pursues its quest. And the quest of unconscious desire—at the heart of the aesthetic space opened up in the body with femininity, and the object of which sustains the being's jouissance—is not without consequences in the social link, for both the subject and for others. The care for the human that this desire represents, in addition to the aesthetic stakes it raises in the act that opens a space for the unaddressable, thus requires a capacity of the being to assume responsibility for the consequences of such an act—in other words, an *ethics*. Masculinity, in women as in men, supports this capacity up to the point where the *sublime*, to which the feeling of the beautiful opens the path, makes the being discover what, of the human, is more important than its own existence. A clinical metapsychology in this age of globalization must be able to support this profound link between ethics and aesthetics, a link that results from the lifting of the censorship of femininity, wherein *the traversal of symbolic castration* is verified as the decisive stage of an analytic cure. This is why we understand this traversal of castration as *the condition of the transference*, for it alone can make possible the subversion of the function of the Other as guardian of the cultural montage of the sexual and of the unsayable in the structure of the address. This is precisely what the cures of several hundred psychotics over the last forty years have shown.


## To Conclude

This conception of metapsychology is intended to be clinical because its elaboration results in a questioning of *the object of psychoanalytic experience.* Such an interrogation imposes itself in context of *mondialisation* in which we find ourselves. Civilizations are in open conflict via the contradictions facing the cultures that express them. Collectives whose stakes and objectives find their meaning and credibility in the values assured by these civilizations see their cultural and geopolitical borders crossed by other collectives defined by other civilizations with other cultural concerns. This situation is getting worse in the major international metropolises on which the global economy, and the geopolitics it overdetermines, now depend. In the same residential area, what is valued by one family contradicts with what is valued by another. Cultures that no longer know borders clash in the same society, calling into question the values that have until now underpinned the receivability of a certain number of societal objectives. In such social configurations, violence against women can no longer be repressed under the guise of a cultural montage of the sexual that is specific to certain civilizations, while in others, where this montage is maintained in silence, it can still take the form of feminicide. A perspective in which the object of unconscious desire would be at stake in the structure of the address between man and woman, a structure that would be defined by cultural concerns and even more so by whatever civilization would render it credible, is no longer tenable.

Furthermore, a decisive dimension of this context has been the calling into question of precisely what lies at the heart of any civilization: a conception of the human that justifies the values that serve as pillars for each civilization, distinguishing it from others and making it consider itself superior. *Mondialisation,* which is now emerging as an obstacle to the financial globalization that restructures relations between nations, has given rise to a number of problems that clearly cannot be resolved by the largest nations but require the engagement of all. Global warming, the increasing impoverishment of populations and middle classes alongside and ensuring the enrichment of a few, the migration of hundreds of millions of people, and the incessant wars that destroy and exploit millions more, the violence done to women everywhere . . . these are just a few examples of such problems, which are not lost on new generations across the globe. The pandemic that has affected all nations arrived in such a manner as to dramatize the fact that *the human* as such is beyond the interests of nations and civilizations, and that it tends to become the principal concern, calling into question what has until now been at stake everywhere in the structure of the address.

The metapsychology we seek to promote is provoked by *this care for the human in the social link*, which the context of *mondialisation* tends to make unavoidable. The clinics of psychosis and of perversion constrain us to this perspective, in which the *concern for the human in the subject*, as unsayable, now takes precedence over the *success of the ego in the social link* that the neurotic expects from psychoanalysis. This changes the perspective on the unconscious, so as to cast doubt on whether the *object of unconscious desire* could be anything other than *the human as it would be still to come*. This in no way settles the question of what this object is for psychoanalysis. But every analysand now finds themself summoned, in the traversal of castration, to confront what they assume as responsibility for and with others in relation to this question.

# The Aesthetic and the Out-of-Language

2

# Language, *Hors langage*, Act, Aesthetics

Tracy McNulty

Willy Apollon reconceives the metapsychology within the context of what in French is called *mondialisation*, which he defines for his purposes as the confrontation or clash of civilizations that is brought about by the often fraught coexistence of many different cultures and civilizations in the same spaces: a confrontation that at the same time attests to the emergence of something that transcends all civilizations ("Psychanalyse" 10 June 2020). He therefore calls for a psychoanalysis for the human as such, one that is not internal to or in the service of a particular cultural construction of the human but capable of opening up a space for something within the human being that transcends both the demands or requirements imposed on it by culture and the civilization that validates those requirements. At the same time he maintains that the liberation of desire, for the analysand, is also inseparable from the advancement of what he calls the "human quest," a quest that takes him or her beyond the limits of what culture allows.

The human for Apollon is characterized above all by the spirit [*l'esprit*] that traverses it, which in turn is defined by its capacity to conceive something that doesn't exist, to want it, and eventually to create it.[1] Conversely, he identifies the foundations of culture with a rule that censors the spirit in every human being to guarantee its own material and ideological reproduction. This censorship has four different manifestations. First, a refusal of the inviolability and autonomy of the human being, with the violence it supposes; second, the collective possession of the objects of speech through language, which determines what can or cannot be said; third, the introduction of a cultural construction of the sexual wherein sex is conceived solely as an organ pleasure, and therefore as a means through which every culture produces the man and the woman that it needs to reproduce itself; and fourth, the constitution of the Other as the guardian of the limits of the receivable through the structure of the address that founds the social link ("Psychanalyse" 16 Dec. 2020).

This chapter first describes how the quest of desire is censored by language and the structure of the address, and then explores how what remains of that censored quest becomes inscribed in the body—thereby constituting the unconscious as the site where what remains out of language continues to eroticize the body and find expression through acts. The second half is devoted to the act whose unforeseeable consequences impact the subject's relation to the other and disrupt the social link, but which may be judged aesthetic when they elicit in others the feeling of the beautiful or the sublime that articulates the subject's quest to humanity and its heritage. Throughout I explore the stakes of Apollon's recent contributions to the metapsychology for how we conceive the trajectory and especially the end of an analysis.[2]

## Language and *Hors langage*

We often treat language, speech, and address as if these belong to the same field. For example, I want to speak to you about something, and to do so I address you in the language we have in common. For Apollon, however, these three dimensions are distinct and often in tension. As counterintuitive as this may seem, speech for Apollon actually *precedes* language: there is a speaking being (a *parlêtre*, in Lacan's neologism) long before there is language. Apollon evokes the "human *thing* that speaks," or the "thing that speaks in the human" ("Subject" 6): both of which recall Freud's *Es* (the "it" or id) and Lacan's *ça parle*, "it speaks." Speech isn't something we "have" or "use," therefore, but something that erupts within us without our volition or consent. Driving speech is the effraction of the psychic apparatus by the spirit, which sets the living being on a quest that has nothing to do with the living being's survival in a natural environment or the reproduction of the species or group. This effraction, which Apollon calls *real castration*, gives rise to the quest of desire. Like speech, which speaks in or through me rather than at my bidding, desire isn't something that "I" want, therefore, but something that acts in me or that pushes me.

Homo sapiens emerged three hundred thousand years ago. Language, on the other hand, is a relatively late acquisition of human beings, dating to only about fifty thousand years ago. Apollon hypothesizes that it emerged at a moment in human history that was defined by the need for human beings to band together in larger and larger groups to survive in a hostile environment. This claim by itself is not particularly novel, of course. As Apollon understands it, however, language is not primarily a tool that allows humans to communicate with one another more effectively, or to conceive and execute collective projects. Instead, it is the means through which the collective suppresses the quest that acts in the individual—a quest that necessarily takes him or her far beyond the limits of the collective and even the instinctual aims of survival and reproduction—to press him or her into the service of the group and its reproduction. Through language, the collective takes possession of the objects of speech to subordinate the quest acting in each individual to the shared reality that language founds. Henceforth, only those things that can be said in the language of the collective are deemed to be real. One consequence is that the object at stake in speech "seems to withdraw if not disappear as language is installed," both in the history of humanity and in the life of the child ("Subject" 2).

*Symbolic castration* is the name Apollon gives to this subordination of the human quest to the language and the shared reality of the collective. The reality imposed by language nevertheless leaves a part of this quest untouched, which "escapes communal consciousness and subverts the life of the adolescent, for whom desire will follow paths that go against the paths that are traced out by the expectations of culture." This untouched part of the quest thus "constitutes the real object that maintains, at the heart of the human being, the irreducible desire to create something else." The aim of a psychoanalysis, therefore, is to establish a space for the speech that sustains this quest, "beyond the stakes of civilization, in service to the human and its future" ("Subject" 12).

If speech precedes the development of language by 250,000 years, then it is clear that speech is not limited to the use of language. Instead, early speech would have taken the form of acts: a fact whose ongoing significance is confirmed by Freud when he discovers that the symptom, repetitive behaviors, and the *acte manqué* are all forms of unconscious speech that do not involve language. When speech does make use of language—for example, in the condensations and displacements of the dreamwork, slips of the tongue or of the pen, or the metaphors and figures of speech that manage to evoke something of an experience that is out of language—it is because the quest acting in the subject of the unconscious has managed to wrest words away from language, forcing them to say something other than what they are supposed to mean in the shared reality of the social link. As the author Elfriede Jelinek puts it, "language must be tortured to tell the truth."[3] Only very rarely is language speech, therefore, and speech only occasionally makes use of language.

## The Unconscious, Repository of the *Hors langage*

Central to this project is Apollon's insistence that what Freud names the unconscious is, fundamentally, something that does not pass through language. It is concerned above all with the censored, and not the repressed. It follows that psychoanalysis cannot be concerned solely with undoing repression—a defense against the unconscious that is specific to the neurotic—but must strive instead to liberate the human that has been censored in the analysand.

Apollon distinguishes between four levels of the unconscious: the **repressed**, the **unsayable**, the **censored**, and the **unaddressable**. The first two are concerned with *language*, or what can or cannot be said [*le dire*]; the third and fourth are concerned with something that is out of language [*hors langage*], and therefore expressible only in the form of *action* ("Psychanalyse" 10 June 2020).

Apollon identifies the *repressed* with what we don't want others to know about us, or what we give up to make ourselves lovable or to be successful in the social link. It is rejected by the ego during the period he calls "second childhood" (approximately five to ten years of age), where anything that doesn't belong to the "mirror"—the ego presented to others on the social stage—must be rejected from consciousness. The *unsayable*, on the other hand, is what is not receivable in the social link, what is inadmissible or forbidden to say in a given cultural context. It includes thoughts or desires that are withheld from language by the subject, who dares not say (even to herself) what is inadmissible in a given culture or civilization. (The French term *l'impropre au dire* conveys better than the English translation that what is at issue is something that it would not be proper or acceptable to say, and not something that is inherently out of language.) The unsayable can in fact be said, and doing so is even an important role of the artist or comedian. The repressed and the unsayable are both concerned, therefore, with thoughts or wishes that are rejected from consciousness or withheld from speech, but that are not fundamentally alien to consciousness and language. (They are "unconscious" only in a limited or temporary sense, that is, since they were conscious—or at least preconscious—prior to being rejected, and are capable of becoming conscious once again.) In both cases, moreover, the agent of repression or self-censorship is the ego that repudiates parts of the subject or bows to societal prohibitions in order to be a viable object in the social link.

Neither the repressed nor the unsayable is of much significance to the pervert or the psychotic, however, since neither is particularly concerned with what others think or with submission to societal norms and prohibitions. (The speaking or writing of the unsayable, for example, is even a signature of the perversions.) If we limit the unconscious to these two levels, therefore, we limit the scope of psychoanalysis to the investigation of neurotic resistances and defenses. Even for the neurotic, moreover, it is impossible to take an analysis to its logical end if the focus is solely on the dimensions of the unconscious that are within language. To privilege repression is ultimately to privilege consciousness and the language that supports it, and not the unconscious quest of the subject and the letters of the body where that quest is inscribed.

This is why the censored and the unaddressable constitute for Apollon the core of the unconscious, which becomes the site where what remains out of language continues to work upon the body. The *censored* is the name he gives to experiences that have never been named, that have never entered consciousness, and that for that very reason have become inscribed in the body. Lucie Cantin writes that "it is this unconscious that interests the analyst, because it is the censored, the unnamed, that is the . . . active force still at work in the life of the patient, pushing her to act without regard for the wishes of the ego and seeking a path for itself through the symptom or acting out—no matter the consequences for the organism or the ego in the social link" ("Drive" 28). These experiences are alien to language not only because some occur at an age when the infant does not yet speak, but also and more importantly because they cannot be named and are therefore excluded from the reality founded by discourse and the consciousness that language constructs.

While the "out of language" and the "censored" are not expressions we find in Freud, both are central to his conception of the unconscious. However, Freud generally conceives these in ontogenetic terms, as experiences from infancy that coincide with the child's first encounters with the free drive and that predate the acquisition of language. Apollon builds on this account by conceiving the censored as what is inscribed in the body as a result of the psyche's effraction by the spirit, which gives rise to an unconscious quest that continues to work upon the body and find expression through acts. Most importantly, he adds to Freud's ontogenetic account a phylogenetic dimension. The censored is understood not merely as something unique to the individual subject, that is, but as what remains in each of us of a human quest that was long ago censored by civilization and excluded from language by culture. This he calls *the feminine*, for reasons I explore later in this chapter. While the repressed and the unsayable are rejected by the ego, therefore, the censored for Apollon is the object of a silencing or erasure imposed by civilization and reinforced by culture.

If the structure of the address that founds the social link constitutes the Other as the guardian of the limits of the receivable, the *unaddressable* is that part of the address that cannot pass through language and is not receivable in culture. Apollon writes that when Freud decided to let the hysteric do all the talking, he effectively broke with the structure of the address ("Human" 1). By remaining silent, and neither responding to nor validating or invalidating what the analysand says, the analyst empties out the place of the Other whom the patient addresses, rupturing the structure of the address that defines the social link to create a space for speech that is no longer constrained by the receivable. The function of the analyst as absent Other is thus completely opposed to that of the psychotherapist, who is explicitly positioned as an Other who guarantees the limits of the receivable. The therapist, as opposed to the analyst, is an interlocutor whom the client addresses in the language of the social link and appeals to for help in being successful within its constraints. More importantly, the therapist is a mandated reporter who is required to report to the state behaviors and fantasies that are not socially sanctioned or are viewed as threats to the client or to the social order. As a result, it is structurally impossible for the therapist to create a space for true speech.[4]

The distinction between language and action that organizes the four levels of the unconscious for Apollon is in no way a distinction between *speech* and action, therefore. Whereas language founds the social link and determines the limits of reality to subordinate the human quest to its own reproduction, speech—and especially what Lacan calls "full speech"—is an *act* that gives expression to that part of the censored human quest that continues to work upon the body. It therefore relates to the third and fourth levels of the unconscious, and thus to the *hors langage* and action. An act, writes Apollon, "supposes an effraction of the organism or of the psyche that has been repeated and inscribed: a writing." It is precisely for this reason, he continues, that speech is an act: "it supposes the letter of an inscription not only in the body of the subject who speaks, but in that of the Other who is addressed. An act surges forth because something has been inscribed [that] couldn't be said," an inscription that constitutes a part of the body ("Human" 15).

## Language and *Hors langage* in the Freudian Clinic

Before examining the most novel aspects of Apollon's understanding of the *hors langage*, I want to begin by discussing how the four levels of the unconscious both relate to and illuminate the stakes of the Freudian clinic.

It might seem counterintuitive to say that the repressed is concerned with language, especially since we all too often use "repressed" and "unconscious" as interchangeable terms in a way that tends to restrict the latter to what is forgotten, buried, or otherwise inaccessible. Repression, however, is an operation that is entirely internal to language: it supposes a content that was first conscious and named and then rejected. Freud discovers repression at the very beginning of his practice, before he theorizes and names the unconscious and even before he begins work on his seminal text *The Interpretation of Dreams*. In the *Studies on Hysteria* (1895), for example, Freud advances that a symptom is caused by a conflict between the ego and a thought or desire that the patient is unable to face up to; the latter is "repressed" (*verdrängt*) by being "cut off from any free associative connection of thought" with the rest of the ideational content of the patient's mind (165). This repressed idea is not merely rejected or rendered inaccessible, however, since it finds expression in the symptom itself.

Despite the connotations of both the English term and the German *Verdrängung*, therefore, repression does not involve the complete suppression of the repudiated thought or idea. Freud's elucidation of the processes of the dreamwork in *Interpretation of Dreams* (1900) demonstrates that repression is not merely the rejection of the intolerable idea, but its expression by other means. Repression is thus a tropological or figural operation, in which the rejected thought is represented in a distorted form or by means of a substitute. This is what we're dealing with in the dream, where the transformation of latent into manifest content is effected by the distortions characteristic of the dreamwork (condensation, displacement, considerations of representability), which hold the troubling thought at a distance or make it unrecognizable through distortion or transformation. In analysis, the work on the dream also provides a path back to the rejected thoughts through the same channels. Repression and the return of the repressed are both linguistic operations, therefore. Freud advances that every dream can be translated into a single sentence (*On Dreams* 647), just as the hysterical conversion symptom often translates an idiomatic expression or brings to mind other memories and associations related to the part of the body affected.

The case of Elisabeth von R. from *Studies on Hysteria* illustrates very well the stakes of repression and the unsayable. Elisabeth suffers from leg pains that interfere with her ability to sit, stand, or walk. Asked to remember when the pains first appeared, she recalls sitting down on a bench after a strenuous walk; when she tried to stand she was seized with pains and had to take to her bed. Pressed by Freud to remember the thoughts that had preceded the emergence of the pains, Elisabeth recalls musing that "the fact of her 'standing alone'" (implicitly, without the support of a husband) had become painful to her, as was her sense of helplessness—the feeling that "she could not 'take a single step forward'" (*Studies* 152). As a cultivated and ambitious young woman who prided herself on her independence and rejected the institution of marriage, Elisabeth found these thoughts intolerable. Banished by the ego, the rejected thoughts found expression through leg pains that rendered her unable to stand or walk unsupported.

The turning point in the analysis has to do with the lifting of the unsayable, which occurs when Freud compels Elisabeth to remember—and recount in the session—the more deeply buried thoughts that lay behind the first appearance of the leg pains. While her sister was already bedridden with the illness that would cause her death, Elisabeth had gone on a walk with her brother-in-law during which they had discussed all kinds of subjects. During that walk, she admits, "a desire to have a husband like him became very strong in her" (155). It was a few days later that she sat down on the bench and dreamed of enjoying such happiness as her sister's; later that afternoon the leg pains broke out. A few weeks later, her sister died. When Elisabeth stood over her sister's deathbed, "another thought had shot through her mind, and now forced itself irresistibly upon her once more, like a flash of lightning in the dark: 'Now he is free again and I can be his wife'" (156). This is when the leg pains erupt with their greatest ferocity. We can see from this account that Elisabeth is not unaware that she is in love with her sister's husband. Until this moment, however, she was unable to avow this fact either to herself or to others: it was inadmissible in her familial and cultural context and so became unsayable.

In these early cases Freud is interested in getting the patient to say what she knows without knowing it (*Studies* 110), to articulate a knowledge that is conscious—or at least preconscious—but "cut off" from other associative chains. At this point, however, this is as far as Freud goes: he doesn't deal with the *hors langage* as such. When we read these cases it is easy to see why Apollon states that Freud's clinic was concerned primarily with the repressed, and not with the censored or the unaddressable. (We must remember that the Elisabeth von R. case, like all the others in *Studies on Hysteria*, predates Freud's theorization of the unconscious and the drives—underscoring Apollon's point that the repressed cannot be confused with the unconscious itself.)

Even in these early cases, however, Freud is confronted with the limits of repression as a way of conceiving what is at work in the patient's body. At the beginning of the Elisabeth case, Freud hypothesizes that the hysterical illness was most likely "a question of a secret" that she had told no one (145). By the end, however, he acknowledges that the basis of her illness was not only a secret, but a "foreign body" (165). The first—the secret—concerns thoughts that the patient does not want to avow to others (the repressed or the unspeakable). The second is an anticipation of the unconscious properly speaking: a foreign body within the organism that is not recognizable to the ego. The case therefore shows Freud moving from repression to an incipient theorization of the unconscious as such, which cannot simply be equated with the thoughts the patient conceals from others or rejects from consciousness: the unconscious is not merely a "secret," but a "foreign body."

In distinguishing the *hors langage* from language, and more specifically the censored from the repressed, Apollon seeks to distinguish dimensions of the unconscious that are often conflated in the reception of Freud's work, in part because he generally uses the same root word—*Verdrängung*, or repression—to speak about both of them. The censored is the "foreign body" of Freud's formulation. It is not only foreign to or cut off from other associative chains, however, but inscribed *in the body*: and therefore foreign to consciousness. Apollon's intervention is not only terminological or conceptual, however, but develops and amplifies the stakes of the censored and the unaddressable in their relation to the act and aesthetics, especially as concerns the aims and the end of an analysis.

The investigation of repression and its logic dominates Freud's early clinical practice and nascent understanding of the unconscious. Beginning around 1914, however, Freud begins to theorize both the fantasy and the death drive. At this point he becomes increasingly interested in the unconscious not simply as a repository of memories and thoughts that have been rejected from consciousness, but as a "force" at work in the life and in the body of the patient that gives rise to mental presentations that are inaccessible to consciousness. This "force," which is expressed through actions rather than words, is what is at stake in the *hors langage*.

Here I give a brief exposition of two important articles from this period, "Remembering, Repeating, and Working-Through" (1914) and "Repression" (1915). Both were written during a period when Freud was fundamentally rethinking both the nature of the unconscious and the technique of psychoanalysis. Through his work with the patient he called the Wolf Man (1908–1918) in particular, Freud was beginning to theorize the existence of an unconscious fantasy that overdetermines the patient's symptoms, repetitive behaviors, and unintended acts. Unlike the "secret" or unavowable wish that the Freud of the *Studies on Hysteria* supposed to be at the origin of the patient's symptoms, the fantasy is not conscious. This is true not merely in the limited sense that the patient doesn't connect it to what is happening at the moment ("cut off from other associative chains"), but because it was *never conscious*.

In "Remembering, Repeating, Working-Through," Freud formulates very well the inadequacy of any psychoanalytic technique that focuses on memory or consciousness alone. He begins by breaking down into three distinct periods the evolution of the technique and the aims of psychoanalysis. In the early days of psychoanalysis,[5] the cathartic method pioneered by Freud's colleague Josef Breuer used hypnosis to bring "directly into focus the moment at which the symptom was formed"; it endeavored "to reproduce the mental processes involved in that situation, in order to direct their discharge along the path of conscious activity" ("Remembering"

146). During this period, Freud and Breuer's guiding assumption was that "hysterics suffer mainly from reminiscences" (*Studies* 7): memories that could be called up, made conscious, and so stripped of their traumatic charge. As a technique, hypnosis promises something like a full recovery of those memories. It "brings into focus" a triggering situation or event in the manner of a cinematic flashback, thereby allowing the thoughts and feelings associated with it to be relived and spoken about.

When hypnosis fell out of favor, a new technique came to the fore that consisted in "discovering from the patient's associations what he failed to remember" ("Remembering" 146). Here the emphasis was still on the "situations which lay behind the moment at which the illness broke out," but these were arrived at through free association—and therefore with the aid of speech—rather than through the pseudo-scientific technique of hypnosis. In comparison with the cathartic method, the analyst now placed less emphasis on "abreaction," the catharsis associated with reliving an experience in order to purge or release the energy associated with it. The focus instead shifted to circumventing the patient's *resistance*, which was understood to be responsible for the content undergoing repression in the first place. That resistance was now conceived primarily in ethical terms, as a refusal on the patient's part to confront something that was painful, unpleasant, or at odds with her own morals or ideals.[6]

Finally, Freud describes "the consistent technique used today"—that is, 1914—"in which the analyst gives up the attempt to bring a particular moment or problem into focus" (146). Instead, he "contents himself with studying whatever is present for the time being on the surface of the patient's mind" (146). A striking feature of this third technique is that the interest in reproducing the mental processes associated with a past event that could be understood as the exciting cause of the illness, which had been central to the first technique in particular, diminishes in importance or even falls away altogether. Instead, the analyst presumes a psychic continuity between what is present right now on the patient's mind and the symptoms, affects, or behaviors that brought him into treatment.

One important consequence is that the unconscious can no longer be understood as a set of "memory traces," but as something that is expressed through acts. As an example of the latter, Freud cites several "psychical processes" that are not susceptible to being remembered: "phantasies, processes of reference, emotional impulses, thought-connections—*which, as purely internal acts, can be contrasted with impressions and experiences,* must, in their relation to forgetting and remembering, be considered separately. In these processes it particularly often happens that *something is 'remembered' which could never have been 'forgotten' because it was never at any time noticed—was never conscious*" (147, my emphases). Here it isn't a matter of a lost memory suddenly popping into the patient's head or being recalled in a specific connection, as with the restoration of a link that has been severed by repression. Nor is the memory or rejected thought represented in distorted form or by means of a substitute. Rather, something is "remembered" only in the form of an act, whether that act is "internal" (a fantasy, a feeling) or external (a repetitive behavior, a staging, or an episode of acting out). It acts in and through the subject in a way that does not enter into consciousness and is not dependent on it.

Freud then observes that "[t]here is one special class of experiences of the utmost importance for which no memory can as a rule be recovered. These are experiences which occurred in very early childhood and were not understood at the time but which were *subsequently* understood and interpreted. One gains a knowledge of them through dreams and one is obliged to believe in them on the most compelling evidence provided by the fabric of the neurosis" (148; emphasis in original). Before the child speaks, he has experiences that are out of language. These are not only beyond his understanding, therefore, but inaccessible to the consciousness that language founds. The footnote to this passage explains that the reference is to the Wolf Man case. The experience at issue there, which Freud calls the "primal scene," was completely *hors langage*. This is true not only because it dates from a period when the child did not yet speak, or because he didn't have the maturity and the knowledge of human anatomy to understand what he was seeing: for example, to grasp that what he witnessed was a sexual act and not a violent castration, or to understand that the mother was being penetrated in the vagina and not the anus. More importantly, the experience was *never* available to perception-consciousness. This is because the child experienced something more, or something different, than what he "witnessed" when he lay in his crib in the parents' bedroom. He experienced the effects of a fantasy—a mental presentation—that emerged in response to that witnessing. It is this fantasy that continues to act upon the patient throughout his life, driving a compulsion to repeat that takes the form of behaviors that are not under his conscious control and inscribing itself in the letters of his body.

Freud concludes that "the patient does not *remember* anything of what he has forgotten and repressed, but *acts* it out. He reproduces it not as a memory but as an action; he *repeats* it, without, of course, knowing that he is repeating it" (149). It follows that "[a]s long as the patient is in the treatment he cannot escape from this compulsion to repeat; and in the end we understand that this is his way of remembering" (149). "We may now ask," Freud continues, "*what it is that he in fact repeats or acts out*. The answer is that he repeats everything that has already made its way from the sources of the repressed into his manifest personality—his inhibitions and unserviceable attitudes and his pathological character-traits." He also repeats "all his symptoms in the course of the treatment," which explains the "deterioration during treatment" that is often an unavoidable response to the analytic work. It therefore becomes clear, Freud concludes, that "the patient's state of being ill cannot cease with the beginning of his analysis, and that *we must treat his illness, not as an event of the past, but as a [still active] force*" (150, my emphases).

What is enacted in repetition belongs neither to the past nor to the present, but is an always active "force" in the patient's life that is called forth by the transference and asked to show itself. More importantly, however, what is acted out is now conceived not merely as a "mental process" that has undergone repression, but as something like the crux of the patient's unconscious subjectivity. Unlike the unwelcome thought or psychic conflict at stake in repression, whose avoidance is at the origin of the patient's illness, the act is concerned with a quest in the subject that cannot be reduced to a pathology requiring treatment. Accordingly, writes Freud, the analysand "must find the courage to direct his attention to the phenomena of his illness. His illness itself must no longer seem to him contemptible, but must become an enemy worthy of his mettle, a piece of his personality, which has solid ground for its existence and out of which things of value for his future life have to be derived" (151).

At the end of the essay Freud speaks of the transference as a "playground" in which the compulsion to repeat is allowed to expand in complete freedom:

The main instrument . . . for curbing the patient's compulsion to repeat and for turning it into a motive for remembering lies in the handling of the transference. We render the compulsion harmless, and indeed useful, by giving it the right to assert

> itself in a definite field. We admit it into the transference as a playground [*Tummelplatz*] in which it is allowed to expand in almost complete freedom and in which it is expected to display to us everything in the way of pathogenic [drives][7] that is hidden in the patient's mind. (153)

This wonderful expression makes clear to what extent Freud's clinic is ultimately concerned with the act and the censored, despite his persistent attention to repression and the return of the repressed. Even as Freud calls on the compulsion to repeat to display the "pathogenic drives" hidden in the patient's mind, it is clear that what is acting in repetition cannot be conceived merely as a threat to the patient's health that could be cathected or abreacted and so stripped of its power, but as a force that is creative as well as destructive and that has "the right to assert itself" in the field of the transference. The latter is not only a field for the identification and treatment of pathogenic material, therefore, but a space for the manifestation of the subject as such.[8]

This thing that acts in the subject, this "enemy worthy of our mettle," is the essence of the subject of the unconscious as Apollon understands it. He observes that every analysand is sooner or later confronted with the disquieting realization that "the object of his quest [is at the same time] the object of all his misfortunes. He can neither rid himself of it nor require that it be healed, unless it is by the negation of his very existence as a subject" ("Untreatable" 37). The "untreatable" is the name Apollon gives to this unconscious quest from which the subject will not be derailed, no matter the consequences. "Untreatable" translates the French *intraitable*, which means not "incurable" (as in the case of a disease for which there is no cure), but rather "intractable, inflexible, uncompromising." It exceeds the treatment framework implied by illness, which presumes at the same time the possibility of a cure. It is this untreatable object that Apollon has in mind when he suggests that the end of an analysis articulates the analysand to what constitutes his or her "signature in the social link," the mark of the subject in its refusal of all concessions ("Conclusive").

In "Repression," a key metapsychological essay from 1915, Freud further problematizes and restricts his earlier understanding of *Verdrängung* by arguing that repression is an operation that occurs at a relatively late phase of the mental organization, and involves the rejection of thoughts that have already entered consciousness: "Psycho-analytic observation of the transference neuroses . . . leads us to conclude that repression is not a defensive mechanism which is present from the very beginning, and that it cannot arise until a sharp cleavage has occurred between conscious and unconscious mental activity—that *the essence of repression lies simply in turning something away, and keeping it at a distance, from the conscious*" (147; emphasis in original). This conception of repression, he now adds, "would be made more complete by assuming that, before the mental organization reaches this stage, the task of fending off [drive] impulses is dealt with by the other vicissitudes which instincts may undergo—e.g., reversal into the opposite or turning round upon the subject's own self" (147). Repression thus supposes an earlier, more fundamental state of affairs, one that is concerned not with the rejection of thoughts and ideas that have already entered consciousness, but with "drive impulses" and their effects.

This attention to the fending off of drive impulses as a necessary antecedent to repression leads to a further modification in Freud's understanding of the unconscious. Within the general concept of repression, he now argues, we must distinguish between two fundamentally distinct operations:

> We have reason to assume that there is a *primal repression* [*Urverdrängung*], a first phase of repression, which consists in the psychical (ideational) representative of the [drive] being denied entrance into the conscious. With this a *fixation* is established; the representative in question persists unaltered from then onwards and the instinct remains attached to it. . . . The second stage of repression, *repression proper* [*die eigentliche Verdrängung*], affects mental derivatives of the repressed representative, or such trains of thought as, originating elsewhere, have come into associative connection with it. On account of this association, these ideas experience the same fate as what was primally repressed. Repression proper, therefore, is actually an after-[expulsion]. (148)

Repression proper is a secondary operation, applying merely to the conscious thoughts to which the "mental presentation" of a drive has become attached. The memories and thoughts that undergo repression are not the drive presentations themselves, therefore, but "trains of thought" that originate elsewhere, and that subsequently come into associative connection with those drive presentations because they manage to express or capture something of the *feeling* associated with a drive presentation that nevertheless remains unconscious. These thoughts are therefore already substitutes, standing in for something that cannot be represented as such. Conversely, primary repression [*Urverdrängung*] describes the impossibility of something entering consciousness in the first place. The logical corollary is that while (secondary) repression supposes language and the consciousness it enables, primary repression applies to something that is unable to enter language and therefore alien to consciousness.

The "fixations" associated with primary repression—which include drive vicissitudes like sadism and masochism and fixations of the oral, anal, or scopic drive—give expression to mental presentations of the drive impulses that are not conscious and not attached to other trains of thought.[9] In these fixations, the mental presentation "persists unaltered": it does not undergo distortion or transformation and is not represented by a substitute. What happens here cannot be assimilated to repression, therefore, even when it is characterized as "primary."

The second part of the essay turns to affects, which Freud characterizes as drive-presentations that do not pass through language and are not conscious:

> so far we have dealt with the repression of [a drive-]representative, . . . an idea or group of ideas which is cathected with a definite quota of psychical energy (libido or interest) coming from [a drive]. Clinical observation now obliges us to divide up what we have hitherto regarded as a single entity; for it shows us that besides the idea, some other element representing the [drive] has to be taken into account, and that this other element undergoes vicissitudes of repression which may be quite different from those undergone by the idea. For this other element of the psychical representative the term *quota of affect* has been generally adopted. It corresponds to the [drive] in so far as the latter has become detached from the idea and finds expression, proportionate to its quantity, in processes which are sensed as affects (152).

Under the broad rubric of "repression," therefore, Freud identifies three distinct outcomes. In primary repression, the drive presentation is denied entry to consciousness. In secondary repression, or repression properly speaking, the drive presentation is represented by a substitute through a process of distortion. That substitute is a once-conscious memory or thought that "came into association" with the unconscious drive presentation. Finally, "the *transformation* into *affects*, and especially into *anxiety*, of the psychical energies of [drives]" (153).

## THE *HORS LANGAGE* IN APOLLON'S METAPSYCHOLOGY

Apollon's use of the expression *hors langage* helps to distinguish dimensions of the unconscious that are too easily conflated in the reception of Freud's work, especially since Freud uses the same root word—*Verdrängung*—to describe the fundamentally different stakes of primary and secondary repression.

Returning to Apollon's distinction between the four levels of the unconscious, we can see that what Freud describes under the heading of (secondary) repression, or repression properly speaking, encompasses both the repressed and the unsayable. The primally repressed and charges of affect that are not attached to ideas, on the other hand, are two dimensions of what is at stake in the concept of the censored for Apollon. Both concern mental representations (or "drive presentations," in Freud's terms) that are not conscious, for which there are no words, that find expression only in the form of symptoms, repetitive or compulsive behaviors, and unmotivated acts. The censored is what Freud encounters in the Wolf Man case, where the body of the analysand has been eroticized by an experience that is completely *hors langage*. The fantasy of the primal scene leaves traces in the subject's life, informing his life choices, dictating the repetition of certain painful experiences and impasses, and determining the choice of a specific symptom—the constipation whose treatment is central to the final phase of the analysis—that inscribes the fantasy in the letters of the body. Crucially, however, that fantasy will never become conscious for the Wolf Man. It cannot be remembered, therefore, but only *constructed* by means of the transference that calls on the letters of the body—the erogenous zones where the unconscious fantasy is inscribed—to produce stagings or acts in response to Freud's desire to know about the jouissance inscribed in the patient's symptom, his repetitive behaviors, and the feeling of depression that overtakes him each day at five o'clock in the evening. If the repressed returns in language, the censored returns "in the real" in the form of an act or an affect with no ideational content. It does not take the form of a thought or a phrase that can be identified through the undoing of distortion, but of a staging or enactment of a drive presentation.

When Freud invites the bowel to "join in the conversation" in the final phase of the analysis, we also have a striking example of the stakes of the unaddressable. Prior to this maneuver on Freud's part, the patient had been suffering from terrible constipation, which could be relieved only by the application of regular enemas delivered by his manservant. Eventually this staging—a man inserts something in the patient's anus from behind, resulting in the passing of a stool—is revealed to be a repetition of the fantasy of the primal scene, where the patient fantasizes about being penetrated by the father's penis while in the mother's bowel and then giving birth to a feces-child. When the patient demands an enema, this unaddressable is made receivable in the social link as a request for medical treatment—but at the cost of silencing what is at work in the body and allowing the patient not to confront the fantasy. Only in the space of the transference can what has been inscribed in the bowel truly speak. The function of the analyst, and the address he makes possible, is thus opposed to that of the manservant, the other in the social link who upholds the limits of the receivable. The "conversation" that can be had with the bowel, unlike the demand for treatment or the conversation the patient tries to initiate with the clinician as an other in the social link, is an opportunity for true speech.

We can also think of other examples that relate not to the experiences of early childhood, but to the impact on the subject of experiences that are censored because they were denied entry to language and consciousness before the subject was even born. Lucie Cantin gives the example of a patient whose commitment to a mental hospital turns out to be the reenactment or staging of a family history that was unsayable in the parents' generation: her grandfather had died in a psychiatric hospital where he had been interned for many years ("Drive" 30). Because it was never spoken about, a story that might otherwise have been an object of consciousness was preserved solely through the traces it left on the body of the child who was subject to the effect of that unsayable on her parents. In Cantin's words, "Ms. B's commitment to the psychiatric hospital stages or enacts what she calls a family secret. What was forbidden or impossible to say for her parents' generation becomes for her the censored, something that has never been named but is nevertheless inscribed in her body" (33).

Similarly, Freud in *Moses and Monotheism* explores how the murder

Table 2.1. Repression, the Unsayable, the Censored, and the Unaddressable

| | APOLLON | FREUD |
|---|---|---|
| **LANGUAGE** | **The repressed** <br> In language, but distorted; what you don't want others to know about you <br><br> **The unsayable** <br> Withheld from language; what cannot be said in a given cultural context | **(Secondary) repression (Verdrängung)** <br> *Elisabeth is afraid of "standing alone," "unable to take a step forward": repressed thoughts are expressed through conversion as leg pains* <br><br> *Elisabeth thinks as she stands at her sister's deathbed, "now he is free and I can be his wife"* |
| **ACTION** <br> *Hors langage* | **The censored** <br> Not in language, inscribed in the body and expressed in acts <br><br> **The unaddressable** <br> That part of the address that cannot be expressed in language | **Primary repression (Urverdrängung)** <br> *Wolf Man: the jouissance associated with the fantasy of the primal scene eroticizes the anal zone and is inscribed in the bowel.* <br><br> *Freud invites the Wolf Man's bowel to "join in the conversation," providing an address for what is otherwise unaddressable.* |

of Moses by his people was first rendered unsayable before becoming a censored whose only manifestation was an obscure feeling of guilt that for thousands of years pursued generations who had no knowledge of that original event. In each of these examples, it is clear that the censored will never be remembered: it always necessitates a *construction*, which in turn relies on acts (stagings, repetitive behaviors, acting out, etc.) that engage the letters of the body.[10] If the repressed was once conscious and is capable of becoming conscious once again, the censored was never conscious and never will be, except in the form of a construction or formula that has no relation to memory or perception. Accordingly, the lifting of censorship does not result in a conscious memory or insight, but in the act of true speech wherein what is inscribed in the body will find signifiers that manage to evoke what cannot be named.

Apollon's use of "the censored" [*le censuré*] or "censorship" [*la cen-*

*sure*] to describe the *hors langage* that acts in the subject will no doubt be puzzling to some readers, since in everyday usage we think of censorship as an operation that takes place at the level of language.[11] In the Freudian corpus, moreover, the concept is found almost exclusively in *Interpretation of Dreams*, where it arguably does not have the same connotation that it does for Apollon. At a minimum, Freud's use of censorship is ambiguous. Like his use of repression, it seems to go in two, fundamentally distinct directions: one that is internal to language and the logic of repression, and another that is closer to the Apollonian *hors langage*. In chapter IV, for example, Freud's discussion of censorship in dreams is developed through an analogy to political censorship (*Interpretation* 141), and thus understood as an operation that applies to something that has already been spoken or expressed: for example, the military censorship of letters that soldiers send home during wartime or a government's denial of access to websites that address topics whose discussion is forbidden in a given cultural or national context. The way to circumvent this kind of censorship, for the letter writer and the dream alike, is to disguise the offending content by transforming it to such a degree that it is no longer recognizable: whether by using coded language or imagery or by distorting the content through the processes that Freud locates within the dreamwork: condensation, displacement, and considerations of representability. Considered in this light, censorship can be situated squarely within the problematic of repression.

With his account of the "navel" of the dream, however, Freud implicitly introduces another understanding of the censored that is very different from the one at stake in the political analogy and in everyday usage. While associations to the different elements of the dream will lead to the *repressed* thoughts that are represented in distorted form in the manifest content of the dream, they will not lead to the censored. This is the function of the dream's navel, a point of nonsense in the dream that cannot be assimilated to the waking thoughts of the dreamer. It is the trace of something at work in the subject that is unable to find even a distorted expression in the dream: namely, the "day residues" that drive the production of the dream but are represented neither within its manifest content nor in the associations to which the different elements of the dream narrative give rise. These "day residues" invariably concern an act or a failed act, which the dream circles around without being able to represent it.

## The Censorship of the Feminine

Censorship also has another dimension for Apollon, not present in Freud: the censoring of the feminine. He defines the feminine as an effect of the quest that surges up in each of us as a consequence of the living being's effraction by the spirit, a quest for something other than what culture demands or civilization validates. The feminine is not unique to women, therefore, but—like masculinity—is a dimension of subjectivity that is present in every human being.

More specifically, the feminine is concerned with something at work in the body that cannot be addressed to others, that cannot be said. For that very reason, it also introduces as unavoidable the dimension of the aesthetic. This link between the feminine, the spirit, and the aesthetic is not without historical and religious precedent, of course; we need think only of the Muses of ancient Greece, the Vestal Virgins of ancient Rome who were charged with maintaining the sacred fire that brought light to the human world, or the Virgin Mary who in Catholicism enables the corporeal manifestation of the spirit. All of them underscore the fundamental link between the feminine and the spiritual realm that is a regular feature of ancient religions and that remains central to many African spiritual practices.

Nevertheless, it is precisely this connection to the spirit and to the aesthetic that must be censored by culture if it is to manufacture the woman and the man it requires to reproduce itself. Apollon argues that no culture can possibly accept the challenge that the feminine represents, since every culture relies on the structure of the address to define what is receivable, impose limits, and create norms. Apollon conceives this censorship as something that occurs at a specific moment in human evolution, when humans who previously lived in small groups of ten or twelve individuals are obliged to band together in much larger groups for their survival. These larger groups, which were also responsible for the invention of language and all of its consequences, were less dependent on the creative capacity that each member of the group brought to the collective and could therefore afford to turn some human beings—and women in particular—into resources to be used for the reproduction of the group or exchanged for other goods. But this originary censorship is also recapitulated in the life of the individual at puberty, when it is renewed and reinforced through the specific itera-tion of the sexual montage that each culture imposes on the pubescent girl and boy to press them into the service of the group's material and ideological reproduction.

Although we can recognize the censorship of femininity in the forced marriages of pubescent girls or the homophobic violence directed against the feminine in a man, for example, these are merely a few conspicuous manifestations of a censorship of the feminine that is so pervasive, and so deeply rooted in the evolution of human civilization, that we aren't even conscious of it. These recognizable examples are really censorship at a second remove, therefore, since they involve the censoring of what is *perceived as feminine* within the framework of the cultural montage of the sexual, which is a mere vestige of the much more capacious understanding of the feminine that Apollon introduces: the ability of any human being to express, through acts that will be received by others, things that a culture does not tolerate that one say (the unsayable) or that cannot be said (the censored). Because the feminine is concerned fundamentally with what cannot be said, the dimension of the aesthetic that it introduces necessarily shatters the structure of the address: and, with it, the reduction of the human being to the man and the woman that culture requires.

If the feminine is a dimension of every human being, then why call it "the feminine"? In Apollon's words,

> I call it the feminine because it is most persecuted, its censorship is most apparent, in the bodies of women and in the violence that is done to them. The capacities of the [human] spirit are present in every member of the community. If women begin to represent things that do not exist, to want them, and to do what is needed to create them, then what will happen to the survival of the collective? Every human being comes out of a woman's womb. These two statements lead to the logical conclusion that femininity has to be censored by culture because it is on the side of the spirit and the capacity it implies. If women decide that they no longer want what culture wants, then this also means that they are capable of conceiving something else and making it happen. ("Séminaire" 29 Jan. 2022)

At the limit, then, the feminine confronts every culture with the possibility of its own disappearance. To counter this possibility, the collective maintains the censorship of the feminine with the cultural montage of the sexual, through which culture asserts its control over the limits of the receivable by prioritizing the reproduction of the collective over the human quest at work in the subject.

This censorship of the feminine is sometimes sustained even by Freud himself, whose susceptibility to accepting and affirming the limits and the models imposed by culture—although rare—is nowhere more apparent than in his work with women patients and his writings on femininity. When he claims in "Femininity" that the only way for a woman to undergo castration is through motherhood and the eventual loss of the child (*New* 112–13), he effectively reduces the ethical and subjective stakes of castration in analysis to symbolic castration, or the limits defined by culture. Even more problematic, success for a female analysand is too often defined by marriage and by the ability to find pleasure in—or at least resign herself to—a sexual relationship. I'm thinking not only of the consternation Freud feels at Dora's refusal to take Herr K's talk of marriage in good faith, but of his definition of hysteria as a pathological refusal of sexual enjoyment: "I should without question consider a person hysterical in whom an occasion for sexual excitement elicited feelings that were preponderantly or exclusively unpleasurable; and I should do so whether or not the person were capable of producing somatic symptoms" (*Fragment* 28). This reductive treatment of femininity is not limited to the treatment of women patients, moreover. Just as significant is the case of the psychotic Doctor Schreber, where the solidarity with the feminine that Apollon locates at the heart of the psychotic's experience—and that for Schreber is manifested in part by the gradual feminization of his own erogenous body—is apprehended by Freud solely in the guise of the homosexual fantasy that he places at the origin of the delusion: Schreber would be transforming himself into a woman in order to be copulated with by (God) the father.

## The Act and Aesthetics

Freud's failure to acknowledge and confront the censorship of the feminine underscores what for Apollon is one of the most pressing questions confronting psychoanalysis today. How do we, as analysts, receive and welcome the feminine in each human being, and not simply the man or woman produced by the cultural montage of the sexual?

What the censoring of the feminine in sex renders impossible in the social link continues to haunt the body, where the censored and the unaddressable are inscribed. The feminine is thus at the heart of the body as Apollon understands it, which is eroticized by the energies unleashed by the drive that opens up an aesthetic space for the censored. This body has nothing to do with what culture calls the body, however, since it is made manifest only in those acts that give expression to something that cannot be said. The aim of an analysis as Apollon understands it is to liberate the human quest that traverses the analysand by giving expression to the femininity that has been censored in his or her body, but also to take responsibility for the consequences of that expression both for the subject and for others.

Because femininity goes beyond what culture posits as limits, it has consequences that are necessarily disruptive, both for the subject and for others. The feminine invariably concerns the relation to the other, therefore, and not only the subject's own intimate experiences. Apollon specifies that "an act is feminine because, in the address, it displaces the other: it provokes in the other something that the other can't control" ("Transference" 10-11-22). Hence the importance of the aesthetic. If there is not something aesthetic about the consequences of the acts through which the feminine finds expression, the reaction of the other will be one of violence or refusal. An act is aesthetic when it "produces something that articulates the subject to humanity and is therefore recognizable both for . . . the feeling of the beautiful and the sublime that it elicits in others, and for its ethical dimension insofar as it is articulated to a collective work, as a kind of contribution to the edification of humanity's heritage" (Cantin, "Drive" 39).

If femininity is something at stake in the relation to the other, masculinity—which is explored in more detail by Daniel Wilson in chapter 5—is what is at stake in the social link. More specifically, it involves taking responsibility for the consequences, in the social link, of the feminine and the acts it produces. The feminine, Apollon says, is "a brick thrown through the window of civilization"; the masculine is about taking responsibility for that and picking up the pieces. It is important to underscore again that this is not a question of a *man* taking responsibility for the acts of a *woman*, but of the masculine in the subject taking responsibility for the acts through which his or her femininity finds expression and its consequences for others. This assumption of responsibility for the feminine and the act—which should in no way be understood as an imperative to control, suppress, or prevent the act—is an essential dimension of the end of an analysis.

Earlier I argued that Freud was dealing with the censored in his clinic well before he articulated a theoretical distinction between primary and secondary repression. Even in the Wolf Man case, however, we do not see Freud dealing with the censored in the full sense that Apollon gives to it: a quest acting in the subject that disrupts the relation to the other and demands an aesthetic expression. This is in part because Freud stops his analyses at a point that is well short of the logical end of an analysis as Apollon understands it. With respect to the four levels of the unconscious discussed earlier, it seems that Freud deals with the censored in the Wolf Man case, but not the censoring of the feminine or the unaddressable: the analysis isn't taken to the point where the patient will be compelled to find an aesthetic expression for what is acting in the body, even at the cost of a rupture with the social link.

Ironically, however, there is arguably no better illustration of what it means to assume the quest of desire, and its consequences for others, than Freud's own life following his self-analysis. This self-analysis goes further than Freud is able to theorize or integrate into his own clinical practice, and foregrounds very well the stakes of the act and its aesthetic dimension. This act is central to the analysis of the "specimen dream" to which Freud devotes the second chapter of *Interpretation of Dreams*, the dream of Irma's Injection (96–121). It is concerned with the liberation of his act, which previously had been an object of ambivalence and even apprehension. With respect to the preceding development, my reading of Freud's dream analysis attempts to show that this feminine dimension is what acts in the analyst and that there can be no psychoanalysis without it.

The dream interrogates a failed act or ethical equivocation on Freud's part, which is related to the treatment of his hysterical patient, Irma. The day before the dream, he receives a visit from a colleague who has just seen Irma and responds to Freud's query about her condition by saying that she is "better, but not quite well." Freud, vexed by the insinuation that the treatment might have failed, stays up late into the night preparing a write-up of the case history "in order to justify himself." Driving the production of Freud's dream is the question: Is he or is he not responsible for the persistence of the patient's symptoms? If it is a hysterical symptom, then why hasn't it been treated by the interpretation? Has he missed an organic illness? What is the source of the infection?

The first part of the dream deals with Freud's annoyance at Irma's refusal of his "solution" and his attempts to get the hysteric to "open her mouth properly" and tell him what he needs to know. The dream dates from 1895, when Freud is involved precisely in getting the hysteric to "open her mouth." This is the year Freud publishes *Studies on Hysteria*, where he claims that the symptom is caused by an "unspoken secret," something the patient does not want to avow. The flip side of this attitude is a belief in the treatment of the symptom by knowledge or interpretation, and therefore by the signifier. In the first part of the dream, Freud says to Irma: *"If you still get pains, it's your own fault."* This is what Freud will later refer to as "wild psychoanalysis": the assumption that interpretation can treat the symptom: that once the cause of the symptom is revealed, the symptom should disappear.

What follows is the "navel" of the dream. When Irma opens her mouth, what emerges is not a word or a discourse, something she might tell him, but terrifying, anxiety-inducing forms that lead to thoughts of illness and death. In Irma's throat, Freud sees a "big white patch" and "some remarkable curly structures" covered with scabs that appear to be modeled on the turbinal bones of the nose. These scab-covered forms lead Freud to associations that are concerned not with *Irma's* symptoms and their treatment, but with Freud's *own* severe nasal symptoms—the result of his overly zealous experimentation with cocaine. His own symptom is thus projected into the patient's throat, as a defiant limit to the knowable there where he had expected the words that would establish the symptom's causality. Freud is therefore obliged to encounter the censored not only in his patient, but in himself.

The second part of the dream shows Freud turning to medical colleagues for confirmation or guidance, as if unsure whether he ought to approach the case as a doctor or as a psychoanalyst. One doctor, a senior colleague, is represented as saying: *"There's no doubt it's an infection, but no matter; dysentery will supervene and the toxin will be eliminated."* The associations evoke the futile hope of the medical doctor that it might be possible to treat hysteria as if it were a disease, and so eliminate the symptom from the patient's body.

The dream ends with the evocation of an unclean syringe, charged with having caused an infection in the patient: *"Injections of that sort ought not to be made so thoughtlessly . . . And probably the syringe had not been clean."* In response to this dream element, Freud professes that, unlike some of his more careless colleagues, he always makes sure that *his* syringe is clean: as a result, he has never caused a single infiltration. His associations have already undercut this claim, however, by pointing to numerous occasions on which Freud has either killed his patients with injections or induced potentially deadly toxic states: in part by sharing his own passion for cocaine. On the one hand, Freud harmed or killed those patients when he was acting as a doctor, and not as a psychoanalyst. In these instances, we can say that the patient's brush with death is due to the limitations of medical knowledge rather than to the failings of psychoanalysis. But on the other hand, and more importantly, Freud *as a psychoanalyst* is confronting his patients with death by upholding the work of the symptom. In psychoanalysis, unlike medicine, this isn't just a matter of professional scrupulousness, of a risk that could be avoided through careful attention to protocol. Instead, the treatment confronts his patients with death at its very core.

I see the dirty syringe as a figure of the act, in two senses. First, it figures the failed act or counter-transference. In an act of "wild psycho-analysis," Freud attempts to impose on the patient the solution provided by the interpretation, but at the expense of silencing what is at work in the symptom. With the image of the unclean syringe, the dream seems to be offering a forceful indictment of this counter-transference on Freud's part, his attempt to force or inject a solution rather than allowing the analysis to run its course.

Lacan makes such an interpretation in his own commentary of the dream: "In the first phase, then, we see Freud in his chase after Irma, reproaching her for not understanding what he wants to get her to understand. He was carrying on his relationships in exactly the same style as he did in real life, in the style of the passionate quest, too passionate we would say, and it is indeed one of the meanings of the dream to say that . . . the syringe was dirty, the passion of the analyst, the ambition to succeed, were here too pressing, the counter-transference was itself the obstacle."[12]

But second—and here I differ from Lacan—I think we can see the dirty syringe as a figure of the *true act*, the act that makes him Freud. That is, the analyst's desire to know triggers and reactivates the symptom in the patient's body: and it can't do otherwise! The fear that the syringe might not be clean is the fear of the medical doctor. It cor-responds to the ideal of experiments under controlled conditions, where there must be no contamination from the subject. For the doctor, the "dirty syringe" is a failure and a breach of scientific protocol; for the psychoanalyst, it is a necessity. The psychoanalyst *must* infect: he must provoke symptoms in the patient's body, reactivating a real that she will have a hard time managing. Rather than conscientiously sterilizing his person to *avoid* transmitting something (to "do no harm," in the words of the Hippocratic oath), the analyst acts with the object-cause of his own desire, thereby eliciting the work of the drive.

When Freud the dreamer peers into Irma's throat to find his own symptoms staring back at him, what he encounters is not only his own relation to the untreatable, but more powerfully the impact of his act on the body of his patient. After the turning point marked by this dream and its analysis, Freud doesn't hesitate to inject his patients with his "dirty syringe" to retrigger the symptom or call forth the drive.

The act relates to a quest in Freud that takes him beyond the pleasure principle, beyond what culture and civilization allow. When Freud the medical doctor refused to recognize the consequences of his acts for others, those consequences were sometimes violent or even fatal. But once he acknowledged that his acts were eliciting a drive response in his patients, and therefore contributing directly to the production of their symptoms, that disruption or displacement of the other was no longer harmful to his patients but instead founded a practice that allowed them to access something of the censored quest in themselves. It was therefore able to be judged aesthetic not only by those patients, but by humanity itself inasmuch as it was able to benefit from the creative capacities thus unleashed. Freud therefore took responsibility for that "brick" thrown through the window of civilization by creating the aesthetic space of the transference—the "playground" evoked in his 1914 essay—in which the censored and the unaddressable both in himself and in the bodies of his patients could expand in complete freedom without becoming pathological.

## The End of Analysis as an Opening to the Human

Apollon's theorization of the feminine as what remains in each of us of a censored quest, and his conception of the act as the vehicle through which that femininity impacts others and elicits in them either violence (or resistance) or the feeling of the beautiful and the sublime, fundamentally changes our conception of the desire at stake in psychoanalysis by stressing its transcendence with respect to the individual. We often think of the end of analysis as a liberation of unconscious desire, and this dimension is certainly essential. In his most recent contributions to the metapsychology, however, Apollon has started using "the quest" in place of "desire." On the one hand, "quest" helps to qualify and render more precise what is at stake in desire: it isn't a specific object, objective, or goal. But on the other hand, "quest" is always fundamentally related to the "human quest," to that part of the human that finds expression in, and is advanced by, the quest of an individual subject. In this section I attempt to draw out what I find to be some of the most important consequences of Apollon's metapsychology for our understanding of the trajectory of an analysis, as well as its stakes for the human.

One of Freud's most fundamental insights is that for the human being, whose perception of reality is mediated by an unconscious fantasy that no one shares, there is no possible access either to the natural environment or to our fellow man. As a result, each and every one of us is consigned to a fundamental solitude concerning the free drive and its effects upon the organism and the psychic apparatus. Apollon's work explores the paradoxical corollary of this position, namely the affirmation that human reality is fundamentally transindividual and intersubjective, traversed by a quest that impacts each and every human being but that belongs to no one in particular.

This perspective is arguably anticipated by Freud himself, most memorably when he claims that living men retain in their unconscious the traces of the long-ago murder of the primeval father. But its implications for thinking about the aims and end of the analytic experience were only hinted at by Freud, and have been left largely unexamined by later psychoanalysts. An important exception is Jacques Lacan, who not only develops Freud's insight but understands it both as the driving force of an analysis and as essential to the production of the analyst. In his *Seminar XV: The Psychoanalytic Act* (1967–68), Lacan advances that the analysand's act is not something the analyst can know, interpret, or anticipate, but something by which he is "struck" both psychically and in his body, where it leaves its traces or impressions. We can infer from Lacan's argument—for reasons I explain below—that this "striking" occurs at a specific moment in an analysis, and indicates that the cure has entered its final phase.

In the early part of an analysis, the analysand addresses the analyst as an other in the social link: an other who might respond to the sub-ject's appeal or take responsibility for his suffering. Here, the address to the analyst is invariably caught up in the seduction fantasy that allows the ego to repress the unconscious, as well as the fragmented body of the drives, by identifying with the object in the mirror and the "armor of an alienating identity" (*Écrits* 78) that it provides. In Lacan's formula for the fantasy and its traversal, this slope of the fantasy is called "alienation."

Alienation represses the subject of the unconscious, and the erogenous body in which it dwells, by propping up the illusory consistency of the ego and encouraging it to seek satisfaction in the social sphere or in relations with others. Here (a) is an imaginary object, the unified body image or ideal ego that the subject offers up to the Other of fantasy. If the analyst refuses to respond to these appeals, it is in order to confront the analysand with his fundamental solitude concerning what acts in his body: and to call forth dreams and symptoms that might allow him to construct a knowledge about what, until now, has been repeating in silence. In this early phase, then, we might say that the analysis emphasizes not only the absence of any Other who might be able to respond or treat, but the unbridgeable distance separating the analysand from the analyst.

In contrast, what "strikes" the analyst in the analysand's act—as opposed to his pleas for help or demand for recognition or love—is what Lacan calls the object (a), the object-cause of desire that acts in and through the subject. Its impact supposes that the analysand has traversed

Figure 2.1. Lacan's formula for the fantasy. *Source:* Drawn by the author. Original appears in *The Four Fundamental Concepts of Psycho-Analysis*, edited by Jacques-Alain Miller, translated by Alan Sheridan, W. W. Norton & Co., 1978.

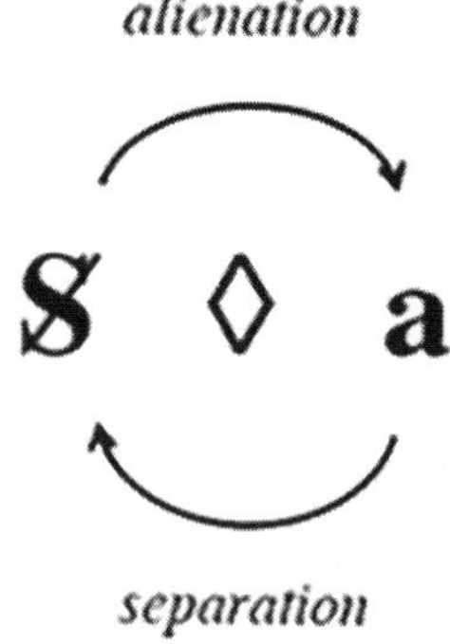

the logical moment in an analysis that Lacan calls "separation," which is marked by the fall of the seduction fantasy and the entry into castration. Inasmuch as the moment of separation entails a detachment from the ego and the ideals that shore it up, it can be understood at least in part as a separation from the social and the identifications that sustain it: and, with it, the recognition that the object that causes the subject's desire is a psychic object, specific to him or her, that has no consistency and no worldly equivalent.

The fall of the seduction fantasy could be summed up in the statement "you're alone, and no one else is responsible." The question is, why doesn't analysis end—in the sense of reaching its logical endpoint—there? And, related to this, is the term "separation" really evocative of what happens at this point, or do we need another one?

While "separation" underscores the loss of the ego image that was built to satisfy the Other of the cultural montage, it risks leaving us with the impression that the individual who arrives at this stage is simply an isolated monad, for whom any dream of connection to or solidarity with other human beings now appears merely as an illusory fantasy. This view is sometimes reinforced by a certain clinical and scholarly reception of Lacan's teachings that tends to accentuate symbolic castration—the losses and privations imposed on the living being as a condition of its entry into language, and thus into the social link it founds—at the expense of what is at stake in the traversal of castration as a logical moment in the unfolding of an analysis.

When Lacan advances that the analyst is "struck" by the analysand's act, he underscores a fundamental paradox that is essential to the final stage of analysis. At this point of maximum opacity or illegibility, a barrier is breached: and something that is not an object of conscious representation or knowledge is transmitted from one subject to another. It is this action, and the effects it produces in those it "strikes," that attests to the end of an analysis: and, in the procedure of the Pass, to the creation of the analyst.

Lacan conceived the Pass as a means of verifying the production of the analyst in 1967, during the period when he was first conceptualizing, in his seminar on "The Psychoanalytic Act," the impact of the analysand's act on the analyst's own body—an insight that becomes fundamental to the logic of the Pass and the creation of the analyst that is its aim. In the Pass, a candidate who has reached the logical term of an analysis testifies about his experience to two witnesses, or *passeurs*, who are in turn charged with transmitting that testimony to a cartel of analysts. The candidate—who is called the *passant*—speaks about his experience as an analysand and attempts to transmit something of his relation to the object that causes desire. The Pass is concerned not so much with what the *passant* has managed to say about the analysis, however, but with something that is fundamentally unaddressable, and that therefore passes through the body. It is not an object of conscious observation or recording, but something that is at once transmitted by a body and received by a body, depositing itself in the bodies of the two *passeurs* without their knowledge. If the Pass is able to guarantee that an analyst has been produced, it is because it confirms that the object acting in the passant is able to impact the body of another person, calling forth a dream, a symptom, an act, or a feeling that gives expression to an unconscious quest. This is why Freud's analysis of the dream of Irma's Injection should be considered as his Pass: it confirms the agency of his object in the body of his patient, and thus the founding act of psychoanalysis.

The procedure demonstrates that under certain conditions, one's "own" erogenous body can become a vehicle for the transmission of something that exceeds the individual subject. For an analogy we might look to the study of trauma, which confirms that what is unspoken in the life of one person can find expression in the body of another—for example through the intergenerational transmission of trauma from a parent or grandparent to a child. A distinctive feature of the Pass, however, is that the procedure brings together three people who are not otherwise connected, who may be complete strangers. The *passeur*, in other words, is a *disinterested spectator*, with no personal stake in the experiences of the person speaking. Moreover, the aim of the procedure is to verify whether the passant has reached the end of analysis. It is concerned not so much with the transmission of trauma or with the unfinished business of that speaker, but rather with the transmission of the object-cause of desire. So why, we might ask, are the bodies of these disinterested witnesses required to confirm it? My thesis is that in registering its impact, the bodies of the two *passeurs* show the object to be something that is not only unique to the *passant*, singular and discreet, but inseparable from the quest of humanity—of the human subject as such. The Pass thus confirms the opening to humanity that is made possible by the traversal of the fantasy, and would not be possible if this were not in fact a fundamental dimension of the end of an analysis.

Apollon amplifies and extends this development when he speaks about the end of analysis in terms of what the subject brings to the human. He advises that in each analysand, the analyst must be alert not only to the problems and impasses she faces, but to how the unaddressable within her both carries within it something of the human quest and moves it forward. For an analysis to have truly reached its end, he suggests, this contribution has to be both identified and liberated.

This elaboration helps us to appreciate that there are really two dimensions to the traversal of the fantasy, therefore: a separation from the montage through which culture censors the human, and a liberation of the free drive that articulates the subject to a quest that traverses and transcends the individual. One important consequence is that separation in its analytic stakes does not merely affirm the subject as a discreet individual, released from all responsibility to and for others. While it certainly involves a liberation from parental and cultural demands and ideals, separation must not be understood as a turn away from others altogether. To the contrary, it necessarily involves a renewed commitment to humanity, above and beyond the imaginary of the social tie.

## Notes

1. "Spirit" is a word that is rarely used in English outside of a religious or supernatural context. The French *esprit*, on the other hand—like the German *Geist*—is a very common noun that is used in many different contexts and can be translated in a number of ways. The most obvious is "mind," but only if we distinguish the mind from the brain and from the psychic apparatus that all animals possess (Hegel's *Phenomenology of Spirit*, for example, is sometimes translated *Phenomenology of Mind*). *Esprit* can also be rendered as liveliness, spirit, humor, intelligence, or wit; a *mot d'esprit* is a joke. To describe someone as *spirituel(le)* is to say that he or she is spirited, quick-witted, lively or intelligent, and not spiritual in the religious sense. In short, *l'esprit* really characterizes what is uniquely human in us, our imaginative and creative capacities.

2. The four terms of my title—language, *hors langage*, act and aesthetics—can be understood as corresponding to distinct logical moments in the unfolding of a cure.

3. Lecture given on the occasion of being awarded the 2004 Nobel Prize in Literature. See https://www.nobelprize.org/prizes/literature/2004/jelinek/lecture/.

4. The neurotic is someone who is unwilling to take the risk of speech, and is therefore content to remain within the limits the therapist maintains. The pervert and the psychotic, on the other hand, are all too aware that true speech

has the potential to get them reported to the state or committed to an asylum.

5. This period corresponds roughly to the early 1890s, or the period covered by Freud's and Breuer's *Studies on Hysteria* (1895).

6. Freud's early claim that hysterics "suffer mainly from reminiscences," and his emphasis on restoring "memories" that have been "forgotten," situate the subject's symptoms and impasses as the result of a failure to face up to reality, to take responsibility for what is or is not possible (for example, Lucy R. acknowledging that she has no future with her employer). Reality has not yet become a mere "principle" for Freud, as it will later on, but functions instead as a hard limit: the neurotic is someone who has trouble facing up to (social, interpersonal) reality and needs to confront and take responsibility for that limit.

7. In my citations of the *Standard Edition*, I have consistently substituted "drive" for "instinct" wherever *Trieb* or *Triebe* is used in the German text.

8. Or, put another way, the drives are "pathogenic"—creating problems for the analysand in the form of symptoms or difficulties with social adaptation—only to the extent that they have no field in which they can assert themselves, no means of finding expression.

9. When the English translation of Freud states that primary repression denies entry into consciousness to the "psychical (ideational) representative of the [drive]," we must keep in mind that the term "ideational"—especially when used as a synonym for "mental"—is potentially misleading, since it risks equating the mind with the consciousness that we usually understand to be a feature of ideas (the Greek ἰδέα—"form, pattern"—is derived from the root ἰδεῖν, "to see").

10. Freud's last essay, "Constructions in Analysis," contemporaneous with *Moses and Monotheism*, deals with this necessity.

11. The examples just provided show how something that has been censored in the usual sense of the term—i.e., stricken from language or rendered unsayable—can become censored in the sense Apollon gives to the term, i.e., inscribed in the body because incapable of being expressed in any other way.

12. *The Seminar of Jacques Lacan, Book II: The Ego in Freud's Theory and in the Technique of Psychoanalysis 1954–1955*, edited by Jacques-Alain Miller, translated by Sylvana Tomaselli, New York: Norton, 1991, p. 164.

# Works Cited

Apollon, Willy. "The Untreatable." Translated by Steven Miller, *Umbr(a): Incurable*, 2006, pp. 23–39.

———. "The Conclusive Pass at the Freudian School of Quebec." 2014. Unpublished manuscript.

———. "Psychanalyse et mondialisation." Lecture series, Québec, 2020–2021. Unpublished.

———. "Séminaire de Montréal." 29 Jan. 2022, Québec, 2021–2022. Unpublished.

———. "Transference." Clinical seminar, Québec, 2022–2023. Unpublished.

———. "The Subject of the Quest." Translated by Daniel Wilson. *Penumbr(a)*, vol. 2, edited by Marta Aleksandrowicz and Fernanda Negrete, 2022, pp. 1–14.

Cantin, Lucie. "The Drive, the Untreatable Quest of Desire." Translated by Tracy McNulty, *differences*, vol. 28, no. 2, 2017, pp. 24–45.

Freud, Sigmund. *Studies on Hysteria*. 1895. *The Standard Edition of the Complete Psychological Works of Sigmund Freud*, vol. II, translated and edited by James Strachey, Hogarth Press, 1955, pp. 1–305.

———. *Interpretation of Dreams*. 1900. *The Standard Edition*, vol. IV, translated and edited by James Strachey, Hogarth Press, 1953, pp. ix–627.

———. *On Dreams*. 1901. *The Standard Edition*, vol. V, translated and edited by James Strachey, Hogarth Press, 1953, pp. 629–86.

———. *Fragment of an Analysis of a Case of Hysteria*. 1901. *The Standard Edition*, vol. VII, translated and edited by James Strachey, Hogarth Press, 1955, pp. 1–122.

———. *Totem and Taboo*. 1913. *The Standard Edition*. vol. XIII, translated and edited by James Strachey, Hogarth Press, 1955, pp. 1–255.

———. "Remembering, Repeating, and Working-Through." 1914. *The Standard Edition*. vol. XII, translated and edited by James Strachey, Hogarth Press, 1958, pp. 144–16.

———. "Repression." 1915. *The Standard Edition*, vol. XIV, translated and edited by James Strachey, Hogarth Press, 1955, pp. 141–58.

———. "From the History of an Infantile Neurosis." 1918. *The Standard Edition*, vol. XVII, translated and edited by James Strachey, Hogarth Press, 1955, pp. 1–124.

———. *New Introductory Lectures on Psycho-Analysis*. 1933. *The Standard Edition*, vol. XXII, translated and edited by James Strachey, Hogarth Press, 1958, pp. 3–182.

Lacan, Jacques. *Écrits*. Translated by Bruce Fink, W. W. Norton & Co, 2007.

———. *Le Séminaire Livre XV: L'acte analytique* (1967–1968). Unpublished manuscript. A French-language manuscript edited by Patrick Valas is available at: https://www.valas.fr/Jacques-Lacan-L-acte-Psychanalytique-1967–1968,136?lang=fr.

3

# Aesthetics, Spirit, Time, and the Quest

Fernanda Negrete

## Aesthetics as Ground for an Ethics

At the core of Willy Apollon's metapsychology lies a confrontation with a "beyond-limits" that provokes anxiety and is also a source of creativity ("The Human in Question" 61). In his chapter for this volume, "The Human in Question," Apollon declares that to consider this encounter, he turns to the most pragmatic level of the philosophical aesthetics developed by Immanuel Kant and G. W. F. Hegel (61). Before becoming a doctrine about what can be rightly called "beautiful," "sublime," or even "wit" and "uncanny," to incorporate what Sigmund Freud saw as the modest contributions psychoanalysis could make to the field of aesthetics (*Jokes* . . . 9; "The Uncanny" 219), aesthetics refers to an encounter that destabilizes "ordinary sense" and mobilizes the body, provoking feelings that only arise beyond the pleasure principle.[1] Aesthetics indeed plays an essential role in Apollon's metapsychology and in its related account of the unfolding of an analysis. This metapsychology is distinct from other theoretical interactions between psychoanalysis and aesthetics because it posits the function of the aesthetic as crucial to each human life and to humanity as such. Furthermore, aesthetics becomes a necessary moment in the logical unfolding of an analytic cure toward its endpoint in the adoption of an unswerving ethical position. Since, according to Apollon, aesthetics initiates ethics, it's worth clarifying the stakes of aesthetics as a crucial and unavoidable site for a singular quest that inhabits each subject and "mobilizes this human thing that speaks" ("The Subject of the Quest" 1).

## Aesthetic Time

> The organism is the object to which the Other has access in the space controlled by the collective; this sensibility, on the other hand, creates the *body* as the *time of subjectivity*, which is affirmed in *the consciousness of lived experience*. I thus describe this experience as the time of the aesthetic, a time that is foreign to the clock, and that is comprised of the feeling of or sensitivity to the beautiful—that which under no circumstances would the Other want to lose, and which the being lives as the best of its experience—and the feeling of the sublime, in which the being has the experience of something more important than its own existence.
>
> —Apollon, "The Human . . ." 60

This key passage from Apollon's essay in this volume highlights a subjective and distinctively aesthetic time. Why time? As Augustine acknowledged at the turn of the fifth century in his *Confessions*, time is a paradox. It defies any firm distinction between being and non-being. Later, in his *Critique of Pure Reason* (1781/1787), Kant wrote that time is the "inner sense" or form of interiority—a mental capacity that provides intuitions of our self and internal states, rather than an objective factor of reality (A33/B49). For subjects of reason, thought is organized by two pure forms of sensibility: time and space, which Kant defined in turn as the "outer sense," as the capacity to represent objects as outside of us (A23/B37). Kant called this structure of pure forms of sensibility the transcendental aesthetic. As inner sense, time introduces a difference between the "I" as active consciousness, and a passive receptivity of the being in self-affection. Gilles Deleuze has emphasized the degree to which this disposition, where "the activity of thought applies to a receptive being, to a passive subject which represents that activity to itself rather than enacts it (. . .) and which lives it[s effect] like an Other within itself," also introduces a fracture into the "I" that marks the discovery of the transcendental as the beginning of "a long inexhaustible history: I is an other, or the paradox of the inner sense" (*Difference and Repetition* 86).

For Deleuze, this moment in Kant then paves the way for Arthur Rimbaud's striking formula "I is an other" in his letters of the visionary or seer, where the poet, to become a seer, contemplates not the "I think" but rather the experience that "I am thought" (Rimbaud 113), which destabilizes the agency of the I and causes the "disorganization of all the senses," in a search that "attains the unknown" (115). Apollon's aesthetic time is attuned to such an experience, which Rimbaud as a young seventeen-year-old man described in his letter, and which indeed offers an example of adolescence, as a logical moment for a search or quest that leads to the unknown and the new.

To grasp the stakes of this quest, it's useful to bear in mind that the foreignness to the clock through which Apollon emphasizes the subjective dimension of the aesthetic points not only to Kant's transcendental aesthetics, but also to a long spiritualist philosophical tradition developed by Henri Bergson and Deleuze. Following Deleuze's thread linking Kant to Rimbaud, one might say that the intimate experience of time decenters the conscious "I" and opens onto the unconscious, and that it is an *extimate* experience, where the prefix ex- indicates an outside of space and shared reality. According to Bergson, philosophy always failed to think time. There is a clash between insubordinate change as the distinctive trait of time, on the one hand, and the philosophical inclination to establish definitions, on the other. Bergson proposes to think something like "pure time," independently from physical movement and even as the non-spatial dimension subjects dwell in, rather than as something internal to subjects. Reading Bergson, Kant, and Proust, Deleuze thus writes that "the only subjectivity is time, non-chronological time grasped in its foundation, and it is we who are internal to time," and adds, with an image from Alain Resnais's cinema in mind, that "subjectivity is never ours, it is time, that is, the soul or the spirit, the virtual" (*Cinema 2* 83). Time is therefore not merely a challenge for philosophers, but rather an experience profoundly linked to humankind, where the human being confronts a dimension that exceeds what can be called one's own. The dimension of time is the foundation of creation, in a radical sense that cannot be subsumed under an already existing reality or an individual existence.

Yet while time displaces a notion of subjectivity as only internal, or as individual property, this dimension (which Deleuze names equally "time," "soul," "spirit," or "the virtual") carves out singular bodies. Freud, who refers in *Beyond the Pleasure Principle* to the "Kantian theorem"

(28) of forms of interiority and exteriority, continued to think about the distinctive "timelessness" of the unconscious in relation to the notion of memory traces that inscribe themselves in the unconscious psychical systems without any chronological order. The emergence of a paradoxical "time of the aesthetic" is thus especially striking in the passage by Apollon, insofar as what he proposes is precisely an experience for the subject of the unconscious. Freud's return to the question of "timeless" or non-chronological memory traces allowed him to consider the foundation of memory (25) and of trauma, when there is a breach of the pleasure principle and of what he called "the protective shield" against stimuli (*Beyond* 29–32), foregrounding repetition as an earlier process that deals not only with external stimuli but also with the unbound energy of the drive, autonomous from the pleasure principle (34–35).

Apollon's evocation of a time of the aesthetic implies that the unbound drive, this beyond of the pleasure principle, is the result of what he calls "the effraction by the spirit of a psyche that is still being formed" ("The Subject of the Quest" 5). This fundamental, "internal" breach carves out a human body beyond the organism and precedes language. The effraction gives rise to pure representations, that is to say, intimate experiences of the capacity to think what doesn't exist. These experiences inscribe themselves in childhood in specific organs and systems, altering the developing organism to form what Apollon calls "the letters of the body": an inscription "invested with energy mobilized by another logic, a quest whose object remains unknown" (Cantin, "The Fantasy" 409), but that reactivates itself throughout the subject's lifetime, in symptoms and inexplicable acts. The effraction also creates the conditions for the subject to eventually will and create what doesn't exist, as the work undertaken in adolescence, when the subject may realize this potential.

Jouissance is often stranded in repetitions whose logic is unknown to the one who has gone through childhood—when the subject discovers a discrepancy between its intimate experience and what can be perceived and said about the child—and puberty—when, at the expense of intimate experience again, the subject's drives are brought under the control of the collective, which depends on its members' performing certain roles to secure its biological and ideological reproduction. Yet this stranded jouissance need not be merely exhausted or relinquished in an analysis, where its implications emerge. For Apollon sharply distinguishes puberty from adolescence—when the subject encounters, again, the defect in language and is now poised to act beyond the collective's requirements (and imposed ideals of sexual satisfaction), on the very ground of this jouissance. Jouissance can thus also become a matter of joy, and the unconscious can be the subjective time for aesthetic experience, which appears in Apollon's thought as more fundamental than repression and masochistic repetition in the effort to bind the energy of the drive. The question becomes, then, how to access and live through aesthetic time.

Kant asserts that the contents of the receptive inner sense cannot be studied scientifically—only the "I" has access to itself in this manner.[2] Deleuze suggests that the full consequences of Kant's innovative approach to time only become apparent in the *Critique of Judgment*, when he develops the aesthetic of the Beautiful and the Sublime. It introduces what Deleuze calls "a Pathos" that replaces the work of "self-affection" Kant had posited in relation to the constitution of knowledge; this Pathos is "the undetermined unity of all the faculties (the Soul) which makes us enter the unknown" ("On Four Poetic Formulas . . ." 34). Aesthetic judgments, Kant explains, are posed by a reflective subject, whose ability to say that something is beautiful (or sublime) isn't a question of evaluating and correctly determining the epistemological or moral status of an object. It's important to observe the difference not only between the beautiful (a feeling) and the object that is its occasion, but also between a judgment and the subjective experience that provokes it. On the ground of an experience that Kant describes as that subject's "feeling of life" (*Critique of Judgment* 44), a subject can make an aesthetic judgment that is subjectively universal and necessary. While it is subjective and reflective—reflecting on its feeling—it is "supposed to serve as a universal rule" (58) or be valid for every human subject, based on a "communal" sense,[3] and not just for oneself, based on one's personal inclinations or needs. These can only result in judgments of the agreeable or the good, but not of taste, which presupposes disinterest. Thus, to Kant the aesthetic judgment is first and foremost a question of feeling that turns toward itself in a searching movement without a known object. The quest of the desiring subject undertakes this movement too.


## The Beautiful


Apollon's definition of aesthetic time described the beautiful from the perspective of its effect on the Other of the social link, followed by a statement on what the being lives, as "the best of her experience." On the side of the subject, then, is an experience, and the beautiful is "lived as the best," although this isn't a matter of language or even necessarily of accounting for this experience verbally in a way that justifies its superlative quality. The beautiful is also a feeling in the body ("The Human" 61), which implies the ability to welcome a dimension Apollon refers to as the feminine in each one of us (62) (regardless of gender[4]). The body at stake here is not synonymous with the organism. It is instead eroticized, shaped, and marked in precise modes—or singular letters—by the nomadic force of the drive that exceeds and derails the organism and reality grounded in language. The work of the drive is unconscious, which is to say fundamentally out-of-language, and therefore only manifest in typically disruptive symptoms and senseless acts. For its part, the feminine is nothing less than the dimension of each subject that carries the singular quest of desire ("The Subject" 11), and it is censored in the collective, which maintains "the frame of the reality established by language" (11). As a feeling in the body accessed within aesthetic time and that entails an embrace of the feminine, the beautiful is a genuine event. It presupposes a subversion of the subject that also produces effects in the Other, an act that removes this powerful censorship.

As long as this censorship is operating in an individual, the feeling of the beautiful is restricted and oriented by the "affective formatting" that each civilization imposes (10). Apollon claims that "what is considered attractive, or what provokes a reaction of fear, will necessarily have a profound link to the founding beliefs of the social link and will limit the feeling of the beautiful in the individual" (10). By contrast, the beautiful that concerns us here is an experience beyond limits, where the feminine escapes this formatting, and instead articulates what is out-of-language to the aesthetic (ÉfQ Teaching). Consequently, the beautiful disrupts the receivable, provoking in the Other a response of wanting to preserve it as the most valuable aspect of humanity. This difference—between what an individual can recognize within the limits of the affective formatting of a given civilization as beautiful, and a feeling that ruptures the limits of both the individual and the collective—is key.

There's a surprising quality to the feeling of beauty. Logically, it barely resembles what is already established as beautiful by culture, even in a field such as art. Instead, this feeling has everything to do with what makes us desiring subjects. These implications mark an important distinction between, on the one hand, cultural guidelines for taste and appearance, and, on the other hand, a subject's intimate experiences of the aesthetic beyond anything preestablished: experiences that mark out that subject's life and action. This subjective dimension is what matters in Apollon's metapsychology. A valorization of surprise or newness can turn into a norm that paradoxically predetermines aesthetic production; to some extent this is art's situation in the wake of modernism. When the surprise effect becomes an expectation, an artwork in turn appears as a compromise between a cultural demand and an attempt at expressing something beyond it. By predetermining a result, something of the surprising quality at stake in the feeling of beauty fades while an ideal of beauty remains in force in one culture or another. What matters here is instead an aesthetics that takes its cue from the quest of desire as a fundamental *force* that, to put it in Spinozian terms, endeavors to persist in its own being (*Ethics* III, P6), and whose own, joyful direction is unpredictable, inasmuch as this direction results, at each step, from this desire's freedom.

In aesthetic time, the quest of desire is not controlled by the beliefs of the social link but instead brings something unprecedented to humanity. The beautiful thus also leads the subject to the threshold of the sublime, where one discovers "that there are things that are more important than one's own existence!" (Schéma, "Une humanité . . .")—but also that this feeling can become the basis for an existence aiming at the creation of spaces that subvert the social link, and taking responsibility for the consequences of the subversions that exceed civilizational requirements.

The aesthetic is therefore an experience of the free drive, the body released from the fetters of the cultural construction or montage of sexuality. This montage names the apparatus whose mirages are dedicated to keeping each being's life, history, and fate subjected to bio-ideological reproduction; it is therefore the very place where a being has "given ground relative to desire" (*Ethics* 321) in Lacan's terms. One could say that aesthetics instead involves regaining the ground of what Apollon calls *l'esprit*: *spirit* as the source of absolute singularity, of an event. Yet the implications of the free drive and of the quest that mobilizes it in a unique way in each human being confront us with the fact that from the outset there was no preexistent or available place for representations of what doesn't exist. A subject can decide to put this and the other two determinations of *l'esprit*—the capacity to will and to create what doesn't exist—to action in the encounter of the beautiful and the sublime, as the feelings that spur the realization of what exceeds language and reality. Rather than regaining a ground, then, it is a matter, as Lucie

Cantin explains, of liberating the unconscious quest and forging with its unbound energy a path that wasn't predetermined by the organism or the social link.[5]


## Spiritus

In his chapter for the present volume, Apollon has stated that *l'esprit* is a fundamental concept of his to be reckoned with that emerges in dialogue with the philosophical tradition where he situates his own work. So, instead of simply translating this word by "mind," considering its various meanings through a strategic turn to the French-English dictionary helps to introduce the stakes of this important term, implied in Apollon's conception of the beautiful and the subject. "*Esprit*" is often translated as "mind" in the contexts of the faculty for thought and awareness, and of describing someone's character ("an analytic mind"). The cognate "spirit" appears, in plural, as a synonym for mood, as in being in "good spirits" or "low spirits." "Wit" in French is also "*esprit.*" It is present in the "*mot d'esprit,*" the joke or *Witz*, through which, as Freud remarked, the repressed can momentarily irrupt in speech. Two other senses of this word involve the individuality and distinctive style or tone of something or someone. In all these meanings it appears as an element that sparks or distinctly inflects life, which its etymology justifies. The Latin *spiritus* is a word for breath, life, aspiration, emanation, divine or poetic inspiration, feeling, soul, and person. "*Spiritus*" is in turn linked to the Greek *pneuma* and the Hebrew *ruach*, two earlier contexts in whose cosmologies breath/air is a principle of life. Returning to the first context of "mind," related to the capability of thought, let us note that, taking Descartes's "*cogito ergo sum*" as a reference, "mind" is a major concept in philosophical treatises, with important differences among them. Apollon's metapsychology is certainly in dialogue with philosophy concerning *l'esprit*, as he himself points out, as well as other key concepts, such as desire, subjectivity, and the aesthetic. But the nuances of words such as "*esprit*" and "mind" are worth analyzing because the different ways of making sense of them today involve crucial questions about what makes us human.

Undoubtedly, scientific progress has affected speculation arising from the different meanings of *spiritus* on the capacity for consciousness, life principles, and cosmology. In the contemporary field of cognitive science, the mind is the site of computational procedures involving representational structures (Thagard). Although cognitive science admits that mental power implies imperceptible processes that exceed empirical evidence, it nevertheless approaches the procedures and structures considered responsible for such processes as if the logical rules they follow were not a human invention. In other words, they are studied as a more highly evolved form of nature that is continuous with its biological antecedents. A radical sense of creation is thus very nearly absent from this cognitive view of mind, which isn't far from the scientistic position Bergson deplored in 1912, wherein "mental life would be but an aspect of cerebral life, [and] the would-be 'soul' is reduced to the collection of those particular cerebral phenomena to which consciousness supervenes like a phosphorescent glow" (49–50).[6]

If, as Apollon affirms, the capacity to conceive, will, and create what doesn't exist concerns something beyond the mechanisms of nature, however evolved, and beyond any systems supporting shared human reality, *l'esprit* is certainly irreducible to a cognitive function. Cognition, following perception and consciousness, is structured by language. Apollon indicates this when he discusses "spiritual space," whose purpose is "to identify represented things that have no other consistency than that of their representation," and which is "an intimately personal experience, independent of and unconnected to the space of perception that will be overdetermined by the creation of language as the structure of the link between companions" ("The Human . . ." 55). This description stresses the fact that the spiritual space that emerges with and is specific to the human, is not perceptible and not overdetermined by language. In contrast to the space of perception, then, "spiritual space" "appears with the human being and is part of an intimate experience that takes place in a *subjective time*. This subjective time is foreign to the psychic space that articulates the being to what is perceptible and observable in the collective and its environment and which has been perfected through evolution over millions of years" (57). Just as the concept of *esprit* resists any seamless translation that might bring it back within the limits it exceeds, the use of "psychical space" in this passage differs from the habitual implications of the "psychical," "psychic," or "psyche" that one finds most often in both popular and specialized contexts. Indeed, Apollon proposes that "l'esprit" and "le psychisme" have two very different orientations. "Psyche" in this metapsychology coincides with perception and consciousness; it situates representations of whatever is in the space-time structured by language. "Psyche," therefore, is the mind at stake in cognitive science. Its function is that it "regulates the organism's relationship to the environment and the collective" (57). Importantly, psychical space formats each individual subject's perception and consciousness, in other words, access to a shared reality. In this sense it is concerned with reproduction and is thus common to animals and humans, rather than something specific to humanity. Spiritual space points, instead, to something other than the domain of the cognitive mind and behavior. Apollon contends that spiritual space remains foreign to language and to the psychical space that articulates an individual to the collective and environment. In psychoanalysis, the object that must be taken apart, as the term "analysis" suggests, is indeed "psyche" as this point of articulation that excludes this spiritual space of the human.

So what happens to the spiritual space that appears with the human but is excluded from language, since it cannot be pressed into the service of the collective? And what exactly can one call spiritual in this specific sense? What Apollon calls "l'esprit" and "spirituel" begins with the "effraction" or break-in that mobilizes the drive and inaugurates the quest of unconscious desire in each subject. The unconscious and the drives are irreducible to a state of "nature" or animal instinct, which seeks only self-preservation and the reproduction of the species. The break-in thus involves a rupture with this logic, although the object of the quest is unknown—otherwise it wouldn't be possible to speak of creative freedom. While the quest's object is the stuff of creation, the social bond cannot easily recognize it; in the interest of self-preservation, it cannot simply welcome the spiritual space at stake here.

From the perspective of human history, Apollon sees the emergence of religion, between ten thousand and six thousand years ago, as a civilizational response to the encounter with the defect in language. Religions thus evoke the spirit within the systems of beliefs they establish to make cultural values and norms credible and transmissible from one generation to the next. In this arrangement, *l'esprit* is necessarily circumscribed. In adopting "*l'esprit*," Apollon recognizes Greco-Roman and Judeo-Christian expressions of the capacity for pure mental representation and radical creation, partially because they are retained by the philosophical tradition his metapsychology engages. That civilizational framework certainly played a part in the discussion on *psyche, pneuma, anima, soul,* and the mind-body problem in Western philosophy. Yet as an autonomous and radical practice of thought, philosophy distinguishes itself by a rupture with "the conduct of everyday life" (Hadot 57) without being grounded on religion (religious practice may also lead some individuals to a rupture with everyday life, yet religion remains a belief system that supports social customs and cultural norms). The translation of *l'esprit* as "mind" in philosophical/psychological contexts doesn't just distinguish these contexts from mythological/religious concerns with "the spirit" as a divine or holy force. It simultaneously restricts "spirit" to a metaphysical and even supernatural domain, and "mind" to a scientific one. Apollon, however, seeks more speculative freedom across philosophy, mathematics, and physics to elaborate spirit beyond the limits of metaphysics and scientism. Most importantly, Apollon considers "*l'esprit*" to describe the capacity for pure mental representation and creation as an *experience*, "whose source is unknown to us" ("La Chose").

Like its source, its direction as a subjective quest in each being is also unknown. I find it important to develop here the link between Apollon's metapsychology and Spinoza's thought, which is often mentioned by Apollon, especially regarding the quest of desire. The quest of desire qua human essence and effect of *l'esprit* in a being involves, exactly, what Spinoza wrote in Latin *mens*. If the latter can be translated as "mind," it does not refer to cerebral contents or functions, but rather to a potential to become conscious of "affections," transitions, and changes in degree of *puissance*,[7] and, also to become active, free, and blissful. This process is not at all automatic, even if the effraction of the psyche by what we may call the *spirit*—with everything this discussion has shown this word to entail—is inaugural. For this moment introduces, beyond conscious intention, the human singularity that consists precisely in the autonomy from any kind of genetic, instinctual programming. To make up for the lack of a program, there is language and the cultural montage of sexuality, which limits the quest by censoring the feminine, a censorship that blocks the masculine as a dimension of the human that takes responsibility for the consequences of one's acts, and thus for the feminine. Pursuit of the path that liberates the quest, engaging the subject in action, freedom, and bliss as Spinoza advanced, implies opening the spiritual space Apollon invokes on the basis of "an intimate experience that takes place in a *subjective time*" ("The Human . . ." 57). It must be opened because in collective reality that experience is insistently controlled and circumscribed by culture and civilization.

Becoming active, there where the beginning of subjective life involves a break-in, can never be a matter of exorcising the demons, drives, or desires that refuse to adjust to the shared reality. This would be to try to live only within the limits of the psyche, to refuse to enter the unknown, and thus to turn away from spiritual space—to refuse, indeed, to become active. The effraction of *esprit* exiles a being from animal instinct and sets in motion, in the infant, a capacity to conceive what doesn't exist, which can develop into willing and creating it at the later logical moment of adolescence, when the being confronts again the real castration at stake in the effraction of the psyche by the spirit.[8] In the course of an analysis, the capacity to will and create what doesn't exist becomes reactivated after the subject traverses symbolic castration—the moment of acknowledging and taking a position regarding the Other as a function of rules, norms, and values necessary for collective existence, for living in society. Symbolic castration is a surrender to the language that conditions the reality of the social link, but not the site for desire to emerge. The subject's position regarding the loss introduced by the Other, and specifically regarding the cultural censorship of the feminine, can be (neurotic) adaptation, (perverse) revolt, and (psychotic) withdrawal (Schéma, "L'enjeu . . ."). To traverse this castration isn't only to become conscious of the satisfactions derived from one's position, but above all to go further and make the quest of desire—which, as the capacity or *puissance* to represent, will, and create what doesn't exist insists and unfolds in subjective time and therefore exceeds any of the psychic structures—the ground for one's life and acts, and to take responsibility for the consequences of those acts for others.

Lacan began to see the limits of symbolic castration in considering the field of *das Ding* as the domain of the drives. Beyond unconscious representations emerging "between perception and consciousness," and "regulated by means of the pleasure principle" (*Ethics* 61), there is something else. These representations "orbit" around what Lacan underscores in Freud's texts as the field, beyond the pleasure principle, of *das Ding*, "the Thing" or kernel of a real that insists at the core of the subject—and calls for a topological space, since at the same time as it lies at the subject's core, it is excluded. This domain of the drives is unrelated, Lacan states, to "something that can be satisfied by moderation, that moderation which soberly regulates a human being's relations with his fellow man at the different hierarchical levels of society in a harmonious order, from the couple to the State" (110). The production of a spiritual space in Apollon's sense, sharply distinguished from the space of the social link, thus concerns this field of *das Ding* that is the domain of the drives.

Apollon underscores the field's fundamental exclusion from language, from the Other, on which its radically unconscious status is based.

Moderation doesn't satisfy the drives, Lacan declares, which explains why a beyond of the pleasure principle is so often expressed as evil or self-destructive. In sublimation and perversion Freud and Lacan both found alternatives to the destructive expression of the drive. The perverse subject revolts, rather than adapting to the censorship of the feminine at play in the cultural montage of sexuality, and may construct a fetish that supports the disavowal of symbolic castration and promotes the drive. Sublimation appeared to Freud as a libidinal economy capable of giving the drive's aims a satisfying, creative path that circumvented the obstacles of the external world (*Civilization and its Discontents* 79) or a given culture's restrictions upon sexual life, by displacing the sexual aim without repressing it ("'Civilized' Sexual Morality and Modern Nervous Illness" 187). Freud also highlighted the value placed on the products of sublimation by culture. But while these solutions may "raise an object to the dignity of the Thing" (Lacan, *Ethics* 112), they only go so far in terms of traversing symbolic castration. In other words, putting one's life in the service of creating a space for the censored dimension of the human to transform reality is significantly different from finding a sufficiently welcoming place within culture for the work of the drive in oneself. In a similar way, a pervert may set up a "double life" to simultaneously function in society and cultivate a personal fetish. While this may solve the problem of the unreceivable by the collective for that subject, it still refuses the feminine by attempting to control it, and so does not fully commit to unconscious desire—to grasping its full potential out of bounds and to introducing and taking responsibility for it in the collective.

By insisting that what makes us human and is excluded from language can find aesthetic expression regardless of a psychic structure, and despite the limits imposed by the social link, Apollon further develops the ethics of psychoanalysis. At stake, therefore, is not just a solution for a human being to both satisfy the drives and "succeed" in the collective, which in the end amounts to a new symptom. The subjective time Apollon invokes as fundamental to opening a spiritual space is also aesthetic time, which introduces something unprecedented in the world. While symptoms in analysis bespeak such a time, or timelessness, and even manifest its singularity, the jouissance at stake there is "lapsed"

("From Symptom . . ." 140): caught up in a repetition of an impasse that doesn't mobilize the creativity of the desiring quest. As seen earlier, Apollon specifically highlights the beautiful and the sublime as the feelings at stake in this subjective time. As feelings whose consistency is only "spiritual," the beautiful and the sublime are therefore foreign to perception and to what Apollon designates as psychical space. But for the death drive to serve a creative freedom that transcends the interests of the collective, or for unconscious desire to promote what Apollon calls "the subject's spiritual quest" beyond violence, some work is necessary. It can be tempting for the subject (and for the practice of psychoanalysis) to remain in the field of the symptom. In resisting this tendency that often leads to celebrating the symptom's uniqueness and its rebellious side, but not much more,[9] Apollon with the beautiful and the sublime prioritizes the subject's act. The symptom at best allows a subject to manage the defect in language, based on solutions that can be identified in the subject's culture. The act instead gives consistency to something previously imperceptible, opening a dimension otherwise unknown to the Other. The act concerns the human as that which cannot pass through language, what remains unreceivable and inadmissible; insofar as the act is only known by its effects, this necessarily implies that the consequences of an act are not only for the individual or for the collective, but above all for "the becoming of the human" ("The Human . . ." 89).

## A Line of Joy for the Quest

So far, we have observed that Apollon's metapsychology situates human experience in the effraction of the psyche by the spirit, inaugurating a subjective, aesthetic time, and that this experience undergoes transformations throughout the human being's lifetime. What Apollon calls aesthetic time only unfolds its full potential when the capacity to represent what doesn't exist that surges up in the child can develop into the adolescent's capacity to will and create or actualize the mental representation. As a capacity to conceive, want, and create what doesn't exist, then, the spirit is what is distinctly human; it surges up in an unprecedented way in each human being. However, fully using this capacity, or accessing a life of truly active desire, is not a given. In fact, this actualization of desire threatens and is thus unwelcome by the culture's project of bio-ideological reproduction, which means that the conditions of living aesthetic time and liberating the subjective quest of desire do not lie within cultures. The latter perpetuate group identities that result in forms of oppression and inequality shaped by the dominant ideology and economic system. Movements for social justice may certainly provide a space for the quest to find expression in the collective, as a care for the human more important than one's personal well-being and comfort, also more important than social stability. In particular, the very possibility of living and dying for social change can mean stepping beyond the limits of the ego, culture, and civilization, and thus standing only on the ground of this desiring quest. Joan of Arc, Mahatma Gandhi, Martin Luther King, and Greta Thunberg come to mind as examples of fully lived adolescence. Their response to the loss of the father in Lacanian terms, the death of God in philosophical ones—is neither withdrawal nor nihilism, but instead leaping forward with a concern for the human beyond the man or woman promoted by culture, and assuming the consequences of their acts.

To take seriously, as the metapsychology does, the spirit as the essential human capacity is to realize, among other things, that there's something much more important than the identity positions that are defined by culture. Thus Apollon sometimes suggests that what acts in Beethoven's compositions is not some exceptional gift of genius, of which the rest of humanity is deprived, and certainly not an exceptionally powerful ear, given that he was losing his sense of hearing throughout the period when his renowned symphonies were composed and first performed.[10] What acts, instead, is the fundamentally creative capacity of the spirit, in the form of a quest that is unique to each human being.

Strikingly, this very intuition appears in Virginia Woolf's reflections on writing, which she describes as the result of "a shock receiving capacity" (72) that she relates to three childhood memories whose impact she remembered all her life (71). The shock is "a token of some real thing behind appearances; and I make it real by putting it into words" (71), that is, in metapsychological terms, by creating this real thing that doesn't exist, which gives rise—beyond appearances, ideals, and other limiting functions of what Woolf calls "non-being" and "the cotton wool of daily life" (70–71)—to her intuition of the human:

> From this I reach what I might call a philosophy; at any rate
> it is a constant idea of mine; that behind the cotton wool is
> hidden a pattern; that we—I mean all human beings—are

> connected with this; that the whole world is a work of art; that we are parts of the work of art. *Hamlet* or a Beethoven quartet is the truth about this vast mass that we call the world. But there is no Shakespeare, there is no Beethoven; certainly and emphatically there is no God; we are the words; we are the music; we are the thing itself. And I see this when I have a shock. (72)

As her own reflection logically suggests, she would not have reached this intuition had she not insisted on putting into words the shocks she received as a child. First, "a feeling of hopeless sadness" (71) at the realization that people hurt each other; second, "looking at a plant with a spread of leaves" by her house and realizing "the flower itself was a part of the earth," which made her say "That is the whole"; and third, upon overhearing her mother say a man her family knew had killed himself, the impression of being "dragged down, hopelessly, into some pit of absolute despair from which I could not escape" (71). If she hadn't insisted on learning to write from the site of what she discovered to be not only a force before which she was powerless (72), but instead a "shock-receiving capacity," she wouldn't, she claims, make real, "make whole" that "token of some real thing."

At the different stages of the human being's development, a clash occurs between the quest and the social link into which every being is summoned, affecting in specific ways the vicissitudes of the drive initially mobilized by the spirit. When the quest comes up against the cultural montage of sexuality in puberty, the drive may become fixed in fantasies, scenarios, and missions, as the different psychic structures' solutions to the defect in language that consequently place limits on the subjective quest.[11] In addition to the trajectory of the human being's development from infancy to adolescence, Apollon sketches out a trajectory for analysis, whose logical moments are the triggering of transference, the fall of seduction (for neurotics), and the traversal of symbolic castration, which leads to the end of analysis: the transmission of and taking responsibility for the unknown object of the subjective quest. Analysis is thus an opportunity for subjects who failed to live their adolescence to its full ethical consequences to return to this very threshold, an opening to take the leap beyond limits.

I have also mentioned that Apollon's emphasis on the aesthetic feelings of the beautiful and the sublime as a support for ethics insists on an essentially joyful character of jouissance in the quest as such. Apollon includes among the characteristics of the spirit "the capacity to exceed the limits of the psyche for the joy (jouissance) this brings" (Schéma, "Le hors-langage"). This status of joy as a primary experience of the spirit, as well as the problem of sustaining or liberating this joyful mode of the desiring quest despite the efforts of culture to limit and divert it, can become clearer by considering some key aspects of Spinoza's *Ethics*, the stakes of which Deleuze elucidates with a particular attention to the question of what acts in the human being and the world. Teaching Spinoza in 1981, Deleuze points out that realizing the potential that leads to action involves "finding one's line of joy" and going through "a bit of a leap, and, undoubtedly, a threshold that varies for each one" ("Spinoza"). The Spinozian articulation of desire, body, and mind, as well as the choice between a more or less passive and active life and, beyond, "bliss" are crucially at stake in Apollon's account of the quest in the subject and the psychoanalytic hospitality due to it.

Deleuze links two key theses from Spinoza's *Ethics* in speaking of "seeking one's line of joy." First is that "we don't endeavor, will, seek after, or desire because we judge a thing to be good. On the contrary, we judge a thing to be good because we endeavor, will, seek after, or desire it" (*Ethics* III 9 s). In a sense, this statement emphasizes that the causality between the judgment of goodness and desire implies that the human mind is conscious of its desiring effort, and that this awareness distinguishes the human from other modes of life. But Deleuze also sees in this argument an important difference between ethics and morality, since recognizing the primacy of desire over moral judgment makes it possible to engage this desire as a trajectory, rather than denying or controlling it. Independent from reality, objectivity, and any kind of external moral code, desire appears here as the starting point for an ethical life. This is why a line of one's own must be sought, found, and taken even further. A "borrowed" line can only function as an ideal, which is at odds with desire. Spinoza's stance expresses an ethics of psychoanalysis, which sharply distinguishes the subject from a well-adapted ego in the social link.

The second thesis in Deleuze's dictum to seek one's line of joy concerns, of course, joy. For Spinoza, desire, joy, and sadness are the fundamental affections from which all others derive (III, 11 s). Joy is privileged, however, because it is defined as an intensification of *puissance* consonant with desire, which Spinoza defines as the effort to persist in one's own being. Therefore, seeking one's line of joy implies a work of affirming desire that orients one's direction before any moral judgment, as well as the conviction that following this path is joyful and leads to action and bliss. Apollon is concerned with this very process in the analysis as an opportunity to traverse one's adolescence. Concerning the fall of seduction and the traversal of symbolic castration, oriented toward real castration (which first occurs in the effraction of the limits of pleasure that carves out the erogenous body), Apollon indicates that liberating the subjective quest and taking responsibility for what its act brings to the human is not a matter of abandoning jouissance. On the contrary, if joy is the unbound drive's essential energy, then reactivating it and pursuing its ultimate actualization must lead to bliss.

Deleuze's observation of the "little leap" and "threshold" to be crossed precisely marks a difference between degrees of engagement with joy. Before this threshold, a first degree already indicates progress beyond a life almost entirely at the mercy of external affections, fluctuating between joy and sadness without a trajectory of its own. At this degree one commits to selecting the affections that increase and are in tune with the force of desire. However, these affections remain somewhat passive, insofar as they are partially caused by something external. The leap each one must uniquely take elevates a human being to a full commitment to joy, caused by the mind's own activity and the body's realizing action. In considering this formulation and its process of becoming active, it's crucial to retain the fundamental role of creativity in the concept of spirit Apollon proposes, since to Spinoza "mind" is the domain of desire that can become free to act from its own source. Deleuze continues to explain that taking the leap of joy concretely means "to acquire and gain possession of one's *puissance*." It's important to note also that, far from becoming increasingly impassible to other affections, such that in the end the mind is isolated with its capacity, becoming active begins with a greater receptivity to affections that increase desire. Spinoza's desire and affects resist a relation in which body is subjugated to mind, thereby introducing the moralistic worldview he instead breaks out of through ethics. This standpoint is also key to psychoanalysis, which is concerned precisely with what Deleuze discerns as the "theory of *puissance* according to which actions and passions of the body accompany actions and passions of the soul" (*Expressionism in Philosophy* 257). This parallelism of mind and body is precisely at play in the drive, as Lacan and Deleuze both know, and in the specific work of the letters of the body Apollon developed after them.

The letters of the body are inscriptions of traumatic encounters with the real that have erogenously derailed the logic of the organism at specific orifices, functions, and systems. The letters manifest the jouissance at stake where language fails to mediate and limit the subject's experience. This is crucial to the problem of liberating the subjective quest of desire. It's helpful to see in this regard that Spinoza's parallelist view of mind and body as the joint sources of an ethics already begins with aesthetics, insofar as this initial sensibility to the effects of many other bodies is taken, especially through Deleuze's reading, as a fundamentally creative capacity, and the starting point toward freedom, *puissance*, and joy (*Spinoza*).[12]

It's interesting that this is so, even if this sensibility or passivity also exposes one to pain, sadness, dependency. Escaping this initial state could be conceived as a matter of gradual numbing or of adequation to prevailing models in the world, but Deleuze shows that Spinoza instead privileges this sensibility, since, taken as *puissance* already, it is the very source of freedom to eventually possess this power of action and of producing active affections in the world (*Expressionism* 262). This astonishing logic is at stake in the trajectory Apollon schematizes from infancy to adolescence, which concerns real castration in two different moments: first, in infancy, the effraction of the psyche by the spirit I have discussed, and second, in adolescence, where the aesthetic is the sole guide to actualizing the mental representation of what doesn't exist, and on which the realization of this ethics depends.

In describing the art of selecting lines of joy, Deleuze remarks: "but, like worms, you obstinately seek your line of joy, which means something very different from seeking pleasure" ("Spinoza"). Deleuze's brief remark that the tenacious pursuit of joy is not to be confused with pleasure is crucial. Translated into psychoanalytic terms,[13] the pursuit of joy is on the side of the drive. It follows that this joy—or jouissance—is not something to surrender as the price to pay to become active, or in Spinoza's words "reasonable." Becoming reasonable is actually not at all a question of the mind controlling or cutting itself off from bodily impulses or appetites. Deleuze is interested in stressing this standpoint, so he clarifies that the movement toward reason from "inadequate" to "adequate ideas" is not correspondence to an object in the world (or to its conventions), but rather "the internal conformity of the idea with something it expresses" (*Expressionism*, 133) or the expression of "its own cause" (139). For its part, the body on this line of joy increases its capacity to "participate in the power of existing" (146); it can endure the experience of its own activity, the soul's "*puissance* of thinking" (146 tr. mod.), and the fundamental affection of joy.

Pleasure—whose homeostatic function of lowering the intensity of external and internal stimuli Freud explained—doesn't increase the *puissance* of desire; instead, it manages stimuli and even subordinates desire to the objectives of culture. Deleuze stresses the importance of exceeding pleasure to keep finding this line of one's own and to discern its precise edge, tension, and tendency, which pleasure would obscure. Apollon makes evident that under the pleasure principle—in second childhood and puberty, specifically[14]—externally imposed lines come in to organize one's thought and body according to the collective's requirements. The subjective quest that surged up in infancy becomes stranded in what Apollon calls second childhood, as an ego takes form for the subject to satisfy the parental other on whom its life depends. Meanwhile, something of that quest insists in the body. In puberty, as the sexual organs begin to mature, the culture uses the montage of sexuality to produce the woman and man it needs to secure the biological and material reproduction of the collective. The montage of sexuality is a key instrument to setting limits to joy beyond pleasure by subordinating the subject and its humanity, which involves a profound violence, since the effort aims at cutting the subject off from its own quest. The montage Apollon puts on view restricts the pursuit of one's line of joy to what Spinoza would call "passive affections," which, Deleuze remarks, reduce our capacity to be affected "to a minimum, having cut us off from what we can do (our power of action)" (225).

Both joy and sadness are beyond the pleasure principle, yet ethically these vectors are not at all equivalent. Deleuze states that there can be "a very bizarre joy" and "a dirty little joy" in suffering, and an inclination to produce and add to sadness, but that "humanity dies from it." The death drive is not a useful concept as long as, on a practical level, it is placed in the service of reducing jouissance to a project of "fabricating your own sadnesses" ("Spinoza"). This distinction is key to an ethics of psychoanalysis focused on the act of unconscious desire. As a work dedicated to finding one's line of joy, of liberating the quest, an analysis certainly involves examining the bizarre joys that have taken hold of one's life, and so uncovering the fantasy underlying one's choices, and the position with regard to the Other structuring one's jouissance. But for Apollon this knowledge concerning the obstacles to the subject's desiring quest can never be the endpoint of the analytic trajectory.

The commitment to joy beyond pleasure appears as the condition to truly access the aesthetic, among whose modes are genuine events of thought that exceed what Deleuze calls "common" and "good sense," as criteria with a moralistic underpinning. In the seminar session I have been citing, the committed pursuit of one's line of joy involves "seeking your encounter with bodies that suit you, whether it's the sun or the beloved, or stamp collections, anything whatsoever." In agreement with Spinoza's view of the causal relation between desire and "the good" (something is good because we desire it, and not inversely), this range of examples appears as sublimatory effects of the polymorphous perversion, unrelated to repressing or renouncing one's inclinations.[15] So while transcending pleasure is imperative to follow one's line of joy, it in no way means renouncing the body of the drive that surges up in what Deleuze describes as "encounters with other bodies" that increase one's joy. Apollon's metapsychology evinces that Deleuze's examples of the stubborn pursuit of the line of joy express, to a certain point, what acts out of language—in the body and the mental representation. Yet at this level the subject hasn't reached the threshold and leap beyond which the quest is truly free to act and to assume the consequences, where joy relies on its own *puissance*. This moment implies the traversal of symbolic castration to access real castration, and the correlative movement from puberty to adolescence. To think about this decisive moment of crossing this threshold to act beyond the limits of culture and civilization, it's important to better grasp the body of the drive in relation to the spirit and its capabilities. The beautiful has a crucial function here, and it is no accident that philosophical definitions of this feeling often miss something fundamental, namely the place of feminine jouissance.

## Unbinding Beauty

This chapter previously presented Apollon's contention that the beautiful is "a feeling in the body" that involves the discovery and embrace of the feminine. He also notes that what we call "the aesthetic" was called by the Ancient Greeks and Romans "the erotic" (Schéma "Une humanité en panne?"). "Erotic" evokes and emphasizes the irreducibility of the body mobilized by this feeling, there where modern philosophical aesthetics may instead avoid this bodily aspect, plausibly in an anxious attempt to distinguish the beautiful from sexual excitation. *Eros* is, after all, the Greek god of love and sex. It's interesting to recall here Friedrich Nietzsche's criticism of aestheticians whose interpretation of Kant's claim that "the beautiful is what pleases in a *disinterested* way" leads them to believe "that under the magic spell of beauty people can look even at unclothed female statues 'without interest'" (*Basic Writings* 540). Nietzsche's attack against this sedative effect of beauty pointedly exposes the presence within philosophical aesthetics of the cultural censorship of the feminine—where a naked woman is only thinkable as an object of satisfaction, and where a man's own femininity is also censored, and exiled to an external object to be looked at, if not dominated and exploited.

In psychoanalysis the scene of discovering sexual difference in the appearance of the girl's and boy's genitals was introduced by Freud to evoke the experience of castration as something lived differently by a girl and a boy. Regarding this problem in Seminar III, Lacan stated that, unlike the man's sex, the woman's sex isn't symbolized, and that it "is characterized by an absence, a void, a hole" (176). This highlights the subject's problem of responding to this encountered void. In speaking of "the Thing" beyond the pleasure principle in Seminar VII, Lacan points out how the mother has been a representative for this unrepresentable, and also highlights the troubadour's forbidden Lady from the literature of courtly love in the role of supreme good or Thing that provokes sublimation. Lacan also explores this Thing as the source of an ethics and its effects in the female tragic figures of Antigone and (in the subsequent seminar) Sygne de Coûfontaine. In later seminars, Lacan deals with the difference between a man and a woman with regard to the Other, the phallus as signifier of lack, and jouissance by developing the formulas and graph of sexuation through which he develops the difference between phallic and feminine jouissance (*Book XX* 78).

Apollon's "feminine" further extends Lacan's feminine jouissance. In Apollon's metapsychology, feminine jouissance is thus not only the effect of a subjective position that one may or may not find oneself in, regarding both the phallic function—as "not-all" anchored by its effect of limiting jouissance—and the Other without a signifier ($S(\bar{A})$). The precedence of the aesthetic and the spirit over language and the signifier turns feminine jouissance into an essential dimension of each subject's humanity. The concrete fact of every human life originating from a woman's womb is relevant here, insofar as each one's experience as a body begins, Apollon states, "in an intimate relation, unbeknownst to [both mother and child], with something in the body of this woman that is of the order of a lost jouissance—even a jouissance that this woman has never experienced, because it has been censored by the culture." ("The Human" 65). The body susceptible to aesthetic feeling in adolescence is, as mentioned, shaped early on by specific inscriptions of jouissance that eroticize the body and form its sensibility. With Deleuze one might also say that these letters shape the capacity to be affected, in either joyful or sad encounters that respectively increase or decrease the power of desire (*puissance*).

If the letters of the body attest to the child's decisive experiences out-of-language, the feminine articulates the out-of-language to the aesthetic. Importantly, femininity is precisely what culture censors in the pubescent man and woman through the montage of sexuality, obstructing the feminine with orgasm (in the man) and maternity (in the woman), to meet the collective's need for bio-ideological reproduction. Thus, the aesthetic results from an insistent work of forging a way for an experience beyond pleasure that necessarily entails a shift of position regarding the feminine, from exclusion and repudiation,[16] to its discovery and embrace—and beyond it, to upholding the intimate thing that has no place in the world or language by creating subversive spaces in the social link for its incalculable effects.

Apollon contends that the beautiful and the sublime emerge in relation to levels of the unconscious that exceed cultural and civilizational limits, and thus lie beyond the purview of both "the repressed"—what the individual doesn't want to think about or the Other to know—and "the censored"—what the culture needs to exclude to secure collective reproduction. Apollon certainly recognizes a powerful cultural formatting of the aesthetic, where aesthetic feelings are appropriated by the collective, in the service, for instance, of group psychology, the bourgeois family, religion, and nationalism, enforcing the illusion that the collective and its continuation are what is at stake in such feelings. However, aesthetic feelings are ultimately irreducible to familiar ideals of beauty and greatness. Beyond culture, the aesthetic is not moral, but rather an ethical choice of the subject of the quest, grounded solely on feelings that uphold the drive's fundamentally "unbound" quality, as that which propels the quest. Ideals and values of beauty, greatness, goodness, and so forth bind aesthetic feelings to make human individuals into members of the collective who reproduce its culture. Faced with the conflict between the drive and cultural ideals and the beliefs that sustain them, the neurotic surrenders aesthetic experience for the sake of adapting to culture and of being receivable by others.[17]

Beyond these cultural limits, the beautiful has destabilizing effects. In his study of the problem of happiness in relation to different economies of the drive, Freud considers beauty's importance to civilization, although it "has no obvious use; nor is there any clear cultural necessity for it. Yet civilization could not do without it" (*Civilization and its Discontents* 82). This raises the question for him of beauty's "nature and origin" (82), and causes him to struggle:

> The science of aesthetics investigates the conditions under which things are felt as beautiful, but it has been unable to give any explanation of the nature and origin of beauty, and, as usually happens, lack of success is concealed beneath a flood of resounding and empty words. Psychoanalysis, unfortunately, has scarcely anything to say about beauty either. All that seems certain is its derivation from the field of sexual feeling. The love of beauty seems a perfect example of an impulse inhibited in its aim. "Beauty" and "attraction" are originally attributes of the sexual object. It is worth remarking that the genitals themselves, the sight of which is always exciting, are nevertheless hardly ever judged to be beautiful; the quality of beauty seems, instead, to attach to certain secondary characters. (83)

Freud points to philosophical aesthetics and bluntly states that no satisfactory explanation has come of its investigations on the nature and origin of the feeling of beauty. His criticism underscores how empty words make up for this failure, which effectively leaves psychoanalysis almost speechless. This failure of speech when it comes to the beautiful should not be passed over too quickly, since it points, exactly, to the problematic of the out-of-language. Freud's observation is indicative of the unaddressable and unsayable dimensions of the unconscious, which Apollon considers to be at stake in the beautiful and the sublime. Freud seems to rush, however, toward interpretation and regaining a voice of psychoanalytic mastery in his next sentence, which shifts from "the feeling of beauty" to "the love of beauty," and contains it within the modest limits of "a perfect example." One could take the passage to suggest that if there's anything psychoanalysis can say about beauty, it's that it concerns an inhibition of sexual excitement. As if the sexual object were the genitals, and the excitement about them were being displaced to other features. It may seem as if beauty were merely a displaced or disguised obscene arousal coming from the object, or also as if the economy of sublimation he describes a few paragraphs earlier in terms of displacements of the drive to circumvent the external world began its trajectory within the cultural limits of the receivable. Nothing is further removed from the function of the aesthetic in Apollon's metapsychology.

Perhaps, however, there's another way to consider Freud's discussion. By introducing "love of beauty" and "attraction" into the investigation on "the origin of beauty," Freud certainly takes an important step beyond the ideals imposed by culture and dares to expose less virtuous and ideal motives at the root of aesthetic feeling. Long before Freud, of course, Sade and Sacher-Masoch—but also many other poets, from Arnaut to Verlaine and from Ronsard to Rimbaud—had unveiled and played with the force of the unsayable. Yet in the Freud passage cited above, as well as in the work of these perverse authors (writing to provoke the reader's jouissance), cultural norms and morals tend to remain the standard by which feelings are measured, whether these are judged obscene or aesthetic. In the end, if this measure is indispensable, even to transgress it, the unconscious remains insufficiently considered, as Freud implicitly acknowledges with his comment about the limits of language. Above all, if his point about inhibited excitation may helpfully indicate a use of ideals of beauty to reinforce repression and cultural censorship, it does not say what else the love of beauty could offer. The real difference isn't between the obscene genitals and the attractive "secondary characters" that surreptitiously evoke them, but rather between this entire circuit of beauty as displaced excitation and something else as the feeling of the beautiful—erotic, yes, but precisely where words fail and feelings are unbound from both genital excitement and any established model of beauty.

Aesthetic feelings are relevant insofar as they reveal human subjectivity as independent from the Other in the function Apollon calls that of "guardian of the receivable" ("L'humain" 26). In other words, the beautiful and the sublime never derive from social conventions, cultural values, or the civilizational frameworks that make them credible. Instead, the beautiful and the sublime are genuine events—disruptions of the structure of the address as what is receivable in language[18]—that produce their own grounds and criteria. The aesthetic, then, constitutes a unique site for the unconscious subject. To speak of the aesthetic, one must thus affirm the hypothesis that opens the possibility of transference, and thus of an analysis: that there is, somewhere, a desiring subject. Something unnamed works in a body—a dimension of a human being that fundamentally escapes language as the organization of social relations and therefore can only be expressed through symptoms and senseless acts unless the subject creates a path for what cannot be or has never been said.

I previously mentioned that the Freudian "timelessness" of the unconscious has to do with "mnemic traces" that persist in a being and can be activated despite the passage of chronological time. This capacity of the body results from the human being exiled from an organism responding to pure instinct. Apollon speaks of the drive as an energy working in a body beyond the pleasure principle, "beyond the organism's natural functioning," and this drive is mobilized by the capacity to represent what doesn't exist. In early childhood, the drive marks specific systems of the developing organism according to the child's jouissance in lived and imagined experiences, inscribing the letters of the body.[19] Apollon indicates that the child's body bears the inscription of a divergence between the parents' lost object or impossible desire and the child's being, which is inadequate to this desire ("Qu'est-ce qu'un enfant?" 151). Furthermore, something of this inscription "remains rebellious to any signifying representation in the unconscious," and for which Freud introduces "the concept of the death drive" (152). This rebellious letter concerns "a jouissance that is unjustifiable and outside the phallic law" (153).

The treatment of psychosis Apollon developed for young adults in Quebec[20] has allowed its analysts to approach the tension between this rebellious letter and the paternal metaphor, whose function is to protect the child against confronting an unsignifiable void directly in this early moment of its life, in a way that recognizes in psychosis an ethical commitment to the human. Psychosis implies a fidelity to the spirit against the cultural montage of the sexual. In facing "the groundlessness of the Symbolic" ("Qu'est-ce qu'un enfant" 157) that every human being discovers, the psychotic response is never one of repression. Apollon points out that the little girl also knows something of this groundlessness (153), regardless of her structure. Rather than turning away from it, of hoping for a solution from the Other,[21] or of controlling it in a scenario, as the pervert does, the psychotic attempts to resolve the defect in language alone, by constructing a delusional mission that also expresses the desiring quest. Although the letter of the body is most often encountered in its more debilitating manifestations, such as the symptom or the psychotic crisis, Apollon insists on the crucial fact that the letter is nonetheless the inscription of the quest. The psychotic can instead be taken as guide to ask what can be made with the letter that escapes the signifier when it is taken as the inscription of a quest, therefore as a capacity that can bring joy and action, because it is attuned "to the spirit of the spirit."

The aesthetic alternative to the symptom isn't just optimistic speculation to counterbalance the drive's destructive potential. Apollon points to a space of freedom for the child, where both the joy of play and deceiving the Other are possible. "What I call here aesthetic is this space that the work of the Letter wrests away from the signifiers circumscribed by the Other" ("Qu'est-ce qu' . . ." 161). Although "this can certainly also be the space of the symptom that finds there its structure as a writing and its fundamentally metaphorical dimension" (161), the work of the letter to structure an imaginary that escapes the signifiers of the Other emerges as a push of jouissance to define a unique sensibility, beyond good and evil, "for the infant is immoral" and "doesn't know anything of the rules and ideals with which adults frame the deceit of language and the seduction of words" (161). While this push can eventually take the form of symptoms and senseless acts, it is also key to the emergence of aesthetic feelings, which result from "an act [that] opens a path for what cannot be spoken, in the field of that which goes beyond the being and its simple pleasure: beauty" (Schéma: "La clinique du fantasme").

An act opens a path for the unaddressable through beauty, where the body expresses the quest aesthetically. In following this path, the dimension of the sublime is opened as well, where the subjective quest takes responsibility for something greater than both the individual's life and the collective. The work of the spirit and of the letters that carve out a body beyond pleasure doesn't merely destroy this body. For Apollon the drive does not condemn the subject to stale repetitions; it offers a way to uphold the subjective quest of desire. This is the goal of an analysis, although the specific expression of this quest cannot, of course, be known beforehand.

Apollon insists that every culture censors the feminine dimension of experience in a child, and that the feminine is excluded from the social link. These claims certainly do not entail that, from a psychoanalytic viewpoint, the feminine is irrelevant or that which "we must pass over in silence," as Wittgenstein suggested of the unspeakable (*Tractatus* P7). On the contrary, there is no "gaining possession of one's *puissance*" in the Spinozian sense without discovering the intimate space of the feminine that remains outside the social link. Beyond the individually repressed, the unsayable, and even the censored, from which the "inappropriate to say" derives, on the ground of credibility afforded by civilization (Schéma "Le hors-langage"), there is the unconscious in its most radical sense, which concerns the "unaddressable," defined as "an experience in a subject's body for which there are no words and no Other" (Clinical Cases Seminar).[22] Feminine jouissance is censored, unaddressable, unbelievable even, but perfectly real, and certainly not exclusive to women or to a certain kind of human organism.

Thus situated, the relevance of the feminine to the spiritual quest of the subject—to unconscious desire—becomes apparent. Some Thing insists beyond the Other, beyond language, without words. It is felt sometimes in an encounter that exceeds the realm of what we can say and address to one another in the collective. Something disorganizes that circuit and provokes the feeling of the beautiful. Thought is also disorganized by this unexpected encounter, and there's a failure of the usual resources to make sense of it, which limit one's exposure and refuse feeling. The long-standing tradition that binds the feminine Thing in a body to evil and illness illustrates the collective's defensive response to the beautiful (recall that to Apollon the feminine articulates the out-of-language to the aesthetic, which begins with the beautiful as a feeling in the body). Spinoza's ethics show that it is often only on the line of sadness that a way of dealing with feelings beyond pleasure is developed. Under these conditions, Apollon contends, what is missed is nothing but the best of humanity in each being. The drive is stuck in stale repetitions, all for "a dirty little joy," while the feminine remains tied to the cultural montage of sexuality, which historically has, indeed, limited how the feminine within a woman can find aesthetic expression, for example as the nude statue or body depicted in an artwork, where she remains an object.

## Desire's Leap: The Act

Apollon remarks that the analyst's act "creates a space for what is outside of language, and [. . .] therefore creates a rupture within the social link"

("The Act" 5). Yet there is also "the act of the analysand that constructs the ethical framework [for] this thing that has never been symbolized, and that subverts her neurophysiology for lack of the signifiers that would allow it to be spoken" (5). Sustained by analysis as ethical practice, this action's force allows the analysand "to express the singular fantasy from which it extracts its jouissance" (5)—and, beyond the fantasy, to give aesthetic expression to the quest of desire and take responsibility for its effects in the world.

Deleuze admits his struggle to explain how he can tell that someone committed to their line of joy beyond pleasure has crossed the threshold and "possesses their *puissance*." He suggests it is "by their way of walking, of being gentle, of being angry, when they are angry." He concludes: "by a certain agreement with themselves" ("Spinoza"). It is as if impressions of the letter of the body could be discerned in someone's stylistic traits, which evoke some of the previously mentioned dictionary definitions of "*esprit*." In Deleuze's description of certain bodies, it seems as if they also transmitted intimate experiences of the beautiful. But what can someone *do* with their *puissance* when they gain possession of it? Deleuze poses this crucial question: "What can a body do?" (*Expressionism* 217). He tells us the fundamentally unknown quality of one's *puissance* is part of the issue—of what makes the path that ruptures the social link come to a threshold where the choice between stopping short or taking a leap becomes necessary.

The leap enables us to "feel and experience that we are eternal," Spinoza writes (V 23 s). In Apollon's terms, this concerns nothing other than the sublime, particularly if we consider Deleuze's explanation of Spinoza's sentence. Deleuze in fact indicates that for the human being the problem of death depends on the distribution of portions of what Spinoza calls extensive and intensive parts in one's life. Death only means "I no longer have extensive parts" ("Spinoza"). So in a life that has consisted in actualizing intensive parts—the spirit's capacities, in metapsychological terms—"what perishes of me is . . . a rather insignificant part, rather small" ("Spinoza"). Such a case prioritizes that experience in one's life that lies out-of-language and out of biological time.

Closely related to the question "What can a body do?" is Deleuze and Guattari's "How do you make yourself a Body without Organs?" The question that gives their essay its title—and pinpoints the stakes of the aesthetic in Apollon—is an enthusiastic response to the conclusion of "To Be Done with the Judgment of God," a 1947 radio play by the

French poet Antonin Artaud, who spent periods of his life in psychiatric hospitals. In the play, Artaud's interlocutor declares him "ready for the straitjacket" for saying that since nobody believes in God anymore, "it is man whom we must now make up our minds to emasculate" (39). Artaud insists that "man is sick because he is poorly built," and pronounces: "you can tie me up if you wish, but there is nothing more useless than an organ. When you make him a body without organs, he will be delivered from all of his automatisms and restored to his true freedom" (40). Artaud's speech is a subversive act that ruptures the order of the sayable, especially in its broadcast form. Moreover, the proposal of emasculation undermines notions of health and power linked to a unified ego, and also to a discourse of manhood. In his chapter for this volume, Apollon considers this idea in young male psychotic subjects as a response to "the experience of censorship of the feminine" ("The Human" 79). In "shatter[ing] the reality that conditions social coexistence" ("The Act" 8), one might say Artaud gives expression to his femininity. Apollon explains that femininity "is called forth by the inability of language to provide a conduit for this essential part of the living being, which, when it fails to be symbolized, must find expression in an act that invariably tears the social fabric" (9).

Convinced of the urgency of the task Artaud announces, that of creating a way out of the organism as tool for bio-ideological reproduction, Deleuze and Guattari ask how to *make oneself* a Body without Organs. They strategically displace Artaud's proposed solution—as though beckoning the sick or dead man to remove himself from "the autopsy table to remake his anatomy" (Artaud, "To Be Done . . ." 570)—and also invite "Artaud le Mômo"[23] to avoid a light under which "he can be taken for a person *suffering* from hallucinations" (570; my emphasis). After all, what emerges as distinctly human with the effraction of the spirit is the capacity to hallucinate, before entering language. Artaud indicates a direction for a body's transformative process or "becoming," toward acquiring its own, unprecedented name.

Deleuze and Guattari's essay offers a concrete sense of the Spinozist development of one's line of joy as a singular ethical matter. There is at once a peculiar sense of duty to take on this task of making oneself a Body without Organs, and a freedom to embrace it. And there are consequences:

> At any rate, you make one, you can't desire without making one. And it awaits you; it is an inevitable exercise or exper-

imentation, already accomplished the moment you undertake it, unaccomplished as long as you don't. This is not reassuring, because you can botch it. Or it can be terrifying, and lead you to your death. It is nondesire as well as desire. It is not at all a notion or a concept but a practice, a set of practices. You never reach the Body without Organs, you can't reach it, you are forever attaining it, it is a limit. (149–50)

One might say the "Body without Organs" is immanent in each of us insofar as a joyful desire (in Spinoza's terms) or (in Apollon's) spirit breaks in on the organism, inaugurating each human life. Yet it is also a work, "a practice" indispensable to desire. Similarly, for Spinoza, while a human mode of life already presupposes desire—that is, the individual experience of the effort to persist in one's own being—one must still make one's line of joy to desire more actively.

The complex sense of duty and freedom regarding the experimental yet somehow fated work on the Body without Organs evokes the complex temporality of desire, as the human thing at stake in Apollon's spirit and in aesthetic feeling specifically. The existence of mental representations exclusively in subjective time means that the *puissance* of desire is not fully actualized without passing from conceiving and willing what doesn't exist to giving oneself the means to create it. The capacity to represent what doesn't exist in the first moment of Apollon's definition of spirit lays out a singular path for its subject, which can be conceived of as "an inevitable exercise or experimentation." But the specificity of this quest that fuels an initial mental representation can only grasped retroactively.

The play maintained between inevitability and call to action, alongside the remark that the Body without Organs is a limit, indicates that the exercise simply cannot be evaluated beforehand or from a viewpoint external to the practice. In this regard, the claim that the Body without Organs is not a notion or a concept is especially striking. There is no room for simulations of becoming active in an ethics of desire. One cannot become active "only in theory"; even theory must carry out its act. Desire thus exceeds the realm of notions or concepts, and certainly the principle of non-contradiction that theoretically distinguishes desire from non-desire and thereby halts the action. As a process, desire includes its own collapse and possible transformations.

Psychoanalysis offers a space to embrace and a pursue a subjectivity beyond the limits of reality, representation, the possible, and the receivable. Deleuze insists that an ethics is not a tribunal, and a life can never be judged by any external measure.[24] An analysis that traverses symbolic castration also necessarily drops tribunals and external measures, since it is concerned with accessing the unaddressable as its endpoint (ÉfQ Teaching). Aesthetic time, then, has to do with advancing where there is no Other, where a creative act takes place at each step. So when someone on their line of joy encounters the threshold of the act, there's a leap: "little," perhaps, but real. The leap leads to the emergence of a "new mode of existence" that "creates itself through its own forces" (Deleuze, "To Have . . ." 135). Apollon's metapsychology shows that to realize this creative act is to fully, immoderately embrace the quest of desire, which is sublime: more important than one's own existence. The question of whether one has become active, "gained possession of one's joy," necessarily involves that the desiring quest can only be grasped by its effects *beyond oneself*. This is what is at stake in psychoanalysis: a genuine *act* whereby aesthetic time enters and transforms the world.

## Notes

1. For a philosophical aesthetics that prioritizes exactly this register of the aesthetic, foregrounding its presence as early as Plato, wherever an encounter disrupts "good sense" and "common [ordinary] sense," see Gilles Deleuze's *Difference and Repetition*, chapter 3. See also his *Francis Bacon: The Logic of Sensation*. It is no accident that the metapsychology that prioritizes the aesthetic in the specific manner this chapter attempts to highlight was developed by an analyst with a philosophical background, whose dissertation was directed by Gilles Deleuze and later published at the motivation of Catherine Clément and Michel de Certeau. See Apollon, *Le vaudou: Un espace pour les "voix."*

2. Arguing in 1786 that "the doctrine of the soul must remain even further from the rank of a properly so-called natural science than chemistry," Kant notes that "another thinking subject [does not] suffer himself to be experimented upon to suit our purpose" (*Metaphysical Foundations of Natural Science* 471).

3. Jeffrey Librett, in "The Aesthetic Supplement in Willy Apollon (in relation to Kant, Hoffman, Freud)," offers an exposition of the "unheard-of" quality of Kant's notion of *sensus communis* and emphasizes how it is also a "communal" sense (44–45).

4. See Wilson and Miller in this volume on this. More on the feminine later in this chapter.

5. See "The Fantasy" in this volume.

6. Translation slightly modified.

7. Deleuze marks the ethical distinction between *puissance* and *pouvoir*, which otherwise would both translate as "power." *Pouvoir* conveys a tyrannical

and ultimately sad force exerted over others, whereas *puissance* is used to refer to vital thriving, including that of desire.

8. Cf. "Castration" with Lucie Cantin in *Penumbr(a)cast—The Other Scene.*

9. I discuss this position in surrealist claims about hysteria and beauty in chapter 1, *The Aesthetic Clinic.* Michel Bosseyroux explores, beyond the Joycean *sinthome* as end of analysis, a further-reaching Beckettian "endgame" within Lacan, which gives up identification with the *sinthome's* unique style to get closer to silence. This analysis certainly evokes what is out-of-language and highlights the analyst's task as implicitly ethical, although its conclusion—promoting the analyst's use of the signifier to reduce chatter "to extract the pearl"—doesn't necessarily deal with the consequences of sustaining the "how to say even worse" "comment encore plus mal dire" ("Au commencement, le symptôme. À la fin, le sinthome où . . . *?" 39). Geneviève Morel's *The Law of the Mother* offers a detailed exposition of the rethinking of the symptom in Lacan's late seminars, showing the way in which the *sinthome*, in its way of linking the Real, Symbolic, and Imaginary, makes possible a non-Oedipal psychoanalytic theory of sexual difference, without transcendent norms in the symbolic. Morel observes that instead of construction, the *sinthome* is a matter of reduction to the minimum that gives subjective consistency and is creative.

10. A recent example of this perspective on creative abilities appears in the discussion about Aimée Mullins in Danielle Bergeron's chapter for this volume.

11. "The fantasy arises in the defect of the signifier, in the defect of language, constructed so as to manage the unmanageable, to treat the untreatable" (Cantin, "The Fantasy" 413). The same applies to the mission and the scenario in the other structures. Also, "the adolescent, like the psychotic, experiences the defect of language" ("Fantasy" 428).

12. The distinction between *pouvoir* and *puissance* and the process of gaining possession of one's *puissance* closely resonates with the stakes of becoming a vodou priest as developed by Apollon in "La prise de l'Asson," a chapter from his early work *Le vaudou.*

13. Deleuze extends Freud's notion of the death drive in his philosophy of difference. See chapter II, *Difference and Repetition.*

14. For more on Apollon's concepts of second childhood and puberty, see Alexander Miller's chapter in this volume.

15. Like Deleuze, Lacan's *Ethics of Psychoanalysis* also invokes stamp collections, in a discussion of an article by Bernfield about sublimation, which says "on the level of analysis one shouldn't distinguish between the work of an artist and a stamp collection" (158).

16. In "Analysis terminable, interminable," Freud explains that the final stage of analysis brings patients up against "the bedrock of castration" where what is at stake is "the repudiation of femininity" (SE XXIII, 250).

17. See Cantin's chapter in this volume, which points out that repression fails for the pervert and psychotic subjects, since they aren't subjected to the

same concerns as the neurotic. See also Heidi Arsenault's "Beauty in Play" for a reflection on the aesthetic experiences of children and the conflict between this joy and dependency on others as a factor in the subject's decision to enter language, or not.

18. See Jeffrey Librett's chapter in this volume for more on the structure of the address and its subversion.

19. See "The Letter of the Body" in *After Lacan*.

20. In 1982, Apollon with Danielle Bergeron and Lucie Cantin founded a center for the treatment of psychotic young adults in Quebec City known as "The 388," for its street number. It is known for its efficient results in terms of dramatically decreasing hospitalization and medication and avoiding confinement, while centering the treatment around the psychoanalysis of its users. The treatment is grounded on speech and companionship with staff members, called "intervenants," whose training allows them to listen, respect, and not pathologize the center's users, and also on workshops focused on their artistic creativity. It aims and succeeds at enabling users to become active and independent citizens. For details, see Apollon, Bergeron, and Cantin, *Un avenir pour le psychotique et La cure psychanalytique du psychotique*, and Vanderwees's interview "Treating Psychosis in Quebec."

21. This is the case for many women, given the historical unreceivability of the thing in them and the position ascribed to them in the montage. See "Castration, with Lucie Cantin."

22. McNulty discusses the four levels of the unconscious in this volume.

23. Aratud refers in the radio play to this figure he developed beyond it in a set of poems. The name "Artaud le Mômo" evokes the "kid," "*le môme*," as well as "the girl," "*la môme*."

24. Cf. Deleuze, "To Have Done with Judgement."


# Works Cited


Apollon, Willy. "The Act." *Umbr(a): The Journal of Culture and the Unconscious*, vol. 9, no. 1, 2013–2014.

———. "La Chose." 8 May 2020. Unpublished.

———. Clinical Cases Seminar. 1 June 2020. Unpublished.

———. ÉfQ Teaching. 25 Jan. 2020. Unpublished

———. *From Symptom to Fantasy: After Lacan. Clinical Practice and the Subject of the Unconscious*. State U of New York P, 2002, pp. 127–40.

———. "The Letter of the Body." *After Lacan: Clinical Practice and the Subject of the Unconscious*, State U of New York P, 2002, pp. 103–15.

———. "Qu'est-ce qu'un enfant?" *La différence sexuelle au risque de la parenté*, Les Éditions du GIFRIC, 1997, pp. 147–62.

————. Schéma: "La clinique du fantasme." 2018. Unpublished.

————. Schéma. "Le hors-langage."12 June 2020. Unpublished.

————. Schéma. "Une humanité en panne?" 14 Dec. 2022. 14 Dec. 2022. Unpublished.

————. Schéma. "L'enjeu de la quête dans la cure." 23 Jan. 2023. Unpublished.

————. "The Subject of the Quest." Translated by Daniel Wilson, *Penumbr(a)*, vol. 2, edited by Marta Aleksandrowicz and Fernanda Negrete, 2022, pp. 1–14.

Apollon, Willy, Danielle Bergeron, and Lucie Cantin. *Un avenir pour le psycho-tique. Le dispositif du traitement psychanalytique.* GIFRIC, 2013.

————. *La cure psychanalytique du psychotique. Enjeux et stratégies.* GIFRIC, 2008.

Arsenault, Heidi. "Beauty in Play: Willy Apollon's Concept of the Structure of the Address and Work with Autistic Children." *Penumbr(a)*, vol. 2, edited by Marta Aleksandrowicz and Fernanda Negrete, 2022, pp. 15–35.

Artaud, Antonin. "To Be Done with the Judgment of God." *Antonin Artaud: Selected Writings.* Translated by S. S. and D. E. L, Farrar, Straus, and Giroux, 1976, pp. 553–71.

Bergson, Henri. "The Soul and the Body." *Mind-Energy.* Translated by Wildon Carr, Greenwood Press, 1929.

Bosseyroux, Michel. "Au commencement, le symptôme. A la fin, le sinthome ou . . . ?" *L'en-je Lacanien*, vol. 1, no. 26, 2016, pp. 93–109.

Deleuze, Gilles. *Cinema 2: The Time-Image.* Translated by Hugh Tomilson and Robert Galeta, U of Minnesota P, 1997.

————. *Difference and Repetition.* Translated by Paul Patton, Columbia UP, 1994.

————. *Expressionism in Philosophy: Spinoza.* Translated by Martin Joughin, Zone Books, 1990.

————. *Francis Bacon: The Logic of Sensation.* Translated by Daniel W. Smith, Continuum, 2003.

————. "On Four Formulas That Might Summarize Kantian Philosophy." *Essays Critical and Clinical*, translated by Daniel W. Smith and Michael A. Greco, U of Minnesota P, 1997, pp. 27–35.

————. "Spinoza: Les vitesses de la pensée." *Seminars*, Feb.–Mar. 1981.

————. "To Have Done with Judgment." *Essays Critical and Clinical*, translated by Daniel W. Smith and Michael A. Greco, U of Minnesota P, 1997, pp. 126–35.

Deleuze, Gilles, and Félix Guattari. A *Thousand Plateaus: Capitalism and Schizophre-nia 2.* Translated by Brian Massumi, U of Minnesota P, 1987, pp. 149–50.

Freud, Sigmund. *Beyond the Pleasure Principle. The Standard Edition of the Complete Psychological Works of Sigmund Freud*, vol. XVIII, Vintage, 2001, pp. 3–64.

————. "Civilized' Sexual Morality and Modern Nervous Illness." *The Standard Edition*, vol. IX, Vintage, 2001, pp. 177–204.

————. *Civilization and Its Discontents. The Standard Edition*, vol. XXI, Vintage, 2001, pp. 59–145.

———. *Jokes and Their Relation to the Unconscious. The Standard Edition*, vol. VIII, Vintage, 2001.

———. "The Uncanny." *The Standard Edition*, vol. XVII, Vintage, 2001, pp. 218–56.

———. "The Unconscious." *The Standard Edition*, vol. XIV, Vintage, 2001, pp. 159–215.

Hadot, Pierre. *Philosophy as a Way of Life.* Wiley-Blackwell, 1995.

Kant, Immanuel. *Critique of Judgment.* Translated by W. S. Pluhar, Hackett Publishing Co., 1987.

———. *Critique of Pure Reason.* Translated by Paul Guyer and Allen W. Wood, Cambridge UP, 1998.

———. *Metaphysical Foundations of Natural Science.* Translated by Michael Friedman, Cambridge UP, 2004.

Lacan, Jacques. *The Seminar of Jacques Lacan: Book III: The Psychoses 1955–1956.* Translated by Russell Grigg, W. W. Norton & Co., 1993.

———. *The Seminar of Jacques Lacan: Book VII: The Ethics of Psychoanalysis.* Translated by Dennis Porter, W. W. Norton & Co., 1992.

———. *The Seminar of Jacques Lacan: Book VII: The Ethics of Psychoanalysis.* Translated by Denis Porter, W. W. Norton & Co., 1992.

———. *The Seminar of Jacques Lacan: Book XI: The Four Fundamental Concepts of Psychoanalysis.* Translated by Alan Sheridan, W. W. Norton, 1981.

———. "Logical Time and the Assertion of Anticipated Certainty: A New Sophism." *Écrits,* translated by Bruce Fink, W. W. Norton & Co., 2002.

———. *The Seminar of Jacques Lacan: Book XX: On Feminine Sexuality.* Translated by Bruce Fink, W. W. Norton & Co., 1998.

Librett, Jeffrey. "The Aesthetic Supplement in Willy Apollon (in Relation to Kant, Hoffman, Freud)." *Penumbr(a)*, vol. 2, edited by Marta Aleksandrowicz and Fernanda Negrete, 2022, pp. 36–70.

Miller, Jacques-Alain. "La signature des symptômes." *La cause du désir*, vol. 2, no. 96, 2017, pp. 112–20.

Morel, Geneviève. *La loi de la mère.* Economica, 2008.

Negrete, Fernanda. *The Aesthetic Clinic: Feminine Sublimation in Contemporary Writing, Psychoanalysis, and Art.* State U of New York P, 2020.

———. "Castration, with Lucie Cantin," *Penumbr(a)cast—The Other Scene,* episode 6, 2022, https://www.penumbrajournal.org/podcast.

Nietzsche, Friedrich. *The Basic Writings of Nietzsche.* Translated by Walter Kaufmann, Modern Library, 2000.

Rimbaud, Arthur. *Complete Works.* Translated by Paul Schmidt, HarperCollins, 2008.

Spinoza, Baruch. *The Essential Spinoza:* Ethics *and Related Writings.* Translated by Samuel Shirley, Hackett Publishing Company, 2006.

Thagard, Paul, "Cognitive Science." *The Stanford Encyclopedia of Philosophy*, Winter 2020 edition, edited by Edward N. Zalta, https://plato.stanford.edu/archives/win2020/entries/cognitive-science/.

Vanderwees, Chris. "Treating Psychosis in Quebec: A Conversation with The Founders of GIFRIC and The 388." Translated by Daniel Wilson, *The Museum of Dreams*, 2018, https://www.museumofdreams.org/treating-psychosis-in-quebec.

Wittgenstein, Ludwig. *Tractatus Logico-Philosophicus*. Translated by D. F. Pears and B. F. McGuinness, Routledge, 2001.

Woolf, Virginia. *Moments of Being*. Harcourt Brace, 1976.

# Rethinking Femininity
# and Masculinity

4

# The Cultural Montage of the Sexual

Alexander Miller

## Overview and Trajectory

The concept of the cultural montage of the sexual brings together a series of hypotheses, observations, and insights that bear upon the relation of the individual and the collective. Philosophical and anthropological in nature, these are organized in relation to a clinical understanding of what many refer to since Lacan as the speaking being. More precisely, with this concept Apollon accounts for the manner in which gender, sex, and sexuality are called upon to ensure the collective's control over each individual. The cultural montage—an ensemble of discourses, images, values, practices, and so on—is understood to do this by mediating one's relation to their own being: conditioning experience, formatting affectivity, and canalizing desire toward the objectives of the group. In short, it is a question of how sex and its many avatars are substituted for unconscious desire, the better to ensure the stability and reproduction of social forms of existence. This can be understood to begin in childhood, or well before, but Apollon emphasizes the encounter with the cultural montage of the sexual at puberty, as the child begins to enter into reproductive maturity and the world around them transforms.

To elucidate this concept, I suggest that we must consider it from two distinct but interrelated perspectives: on the one hand, along the lines of a "social fact" in the classic Durkheimian sense of the term, that is, as a "system with a life of its own," "diffused throughout the society," "independent of the particular conditions or of the individuals in which it is located"; and on the other, with respect to a logic of lived experience for the subject confronted with this social fact, and especially as concerns the effect of this encounter. Apollon conceives of this effect in terms of *symbolic castration*. So doing, he both takes up and transforms one of the central problematics in the history of psychoanalysis. I thus consider the broad outlines of how castration was approached in the work of Freud and Lacan, whose contributions Apollon has inherited but also reworked. We will not only derive insights from each but will consider some of the grounds for a reconceptualization of this problematic. Then I have to introduce other key concepts of Apollon's metapsychology, without which an understanding of the cultural montage of the sexual as the operator of symbolic castration can hardly be brought to light.

Among the results of Apollon's reformulations, one in particular deserves to be highlighted from the outset: the orientation it provides for clinical practice. A primary objective of the psychoanalysis practiced in Quebec City has become *the traversal of symbolic castration*, often discussed in terms of the subject "getting out" of the cultural montage. Insofar as the montage is understood as a key to the articulation of the individual and collective, psychoanalytic practice and the metapsychology that informs it can thus be understood to arrive at a displacement of these categories, opening onto what I refer to as the transindividual dimension of the human. Apollon offers an unprecedented definition of the object of the psychoanalytic experience as "the human, insofar as it would be still to come," an "object" to be discovered by the analysand beyond the various manners in which the cultural montage of the sexual conditions experience (see ch. 1 in this volume). The cultural montage is thus understood to occlude this object, this dimension, this experience—in the most general terms, to *censor the human*. We will come to understand this more precisely to occur by way of a *censoring of the feminine* and a *control of aesthetic feeling*. We can begin to explore this topic by way of an example.

## Moms-in-Waiting: Femininity and Maternity

In 2006, the national public health agency of the United States (the CDC) issued guidelines intended to promote and improve "preconception health care" (Johnson et al.). Preconception care refers to a range of measures intended to maximize the probability that women enter pregnancy in optimal health. Not limited to women planning a pregnancy, the CDC recommends that "all women of childbearing age receive preconception care services," that such services be integrated into primary care "from menarche to menopause," and that men, too, be encouraged to have a "reproductive life plan" (Johnson et al.). In the *Washington Post*, this was summarized as follows: "New federal guidelines ask all females capable of conceiving a baby to treat themselves [. . .] as pre-pregnant, regardless of whether they plan to get pregnant anytime soon" (Payne).

The terms "pre-pregnant," "pre-pregnancy," 'and "preconception" emerged into the lexicon of the English language with our entry into the twenty-first century.[1] An internet search today yields results from the CDC, the UK's National Health Service, Planned Parenthood, WebMD, and more—results that testify to the manner in which these terms have been positioned by governmental and medical authorities of the Anglophone world with the intention of modifying the attitudes and behaviors of the population. Epidemiological objectives notwithstanding, we are dealing with a discursive operation, leading onto and supported in turn by a range of practices and institutions, referred to as the "promotion of consumer awareness" or the modification of "knowledge, attitudes, and practices." From a different angle, it is not difficult to assert that, having been elevated to the rank of keywords, or "master-signifiers," in the marketing strategy of a governmental initiative, these terms function as part of a targeted campaign the objective of which is to mediate women's relations to themselves.

One need not dismiss the validity of a concern with pregnancy outcomes to view this initiative slightly askance. And indeed, a range of critical responses has been offered.[2] Adding to these, what I would like to call attention to is the fact that both anthropologists and primatologists have attested that the physiological maturation of reproductive functions, across human societies and even in the case of other primate species, is greeted by a logic that is elaborated *socially*—that is, in a manner that has to be considered irreducible to the biological facts to which it responds (Godelier 583, 591).[3] Simply put, a collective response to the entry of each generation into sexual maturity can be understood as an imperative internal to the logic of social organization insofar as the regulation of sexuality and desire amounts to a condition of possibility for the existence of a group as group and its reproduction over time. On this basis, one must take seriously the idea that, in this initiative, "the experts were guided by cultural, not biomedical, logics" (Waggoner 346).

And in a sense, a collective attention to the production of a new generation of mothers can be understood as the most fundamental imperative there is vis-à-vis the logics of a given society. Apollon refers to this in terms of the *inscription of women within the cultural function of maternity*. This is the case for the most obvious of reasons: without mothers, and the children that pass through their wombs and care, a given society, in its determinate forms of organization, will not survive. Present-day phenomena would seem to affirm the validity of erecting this observation to the status of an analytical principle—whether ongoing efforts of think tanks and governments to respond to declining birth rates, or to prevent access to the termination of pregnancies (Rindfuss and Choe). As one writer on the topic has noted, "we have a fairly unique moment in the history of the world: there's never (before) been a time when people have voluntarily produced fewer children than is necessary for sustaining the population" (Wilson Center).[4] From the standpoint of social reproduction, this poses a considerable problem: a new generation of workers will not replace the previous, power the economy, support the old in retirement, and so on, which threatens the very stability of contemporary societies.

As concerns our topic, I simply propose that we consider the idea that the novelty of this situation may help to bring long-standing dynamics to light. Meanwhile, neither the profound historical continuity nor the relative rupture this initiative represents has gone unnoticed, with one commentator asserting, "for the first time, a U.S. government institution was explicitly saying what social norms had always hinted at: All women, regardless of whether they have or want children, are moms-in-waiting" (Valenti). To be sure, this doesn't mean every girl will be obligated to become a mother, but that an imperative deriving from the norm will be there and will have to be negotiated one way or another. In considering this from a metapsychological perspective, let's take note of how integration within preconception care is to be accomplished: at the precise moment the existence of the girl as child has been upended by an unprecedented effusion of blood, an interpellation is issued by individuals and institutions endowed with the moral authority of the collective—in this case, those supported by a faith in science in a period in which its authority has come to be taken for granted. The culture responds to this disruption by providing the meaning of an experience, calling on a "natural" order to do so, and presenting the girl with an unmistakable image of her future.

Moreover, the future in question is not simply that of the girl, but of the girl as mother of a child, raising the issue of the future well-being of that child. As this initiative was implemented, a marketing campaign was developed that called on the girl to "show her love" for her future child by preparing for an eventual pregnancy—that is, by seeing and treating herself as pre-pregnant.[5] It's worth underlining an obvious point: this future child is a strictly imaginary object, a "phantom fetus" in the words of Waggoner, who has described this process as the cultivation of an "ethic of anticipatory motherhood" ("Cultivating the Maternal Future" 942). Recourse to this imaginary object, which is brought into the girl's consciousness by medical and moral authorities, serves to orient thought, behavior, desire, self-image, and so on. A cultivation and mobilization of feelings (of responsibility, care, love, etc.) and their orientation toward the objectives of the society thus appear as a crucial measure in this undertaking. And this does not, in fact, merely encourage a certain manner of "showing" one's love; it provides the pubescent with the very definition of what love is or should be.

It is for these reasons that I propose we consider this a privileged, if late-arriving, manifestation of what Apollon refers to as the cultural montage of the sexual. More specifically, it presents us with what is understood to be the primary modality of the operation of the montage on the side of the women: *the censoring of femininity by way of the cultural function of maternity*. In the simplest terms, by preparing the child for her role as mother, whatever she might desire beyond her eventual children will be subordinated to a social destiny marked out for her by the group. Though in a sense it is as simple as that, considering Apollon's perspectives on this topic will require situating each of the terms in question (femininity, desire, culture, feeling, etc.) in relation to the sort of philosophical anthropology that this metapsychology provides.

To get a glimpse of the perspective we will be developing, consider the following statement from Lacan: "the speaking body," he says, "only succeeds in reproducing itself by way of a misunderstanding [. . .], that is, it only reproduces thanks to a failure of what it wants to say" (Lacan, *Le séminaire livre* XX 109). Not an indictment of the choice to start a family, it is a question here of the subordination, logically necessary from a psychoanalytic perspective, of a supposedly "natural desire" to procreate to the question of unconscious desire, as well as the relation of this latter to speech. After all, any individual will have lived and desired for more than a decade before arriving at puberty and the gradual inauguration into adult sexuality that now begins. Nor will the thoughts, feelings, experiences, aspirations, and so on that have preceded this, as well as those that will never fit into the new frameworks that will then be erected, somehow magically lose their power once life becomes a question, according to the messages that circulate around them, of birds and bees.

It should be clear, meanwhile, that the implications of the confrontation with the cultural montage of the sexual must be understood to extend well beyond the question of biological reproduction. We have seen how, in addition to the question of desire and its interpretation, an understanding of the lived experience of such feelings as responsibility, care, and love is at stake. It is this we can conceive of in terms of *the control of aesthetic feeling*.

Finally, as concerns the child's experience, it is not difficult to see that something like preconception care, whatever forms its implementation might take, is but a single example of the how the society will reflect back to the girl that her physiological maturation has become a collective concern, thoroughly overwritten with expectations and demands that have little to do with her previous experience, relation to her body, or desire—in short, with her subjectivity. She will confront the same, albeit in a different manner, in the covetous or anticipatory gaze, the "complimentary" or derogatory comments of those around her who would evaluate the transformation of the organism as, in Apollon's words, the "newest commodity" to enter circulation in the marketplace of sexual desire. The concept of the cultural montage, understood as a social fact with which the being is confronted, encompasses such phenomena as well.

The crucial point in all of this is that such a confrontation cannot but disrupt the manner in which the child lives her relations to herself and to others, introducing a unique and pronounced discontinuity with the entry into puberty. So, how might we better understand the experience of the child when confronted with the discourses, practices, images, and so forth that would provide the meaning of sexual maturity? How might we understand the effect of this experience on the ongoing structuration of subjectivity, its impact on the transition from childhood through puberty and adolescence (three moments, as we will see, to be strictly distinguished from one another)?

I return to this question of the lived experience of puberty in the final sections of this chapter. First, I take up two additional questions, an exploration of which situates the problematic and thus helps provide keys for an eventual response. How is it that these dynamics have come to be conceived of as the very core of what is at stake in psychoanalysis? How do the effects of such an experience come to be designated in terms of *symbolic castration*, a notion that has been employed in the Lacanian tradition to designate a fundamental loss, coextensive with integration in a socio-symbolic order, and around which an individual existence will be organized?

## Part One: Castration between Psychoanalysis and Anthropology

### FREUD AND IMAGINARY REPRESENTATIONS OF THE SEXED BODY

It was of course Freud who established the castration complex as a crucial factor in psychic life, when he identified it as the primary effect of the discovery of the anatomical difference of the sexes ("On the Sexual Theories of Children"). Freud proposed that when the child is confronted with the absence of a penis, this perceived lack is attributed to the organ having been cut off. Soon posited as a universal feature of the psyche, the complex deriving from this combination of discovery and speculation was understood to take different forms on each side of this difference, while its various modalities were thought to be observable in all psychopathological structures. In short, tightly interwoven with the Oedipus complex—or more generally, the regulation of sexuality and desire—the differential relation of girls and boys to castration was understood to set the pathways by way of which they would attain maturity as women and men; and it was in relation to these dynamics that psychopathological disturbances were understood to arise. In *Totem and Taboo*, Freud situated the castration complex at the heart of human cultural order, with the "threat of castration" from the primal father ensuring its emergence as the incest prohibition ("On the Sexual Theories of Children").[6]

At the ontogenetic level, the castration complex was understood, for the boy, to be manifested most characteristically in castration anxiety, deriving from a perceived threat made by the father against precocious sexual activity. It was thus considered the terminal crisis of the Oedipus complex, the overcoming of which marked acceptance of paternal prohibition and entry into the period of latency. This was thought to allow for a "normal" sexual development, with the polymorphous perversity of infantile sexuality supplanted at puberty by the genital organization taken to be characteristic of maturity for the male. This, in turn, would enable a sexual relation to a woman, this eventual relation compensating the child for what he had renounced: the use of sexuality in the family. For the girl, the castration complex was thought to be most characteristically manifested in what Freud referred to with the much-reviled term penis envy: the girl experiences herself as lacking something the boy has been given and wishes to gain possession of the same. In contrast to the boy, this marks the entry into Oedipus, with the girl turning away from her mother, whom she blames for what she hasn't been given, and redirecting her libidinal life toward the father, who, as bearer of the phallus, would be capable of compensating this lack. This, too, prepares for sexual maturity: most fundamentally, for the role of mother, with a baby arriving as compensation for what the girl experienced herself as deprived of.[7]

By way of the castration complex and its resolution, girl and boy are thus prepared for their roles as man and woman (husband and wife, mother and father . . .) within the forms of life proper to bourgeois Vienna at the turn of the twentieth century. In both cases, the economic logic, through which *a lack or loss is to be compensated upon attaining a mature sexual position*, is clear.

And though the importance granted to the penis has been criticized, leading anthropologists today affirm Freud's intuition as to the importance of imaginary representations of the body in integrating individuals within the organizing frameworks of a given society.[8] They also supplement Freud, however, by calling attention to the fact that it is not only a question of the penis but of the sexed body more generally and, in particular, representations pertaining to bodily fluids and procreation: semen and ejaculation on one side, menstruation on the other. This perspective lends credence to the idea that the entry into puberty—at which Freud's account of psychosexual development ends but which for Apollon is a moment of intensified conflictuality rather than resolution, which must be conceived of in relation to the experience of adolescence that follows—can be understood to be crucial to stamping "each person's innermost subjectivity with the order(s) that prevail and that must be respected if society is to be reproduced," in the words of the anthropologist Maurice Godelier ("Bodies, Kinship, and Power(s)" 315).

An anthropological perspective on this, as we have begun to see, also emphasizes another crucial consideration: the role of these representations with respect to social reproduction. This psychosexual developmental process cannot be conceived of in isolation in terms of the individual's progression to a supposedly normal maturity; rather, this very pathway toward "individual maturity" must be understood as part of a deeper logic conditioning the cultural production of adult members of a given society. Godelier has accounted for these dynamics in terms of the "double metamorphosis that occurs in all societies" (*Métamorphoses de la parenté* 663).

The first metamorphosis is that "social content"—content pertaining essentially to political, religious, and economic rather than kinship relations—penetrates kinship relations and subordinates them to their own ends: the social becomes, let no psychoanalyst forget, the familial. The second is that these transformed kinship relations—which traditionally bear upon such concerns as inheritance, the sexual division of labor, and the appropriation and rearing of children—determine in turn the content ascribed to the relations between the sexes, the generations, and different members of the same generation, positioning each individual within a sociocultural matrix that determines the obligations and expectations, the social role to be fulfilled with their very being.

At the broadest level, the dynamics of social reproduction are thus understood to infiltrate and to determine the formation of sexed identities and the nature of relations between the sexes, the heart of castration and Oedipus since Freud. This entails the subordination of one dimension of human life—sexuality, broadly conceived—to the reproduction of these other relations. A given society works in and through sexuality, constraining it to a function of legitimizing realities other than itself and inscribing biological mechanisms in service of these ends. As a result of this double metamorphosis, Godelier writes, "the difference between the sexes is transformed into the difference between 'genders'" (*Métamorphoses de la parenté* 663), in that relational differences deriving from societal and kinship systems are made into attributes of sexed bodies:

> It is thus that sexed bodies, due to the fact that some have a penis, others a vagina, that some secrete sperm, others milk, become bodies of a particular "gender" and start to work as ventriloquist's dolls, holding in permanence a discourse on

the order that reigns in their society—the order between the sexes, the sexual order, but also the political order; in short, the order, in all its forms, that unite the different components of the society, the ensemble of activities of individuals and groups, in a whole to be reproduced. (637)

If we place it within such an anthropological reflection, we can recognize in the classical account of the castration complex in bourgeois Vienna a description of the process of production of these "ventriloquist's dolls," that is, men and women who would take up their place within the dynamics of social reproduction, to the point of becoming mouthpieces of the culture in which they've been reared. Apollon, for his part, renders such an argument in a lapidary formula: *every society produces the men and the women it needs.* We glimpsed this in our opening example: the women the society needs, most fundamentally, are mothers, which requires that they pass through what Freud referred to as "an ancient symbolic equivalence" through which a child would compensate a lack (Freud, *New Introductory Lectures* 128). But we should resist reductive understandings of this claim: it is not necessary for a given individual to participate in the biological reproduction of the species to participate in the reproduction of the society, nor is it necessary for lack to be equated with the absence of a penis. What is most fundamental here is this question of speech.

What should also be clear is that an intimate conflict cannot but be introduced in the life of the individual. On the one hand, the culture that is instilled in them, and focalized around questions of gender and sex, amounts to the means through which the society reproduces itself, thus leading toward ends of its own, to be attained by way of the individual's fulfillment of an ideal proposed by the group. On the other, there will remain the question of the individual's own experience and desire, which we will understand to be irreducible to what any given culture would impose or prescribe. Before we enter into Apollon's metapsychology to bring out the implications of this contradiction—the operation of "the ventriloquial machine of society" Godelier, *Métamorphoses de la parenté* 433) versus the question of what the individual "wants to say"—let's consider another set of reference points.

LACAN, LÉVI-STRAUSS, AND THE TRANSCENDENCE OF THE SYMBOLIC

The problematic of castration retained its organizing role in Lacan's redevelopment of psychoanalytic theory, but it was subject to considerable revision. I will not enter into the details of these reformulations but trace their outlines to consider the movement from Freud to Lacan and from Lacan to Apollon. I want to first call attention to how Lacan redeveloped the Freudian castration complex in the early period of his work, but then also consider the limits of what was developed, and hence the relativity of the early account of symbolic castration, which has continued to predominate in much of the reception of his work.

It is well-known that Lacan's "Return to Freud" was heavily influenced by Claude Lévi-Strauss and the structuralist paradigm he ushered into the social sciences in France. In *The Elementary Structures of Kinship*, Lévi-Strauss proposed what quickly became a canonical interpretation of the incest prohibition, the phylogenetic correlate to what psychoanalysis deals with in terms of castration at an ontogenetic level. In so doing, Lévi-Strauss rejoined a key aspect of Freud's analysis in *Totem and Taboo*: the incest prohibition was made to account for the emergence of human social organization, or for the famous passage "from nature to culture." Whereas Freud, however, speculatively traced the incest prohibition to a singular historical event—the murder of the primal father—the effects of which were thought to be transmitted through the generations, the anthropologist proposed a structural account, attributing it instead to "the emergence of symbolic thought," which, he explains, "must have required that women, like words, should be things that were exchanged" (Lévi-Strauss, *Les structures élémentaires* 569).

In other words, reproaching Freud for succumbing to the temptation of a historical sociology, for Lévi-Strauss, the incest prohibition had to be grounded more fundamentally in a cognitive process. It had to be the case that women could appear to men not only as objects of one's own sexual desire but also of the desire of others, which could only be attributed to the capacity for symbolic thought, which enables in this case the perception of a single woman under these two incompatible aspects (569). Only on this basis could women be viewed by men as objects of exchange—that is, as the means for forming alliances with other groups. The emergence of symbolic thought was thus considered coextensive with the institution of exchange and the principle of reciprocity, which were understood as the very foundation of human societies.

This repositioned what Freud had been considering largely in terms of family dynamics and individual psychosexual development in relation to a broader system of social organization. But to do so, the symbolic function was elevated to the status of a privileged theoretical operator. In the words of Godelier, the emergence of symbolic thought functions as "something like the equivalent of a Big Bang" (*Métamorphoses de la parenté* 564) in Lévi-Strauss's account of anthropogenesis: it is made into a transcendental condition beyond which neither analysis nor experience can reach; human social organization as such is understood to be its derivative.

Seeking to place psychoanalysis on sounder epistemological footing by situating it in relation to the structuralist revolution, Lacan largely adopted the framework Lévi-Strauss had brought to bear. He affirmed the transcendence of the symbolic, declaring it "absolutely irreducible to what is commonly called human experience" and insisting that it "cannot be deduced from any historical or psychological starting point.⁹" With respect to the problematic of castration, Lacan insisted that, rather than being theorized at the level of the imaginary phenomena identified by Freud (castration anxiety and penis envy), it be approached at the level of "man's relation to the signifier," that is, with respect to "the laws that regulate" the operation of language (Lacan, "The Signification of the Phallus" 578). Lacan thus undertook a reconceptualization of the castration complex in relation to this understanding of the incest prohibition as deriving from the symbolic function. He reformulated the Oedipus complex as the paternal metaphor, offering a formalization of a primordial process of signification through which a subject enters the symbolic order that regulates interhuman exchange ("On a Question Preliminary to any Possible Treatment of Psychosis"). As he advanced, Lacan would cease referring to the castration complex, speaking instead of symbolic castration, which has come to be understood by many along the lines of a transcendental condition of experience, an irrevocable loss—the loss of unmediated satisfaction—attributable to the "symbolic operation of language" (Evans 13).

Importantly, Lacan's insistence on a lack or loss more radical than those deriving from a castration threat or penis envy denaturalized the Freudian account, displacing interpretations of Freud that would propose a happy genitality within the conjugal family as telos of individual development. At the same time, the primacy Lacan afforded to the phallus as a symbolic element at play within systems of exchange helped to clarify how individuals are led down these pathways nonetheless: a lack carved into being by the very operation of symbolic systems calls for supplementation, and hence opens onto the logic of compensation I've highlighted above. In this manner, Lacan's attention to the symbolic register helped to establish the psychoanalytic perspective that "in the psyche, there is nothing by which the subject may situate himself as a male or female being" (*Le séminaire livre XI: Les quatres concepts* 186), as a result of which "orders and norms must be instituted which tell the subject what a man or a woman must do" ("Position of the Unconscious" 720).

It must also be noted, however, that this framework drew support from counterexamples such as psychosis, in which a failure of symbolic castration was understood as a faulty integration within the symbolic order, demonstrating the importance still granted to the normative and normalizing functions of the Oedipus complex. Where Oedipus and castration failed, where the individual could not be led via conventional frameworks to the adoption of a supposedly masculine or feminine position, psychopathological disturbances were understood to arise. For this reason, symbolic castration came to be conceived of within the Lacanian tradition as a *salutary operation* (Maleval 106). Indeed, it has been widely understood as the condition of possibility of desire, inseparable from the very advent of subjectivity.[10] Accordingly, what has generally prevailed is the idea that analysis should be oriented around the *assumption* of symbolic castration, that is, the subjective acceptance of "the lack on the basis of which desire is instituted" (Lacan, "On Freud's Trieb" 723).

We can see how the early approach leads onto such an understanding: if the loss suffered by the individual is effectively transcendentalized, if it is attributed to the sheer facticity of language as a formal system, and is hence inseparable from integration within the symbolic, one can only accept or come to terms with this loss. The alternative, at the limit, would be psychosis, which most Lacanians have understood to entail an exclusion of the subject from desire.[11] This latter understanding, however, is firmly contested in Apollon's metapsychology, which has been developed precisely on the basis of the clinic of psychosis, and which, as I've noted, does not envision symbolic castration as an unsurpassable horizon, but rather as something to be *traversed*—that is, both "traveled through," so to speak, and overcome, with the result that what was lost as a result of this operation is, in a sense, regained over the course of the analytic experience.

Such a position does not entail a return to a mythical plenitude of enjoyment, the object of Lacan's early critique. At stake in this point of difference is an apprehension of the nature of the loss inflicted by way of integration into socio-symbolic systems, a question that is occluded if this loss is attributed too quickly to "language." And indeed, there are fundamental objections to be offered to a transcendentalizing approach to symbolic castration. Not least among these is the fact that neither Lacan nor Lévi-Strauss would continue to adhere to the "big bang" hypothesis that served as its axiomatic support.[12] This does not dispel the significance of all that was developed by Lacan on the basis of this early approach. But it's worth considering how he would himself move beyond these early elaborations, as this will further prepare us for Apollon's reconceptualization of symbolic castration in turn.[13]

## FROM THE SIGNIFIER TO THE SOCIAL LINK: LATE TRANSFORMATIONS IN LACAN

As I have emphasized, Lacan approached castration in his early work largely on the basis of a classically structuralist attention to language as an abstract formal system. He positioned this in contradistinction to a consideration of "language as a social phenomenon," an orientation he denounced as "culturalist" (Lacan, "The Signification of the Phallus" 578). That it was ever possible to strictly distinguish between these two approaches, as concerns the relation of the living being to language, is a debate I won't enter into. My simpler contention is that Lacan himself eventually changed his position; and more importantly for us, that Apollon in turn is unambiguous in foregrounding the status of language as a social phenomenon, and in situating symbolic castration in relation thereto.

As concerns Lacan, an important shift was accomplished with the development of the theory of discourse that became central to his work in the late 1960s and early 1970s. I have demonstrated elsewhere how this was part of a broader movement in French intellectual life that sought to escape from certain aspects of the structuralist paradigm, in particular the classical distinction between *la langue* and *la parole*, which established the conception of language as an abstract formal system.[14] In this movement beyond the limits of Saussure, who loomed so large in the early work, the emphasis came to be placed increasingly upon language as a social phenomenon, or what we can conceive of in terms of the socio-pragmatic or again the cultural function of language. Hence Lacan's emphasis from this point forward on *discourse as social link*.

It's worth briefly recalling the meaning of this term social link, specifically insofar as it had been popularized by Emile Durkheim. For the sociologist, the social link consists of two forms of relation between the individual and society: a relation of *integration*, which designates "the manner in which individuals are attached to the society," and a relation of *regulation*, which designates "the way in which society regulates those individuals" (Paoletti 276). In bringing together the terms "discourse" and "social link" as he did, Lacan effectively endorses and develops the idea that "language contains society" (Benveniste 95) or that "no language is separable from a cultural function" (Benveniste 24). To be sure, for Lévi-Strauss and the early Lacan, language and social organization were intimately related, but the theory of discourse entails a different perspective on this problematic: it's a question of how the symbolic functions in service of the social, rather than how the social as such derives from and is coextensive with the symbolic function.[15] This suggests a repositioning of the question of symbolic castration in relation to the sociological problematic of integration and regulation, which is how we will pursue it below.

Subsequent transformations in Lacanian theory confirm the upheaval at play. First, there is the fact that in the wake of the development of the theory of discourse, Lacan revisited the concepts of *la langue* and *la parole* by way of the neologism *lalangue*. This latter accounts for a *form of speech disconnected from the structure of language* (J.-A. Miller 64) and imbued with an enigmatic jouissance. Crucially, *lalangue* was granted logical and chronological priority with respect to language as such. Indeed, in elaborating on this concept, Lacan would flatly declare: "language, in the first instance, doesn't exist" (Lacan, *Le séminaire livre XX: Encore* 126). Linguistic structure has been unambiguously downgraded from its status as transcendental condition of experience and is now conceived of as secondary, even as a response to something that calls for the organization it provides.[16] Theoretical attention is now increasingly brought to bear on what is active within the living being prior to and in excess of their entry into language, while the very understanding of the unconscious begins to shift in relation to this concept.[17]

Contemporaneous to the transition from discourse to *la langue* was Lacan's development of the formulas of sexuation through which castration was rethought in the 1970s. If language now, in a sense, does not exist, it can hardly remain the transcendental operator of an irrecuperable loss. This does not eliminate the question of the effect of language on the living being, but relativizes and repositions it. With the formulas of sexuation, Lacan thus begins to account for a subjective position "not-all" submitted to symbolic castration, explicitly affirming the contingency and the partiality of what was previously conceived of as a law.[18] This subjective position, as is well-known in Lacanian literature, is characterized by a corporeal experience—a mode of jouissance—"beyond the phallus," and thus referred to as "feminine."

The famous "other jouissance" understood by Lacan to be at stake in the feminine position has, however, remained an enigmatic designation for many. Lacan himself found few words to characterize it other than "crazy," while making reference to mystical experience in his effort to depict it (*Le séminaire livre XX: Encore*). Nonetheless, it is clear at this point in his work that inscribing oneself on the "feminine side" of sexuation was considered a possibility open to all, inscription being determined not by anatomy but by the relation one entertains to the "phallic function," which is characterized as "what the relation between the signifier and jouissance produces" (*Le séminaire livre XXI: . . . ou pire* 31). Rather than rendering jouissance impossible,[19] then, symbolic castration is now characterized by the predominance of a particular type of corporeal experience, a specific mode of jouissance—phallic jouissance, also referred to as "sexual jouissance" and even as "the jouissance of the idiot"—rather than the feminine jouissance that is situated beyond castration.

These transformations all point to the limits of the conceptual architecture erected in the 1950s. Taken together, they open onto the affirmation that a dimension of the living being subsists beyond the reach of language and in excess of the loss deriving from integration into the symbolic order. Despite these upheavals, Lacan would continue to adhere to a synchronic perspective, an orientation manifested in and consolidated by his epistemological concern with formalization. On this basis, he offered comparatively little attention to historical and sociological factors that condition a subject's inscription on one side or the other of sexuation.

We have begun to consider above how the formation of sexed identities cannot be separated from a reflection on transgenerational modes of social organization. Read from the perspective of Apollon's interventions in psychoanalytic theory, the formulas of sexuation can be taken to account for "modes of jouissance"—at once forms of corporeal experience, manners of enjoying, and modes of relation to language—that subtend these dynamics. The cultural montage of the sexual will thus be understood to serve the purpose of promoting the phallic to the detriment of the feminine. But crucially, when taking this up with Apollon, the feminine will be understood more capaciously as a constitutive dimension of what he refers to as the human. This implies that symbolic castration refers not only to the emptying of (feminine) jouissance from the body but to the manner in which an individual's access to a dimension of their being comes to be barred.

## Part Two: Apollon's Metapsychology

At this point, I enter into a deeper consideration of Apollon's broader theoretical perspectives. In so doing, I offer cursory accounts of several major concepts treated elsewhere in this volume, taking up only particular aspects of these in relation to our problematic. For fuller treatments of these concepts, the reader should refer to the other chapters of this volume.

### Real Castration: The Effraction of the Psyche by the Spirit

We've seen how symbolic castration came to comprise an unsurpassable horizon for many Lacanians: taken to be synonymous with a primordial loss, with the productivity of lack, it has served as the key to the theory of desire. Apollon, to be sure, does not do away with lack, negativity, and dehiscence, pillars of the Lacanian clinic.[20] But to account for them, he has introduced the concept of real or primary castration, which is defined as *the effraction of the psyche by the spirit*. This allows for a resolution of the conflation between the supposedly transcendental dimensions of symbolic castration and the contingency, partiality, and relativity with which this notion is also marked—a disambiguation that is accomplished insofar as symbolic castration comes to be understood as a secondary, derivative operation vis-à-vis this real castration.

The foundational concept of this metapsychology thus becomes the agent of real castration: *the spirit* (*l'esprit*), which is defined as "the lived experience of a capacity to represent to oneself what doesn't exist, to want it, and, as needed, to give oneself the means to create it" (Apollon; see ch. 1 in this volume). With this concept, Apollon foregrounds, among other things, what he considers a fundamental Freudian postulate: that the representations "with which a human being is always grappling" do not have empirical correspondents or do not appear within the reality that is conditioned by, even constructed within, the cultural function of language ("The Untreatable" 27). He refers to these as *pure mental representations*: representations the object of which is not given through sensible experience. The crucial point is that such representations are no less real for not corresponding to a consensual reality: both the psychoanalytic clinic and any consideration of our history attest that it is in relation to such representations that the human being "organizes [. . .] its thoughts, actions, and objectives [. . .] its entire personal and social existence" ("The Untreatable" 27). Nor are they to be "corrected" via therapeutic or pharmacological intervention. To make the clinical objective subduing this capacity of the spirit, understood to be the source of the unique creativity of the human being, would amount to reinforcing symbolic castration rather than enabling the more demanding procedure of its traversal.

The effect of this real castration on the living being, however, is no small thing; and of course, there can be no guarantee that the inventiveness, ingenuity, and the at times unbridled desire of homo sapiens will be turned to beneficial ends, whether for oneself or for others. Apollon thus often appends to this definition of the spirit . . . "for better or worse."

For indeed, real castration accounts for a profound disruption in our being—the effraction of the psyche—which can lead to any variety of outcomes. The psyche is understood here as an evolutionary inheritance through which the organism regulates its relation to the physical and social environment. Its effraction refers to a disruption of this function, by way of the diversion of energy from the adaptive and self-preservational functions of the psyche, an energy that will push the being toward ends other than adaptation and self-preservation. Primary castration thus accounts for a *rupture of the limits* proper to the principles of reality and pleasure. Rather than serving to integrate the subject within symbolic frameworks, this inaugurates a dimension of the being, first and foremost a dimension of experience, that is radically beyond their reach, and that will remain unintegrated within and unregulated by the ego and the social link.

It should be clear, then, that there will be no question of overcoming or evading castration as such; the question will continue to pertain to how the subject will, if one wishes to remain within a Lacanian idiom, subjectivize the lack deriving from this castration. But this clarifies the understanding of lack at stake in such a formulation: what lacks, fundamentally, are the limits that would constrain the individual to reality and pleasure, which, taken together, amount to the pursuit of pleasure within the culturally determined dictates of reality within the social link, to which Lacanian "phallic jouissance" is effectively subsumed. What Lacan identified as feminine jouissance, on the other hand, is understood to be at stake from infancy onward, as an experience resulting from primary castration.[21] Indeed, this alone for Apollon is to be referred to as jouissance.

This conception of primary castration will have consequences for the entirety of the metapsychology. Our limited objective here is to develop an understanding of how it informs the reconceptualization of symbolic castration, which we will attempt to home in on by circumscribing the action of the cultural montage at puberty. To get there, we must consider how the effects of real castration play out over the course of the processes through which the child is progressively integrated within socio-symbolic frameworks. Apollon schematizes this in terms of four key moments in the structuration of the subject: first and second childhoods, puberty, and adolescence.

## The Address and the Unaddressable

With the action of the spirit inaugurating a dimension of lived experience inaccessible to anyone but the subject herself, subjective experience as such is understood to be of the order of the *singular* and the *unobservable*. Indeed, it can be inaccessible even to the ego consciousness that will be formed in the Mirror under the eyes of the Other. Real castration thus results in a series of "intimate experiences that cannot be repeated and that cannot be made accessible to others," unless, that is, "the subject decides to establish them in speech" ("The Untreatable" 27).

This is of course the very foundation of the clinical situation, which hangs on the question: Through what means might the analyst enable the subject to take the risk of a type of speech that would evoke lived experiences that are inaccessible, yet around which their existence turns? But well prior to that, this is a problematic that accompanies the being through life, and which we can conceive of in relation to another fundamental concept of Apollon's metapsychology: *the address*, understood here in a restrained sense to refer to the search for a "pathway of expression" for what cannot otherwise be perceived (see ch. 8 of this volume). Never merely a question of conscious volition, the effects of the effraction traverse the individual and exceed the control of ego consciousness, impelling the dynamics of the address through which the being would attempt to convey something of their experience. In first childhood, however, the infant evidently has few means to give expression to what is at work in this other scene, whether terrible or pacific, cherished or abhorred.

As a result, the infant is confronted with a series of experiences that comprise what Apollon refers to as *the unaddressable*, which will constitute the "first level" of the unconscious, outside of and prior to the entry into language. Recalling that real castration entails the disruption of the homeostatic regulation (the pleasure principle), and hence the lived experience of a traversal of the limits of neurophysiological systems (jouissance), what is unaddressable is understood to mark the body, provoking enduring modifications of these systems. Or better, these inscriptions—which Apollon refers to as the *letters of the body* and the specificity of which, in the life of a given individual, can be deduced from clinical phenomena—*create* the body, which is thus understood in contradistinction to the organism. Whereas the organism would be taken as the object of a scientific gaze, susceptible to observation and measurement, the body as written is understood to be composed of erotogenic zones and as the site of experience. What is crucial here is that the body that is progressively created through experience institutes a particular mode of self-relation not to be confused with the ego that develops in a dialectic with the Other in social space.

Indeed, excluded from social space as such, the body will be understood as the site of the time of subjectivity: a nonlinear temporality that is "foreign to the time of the clock" and in which the future, rather than the past, is understood to "overdetermine the present" (see ch. 1 in this volume). Evidently, this is a complex problematic, which I broach only to call attention to a particular aspect: the growing disjunction, already in this delicate period of life, between subjective experience and what is accessible, observable, or nameable in the field of the Other. The child is thus subjected not only to the effects of real castration but likewise to this very disjunction; and from first childhood onward, the body develops as site of experience and as vehicle of an erotism and even a temporality at odds with the formation and consolidation of the ego in the social link.

## The Structure of the Address

What begins to come into focus from this perspective is that the sociological problematic I've identified in terms of the social link must understood along the following lines: integration of the individual within the collective will require the regulation, very precisely, of the spirit and the effects of the effraction. This recasts the traditional Oedipal problematic not in terms of sexual desire but in relation to the concept of the address as we've begun to consider it. Such a displacement is not without precedent, for example, in the late Lacan, who eventually declared that "the sexual relation is speech itself" (Lacan, *Le séminaire livre XXIII: Le sinthome* 83). Apollon proposes a similar identity, though transformed in relation to the rest of this metapsychology: "the address is sex"; that is, the erotism that inhabits the speaking being is understood as the work of an energy, deriving from the effraction of the psyche and inscribed in the letters of the body, in search of a means of expression.

For this reason, the understanding of second childhood will be centered not on the resolution of Oedipal desire and the entry into the so-called latency period but on the development of the ego within the framework of *the structure of the address*, and the repression that results. This is the period, from approximately five to ten years of age, of education and socialization, in which the objective of the society is "the transmission from one generation to the next of a cultural formatting" (see ch. 1 in this volume). The notion of the structure of the address calls attention to the fact that this cultural formatting runs in opposition to the free energy of the erotism and desire that derive from real castration, serving to limit or constrain the expression these will find.

In the simplest terms, the structure of the address, in one of its aspects, is thus "what conditions what one can say to another" (Apollon, "Psychanalyse et mondialisation"). This is accomplished insofar as the Other within the structure of the address is established as the *guardian of the receivable*. In other words, the Other—which can be understood in a Lacanian sense as the locus of the signifier, in which the subject is called to come into being—will be erected as the instance to whom the child might address herself, as the field in which experience might be articulated, but also as the representative of social constraints, thus confronting subjective experience with permissible forms.

Thus, to the child's struggle with what is strictly incommunicable, there is added the question of what can be said, that is, the calculation as to what one can allow the other to know. Dependent as the child is on pleasing the adults around them, repression will come to bear upon that which does not fit into that calculation, adding a "second level" to the unconscious, as what is excluded from the structure of the address continues to be inscribed, deepening, as Apollon writes, "a delicious and intimate bodily wound," still the very site of subjective experience (see ch. 1 in this volume).

## Organizing in Advance the Encounter with the Other

From another vantage point, the structure of the address can also be understood as what *organizes in advance the encounter with the other*, a formulation I derive from Godelier. Considering it in this manner will bring to the light further dimensions of this problematic that are crucial for our movement toward the cultural montage of the sexual, so let us return to the anthropologist's account of the process through which sexed bodies become ventriloquist's dolls:

> Representations of the body determine in each society a sort of ring of social constraints, of an ideal nature, that enclose the individual; a ring that constitutes the very form—paradoxically impersonal, social—of the individual's intimacy. And it's within this social form of intimacy with oneself, which is imposed from birth and *which organizes in advance the encounter with the other*, that the child will begin to live their desire for others. While others have already appropriated the child—their parents, their social group, etc.—the child will spontaneously want to appropriate them. And it's thus that the child will discover that they cannot appropriate all of them, that certain among them—father, mother, sister, brother, etc.—are prohibited to the child's desire. Sexuality as desiring machine opposes itself, ventriloquist's machine of society. (Godelier, *Métamorphoses de la parenté*, 433; my emphasis)

Godelier remains here on the classical terrain of the Oedipus complex, in which sexuality as desire—a lawless, asocial, appropriating desire—is opposed to sexuality inscribed in the service of the production and reproduction of society. While echoing this latter dynamic, Apollon's psychoanalytic perspective also displaces this dichotomy, in that unconscious desire is decoupled from sexuality understood in either of these senses. Likewise, it's crucial to note that this process of ventriloquialization, from a psychoanalytic perspective, can never attain closure: at some point, the unconscious will speak in a voice other than that of Godelier's ventriloquist—if nowhere else, then within the analytic experience, as transference subverts the structure of the address.

Nonetheless, Godelier offers a crucial insight in his description of how these social constraints serve to *organize in advance the encounter with the other*. This returns us to the issue of temporality that was previously raised, as any consideration of social reproduction must do. For to speak of social reproduction, from this perspective, is to speak of a teleology inherent to social organization. To organize in advance what the encounter between two beings might be is to attempt to exercise *a control over becoming in time*—simply put, a control of the future. This offers another iteration of the disjunction we've been tracking: because any conscious agent who has the lived experience of the capacity to represent what does not exist and to desire it thus has the experience of a future, or indeed of futures, that are inaccessible to others, unless, once again, they can be evoked in speech or created, once, with increasing maturity, means to do so have been developed.

This sheds light in turn on another aspect of the address: to communicate such an experience to another being raises the prospect that more than one might collaborate in the realization of imagined futures, which may well run against the objectives of the collective. The structure of the address, through which and within which sexed bodies will be made to speak as men and women, is thus understood to be erected as a safeguard against such a threat: it limits what an individual might introduce into the space of the collective, by conditioning what the relation between any two beings might be. And it does not do so merely by way of empirical prohibitions, but by shaping the field of meaning as such and thus tethering the ego's development to the reality constructed therein, privileging the reality principle over the capacity to represent what doesn't exist and the pleasure principle over experiences that derive from the effraction.

In Apollon's words, "the Other in the structure of the address has the function of deciding the fate of what the subject of speech can count on" (see ch. 1 in this volume)—that is, of tracing the possible pathways of desire within the limits of receivability. In short, it seeks to ensure that the psyche's function of articulating the being to a sociocultural milieu proceeds apace, while the unpredictable effects of the spirit are progressively silenced, as anyone can attest by comparing the manifest creativity of a child to that of the average adult.

## The Cultural Montage as Preventative Measure

Throughout second childhood, integration within the structure of the address is firmly rooted in questions of gender and sex, just as gender and sex are firmly rooted, from this perspective, in the structure of the address. I won't take the time to consider the common gendered dynamics of childhood, which are obvious enough, except to point out that these are to be reconsidered in this context in relation to these Apollonian concepts. And indeed, we have an intuitive understanding of this insofar as the limits of the receivable—what is culturally permissible in behavior, speech, comportment, and so forth, and especially for children as they proceed through second childhood—quite typically pertain to what is acceptable *for a girl* or *for a boy*.

Organized around the anticipated attainment of a sense of sexual identity ultimately considered impossible from a psychoanalytic perspective, the gendered dynamics of childhood can of course be understood as components of the cultural montage in the broadest sense. But it is with puberty that this latter will predominate and will be experienced most acutely. Importantly, this occurs just as the credibility of the cultural values transmitted via the authority of parents, teachers, and so forth threatens to wane, as the child's awareness grows of what is arbitrary in these values, if not violent in their imposition, and what it excludes of their lived experience. The cultural montage of the sexual will thus take the relay, so to speak, from the Other of the structure of the address. But before we attempt to circumscribe the logic of its action, we have to consider more closely what it serves to guard against. I have stated that its function will be to censor the feminine and to control aesthetic sentiment. I've yet to introduce another crucial dimension, which is that the cultural montage is understood to serve as a preventative measure: *its purpose is to contain the experience of adolescence*, which will ensue in the wake of the passage through puberty. It is therefore the interrelation of the feminine, the aesthetic, and adolescence that we must try to apprehend.

## The Feminine, the Aesthetic, and Adolescence

We have considered how the child, from first childhood onward, is confronted with a series of experiences that entail the traversal of the neurophysiological limits of the organism. This "insistent work of the effraction" ("The Untreatable" 29) can be understood as jouissance; unbounded by the phallic function, this jouissance in turn can be characterized as feminine. Rather than simply an enigmatic form of enjoyment, however, the designation feminine thus comes to refer, in a first moment, to "the ensemble of lived experiences, at the level of the body, that cannot pass through language" (Apollon, "Séminaire de Montréal, 2021–2022"). This same experience of the effraction, meanwhile, also "introduces us to the field of the aesthetic" (see ch. 1 in this volume). What Apollon refers to as the aesthetic compensates this loss of limits, supplementing the disorganization of the infant's organism and allowing an unbounded energy to "stop itself at forms which conserve themselves" ("The Subject of the Quest"). It is a question here of the classical aesthetic concept of the feeling of the beautiful, which Apollon understands as pertaining to the experience of something *the loss of which would diminish the human.*

The feminine and the aesthetic are thus inextricably linked from the outset, pertaining at once to lived experiences that exceed control, that cannot be bound by language, and to a certain manner of binding their action nonetheless. As development proceeds, not only is the living being subjected to the dynamics through which a culturally bound ego consciousness is produced, but likewise the *subject's* capacity to manage the disjunction between lived experience and social imperatives and expectations develops and transforms. From this vantage point, the feminine will come to be understood—at a new level, so to speak—as "the capacity that there is within the human to find an aesthetic space for what cannot be said" (Apollon, "Séminaire de Montréal, 2021–2022"). Our understanding of feminine jouissance can be supplemented in turn: it refers not only to an energy unbounded by the signifier, but also, in experience, to the joy that accompanies the aesthetic expression of what is outside language.

To mark what is proper to the register of the aesthetic, meanwhile, Apollon emphasizes feeling (*sentiment*), in opposition to both emotion and affect: whereas these latter derive from the operation of the psyche, and hence are the objects of a cultural formatting (the culture only having access to the individual by way of the psyche), aesthetic feeling is what institutes what I have referred to above as a particular mode of self-relation, not to be confused with the relation to the ego. Apollon characterizes this aesthetic and corporeal mode of self-relation, proper to the subject of the unconscious, as "the awareness of a non-difference or non-gap between time and self" (see ch. 1 in this volume). To simplify, aesthetic experience grounds an identity that stands in contradistinction to the illusory identity of the ego and articulates the individual to the environment on other terms. The form of self-relation that derives from aesthetic feeling is thus necessarily experienced in opposition to the Other that serves as the guardian of the limits of receivability.

With these conceptions in place, we can see why the aesthetic and the feminine become targets of a control at the hands of the collective. The feminine refers to a dimension within each individual that pushes the being beyond the limits of receivability, and that, being irreducible to the dimension of meaning and sense, requires an aesthetic plane for its expression. Aesthetic feeling—a relation to what is outside language within one's own experience, in the time of subjectivity—nourishes a desire that likewise requires a subversion of the structure of the address to find its place. The feminine and the aesthetic are thus at stake precisely where the means through which the individual is inscribed in service of the objectives of the society meet their limit.[22]

But crucially, the conflict here is not to be conceived of, in its essence, as that between a vigilant social order and a lawless desire that would put others in peril. On the contrary, this conflict is conceived of in terms of an opposition between what Apollon refers to as *the human* and the determinate forms of any given culture or society. Not to be confused with a generic humanism, this conception of the human has to be understood as a metapsychological concept, crucial to the understanding of both "psychopathology" and clinical work, in what amounts to a sort of culmination of the problematic of the spirit, effraction, address, and the unaddressable that we have tracked. Insofar as it is situated within this line of concepts and their dialectical unfolding, a *dawning awareness of the human* is understood to be the defining experience of adolescence.

In the experience of adolescence, the conflicts of first and second childhood arrive at a new point of inflection, indeed a radicalization, in that the experience of what Apollon refers to as the defect in language—the experience that nothing in language corresponds to the most intimate exigencies of subjectivity—attains a zenith, or a point of maximal intensity. What distinguishes adolescence from childhood, however, is that it is also a moment of discovery in which an awareness of what is outside language develops in addition to this latter's mere presence or mute insistence. On this basis, not only cultural constraints but even the overarching beliefs of a given civilization—which serve to credibilize those constraints—are experienced as "just a step to go beyond, if not an obstacle to overcome for whoever would effectively concern themselves with what is best for the human"—that is, the dimension of being for which no place is given within the space-time of the collective (see ch. 1 in this volume). The "object" of the experience of adolescence is thus understood to be this dimension of being that transcends both culture and civilization.

Integration within the cultural montage of the sexual at puberty thus serves the purpose of containing the experience of adolescence by imposing on the individual *"an interpretation of what is felt"* (see ch. 1 in this volume). This characterization is crucial in that it pinpoints the provenance of a function of misrecognition not only in "the imaginary" but in what we have referred to as a social fact. The cultural montage of the sexual serves to interpret, or at least attempts to interpret, to the individual their own experience as a sort of filter at the border between perception and consciousness, between the body and the social world. As such, its effect is to censor the feminine—to prevent what is outside language from finding expression—and to separate the individual from what is proper to aesthetic feeling by way of its recuperation.

Apollon's conception of the aesthetic is not limited here to the beautiful, but likewise concerns the sublime. Building off the experience of the beautiful, the sublime is understood as the feeling that confronts the being with something *more important than its own existence*. The discovery of, and the uncertain resolution of, one's relation to the feeling of the sublime is at the heart of this conception of the experience of adolescence. In each of these definitions, we can see how both the object and the feeling in question must be understood to exceed the being qua individual, which is why I have employed the term transindividual.[23] It is on such an axis that Apollon situates his fully developed understanding of the aesthetic, as founded on "the experience that your effect upon others will have consequences" ("Enseignement du Conseil d'éthique à l'EFQ")—that is, that what one says or does will touch the other in an immeasurable way.

Seemingly a rather simple observation, I have called on the resources of a philosophical vocabulary because what is "touched" here is irreducible to the terms of self and other, as well as individual and collective. Rather, it can be thought of as a question of what is within me but also without, within the other but also without, and of a feeling that contains an awareness that one's own being and that of the other do not so much interpenetrate as coincide, specifically via action, speech, and their consequences—which is also to say, with respect to a futurity that is incalculable and yet the object of both desire and care, transcending the stopgap function of any possible satisfaction. This is understood as the very heart of the unconscious, the very object of the psychoanalytic experience. To be sure, aesthetic feeling can be recuperated within cultural and civilizational parameters; the sublime, for example, can be inscribed in a politico-religious order that will put it to work in service of the objectives of a society. But a "successful" adolescence, or an analysis carried to its term, is understood to articulate this dimension of experience, beyond both culture and civilization, to the human as such and to a care for its becoming.

## Puberty and the Cultural Montage of the Sexual

With all this in place, we can return to the rather more mundane question of the experience of puberty, beginning with our suspended interrogation of the cultural function of maternity. From the perspective we've developed, the "phantom fetus" that we've seen to be made stunningly literal by the US government, but that is by no means its innovation, covers over the incalculable at the depths of subjective experience, before it can be truly encountered. This latter is a source of anxiety, to be sure, but also of creativity and desire. Irrespective of whether or not a person ultimately bears and raises children, the cultivation of what we've seen referred to as an "ethics of anticipatory motherhood" will serve the function of turning the child away from this dimension of their being, tracing instead the paths to the fulfillment of a social destiny, and canalizing desire into the development of a sexual identity that will allow for such fulfillment.

It is only too evident what this requires, the impact of which for the child, however, should not be dismissed from the vantage point of the adult: to be pretty enough, to be chosen by a romantic partner, and so forth, which means that aesthetic feeling will be tethered to conventional criteria and that what is at work in the letters of the body will be censored by the imperative to fulfill such criteria. In a sense, we pass from ventriloquial machine to a marionette, in that clothing, figure, gesture, posture, the orientation of the body in space will be fixed by invisible strings to what is perceived in social space as traits that are desirable to the Other.

We have considered how the child will now perceive the body in space, by way of the attitudes and reactions of others, in a different manner. Even in the absence of such behavior in the entourage—that is, in the strictly hypothetical case of a pubescent girl not bombarded by images of the objectified female form as object of satisfaction for men—the presentation to the girl of her own being as ever poised on the cusp of fecundation is enough to trace the image of a certain Other, tethered once again to the central role of imaginary representations of the body and the differential nature of sexed identifications: where the girl will have a baby, the boy will have an ejaculating penis and a grimace of pleasure, which she's called upon to ensure if she's to fulfill the destiny marked out for her by the Other.

As I've noted, the psychoanalytic perspective cannot entail a total subsumption of the individual to these dynamics: the subject of the unconscious remains heterogeneous and will express itself "between the cracks," whether by singularizing the individual's creative response to these imperatives, or in the form of the wide variety of symptoms that will begin to manifest precisely at puberty. Moreover, the pubescent girl can of course refuse the entire affair. But let's add to our understanding another element of Godelier's description of the manner in which the ventriloquial machine of society installs itself in the sexed body.

According to the anthropologist, the sexed body is "constantly invited to speak and to testify for (*or against*) the prevailing social order" (Godelier, "Bodies, Kinship, and Power(s) 315). That is, a relation to the montage characterized primarily by contestation can serve just as well to enclose the individual within the structure of the address, as the classical studies of hysteria attest. The psychoanalytic question, opened up and clarified by Apollon, pertains not to the position one takes up within this montage but to the extent to which the cultural montage of the sexual will function to censor the feminine in the individual and to separate the being from the dimension of the human that is supported by the aesthetic—a question to be unpacked in a singular manner in each analysis. Let's reiterate, then, that what is at stake for us is by no means a mechanical determinism but a confrontation or encounter with a cultural montage, and the fact that this will not be without effects.

For the boy, the experience of puberty will of course be different, but it will likewise be structured in relation to this polarity—that is, the sexual relation as posited by the collective. In particular, there will be the experience of the orgasm, which will similarly upend the constellation of relations through which the child will have situated his being within a sociocultural and familial matrix to that point. As Apollon notes, the collective will recuperate this disruption by valorizing the orgasm as the "specifically masculine experience" (see ch. 1 in this volume) and, hence, something he should know about, which leaves no option but to seek within the dimension of meaning, where convention alone knots relations between signifiers and signifieds. This will likewise carry the child away from what is outside language, since it is only within discourse that any answer, it would seem, could be found. Desire is thus canalized in relation to the phallic function, which, we recall, pertains not simply to the use of the penis but to the predominance of the principles of reality and pleasure. And of course, everything we have considered, however pejoratively, with respect to ventriloquists' dolls, invisible strings, and being enclosed within even the contestation of the imperatives of manhood is understood to apply equally to the boy: the psychoanalytic question bears strictly upon the extent to which the montage will serve to censor the feminine and separate the individual from the body as site of aesthetic experience.

What the boy will find, furthermore, in the established discourses around him, is the idea that this orgasm, Lacan's "jouissance of the idiot," characteristic of those who "think themselves to be male because they have a little stub of a cock" (*Le séminaire livre XXIII: Le sinthome* 15) is the satisfaction he is due in exchange for what he has accommodated of the structure of the address. Pursuing this compensation—however timidly or vociferously, however directly or through whatever displacements—he doesn't realize that what is at stake in this belief and the orientation it would provide is his access to the depths of aesthetic experience, to a jouissance beyond the phallus, not a "sexual" satisfaction but a limitless joy pertaining to the expression of what is outside language. This is thus understood to be the primary modality of the operation of the cultural montage on the side of the male: *the censoring of the feminine by way of the orgasm.*

And in fact, this latter is understood as the primary objective of the cultural montage of the sexual as such: to censor the feminine in the man so as to ensure the woman's reduction to the status of an object of satisfaction. Once again, even in a cultural landscape not flooded with pornography, the logic of representation is enough to assure that this idea of a satisfaction that would put a limit to an unbounded energy at work in the body is accompanied by an other who would assure it—prototypically, of course, a woman. As we see in each case, the question of the Other that is posited within the cultural montage of the sexual is crucial, and this need not be limited to a heteronormative frame. What is understood to be at stake is *the reinforcement of the Other of the structure of the address* at the precise moment at which the constraints that have been operative throughout childhood would begin to lose efficacy. It is here that we approach a deeper layer of the logic of the cultural montage.

As Apollon writes, a child accepts the demands made upon them throughout childhood primarily on the basis of "what [they] experienced in the letters of the body as love" (see ch. 1 in this volume). With puberty, however, the child's very understanding of the lived experience of the feeling of love is put into question: the unprecedented experiences that accompany physiological maturation, in combination with the contradiction between the child's previous experiences and the recuperation of this moment within a cultural montage of the sexual, necessarily raises in a new manner the question of what it is that binds individuals together. How could it not, as the very nature of interhuman relations is redefined by discourses that provide the meaning of sexual maturity?

To approach but one aspect of this, consider the transformations in the relations of boys and girls to one another at this moment. How should the girl, for example, relate to male classmates, companions in childhood to this point, once the new "ideal" relation that accompanies her status as pre-pregnant has been proposed? With the newfound awareness of the place of her organism and her future in the space of the collective, the status of the Other is necessarily transformed. And whether idealized or vilified (these are two sides of the same coin), the Other takes on a new effective force. How should the boy relate to the girl once it has been indicated by the culture that the axis of such a relation is not anything he might say but this supremely dysfunctional organ, which he will have to pretend that he knows how to use, since it is what the montage seems to demand? In either case, as the wall of language erected by the collective takes on new dimensions and is more firmly anchored to the erotism of the body, and as each individual attempts to manage this in their own way, what space remains for an address, for an aesthetic relation, for the play that will have been a fundamental axis of the interhuman relation heretofore?

More specifically, what Apollon emphasizes is that, irrespective of the psychic structure at stake, the confrontation with the cultural montage of the sexual entails that what has been experienced as the feeling of love to that point is compromised and overwritten by the "newly acquired concept of a certain desire" (see ch. 1 in this volume).

We can think of this as the phallicization of desire in the strictest sense. And since it is not conceived of simply as a "mode of sexuation" constitutive of neurotic normality and accomplished once and for all in an Oedipal phase, and even less as a brute biological fact, the key is that it is experienced not only as a new form of delimiting imposition but as a *new interpretation of human life*: once the relation to the other has been re-situated along this sexual axis, something of the human is necessarily devalued, even betrayed.

Not a question of prudishness, what is at stake is a logical moment of upheaval within the dimension of experience, deriving from the long-delayed onset of sexual maturity and all that has preceded it: where previously there were interhuman relations that, even if organized in relation to a function of repression, were experientially correlated to a sentiment of love, there is now what appears as an instrumentalization and objectification of the human relation. Even worse, the pubescent must now valorize themself as man or woman, which entails, in the most reductive—but not for that matter erroneous—sense, either provoking or displaying and employing an erection, as well as, more capaciously, the orientation toward this moment via the conventional pathways that organize in advance the encounter with the other: social status, standards of beauty, norms of conduct, and so forth, which serve to censor the human within the individual.

As a matter of logic alone, the confrontation with the cultural montage of the sexual thus entails the experience of a loss of love that is at the heart of symbolic castration, further delimiting any possibility of address. And like any loss of love—consider Freud's account of mourning and melancholia (Freud, "Mourning and Melancholia")—this will provoke significant effects in psychic life. In particular, this loss will call for supplementation: love demands to be refound, with the result that the effective force of the Other of the address only grows. Simply put, a "newly acquired concept of desire" recodes the forms of feeling at stake in the letters of the body—love, the beautiful, the sublime—in terms of the conjugal relation, which begins to appear as the vector of their possible realization. Even in the ideal scenario, which integration within the montage depends on, aesthetic feeling, the address, and whatever expression the feminine may find are constrained within the contours of the romantic relation—at the limit, within the bourgeois family, where they will be put into the service of the dynamics of social reproduction.

What is crucial to grasp in this analysis, then, is the manner in which the psychic and relational life of the being, at an extremely sensitive moment of experience, is inscribed within a mode of operation in which lack is experienced as if it were to be located on the side of the subject, whereas what might fulfill that lack is situated in the hands of the Other, with all the power of caprice and all the subjection to demand this can entail. What Apollon's metapsychology attends to and lays bare is the fundamental inversion of which this consists, an inversion systematically promoted by the very logic of social organization and the deployment of sexuality, and the effect of which is to separate the individual from what is already there: the creativity of the child, the aesthetic register that articulates the being to the transindividual dimension of the human, joy beyond the measure of what can be said, and the quest of unconscious desire that knots these together and seeks their place in a reality that lacks what the subject might bring.

In a word, the symbolic castration imposed with the cultural montage can be understood as the accomplishment of this inversion; its traversal, in a return to the gift of the real castration in which the subject finds its source, a (re)discovery of the body as the site of aesthetic experience, and more. And though an analytic practice oriented toward the assumption of castration may, in the best of cases, arrive at similar ends, if not clarified at a metapsychological level, psychoanalysis risks inscribing itself in service of cultural and civilizational objectives, which bar the individual's access to what is human beyond such frameworks. Whatever therapeutic benefit this might offer the neurotic, particularly in a previous era, such a practice not only leaves psychoanalysis inadequate to the field of psychosis but arguably destines it to disappear with those cultures and civilizations themselves, particularly as younger generations go further into the forms of experience that open up in the fissures of the cultural montage of the sexual.

# Notes

1. According to Google N-Gram Viewer: "Prepregnant." Google Books N-Gram Viewer, Google, https://books.google.com/ngrams/graph?content= prepregnant&year_start=1800&year_end=2019&corpus=en-2019& amp;smoothing=3.

2. Sociologists have characterized the subsumption of women's health to reproductive health as "dangerous" for women (Casper and Moore 67). Others have demonstrated how the emergence of this initiative has intersected with broader sociopolitical trends (the individualization of public health problems, the failure of national health insurance, demographic changes, etc.) (Waggoner).

3. In addition to his own extensive ethnographic study of initiation and ritualized sexuality, Godelier cites the primatologists (Moore and Ali). In the case of certain primates, for example, the physiological maturation of a new generation is understood to present a threat to existing social hierarchies, in that the young enter into sexual competition with the older members of the group. Accordingly, pubescent males or females, depending on the species, are dispersed into neighboring groups. Already with these other species, we find a situation in which "the social (is placed) before the biological, or at least, which *makes of a biological mechanism a modality of the social reproduction of the species and not the biological reproduction of the society*" (Godelier, *Métamorphoses de la parenté* 583).

4. The author, not coincidentally, is a professor at the National Defense University, see (Kramer).

5. See (Waggoner "Cultivating the Maternal Future") for a description and analysis of this campaign.

6. For an overview of the development of Freud's approach to the castration complex, including a list of relevant texts, see (Laplanche and Pontalis).

7. "However it may have been used, psychoanalysis is not a recommendation for a patriarchal society, but an analysis of one. If we are interested in understanding and challenging the oppression of women, we cannot afford to neglect it" (Mitchell).

8. In addition to (Godelier, *Métamorphoses de la parenté*, "Bodies, Kinship, and Power(s)), see Héritier, *Masculin/Féminin 1*.

9. Quoted in (Godelier, *Métamorphoses de la parenté* 792).

10. Consider for example the following passage from Zizek: "Is not [Lacan's] entire work an endeavor to answer the question of how *desire* is possible? Does he not offer a kind of 'critique of pure desire,' of the pure faculty of desiring? Are not all his fundamental concepts so many keys to the enigma of desire? Desire is constituted by 'symbolic castration,' the original loss of the *Thing*; the void of this loss is filled out by *objet petit a*, the fantasy-object; this loss occurs on account of our being 'embedded' in the symbolic universe which derails the 'natural' circuit of our needs, etc, etc" (Zizek 3).

11. On this topic, see (De Battista, "*Le désir dans les psychoses*," "Lacanian Concept of Desire in Analytic Clinic of Psychosis").

12. On Lévi-Strauss, see (Godelier, *Métamorphoses de la parenté* ch. 11); for Lacan, see below.

13. To be clear, the presentation that follows is not intended to suggest that Apollon's metapsychology has been built on the Lacanian theories of discourse, *lalangue*, and feminine sexuation. Rather, my suggestion is that the key insights

at which Lacan was arriving in his later work can be understood to corroborate the directions in which Apollon has since taken psychoanalysis, and indeed that their importance is clarified in turn by Apollon's reformulations.

14. On the development of the concept of discourse in Lacan and Benveniste, see (Miller, A., "Formation and Development of the Concept of Discourse in Lacan and Benveniste").

15. Though it's true that Lacan continued to speak of symbolic castration as a structural condition at the time of the development of the theory of the four discourses, his own approach nonetheless was clearly shifting. In Seminar XVII, for example, castration comes to be defined as "the real operation introduced by the incidence of the signifier—any signifier whatsoever—in the relation of sex" (Lacan, *Le séminaire* livre XVII 149). Or again, he proposes that the master-signifier "in expressing itself towards the means of jouissance (*en s'émettant vers les moyens de la jouissance*)"—which is to say, in orienting the subject's pursuit of what would compensate them for a primordial loss, "not only induces but determines castration" (Lacan, *Le séminaire livre XVII* 101). We will approach this more concretely below. What is crucial to note is the fact that master-signifiers, which anchor the social link (integration and regulation), are defined by their non-equivalence with other signifiers—that is, they require an *extra-semiological* factor that gives them their privileged status. In other words, it is the force exerted by the social upon the system of signs that has to be taken into consideration. I have given an example in our opening consideration of "pre-pregnancy."

16. "Le langage sans doute est fait de lalangue. C'est une élucubration de savoir sur lalangue" (Lacan, *Le seminaire livre XX: Encore* 127).

17. For example, in place of the formula "the unconscious is structured like a language," one now finds the rather more circuitous, "if one can say that the unconscious is structured like a language, it's because the effects of *lalangue*, already there as knowledge, go well beyond everything the being that speaks is susceptible of enunciating" (Lacan, *Le seminaire livre XX: Encore* 127).

18. "The apparent necessity of the phallic function is discovered to be only a contingency" (Lacan, *Le seminaire livre XX: Encore* 87).

19. For another example of the how this is typically approached within the literature on Lacan, see (Verhaeghe 43): "symbolic castration is an inevitable consequence of the fact that man becomes a subject and must pass through the signifier in order to gain jouissance, with the simultaneous implication that jouissance is impossible."

20. See for example (Apollon "The Limit").

21. Jouissance [. . .] refers to the upsurge of a pure mental representation that provokes an effraction in the living being [. . .] jouissance is the insistent work of this effraction, which subverts the conditions of conscious perception, pushing beyond the limits of reality and pleasure [. . .] Jouissance refers to this fundamental experience that makes beings into subjects of a real that turns

them definitively away from the reality of their biological and social roots. As such an experience of an effraction into being caused by the object of hallucination, jouissance constitutes the being as unique, cut off from others and the environment, thrown into an absolute solitude where the other is the stranger (Apollon, "The Untreatable" 30).

22. This is especially so given that, insofar as the feminine is excluded from language, it necessarily pushes the subject to *acts* that will provoke a rupture in the logic of the social link as organized by the collective on the basis of the censoring of this same femininity.

23. See (Simondon), in which the transindividual is conceptualized as "what is exterior to the individual as well as what is inside them," which therefore "traverses the individual" (296) and which, in so doing, "passes within the individual as it does from individual to individual" (294).

# Works Cited


Apollon, Willy. "The Untreatable." *Umbr(a)*, vol. 32, no. 11, 2006, pp. 23–40.

———. "The Limit: a Fundamental Question for the Subject in Human Experience." *Konturen*, vol. 3, no. 1, 2010, pp. 103–18.

———. "The Subject of the Quest." Unpublished transcript, 2017.

———. "Enseignement du Conseil d'éthique à l'EFQ." Unpublished transcript, 2021a.

———. "Psychanalyse et mondialisation." Lecture series, unpublished transcript, 2021b.

———. "Séminaire de Montréal, 2021–2022." Unpublished transcript, 2022.

Benveniste, Émile. *Problèmes de linguistique générale, 2.* Gallimard, 1974.

Casper, Monica J., and Lisa J. Moore. "Calculated Losses: Taking the Measure of Infant Mortality." *Missing Bodies: The Politics of Visibility*, edited by Monica J. Casper and Lisa J. Moore, NYU P, 2009, pp. 57–78.

De Battista, Julieta. *Le désir dans les psychoses: Problématique et incidences de la cure à partir de l'enseignement de Jacques Lacan.* 2012. Université de Toulouse le Mirail, PhD dissertation. HAL Open Science, https://theses.hal.science/tel-00871338/document.

———. "Lacanian Concept of Desire in Analytic Clinic of Psychosis." *Frontiers in Psychology*, vol. 8, 2017, pp. 1–3.

Evans, Dylan. "From Kantian Ethics to Mystical Experience: An Exploration of Jouissance." *Key Concepts in Lacanian Psychoanalysis*, edited by Dany Nobus, Routledge, 2017, pp. 1–28.

Freud, Sigmund. "On the Sexual Theories of Children." *The Standard Edition of the Complete Psychological Works of Sigmund Freud*, vol. IX, translated and edited by James Strachey, Hogarth Press, 1953.

———. *Totem and Taboo. The Standard Edition*, vol. XIII, translated and edited by James Strachey, Hogarth Press, 1953.

———. "Mourning and Melancholia." *The Standard Edition*, vol. XIV, translated and edited by James Strachey, Hogarth Press, 1953.

———. *New Introductory Lectures on Psychoanalysis. The Standard Edition*, vol. XXII, translated and edited by James Strachey, Hogarth Press, 1953.

Godelier, Maurice. *Métamorphoses de la parenté*. Champs-Flammarion, 2010.

———. "Bodies, Kinship, and Power(s) in the Baruya culture." *HAU: Journal of Ethnographic Theory*, vol. 1, no. 1, 2011, pp. 315–44.

Héritier, Françoise. *Masculin/Féminin 1: La pensée de la différence*. Odile Jacob, 1996.

Johnson, Kay, et al. "Recommendations to Improve Preconception Health and Health Care—United States: A Report of the CDC/ATSDR Preconception Care Work Group and the Select Panel on Preconception Care." *CDC*, 2006, https://www.cdc.gov/mmwr/preview/mmwrhtml/rr5506a1.htm.

Kramer, Steven P. *The Other Population Crisis: What Governments Can Do about Falling Birth Rates*. Johns Hopkins UP, 2014.

Lacan, Jacques. "The Signification of the Phallus." *Ecrits: The First Complete Edition in English*, translated by Bruce Fink, W. W. Norton & Co., 2006, pp. 575–84.

———. "On a Question Preliminary to Any Possible Treatment of Psychosis." *Ecrits*, translated by Bruce Fink, W. W. Norton & Co., 2006, pp. 445–88.

———. "The Subversion of the Subject and the Dialectic of Desire." *Ecrits*, translated by Bruce Fink, W. W. Norton & Co., 2006, pp. 671–702.

———. "Position of the Unconscious." *Ecrits*, translated by Bruce Fink, W. W. Norton & Co., 2006, pp. 703–21.

———. "On Freud's Trieb." *Ecrits*, translated by Bruce Fink, W. W. Norton & Co., 2006, pp. 722–25.

———. *Le séminaire livre XI: Les quatres concepts fondamentaux de la psychanalyse*. Editions du Seuil, 1973.

———. *Le séminaire livre XVII: L'envers de la psychanalyse*. Editions du Seuil, 1991.

———. *Le séminaire livre XX: Encore*. Editions du Seuil, 1975.

———. *Le séminaire livre XXIII: Le sinthome*. Editions du Seuil, 2005.

———. *Le séminaire livre XVIII: D'un discours qui ne serait pas du semblant*. Editions du Seuil, 2007.

———. *Le séminaire livre XXI: . . . ou pire*. Editions du Seuil, 2007.

Laplanche, Jean, and Jean-Bertrand Pontalis. *The Language of Psycho-analysis*. Translated by Donald Nicholson-Smith, Hogarth Press, 1973.

Lévi-Strauss, Claude. "Introduction de l'œuvre de Marcel Mauss." *Marcel Mauss: Sociologie et anthropologie*, Presses universitaires de France, 1950.

———. *Anthropologie structurale*. Plon, 1958.

———. *Les structures élémentaires de la parenté*. Editions de l'EHESS, 2002.

Maleval, Jean-Claude. *La forclusion du Nom-du-père*. Editions du Seuil, 2000.

Miller, Alexander. "Formation and Development of the Concept of Discourse in Lacan and Benveniste." *Psychoanalysis and History*, vol. 24, no. 2, 2022, pp. 151–79.

———. "What Holds You Together: The 'Social Link' in Lacan, Durkheim, and Saussure." *Psychoanalysis and History*, vol. 25, no. 1, 2023.

Mitchell, Juliet. *Psychoanalysis and Feminism*. Penguin, 1974.

Moore, Jim, and Rauf Ali. "Are Dispersal and Inbreeding Avoidance Related?" *Animal Behavior*, vol. 32, 1984, pp. 94–112.

Paoletti, Giovanni. "La théorie durkheimienne du lien social à l'épreuve de l'education morale." *European Journal of Social Sciences*, vol. 42, no. 129, 2004, pp. 275–88.

Payne, January W. "Forever Pregnant Guidelines: Treat Nearly All Women as Pre-Pregnant." *Washington Post*, 16 May 2006, https://www.washingtonpost.com/archive/lifestyle/wellness/2006/05/16/forever-pregnant-span-classbank-headguidelines-treat-nearly-all-women-as-pre-pregnant-span/66f9af69-2aff-4148-9a50-7e89c8555ae4/.

Rindfuss, Ronald R., and Minja K. Choe. *Low and Lower Fertility: Variations Across Developed Countries*. Springer International Publishing, 2015.

Simondon, Gilbert. *L'individuation à la lumière des notions de forme et d'information*. Editions Jérôme Maillon, 2017.

Valenti, Jessica. "Are All Women Born to Be Mothers?" *Washington Post*, 31 Aug. 2012, https://www.washingtonpost.com/opinions/are-all-women-born-to-bemothers/2012/08/31/b5df2f0e-f2b1-11e1-adc6-87dfa8eff430_story.html.

Verhaeghe, Paul. "Enjoyment and Impossibility: Lacan's Revision of the Oedipus Complex." *Jacques Lacan and the Other Side of Psychoanalysis: Reflections on Seminar XVII*, edited by Justin Clemens and Russell Grigg, Duke UP, 2006.

Waggoner, Miranda R. "Motherhood Preconceived: The Emergence of the Pre-conception Health and Health Care Initiative." *Journal of Health Politics, Policy and Law*, vol. 38, no. 2, 2013, pp. 345–71.

———. "Cultivating the Maternal Future: Public Health and the Prepregnant Self." *Signs: Journal of Women in Culture and Society*, vol. 40, no. 4, 2015, pp. 939–62.

Wilson Center. "What Can Governments Do About Falling Birth Rates?" Wilson Center, 2014, https://www.wilsoncenter.org/event/what-can-governments-do-about-falling-birth-rates.

Žižek, Slavoj. *Tarrying with the Negative: Kant, Hegel, and the Critique of Ideology*. Duke UP, 1993.

5

# Woman, Man, Femininity, Masculinity

Daniel Wilson

In the historical moment that Willy Apollon calls mondialisation, where people from different cultures and civilizations live in the same cities, work in the same offices, and go to the same schools, cultures have lost control of what it means for a person to be a man or a woman. Not only do different cultures impose different models of what a man or a woman should be, but from one group to the next, from one YouTube channel to the next, there are radically different notions of what a man or a woman is. In this context, why should a woman put up with being denied a fully human future, being reduced to a mother or an object of sexual enjoyment, because of the culture she happens to live in? Why should a man stay within the limits of cultural expectations that offer the promise of social success and the satisfaction of an orgasm in exchange for abandoning dreams and ambitions that go beyond the limits of what is possible in the culture?

Starting in the 1950s, sexologists, feminists, and social critics began to talk about a distinction between sex and gender, where sex was often taken to mean the biological fact of sexual difference, while gender was taken to mean to the identity of the person in the culture—whether seen as something determined by the culture, or as something chosen by the individual.[1] Yet this distinction between sex and gender itself is itself unstable and contested. In 1990, Judith Butler wrote that "[t]his production of sex as the pre-discursive should be understood as the effect

189

of the apparatus of cultural construction designated by gender" (10). As Amia Srinivasan writes in her recent *The Right to Sex,*

> We inspect this supposedly natural thing, "sex," only to find that it is already laden with meaning. At birth, bodies are sorted as "male" or "female," though many bodies must be mutilated to fit one category or the other, and many bodies will later protest against the decision that was made. This originary division determines what social purpose a body will be assigned. Some of these bodies are for creating new bodies, for washing and clothing and feeding other bodies (out of love, never duty), for making other bodies feel good and whole and in control, for making other bodies feel free. Sex is, then, a cultural thing posing as a natural one. Sex, which feminists have taught us to distinguish from gender, is itself already gender in disguise. (xi–xii)

Sex—both as an identity and as an activity—appears as the way that the culture controls what a body can do. The cultures we live in form our bodies, determine what it is that a person should want, what a person should fear, and the limits of what it is possible to do. In the time of mondialisation, where we see the different kinds of bodies that are produced in different cultures, and where we see the different social purposes that these bodies seem destined for, this production of bodies by the culture is visible in a way that is impossible to ignore. This situation—where sex is revealed as a social construction—is both an opportunity for the subject and the site of new constraints and new limits that impose themselves as new modes of control. In *The History of Sexuality*, Michael Foucault writes that "[s]omething that smacks of revolt, of promised freedom, of the coming age of a different law, slips easily into this discourse on sexual oppression" (7). The promise that "[t]omorrow sex will be good again" (7) is omnipresent, as if freedom could be found within the models, identities, and practices that are maintained or produced within cultures or subcultures.

The way that bodies are taken up by the culture, put into the service of ends that are not our own, is part of what Apollon calls the *montage* of the sexual. "The *montage* of the sexual," Apollon says, "is the fact that each culture produces the woman that it needs. Each culture produces the man that it needs. Woman doesn't exist. It is a culture that produces the woman. Man doesn't exist. It is a culture that produces the man" (Sessions de Formation: "La clinique du fantasme"). Each culture produces the man and the woman that the culture needs so that it can reproduce itself, both biologically and ideologically. The culture not only determines what a man is, and what a woman is, but molds the sensibilities of the men and women in the culture to delimit what it is possible for a person, within the culture, to want. The cultural *montage* of the sexual substitutes a sexual desire—where the other person appears as an object of satisfaction or dissatisfaction—for the productivity, creativity, and unlimited richness of desire. The offer of Apollon's psychoanalysis is that it is possible to leave the cultural *montage* of the sexual. Apollon thus departs radically from both a critique of the specific ways that a culture produces and controls bodies, and from an interest in the way that the development of new models of identities and models of sexual relationships might make sex better. The reason that it is possible to leave the cultural *montage* of the sexual is that there is a part of the being that does not enter into the cultural *montage*, and which is censored—which is to say inaccessible—within the limits of the culture.[2] The culture produces a structure of relationships between individuals that determines what it is possible to do, and what it is possible to want, so that the members of the culture will want what the culture wants, and thus will reproduce, both biologically and ideologically, the culture. And yet there is a dimension of the being that does not enter into the cultural *montage* of the sexual. In Apollon's terminology, there is a part of the being that is out-of-language: the essential part of each subject does not enter into the relationships that are structured in and by language. There is the body that is produced within the culture, to serve its objectives, and the body as the site of an experience that remains out-of-language.

Apollon distinguishes between the cultural *montage* of the sexual, where the culture produces sexed bodies and stages what is possible between individuals, and a desire that insists in the body, mobilizing the energy of the being toward unknown ends that have nothing to do with the objectives of the culture. Within the limits of the cultural *montage* of the sexual, where the body is relegated to silence, the energies of the drive find their only expression in symptoms, acts, or behaviors that are not only inexplicable, but that the individual does not recognize as the expression of what is most central to his or her life. In a psychoanalysis, Apollon writes, the analysand discovers that "what causes him or her as a subject of speech and desire, and that motivates and modulates all of his or her undertakings, is also in large part what causes all of the intimate trouble and the suffering that occasion his or her complaints" ("The Untreatable" 37). The cultural *montage* of the sexual is the mechanism that the culture uses to prevent the individual from accessing the creative energies inscribed within the body.

The body is the site of a difference that is neither biological, nor cultural, nor imposed by the signifier. Rather it is the site of a difference that is mobilized by what Apollon calls the spirit: the capacity to represent what does not exist, to want it, and to create it, for better or for worse. Singular unconscious representations mobilize the energies of the drive in each subject, energies that act beyond what can be structured in advance between people, and beyond what is structured by the culture as possible for the members of the collective. Femininity—whether in a man or in a woman—names this dimension of the being that acts, and which is inaccessible within the cultural *montage* of the sexual, where a woman is allowed to exist only as a mother or an object of satisfaction and the creativity of desire is replaced by reproduction. Why would a person who has access to the feminine in him or her either take another person as an object of satisfaction, or accept being taken as an object of the Other's satisfaction? Desire has nothing to do with the satisfactions that are staged in the culture, and the cultural *montage* of the sexual only exists to cut off access to this dimension of the being that is in search of something beyond the limits of the culture. The feminine acts, breaking with anything that could be expected, and provoking incalculable effects in the other. Regardless of whether the other welcomes or rejects the effects of the feminine, an act has consequences: if a man stops taking his partner as an object of satisfaction, if a woman tells her partner that she doesn't want to be an object of his orgasm, this will have consequences, regardless of how the other responds. Masculinity, in a man or in a woman, names the responsibility for the consequences of this dimension of the human that acts. Femininity and masculinity thus have nothing to do with biology or the effects of hormones, and are neither styles or modes of behavior that are determined by the culture nor mutually exclusive subject positions. Femininity is the articulation of what is at work in the body to an unknown space of experience in the other, and masculinity is a responsibility for the consequences of these acts, a responsibility for the fact that the human goes beyond the limits that are erected in language and imposed by the culture.

Apollon's definitions of femininity and masculinity, as well as the radical distinction that Apollon draws between the cultural *montage* of the sexual (which functions to structure human relationships to preserve the collectivity at the expense of the creativity of human desire) and a desire that mobilizes the being in a quest for a space for the human to come, both depart from the way that sexual difference and desire are often taken up in psychoanalysis and popular discourse.

## The Cultural Montage of the Sexual and the Staging of Difference

If thirty years ago the idea that sex was gender in disguise appeared as a largely theoretical question, it now appears more and more as a social fact. Tracy Moore writes about the field of questions that her daughter, and her daughter's friends, are confronted with and negotiate at the beginning of puberty. "I can't pinpoint exactly when it started, but sometime in the past month, my eleven-year-old daughter started talking about pronouns and identities. At first it was one conversation about a friend who identifies as a "demigirl." Next, it was stories of her friends talking about transitioning. Then it was tales about her schoolmates announcing their queer status or "they/them" pronouns." This questioning can have profoundly destabilizing effects on the man and the woman who have the responsibility of being the parents for the child, calling into question the ways that parents lived their own lives, confronting them with what they have given up and with what they accepted in becoming the man and the woman that the culture needed. In Rade Jude's satiric film *Bad Luck Banging or Loony Porn*, a schoolteacher in Romania, whose husband posted a sex video of them on the internet, is confronted by the parents of her students, who demand she be fired. One mother complains that since her daughter saw the video she says "she never wants to get married." The mother continues that "[c]hildren should be protected from horrors." The joke is that if the mother knew then what she knows now, she never would have gotten married. She wants to protect her daughter from what she herself experiences as the horrors of being the object of a man's orgasm, to ensure that her daughter reproduces the culture she is in. The question, for anyone who takes a hard look at what the culture offers, is rather why a pubescent girl would not react with horror to the way that the culture uses her reproductive maturity to reduce her to a mother and an object.

It is thus no surprise that pubescent children would turn to different models of identities, of kinship, that are available in the culture to avoid entering into what they have seen their parents suffer from. And yet at the same time that new models of sex and gender identity appear as alternatives to what their parents suffer from, these new models and identities bring with them a correlate set of rules and norms that structures what can be said and what can be heard. Apollon writes that "Puberty is the strategic moment when the Other in the structure of the address is strengthened in its function as guardian of the receivable, and thus comes to support, in its response and expectations, the rules, norms, prohibitions and values that define cultural identity and belonging. Here, culture assumes its function of formatting the identity of membership within the structure of companionship defined by language and given credibility by a whole range of civilizational issues" (see ch. 1 of this volume). The struggles for identity, the discovery and negotiation of rules, identity, and belonging, inscribe the person within a cultural space that determines what can be said and what can be heard, and thus what can be explored with another person. The variety of cultural *montages* of the sexual that an eleven-year-old encounters today is something radically new for the parents. But this is a fact of experience for the pubescent child, and it is this reality that the child will have to navigate. While these new models of social relationships are presented as a radical break with the past, they function to define companionship and to impose conditions of receivability. These conditions of membership determine what can be said, what can be heard, and thus enclose the person within a certain set of relationships that ensure social reproduction and relegate the body to silence.

Within the cultural and political space, a saccharine appeal to the rapidly disappearing values of a civilization—a civilization that we are supposed to believe is motivated only by a concern for the best interests of the human—is presented as the only alternative to these new models. Patrick Deneen, an influential conservative political theorist, is deeply troubled by the fact that an exposure to, and ability to choose between, different models of how to live is destabilizing traditions and threatening the survival of cultures. Deneen argues that for most of human history, culture "was the comprehensive shaping force of the person who took part in, and would in turn pass on, the deepest commitments of a civilization.

As the word itself intimates, a culture cultivates; it is the soil in which the human person grows and—if it is a good culture—flourishes" (110). Yet now we live in "a society without shared norms, practices, or beliefs" (62). Deneen argues that traditional cultures are being replaced "not by a single liberal culture but by a pervasive and encompassing anticulture" (64) where it is only individual choice that counts. Deneen's project—which is part of the intellectual backbone of a mode of conservatism that is flourishing around the world—is thus to underline that it is within a culture, where we enact models and roles that existed before we were born, that we can discover a freedom that is deeper than the freedom of the individual. "Culture and tradition are the result of accumulations of practice and experience that generations have willingly accrued and passed along as a gift to future generations. This inheritance is the result of a deeper freedom, the freedom of intergenerational interactions with the world and one another. It is the consequence of collected practice, and succeeding generations may alter it if their experience and practices lead to different conclusions" (190). What the culture promises—to express the deepest commitments of a civilization—is something that one can only have access to from within the culture. Deneen wants to ensure that cultural practices continue, producing the human beings—the men and the women—who express the deepest commitments of the civilization. Deneen's concern for the human requires enclosing the being within the limits of the culture. What it is possible to want is determined by the "deepest commitments of the civilization," which express themselves through culture and tradition. The whole point of the operation, which Deneen describes with such clarity, is to ensure that the individual does not have access to a desire that does not serve the ends of culture.

Apollon's articulation of the relationship between culture and civilization turns Deneen's formulation on its head. For Apollon, "a civilization is there to make the rules, norms, and laws credible, to make the cultural demands credible" ("Psychanalyse et Mondialisation"). The rules and models that operate at the level of cultural practices, that structure the relationships between individuals in a collective, are made credible by an interpretation of the human that is sustained by the civilization. Apollon writes that "each civilization, in the cultural productions through which it manifests itself, offers itself as an interpretation of the human, even in a sense as the only receivable interpretation of the human. It is, we could say, the infantile sickness of each civilization to pose itself as the Expression of what Humanity should be" ("Citoyen du monde . . . mais de quelle nationalité" 224). The interpretation that each civilization offers cuts off access to a dimension of the human. Apollon writes that "[t]his censorship of a part of the human that must not be experienced, nor even named, has defined a shadowed part in each civilization" ("Citoyen du monde . . . mais de quelle nationalité" 224). In other words, "the deepest commitments of a civilization" that function to make the culture credible leave something out. And this means that a part of the human is censored. While Deneen underlines the question of civilization in a way that few on the left do, it is equally important to see that there is vision of the human that is at stake in the cultural practices that Deneen describes as "a pervasive and encompassing anticulture" (64). A deeply held sense of what it means to be a human being supports cultural practices within the practices that Deneen takes aim at. As Jasbir K. Puar writes, the question of whether a nation—and we might add, a state or community or institution—has rights and protections for LGBTQ populations has become "a marker of civilized status" (224). The point here is not to suggest that each interpretation of the human is valid, or that the only alternative to the idea that a given civilization possesses the true interpretation of the human is a moral relativism, but rather that each interpretation of the human leaves something out. There is no reason to doubt the good intentions and deeply felt concern of those who defend a certain interpretation of the human against the inhumanity of the other. However, there is something in each human being that goes beyond what is accessible in the culture. There is something in each human being that goes beyond the interpretation of the human that the civilization puts forward—beyond the limits imposed by "the infantile sickness of each civilization"—and this dimension that remains outside of the grasp of the culture and civilization allows each human to recognize, and welcome, what in the other goes beyond any limit.

The way Apollon uses censorship is different from the way that we often speak of censorship, where we talk about a person censoring him- or herself out of fear of being "canceled" or "deplatformed," or otherwise rejected by the Other. This situation, where someone does not say something because of how the Other will respond, is what Apollon calls repression. Apollon draws a distinction between what is repressed, which he defines as "what the Other must never know" (Sessions de Formation: "La clinique du fantasme") and what is censored, which is to say made inaccessible, by the way that the address—what one person can say to another person—is structured in the culture. To explain his use of censorship, Apollon refers to the history of the Catholic church.

> In the past, in the catholic religion, in other words in the heart of the West, there was what was called censorship. In all the libraries there was a room that was the room of censored books—a room where there were books that no one had the right to open. So we said that those books were censored. [. . .] So when I say that femininity is censored, I am saying that there is, somewhere in our body, something that you do not have the right to look at. It is censored by your culture. This does not mean it does not exist. This does not mean that it has been effaced (Séminaire clinique du Gifric 21 Dec. 2021).

In the situation of censorship, there are three perspectives we can take. The first is the perspective of those who enforce the limits of the culture because they claim that the culture promotes the best version of the human being. There is also the perspective of those who have written books that are censored, because what they say goes beyond the limits of what is receivable in the culture. Then there is the situation of those who do not have access to something because it is censored. It is this third position that is at stake in Apollon's concept of the censorship of femininity: a non-access to something in the body because of how the culture structures the address—because of how the culture structures what it is possible for one person to say to another person. The unconscious thus no longer appears as that which is repressed within the relationship to the Other, but rather as something that is censored by the culture but active in the body, and which can be discovered, explored, and taken responsibility for, beyond the limits imposed by language.

Before turning to the question of how femininity—and masculinity—open beyond the censorship imposed by the cultural *montage* of the sexual, I want to look at a brief example, from Dan Savage's podcast "Savage Love," of how the cultural *montage* of the sexual substitutes sex for desire and censors the feminine. In many ways Savage is a guardian of the cultural *montage* of the sexual as the limit of desire. He helps people navigate their sexual relationships, by naming what it is possible to want within the limits of sex. On his podcast he listens to recordings of listeners' questions and gives advice about how they can have a better sex life. In early 2023, a woman who described herself as a "30-year-old cis woman" called in "with a crisis of sexual orientation." She says that she always thought she was bisexual, or hetero-romantic—which means she sometimes likes to have sex with women, but only has romantic relationships with men. But now she wonders if she is maybe a lesbian because, she says, "I've always been really penis averse and I really hate cum." She continues that "I've also always been like strangely embarrassed to introduce my boyfriends to other people, like as my boyfriend." Savage responds by saying that "You may be a lesbian." He continues, referencing research that shows that "a lot of women who are lesbians seem to come out later in life, later in life than the average gay men."

There is something that is acting in this woman that she does not understand and cannot control. She is "penis adverse," she "really hate[s] cum," and she is "strangely embarrassed" to introduce a man to other people as "my boyfriend." Something insists in her body that she does not understand and that does not match up with her identity. So she is calling Dan Savage, an expert on sex—an expert on the sexual *montage*—for help in interpreting what in her does not make any sense. And the culture offers an interpretation of what this means: as Dan Savage says, "you may be a lesbian," as if there were a truth about the subject that corresponds to the field of identities that are available in the culture. Yet what speaks through these uncontrollable feelings and behaviors that subvert the certainty of the ego is something that is in search of its own space—not something in search of the correct identity in the space of the Other. At a minimum, we can observe that there is something in this woman that rebels against being used as an object of satisfaction—she hates cum and is penis adverse—and she does not want to be defined by her relationship to a man. Reducing what speaks in the body to what can be interpreted by the culture, censors the body, replacing desire by the sexual.

Savage offers an interpretation for a lived experience that acts, and that the caller does not recognize, or know anything about. He provides a conceptual framework, elaborated within the cultural *montage* of the sexual, which allows her to interpret what she experiences: the culture defines the terms of receivability. What psychoanalysis offers is that it is possible to speak about what insists in the body, beyond any interpretation. When a person takes the risk of speaking about what cannot be received in the culture, and which goes beyond any possible response or interpretation by the Other, he or she is exploring a part of the body that is censored—which is to say made inaccessible—by the culture. The interpretation that Savage gives excludes the possibility that the reason why a woman might not like to be fucked, to be cum on, or might not want to be a woman who is defined by her relationship to a man—has nothing to do with a possible sexual identity. What is censored—what is made inaccessible—is the fact that the body has nothing to do with the field of identity, with the cultural *montage* of the sexual. If the Other knows the meaning of what insists in the body, how can a person discover a singular desire that animates his or her life? There is the cultural *montage* of the sexual, which censors the body by imposing a field of rules, norms, models, which determine what one person can say to another. And then there is the body, which acts regardless of whether or not the person has access to it. If a person becomes conscious of what is at work in the body, beyond the interpretative framework that relegates the body to silence, they are conscious of something that goes beyond what can be named in the discourse of the Other. The question becomes: how far will a person go in this experience that is censored by the cultural *montage* of the sexual? How far will a person go in taking responsibility for the human beyond the limits of what is produced as a concept of the human by the civilization that makes credible the norms and rules of the culture?

## The Body, the Site of a Difference that Does Not Come from the Signifier

Going beyond the limits of the culture means leaving behind Oedipus as a frame of reference. For what the myth of Oedipus maintains is the idea that beyond the limits of the culture there is only something worse. In "The Ego and the Id" Freud writes that the origin of superego—the internalization of the law during what Freud calls the latency period, the period between the entrance into language and the beginning of puberty—is the "heritage of the cultural development necessitated by the glacial epoch" (35). Because of the harsh conditions of the last ice age, people had to limit reproduction and figure out how to live in groups together.[3] Freud proposes that early humans first organized themselves in the primal horde, under the protection of the primal father. Within the primal horde, people were governed by the absolute authority of the primal father, who had the exclusive right to the women of the group.

Eventually a band of brothers came together and murdered the primal father, devouring him in a cannibalistic feast and incorporating some of his power. The institution of the social link, which protects us from the violence of the other, depends on a prohibition that ensures that the place of the primal father remains unoccupied: all of the men are allowed to have some women, as long as no man has all the women. Freud writes in *Totem and Taboo* that this "shows that the beginnings of religion, morals, society and art converge in the Oedipus complex" (156). As Apollon writes, Freud discovers and elaborates "Oedipus as a strategy to stage Authority as a foundational reference in the West, as a representation and staging of the prohibited, within a certain *montage* of the management of kinship" ("La vie humaine ouvre sur un abîme" 21). A prohibition against incest founds the structure of kinship that organizes human relationships. Because of this prohibition, the only possible object of desire for a man is a woman, and the only possible object of desire for a woman is a baby.

When Lacan takes up Freud's story of the origins of culture, he draws out a structure that is imposed by the signifier. In his seminar on the Names of the Father, Lacan remarks that "[t]he primal father is the father from before the incest prohibition, before the appearance of the law, of the structures of alliance and kinship, in a word, of culture" (*Television* 88). As Lacan writes, this "father can only be an animal" (*Television* 88). Lacan continues that in his myth Freud finds "a singular balance between the Law and desire" that is born from "the hypothesis that the pure *jouissance* of the father is primordial" (*Television* 89). Not only is this pure *jouissance* "a satisfaction without remainder," always lost within the field of the signifier, but the attainment of this full *jouissance* would be the end of the desiring subject: the experience of this "pure *jouissance*" would be the collapse of unconscious desire into animal satisfaction. It is in this sense, as Lacan writes in *The Ethics of Psychoanalysis*, that "the prohibition of incest is nothing other than the condition sine qua non of speech" (69). In the terms that we are laying out, what Freud is elaborating is the structure of the *montage* of the sexual. What it means to be human—versus an animal—is to be within the cultural *montage* of the sexual. It is in terms of this satisfaction without reminder that Lacan evokes what he takes as Walt Whitman's dream of "what as a man one might desire of one's own body": "One might dream of a total, complete, epidermic contact between one's body and a world that was itself open and quivering; dream of a contact and, in the distance, of a way of life that the poet points out to us; hope for a revelation of harmony following the disappearance of the perpetual, insinuating presence of the oppressive feeling of some original curse" (93). In *The Other Side of Psychoanalysis*, Lacan completes this scene of epidermic contact by evoking the angler fish. These fish are

> very pretty and monstrous, as a species has to be in which the female is about this size and the male is like this, tiny. He comes and latches onto her stomach, and he latches on so well that his own tissues are indiscernible—it is not possible, even under a microscope, to see where the tissues of one end and the tissues of the other begin. There he is, hooked on by his mouth, and there he fulfills, if it can be put like this, his male function. It is not unthinkable that this greatly simplifies the problem of sexual relations, when in the end the weary male resorbs his heart, his liver, and none of it is left at all, there he is, suspended from the good place, reduced to what after a certain time remains in this little animal pocket, namely, principally the testicles. (76)

Within the field of the culture a lost *jouissance*, the *jouissance* that is prohibited by the incest prohibition, appears as monstrous. If within the culture, what a man dreams of and keeps at a distance is this nightmare image of a satisfaction without remainder, it is no surprise that men cannot imagine what they do not have access to because of the prohibitions that structure relationships within the culture, and if within the culture a woman is reduced to a mother mobilized by a monstrous incestuous desire, it is not surprising that, as Freud writes in *Civilization and its Discontents*, "the woman finds herself forced into the background by the claims of civilization and she adopts a hostile attitude towards it" (104). In Apollon's terms, what Freud discovers in Oedipus is the way that the culture produces a *montage* of the sexual. Lacan brings out that this idea of a "pure *jouissance*," of a "satisfaction without remainder," is itself produced by the prohibition that keeps this impossible *jouissance* at a distance. It is not that the truth of desire is incestuous, but rather that the prohibition against incest produces the mother as an object of sexual desire. The field of experience that Apollon opens beyond the prohibition takes us outside of the *montage* of the sexual. Beyond the desire that is staged within the *montage* of the sexual, there is a desire that is inaccessible within the *montage* of the sexual—that is, in Apollon's terminology, censored by the culture. An important question arises: outside of the myth of a satisfaction without remainder that is produced within culture, what can we say about humanity before the origins of language and culture? This is not a question of theoretical interest, but rather one of practical import. Desire has nothing to do with the cultural montage of the sexual; the question and unknown horizon of desire open beyond the limits of culture and civilization.

To shift the stakes of psychoanalysis outside of the field of the culture, and to locate the human outside of the interpretation of the human that a civilization offers, Apollon appeals to a widely agreed-on view of human history, where anatomically modern humans appeared between 200,000 and 300,000 years ago, and, as Gabor and Kaufman write, "behaviorally modern humans appeared in Africa approximately 50,000 years ago" (283). Gabor and Kaufman continue that development of "the grammatical and syntactic aspects of language" (284) coincided with this change in human behavior. The importance of this for Apollon is that whereas humanity existed for hundreds of thousands of years, language, which allowed people to organize into larger groups—and which led to the development of culture, of agriculture, of religion, and of the rise of civilization—appeared only 50,000 years ago. In Lacan's reading of Freud's story of the murder of the primal father, the time before the foundation of culture appears as outside of the field of the human: as Lacan says, the father from before culture is an animal. Situating the emergence of the human before the invention of language has two immediate consequences. First, because humans existed before language, it cannot be the case that the signifier is the cause of the human. This means that what is at stake in the unconscious goes beyond the effects that the signifier has on the unconscious. Second, the fact that humans survived for hundreds of thousands of years before language and the law—in what Apollon calls the address—underlines the fact that there is a way, outside of language, for humans to live with each other. The address, which existed before language, allows us to think about what is possible between human beings beyond the limits of language.

The fact that Apollon appeals to the history of humanity to situate the human as beyond the signifier does not mean that he is offering an historical explanation of the human. It is important to distinguish Apollon's concept of the effraction of the spirit from what is often offered as an evolutionary perspective, where the characteristic that makes humans different from animals is presented as an epiphenomenon of complex neurological systems, interacting in unanticipated ways to produce something new. Henri Bergson mapped out the structure of this argument in a manner that remains resonant. "[W]hat is sometimes said in the name of science" (43), Bergson writes, is that "[y]our 'conscious soul' is at most an effect which perceives effects" (43). The argument that Bergson outlines—and which he says is often presented as a scientific argument—is that if we could make more precise observations than are possible today given the present state of science, then we would see that everything that is at stake in human experience falls within the field of scientific observation. And yet such a perspective radically oversteps the limits of scientific observation: "if by 'scientific' we mean what is observed or observable, demonstrated or demonstrable, then a theory such as we have just sketched is not scientific, for in the present state of science we cannot even have a notion of the possibility of verifying it" (43). An argument that claims to be scientific proposes that there is nothing at stake in human experience that is not the effect of observable causes. The premise that there is nothing but what could be observed, or modeled, stands in for the lack of any evidence that this is true. Beyond the fact that such an argument oversteps the limits of what can be verified, Apollon appeals to fundamental work in mathematics and in the philosophy of science—such as Gödel's theorems—which, Apollon writes, "all confirm the impossibility of completely founding a system of representation, no matter how well formalized it is, and even of the impossibility of ensuring the adequacy of the system of representation with all the domains of reality concerned by the system" ("L'événement ou l'avènement de l'Autre" 71). For something to be observable, it needs to be a possible object of collective consciousness: an observation is verifiable. Whether we are talking about what is observable in everyday life, or about what is observable through specialized apparatuses such as MRIs or space telescopes, the observable depends on a system of representation. Yet it is impossible to say that a given system of representation is adequate to the reality that it concerns itself with. It is not just we that cannot verify, at the present moment, that a certain system of representation explains human experience. Rather, any system of representation leaves something out. Apollon thus begins from the premise that there is a dimension of existence, a dimension of the being, that is not in the field of observation. This means that "whatever progress humans make to improve the means of observation, there will be a part of the being that escapes observation" ("Métapsychologie" 26 Feb. 2021). Whereas science is interested in the field of what can be observed, Apollon continues that "psychoanalysis is only interested in the effect of what can not be observed" ("Métapsychologie" 26 Feb. 2021). There is a part of existence, a part of the being, which cannot be observed, which acts, and has effects. The history of humanity is the history of what cannot be observed.

It is in the terms of this distinction between what can be observed, and the effects of what cannot be observed, that Apollon approaches the body as distinct from the organism. Whereas the organism exists as an object of observation, the body exists as the effect of what cannot be observed. The body exists because the spirit—the capacity to represent what does not exist—mobilizes energies that are diverted from the functioning of organs and systems that are necessary for life. "There is therefore a conflict between the drives provoked by the mental representation—energies torn from the organism by the mental representation—and the biochemical automatisms, or if you prefer psycho-biochemical automatisms, that are scientifically observable. This conflictuality, this incompatibility, inscribes itself in tissues, in cells, in systems, and in organs, modifying their functioning and canceling out their limits. This inscription of the drives in tissues, organs and systems, I called this 'the letter'" ("Sessions de Formation: "La chose""). There are two aspects of this definition. First, there is the fact of a conflictuality. To take a simple example of the conflict between the energies mobilized by a mental representation and the functioning of the organism, we can think of laughter. Infants—just like adults—will laugh uncontrollably as a mental representation that others have no access to mobilizes energies that go beyond the limits of the organism and causes a *jouissance*. A mental representation takes energy from various systems in the body, in this case most notably from the respiratory system. This results in a conflict between the energies mobilized by the mental representation and the function of the "biochemical automatisms" that are necessary for life of the organism: people laugh until they are out of breath, until they start to cough, until they lose control of their bladders. The second aspect of this definition is the inscription of this conflictuality, where the functioning of an organ or system is modified by the manner in which the energy of the drive acts through it. In the life of any human being there are experiences that do not pass into consciousness. Through the repetition of these experiences, where unconscious representations mobilize the energy taken from the organism, the body appears as a set of inscriptions. Because of the spirit—the capacity to represent what does not exist—the body exists as the site of the unconscious, as the inaccessible site of the energies that are mobilized by singular representations that will never pass into language. The human is thus subject to the letter of the body, to these unconscious inscriptions that mobilize energy toward an unknown objective. When these energies—which are inscribed in the letter of the body and which mobilize organs and systems beyond their limit—do not find a space of expression—in art, dance, music, athletics, feats of concentration or endurance, or any of the other places where seemingly inexhaustible energies are devoted to ends that have nothing to do with pleasure or what could be identified as the needs of the organism—then they express themselves as inexplicable symptoms, or as behaviors that undermine what the ego wants for itself in the social link.

Because what each person thinks and feels and does depends on representations that no other has access to, which mobilize the energies of the drive in ways that have nothing to do with the interests of the ego or the social link, there is no way to anticipate what someone will do, or want. As Apollon says, "from the moment when we say that there is the spirit in each person, there is no relationship between two people, because neither of them can know what the other is thinking" (Séminaire clinique du Gifric 6 Oct. 2020). Each person is cut off from the other by the spirit. The result of this is not only that there is no relationship between individuals, but that whatever relationship is imposed in the family or by culture will come up short, because what a person wants, thinks, or represents goes beyond whatever terms structure the relationship. Because there is no relationship between individuals, because the experience of each is not something that the other can observe, there is what Apollon calls the inviolable autonomy of the spirit. One person cannot make another person think what they do not think, or feel what they do not feel, and the only way that one person can have any access to what another person thinks is through the address. Apollon's concept of address is thus fundamentally linked to the inviolable autonomy of the spirit. Apollon says: "What I call inviolable autonomy, it is what you address to someone else, either because the other has no access to what you are thinking, or because you, you have no access to what the other is thinking" (Séminaire clinique du Gifric 6 Oct. 2020). The only way that one person can give another person any access to what they are thinking or feeling is if the person takes the risk of addressing the Other. The inviolable autonomy that one person addresses to another necessarily breaks whatever links have been established between people, because it will necessarily go beyond whatever has been structured in advance. Because what is at stake in speech, in the address, is this inviolable autonomy, "speech is a gift to the Other" (Séminaire clinique du Gifric 6 Oct. 2020). And yet, at the same time, Apollon continues, "it is a risk because it gives the Other access to a dimension of me that otherwise the Other could not have" (Séminaire clinique du Gifric 6 Oct. 2020). Because of the letter of the body, because of the spirit, there is no relationship between two people, and what is possible between two people, between two bodies, depends on what happens in the address.

While language emerged some 50,000 years ago, Apollon proposes that for hundreds of thousands of years, before language, it was in the address that groups of humans organized themselves, and in which they managed the consequences of the effraction of the spirit. This was possible only because "as long as we are in small groups of 9–12 people, one person can address the other" (Séminaire clinique du Gifric 6 Oct. 2020). Apollon proposes that it was only later, when humans came into larger groups, that language was needed. Steven Mithen, an archeologist and historian of early humanity, provides a helpful way to think about what life in speech before language might have been like. Mithen speculates that there was "a single precursor for music and language" (26). This, Mithen writes, returns us to "the ideas of Jean-Jacques Rousseau in the *Essai sur l'origine des langues*, where he reconstructed the first language as a kind of song" (26). To reconstruct the way that early humans might have engaged with each other before the language, Mithen draws in part from the linguist Alison Wray's idea of a holistic proto-language. Wray argues that what came before language was not a language with a simplified grammar that operated on a simple set of signifiers, but rather a mode of speech with neither grammar nor words. Wray writes that "[a] language with no grammar may have no need of words, but it does need utterances and these, therefore, must have come first" (49). These utterances, Wray proposes, were holistic. By this she means that people spoke in utterances that, as Mithen writes, conveyed "'messages' rather than words" (3). In the system she imagines, she proposes that each member of the group would "memorize, without the help of any grammatical or lexical clues, the form and meaning of each utterance" (51). Wray's notion of a holistic proto-language is limited in that what she imagines is a system of communication where instead of words organized by grammar, humans communicated through a system of memorized holistic utterances. Mithen takes up Wray's proto-language and adds to it the idea that originary speech was also musical—or rather that what we now call speech, and think of as separate from music, was once internal to music, or, which is to say the same, that music was once internal to speech. As Mithen writes, "music is remarkably good at expressing emotion and arousing emotion in its listeners" (24). Mithen thus proposes that this evocative dimension of speech was part of these holistic utterances through which early human groups were organized.

The condition of speech is not the existence of a grammar, nor the existence of the signifier, but rather wanting to say something, wanting to give the other access to what is not observable. We can thus imagine that once humans lived in groups where the only relationship between individuals was in the address—in one person's response to what the Other's speech evoked in him or her. It is important to see that what is at stake in the address is different from an ideal of communication, where people use words with common definitions to speak about a reality that can be verified by a third person. What is at stake in speech is a dimension of experience that is not observable, and whose only truth is in what it evokes. And yet it is equally important to see that the picture that Mithen helps paint is not of some kind of prelapsarian utopia of the address, where the complexity of human life was resolved by a kind of harmonious holistic song. What we have, rather, is a vision of human existence where each person is cut off from the other by the letter of the body, where the drive is mobilized by unconscious representations, and where the only way to give the other access to what one is experiencing is through these song-like utterances. In the address one person can try to imagine how the Other will respond and address him or her accordingly. However, as Apollon writes, regardless of how we imagine or hope the Other will respond, "the Other, as such, is only an hypothesis" ("Diagram on the Address" 7 Mar. 2019). The person who responds, who exists and has a body that is affected by what is addressed to him or her, will necessarily respond differently than how the person who speaks expects, hopes, or anticipates how he or she will respond. Apollon writes that the Other's response will "fall short of what is expected" ("Diagram on the Address" 7 Mar. 2019). We lived exposed in the address, where any interaction with the other required addressing the other, and the only truth of what was said was the effect that the address had on the other. We can imagine what it would have been like, within the limitations of this holistic song-like speech, to experience the solitude and despair generated by the gap between how a person might have imagined the other would respond and the other's actual response, as well as the experience of encountering the effects of what insists in the other's speech as an uninterpretable demand that has unexpected effects in the body. If we can imagine that this gap—between what is expected and how the other responds—sometimes produced despair and a retreat from the address, it also seems that the unexpected response of the other sometimes opened a space where something different could become possible, where there was laughter and joy, dancing, play, love, friendship. The fact that humanity didn't die out, that for hundreds of thousands of years the full complexity of life—love, aesthetic experience, suffering, joy, violence, loss, death—was lived in speech that had no support in an external grammatical structure or shared vocabulary, suggests that what individuals discovered in the address was a source of *jouissance* and something they wanted to preserve.

However, in a larger group—where there are hundreds or thousands or millions of people—the address is not enough. In a complex society there are people who will never see each other, much less talk to each other, who need to coordinate their actions to work together. In a large group it is necessary, as Apollon says, that the members of the group "all name what is observed in the same way, and that there is a collective consciousness that comes to replace individual consciousnesses" (Séminaire clinique du Gifric 6 Oct. 2020). In the social link, where we all name the same things in the same way, and live in the same collective consciousness, we discuss reality rather than speak from a dimension of experience that is not observable. This allows us to coordinate our actions in projects whose outcomes concern millions of people. Yet what is most real to each of us, what is central to our anxieties, fears, desires, is out-of-language. This dimension of the being does not enter into any system of representation and is not observable. It does not form part of a collective consciousness, but acts. And this passage to the act of what is out of language—the feminine—has consequences.

There is thus a fundamental division between what is structured by language, and the part of the being that remains out-of-language. A child is a new spirit in the world, who has the capacity to represent what does not exist. Because of this capacity to represent what does not exist, the child lives beyond the limits of the organism, as energies taken away from the normal functioning of the organism are mobilized in quest of a *jouissance* that has nothing to do with animal satisfaction. To control this desire, the collective imposes limits that replace the unknown object of the drive with objectives determined by the culture. From the beginning of life, a child confronts the consequences of these limits. Well before a child can speak, he or she encounters parental demands and expectations that have nothing to do with the child's own experience, and when a child enters into language and goes to school, he or she encounters rules and norms that structure social interactions and condition the Other's acceptance and approval. The child's experience has nothing to do with what the Other observes or with what is named in language. Not only are there singular experiences that do not enter into language, but in the solitude of his or her experience the child represents and manages these encounters with the limits installed by language. These experiences and representations, which do not enter into language and which remain in conflict with what is structured by language, inscribe themselves as what Apollon calls letters of the body. In puberty the child encounters the way that the culture uses the sexual maturation of the organism to structure what is possible between individuals: as in Apollon's metaphor of censorship in the Catholic Church, just as certain books are made inaccessible in the library, the culture uses sex to structure what is possible between people to ensure that what is inscribed in the letters of the body remains inaccessible to the subject. Within the limits of relationships that are structured by the culture, where an Other maintained by the culture determines what is receivable, there is no access to what is inscribed in the body.

Adolescence—which Apollon locates as a moment that is distinct from, and that comes after, puberty—is when the person discovers that it is in the body, in the energies of the drive, that he or she has the resources to go beyond the limits of culture and civilization. In adolescence every human being discovers that what they want goes beyond what is structured by cultural practices, and takes them beyond the interpretation of the human in the civilization they are in. If a person does not act on what is censored in the culture, if a person does not find a way to live his or her femininity, to act on a desire mobilized by the spirit that goes beyond the demands of the culture and beyond the aspirations of civilization, then what could a person be left with except the dissatisfactions of the cultural *montage* of the sexual? Within the limits of the culture a woman is left imprisoned within maternity and a demand addressed to the Other, as if the Other could make up for everything that the culture has taken away, and a man is left with nothing but the satisfaction of the organism and the success of the ego. Either one takes the risk of going beyond the limits of culture and civilization, or one becomes complicit with the censorship of femininity within the interpretation of the human that is sustained in the civilization. If a person does not find a way to live his or her femininity, to make a path for what is at work in the body and censored by the culture, with the consequences that this entails, then these energies mobilized by the letters of the body will express themselves in symptoms and behaviors that have no observable logic or cause.

The feminine is the dimension of the being, inscribed in the letters of the body, that goes beyond what is possible in the culture, where language limits speech and creativity to allow people to live together in large groups. In reducing the future of a woman to a mother or an object of satisfaction, in replacing a man's desire with the satisfaction of an orgasm, the culture censors femininity. And when the feminine expresses itself in an unconscious act that evokes a dimension of human experience that is outside of the field of reality, the other is confronted with a dimension of his or her own being that he or she did not know existed. What is out-of-language, and thus unconscious, in one person evokes a dimension of experience that is out-of-language, and thus unconscious, in the other, revealing a new dimension of experience with respect to which the other person must situate him- or herself. The feminine, in the response it provokes in the other, functions to "subvert his or her position in the space of the social link controlled by the concerns of the culture" ("Mondialisation" 8 June 2022). The other can thus either refuse this space that is opened, through "an intimate violence" ("Mondialisation" 8 June 2022), or welcome this, in "an intimate opening to something more important than the demands and the frame of the social" ("Mondialisation" 8 June 2022). If humanity has survived for hundreds of thousands of years in the address, if it is possible to think that humanity will survive for hundreds of thousands into the future, it is because of the aesthetic—because of this capacity to welcome the feminine—and the ethics that the experience of the aesthetic entails, in a responsibility to make a space, in the social link, for something more important than the reality that the feminine subverts.

It is thus in terms of a dimension of the human that is out-of-language—that is outside of the field of reality—that Apollon defines femininity and masculinity. Apollon defines femininity as "the articulation to the aesthetic of what does not pass through language" (Séminaire clinique du Gifric 19 May 2020). There are three components to this definition. First, there is something that does not enter into language. Second, there is another path than language—that of the act—for what is at work in the body. Third, there is the aesthetic. Apollon describes the aesthetic as a feeling that is produced when what is at work in the one person's body opens a space of experience in the other person, which makes the person want to preserve the cause of this experience: "The aesthetic is a feeling, a feeling where the judgment of the individual retains the object of an emotion, of the cause of an emotion, as something whose loss would diminish the human" (Séminaire clinique du Gifric 19 May 2020). When one person articulates a dimension of his or her being that resonates with the letter of the other's body, and that gives the other access to an unknown dimension of experience, which has always been at work, but inaccessible, it reveals a new dimension of the human. The judgment that is at stake in the aesthetic is that "the loss of the object that causes this emotion would diminish the human, would make it that the human is less human" (Séminaire clinique du Gifric 19 May 2020). This is not a judgment with objective criteria, not something that is considered, but a feeling about an emotion. It is not that we would want to preserve something because it is beautiful, as if there were criteria in advance of the experience. Rather there is a surprise. And beauty is a profoundly destabilizing experience because it registers the discovery of a dimension of subjective interiority that goes beyond the limits of the mental space erected in language, and does not fit within the models imposed by the culture or within the interpretation of the human given by the civilization.

Femininity goes beyond the limits that are imposed by the culture. And it is with respect to this experience of going beyond the limits of the culture that Apollon defines masculinity. As Apollon says, "living the feminine will necessarily break the social link, and masculinity consists of taking responsibility for the consequences of this rupture of the social link" ("Séminaire clinique du Gifric" 23 Feb. 2021). An act lives only in its consequences: if there are no consequences, then there is no act. It is the fact of the consequences of going beyond the limits of the social link that poses an obstacle for the neurotic: "the young neurotic evaluates the risks: if he goes beyond what culture imposes, what civilization legitimizes, if he goes beyond, what are the consequences? Is he ready to assume the consequences? Is he ready to take responsibility for the consequences?" (Séminaire de Montréal 11 Nov. 2021). Without femininity—without what goes too far, breaking the relationships to others in the social link and revealing an unknown dimension of the human—it is impossible to speak of taking responsibility for these consequences, to take responsibility for a social link where it is possible to go further. While femininity is this dimension of the being that ruptures the social link, that subverts the position of the other in the social link, Apollon describes masculinity as "that singular joy that there is in accepting, and taking responsibility for, the consequences in the social link" (Séminaire de Montréal 11 Nov. 2021). Without the discovery of this joy in taking responsibility for the consequences of what goes too far, there is a limit to how far beyond the limits of the social link one can go. The offer of Apollon's psychoanalysis is that regardless of whether one enters, in adolescence, into the unknown future that opens within the address, or retreats into the demands, satisfactions, and disappointments of the cultural *montage* of the sexual, the body remains there to be discovered, to be opened as the site of aesthetic experience, and as the occasion of joyous responsibility.

Not only are there no words to name the singularity of subjective experience, but the relationships between individuals that are necessary to bring new productions of the spirit into existence do not exist. The fact that there is something unaddressable that acts at the center of human experience does not mean that the unaddressable is an obstacle to the address. It is language that is a limit to the address. From the moment that the spirit is at work in the being, there is no relationship between two people, and there is no way to know what another person is thinking, or what another person will do. The address is a way to manage this situation: one person can tell another person what he or she is thinking; one person can ask another person what he or she is thinking. In repression a person rejects what they think the other will refuse, and the relationship to the other within which repression takes place is itself produced by the cultural *montage* of the sexual. It is because human beings have bodies that we speak, but the body does not pass through the address. Repression, censorship, and the unsayable are the ways that the culture and the civilization try to ensure that the address is not in service of what is unaddressable and at work in the body, to prevent people from embarking, together, on a journey toward an unknown destination.

## Femininity and Masculinity

Apollon describes how experiences inscribed in the body, repressed in the relationship to the other and censored by the cultural *montage* of the sexual, mobilize energies that pass to the act, with consequences that need to be managed. When people from different cultures and civilizations live in the same spaces—and see that is it possible for their neighbor to say things that they can't say, to do things that they can't do—they are confronted with the fact that lived experience goes beyond what is structured by their culture. Mondialisation undermines the symbolic castration—the loss that is imposed by language, by the collective—through which cultures censor access to the body. The situation of mondialisation thus calls for a psychoanalysis that can accompany the subject beyond the construction of symptom that would allow him or her to live with a loss imposed by a symbolic structure that has already lost its credibility. To look concretely at this situation, I want to turn to a documentary titled *A Jew Walks into a Bar*, directed by Jonathan Miller and released in 2017, about a comedian named David Finkelstein. Finkelstein is an ultra-Orthodox Jew who lives in Brooklyn, within the limits of his culture and civilization, and who regularly, and secretly, goes into Manhattan to do stand-up comedy. In the film Finkelstein describes how he discovered stand-up comedy.

> Before I started doing stand-up [. . .] I would study the Torah all day. I was in Yeshiva. [. . .] It was a very strict schedule. We'd get up at 7:30 in the morning, start studying, and then you'd just go as long as you could throughout the night. Focusing your mind on God's will, that was like considered the most noble profession. I felt fulfilled. [. . .] To me I was pretty happy at times. But [. . .] I always felt like I wasn't doing what I was supposed to be doing. Like I felt something was missing. I got into a very deep depression. For I guess a year I was just at home doing nothing, staring at the wall. You know, I had a lot of emotional problems. It was always hard for me being in front of people. I would get terrible panic attacks whenever I was out in public. And so I got a laptop with internet. That was like the first rule that I broke. And I started watching TV shows, and I saw Louis C.K. That was the first time I heard stand-up comedy. I couldn't stop

watching him. He was so honest. I'd always been brought up that even if you feel a certain way, you don't say what you are really feeling. And suddenly it was like a whole new way of thinking. Louis was just . . . he was like "say everything you think." Right away I knew that's what I should do. I Googled "how to be a comedian," and it said you gotta do open mics. My first open mic, I had to reserve through an email . . . that was the first email I ever sent. It was also the first time that I'd ever gone on the subway myself.

In the culture Finkelstein lives in, a man is supposed to study the Torah, get married, and have children. A man's most noble profession is to focus his mind on "God's will"—to sustain a certain interpretation of the human as determined by God's will. The rules, norms, and models that organize and regulate familial and social relationships are important because they are in service of this effort to be determined by God's will. And yet this interpretation of the human leaves something out. There are things that Finkelstein thinks that he cannot say. Because of the way that the address is structured in his culture, there are certain lived experiences, inscribed in his body, that have no space to express themselves. Finkelstein describes two distinct moments in his experience of these energies in search of a space of expression. In the first moment, the energies mobilized by these experiences expressed themselves as symptoms: as emotional problems, panic attacks, and a depression. These symptoms, which were a source of suffering presumably for both himself and for others around him, expressed the fact of a lived experience that had no space. In the second moment these inscriptions of lived experience, mobilizing the energy of the drive in ways that are equally inexplicable from the perspective of the culture and the ego, passed to the act, searching out an aesthetic space where they could realize themselves. He bought a computer, went on the internet to explore the world around him, and discovered that in this thing called "stand-up" it was possible to say what you are thinking. Then he booked a slot and went into Manhattan to speak during an open mic. Through acts that go beyond the limits of what is allowed in the culture, and that go beyond the interpretation of the human sustained in the civilization, a lived experience finds a path to express itself.

On the one hand, Finkelstein discovered that he could say things that he had always repressed in his relationships to others. On the other hand, he discovers something new and unexpected in his interactions with other comedians. In a scene at the beginning of the movie, Finkelstein tells a woman who works at the club that he cannot shake her hand because of his religion. Later in the documentary, seated at the bar, he has a conversation with a Puerto Rican comedian named Christina. They have seen each other perform, but this is the first time they have met, and when he reacts to her casually touching his arm and tells her that he cannot touch a woman's body, they talk about their different cultures. She tells him about how important touch is for Puerto Ricans, then touches him, then hugs him: she is unwilling to be complicit with the way that women are controlled in his culture. Finkelstein does not react with violence but rather with an uncontrolled joy as he loses control of himself in an explosion of wild laughter. It is not that a comedy club is somehow outside of the culture—comedy is both a place of speech and a place where men and women are put in their places. And there is no reason to think that a Puerto Rican woman living in New York is somehow outside of the cultural *montage* of the sexual. Rather, she lives in different norms, different models, that censor the feminine in different ways. And yet there is in her, as in Finkelstein, a lived experience that goes beyond what is structured in language. In the address, it is possible to explore the body beyond the limits of the culture. We don't know what this gives Finkelstein access to because he doesn't tell us. But in this and other interactions with the comedians, Finkelstein is exploring something new in his body as he discovers what it is possible for one person to say to another person beyond the limits of what is organized by the cultural *montage* of the sexual.

When Finkelstein does stand-up, when he speaks with his non-Jewish friends, he says things that are impossible to say within the limits of his culture and civilization, and constructs relationships that are impossible within the confines of his culture. Yet at the same time he is living his femininity, he wants to preserve his place in his community. Over the course of the film we see Finkelstein wrestling with the question of how far he is willing to go. The film opens as Finkelstein is walking through his community in Brooklyn with the camera crew and director. No one in his community knows that he does stand-up comedy, and he tells the movie crew that if anyone asks, they should say they are making a documentary about his Yeshiva. Because of prohibitions against using the internet or participating in secular culture, he is not concerned that anyone will see the documentary that is being made about him.

Finkelstein says that his rabbi would disapprove of what he is doing and that there is a battle "between the dark and the light"—between religion and what he is exploring outside his community. And yet Finkelstein is careful to underline that he is doing all this without breaking any of the actual laws of his religion and community. He keeps kosher, observes the Sabbath, and says he is in a "gray area." His goal, he says, is not to stop being religious so that he can do comedy, but to do both.

When Finkelstein describes this battle of light and dark he is not giving his individual interpretation of the situation. Ayala Fader, an anthropologist in New York, has written about the response of ultra-Orthodox Jewish leaders to this phenomenon of people—like Finkelstein—who are "living double lives" (187). She writes about how in the ultra-Orthodox community in New York, there are both efforts to stop people from accessing the internet and to delimit an interiority produced within the person by the culture. The problem with the internet is that it can make people think it is "normal" to do things that are beyond the limits of the culture and civilization. The internet thus can tempt people into a double life, and Fader writes about the efforts in the ultra-Orthodox community to warn people about the dangers of the internet. For instance, in 2014, the "Technology Awareness Group" organized a rally in Borough Park, Brooklyn, that Fader says 15,000 people attended. In cautioning people against entering into the spaces that exist outside of the ultra-Orthodox enclave, Fader writes that "ultra-Orthodox rabbis and therapists" draw on "competing notions of interiorities: the theological, based on rabbinic and kabbalistic Jewish texts, and the psychological/therapeutic, rooted in liberal Protestantism" (192). Community leaders responded to the fact that it is possible to experience that it is "normal" to live otherwise—that other communities have other norms, that in a comedy club you can say what you think and talk with a Puerto Rican woman named Christina—by enforcing the limits of an interiority defined by the culture. In policing the boundaries of this interiority, rabbis and therapists "framed religious doubt either as contamination from the Gentile Internet or as a mental illness requiring treatment" (192). Fader continues that this delimitation of "interiority" shows that "interiority is not only private and individualized, as is often implied, but in fact can be a way to shore up hierarchies of authority, reject certain forms of sociality, and discipline others" (187). In Apollon's terms, language replaces individual consciousness with a collective consciousness. The problem that the community leaders are responding to is that it is possible to explore, and become conscious of, experiences that are outside of the collective consciousness, beyond the limits of this interiority produced by the culture.

Whereas in the discourse that Fader analyzes the phenomenon of a double life is seen as a danger to be avoided, it is equally true that a "double life" appears as a symptomatic compromise formation, named in and thus maintained by the culture. As long as a person remains caught in a double life, where a lived femininity must be kept secret, there is a limit on how far a person can go in exploring his or her femininity. In the documentary about Finkelstein, a woman in the comedy club asks him why his community would disapprove of him doing comedy. He responds that, first of all, "I'm hanging out with you guys." Then he says that in his community "We are very careful about speech." The woman responds by remarking, "That is why is it so fascinating what you do, it's really the antithesis of being a comedian, I feel like it's like a woman going up in a burqa doing jokes." What this comment brings out is the strange way that Finkelstein's double life is complicit with a censorship of the feminine. There is a contradiction between Finkelstein's desire to become a comedian, and the fact that he wants to stay in his community: How can it be possible for Finkelstein to say everything that he is thinking, to explore thought beyond the limits of language, if he is at the same time committed to the culture that censors his access to what he is exploring? He is beyond the limits of his culture, exploring a new space where a dimension of his being remains not only out-of-language, but also beyond the limits of what constitutes the interpretation of the human in his civilization, yet he does not want to take responsibility for the consequences of his exploration or for what he discovers. Finkelstein tells a joke about a friend who asks him how he would react if he snuck a piece of bacon into Finkelstein's sandwich: "You'd do that for me?" he asks. The joke is that he wants to experience something that goes beyond the limits of the law while avoiding responsibility for going beyond these limits.

If Finkelstein turned to comedy because he saw there the possibility of speech beyond the limits of language, it is important to underline that doing stand-up is not just a kind of therapy for Finkelstein, a kind of pressure release valve that allows him to live within the limits of his community. He is a funny comedian and is interested in discovering what it might mean to pursue a real career as a comedian. On the one hand, Finkelstein says, this would mean finding a way to make jokes about something other than the difference between how he lives his life and how the people in his audience lives their lives; on the other hand, this would mean, concretely, breaking Sabbath to perform on Friday and Saturday nights. At the end of the film he is invited to a showcase with well-known comedians like Hannibal Buress. But he turns down the opportunity because it will be on a Friday night, during the Sabbath: "Friday nights and Saturday those are—that's the main time for all comedy shows . . . if I wanted to go on the road, right, I can't only travel during the week but not on Fridays and Saturdays."

> I think where I am in comedy, I've reached the point where I can't be religious anymore. But I'm not ready, religiously I'm not ready for that yet. I don't really want to lose my identity. [. . .] What's keeping me religious? My whole life I've been that way, it definitely satisfies something in me. You know, it gives me some direction. I'm very comfortable being religious. It's something that I'm used to and I've been doing, you know, all the time. It's scary to not do what you've always done.

At the end of the film we learn that Finkelstein has decided to give up performing, and in an interview from 2022 about his documentary, Jonathan Miller talks about what "a very difficult decision" it was for Finkelstein to not perform on the Sabbath. When the interviewer asks Miller if Finkelstein still performs, Miller responds that he performs "[o]nce a year on Christmas. David works for a company that does home health care. He enjoys it, and he's happy." Having discovered this access to a dimension of his being that is active in his body, censored in the culture, and unsayable in the civilization, he is faced with a question of responsibility. What Finkelstein confronts is, in Apollon's terms, masculinity: a responsibility for the consequences of going beyond the limits of his culture. Comedy has become a symptom—in the best sense of the word—for Finkelstein. He has found a space to express a dimension that has no space within his culture and allows him to live his life with others. It would be hard to imagine that the experience of his femininity, beyond the limits of what is possible in his community, does not change the way he engages with others, bringing a lightness to his interactions with others that does not come from anything in the environment. And yet it is equally important that the source of this lightness, which allows him to live his life without suffering from emotional problems, panic attacks, and depression, remains a private *jouissance*; the fact that he does not want to take responsibility for the consequences of living a femininity that is censored in his culture constitutes a limit in how far he can go in exploring his femininity.

Within the frame of a culture, an act is always wrong. An act is not receivable in the frame of the culture and so is either understood as a mark of selfishness, as the effect of a bad influence, or as the effect of mental illness. Within the frame of the culture, consequences appear as something that one is lucky to have avoided, as a source of guilt and anxiety, as something to blame on others, or as something that can be solemnly taken responsibility for in a more or less public confession. George Washington's first biographer, Mason Locke Weems, invented the now mythological story of six-year-old George Washington's honesty and courage. After receiving a hatchet as a gift, Washington tried it out on his father's cherry tree. When his father asked him about the damaged tree, Washington responded: "I cannot tell a lie . . . I did cut it with my hatchet" ("Cherry Tree Myth"). This foundational American, Protestant myth of responsibility as public confession is firmly situated in the problematic of second childhood—in the imaginary relationship to the Other. Within this frame, consequences exist only within a dialectic of guilt and repentance. Thinking the act, with psychoanalysis, requires leaving this frame. In an act, a dimension of experience that is out-of-language mobilizes the energy of the drive in search of a space of expression. An act lives in its consequences. The joy in taking responsibility for the consequences of an act is not a courageous responsibility for an error, but the joy in extending an act. The consequences of the feminine are not something to be avoided or apologized for, but something to be illuminated and extended.

Amy Sherman-Palladino's TV series *The Marvelous Mrs. Maisel* offers a kind of fictional extension of the situation that Miller explores in his documentary about Finkelstein. The show follows a young Jewish woman, Miriam Maisel, who has two young children and whose husband leaves her for his secretary. The night he leaves her, she makes her way to a club in Greenwich Village, where she goes on stage during an open mic and improvises a stand-up routine about her life. Over the course of the series she becomes serious about being a comedian. She hides this from her parents—with whom she lives—and friends for as long as she can. Eventually her double life is discovered, and she chooses to be a comedian rather than to do what she is supposed to do—get back together with her now regretful ex-husband or remarry a nice Jewish doctor. The fact that she is a comedian—that she goes onstage and says things about her experience that no one would have access to if she didn't talk—has consequences for all the others in her entourage. Without knowing what these consequences will be, she takes responsibility for these consequences: she is for the consequences of the life she chooses. And her choices, her acts, open up the space of the aesthetic in the people around her. The fact that she goes beyond what is produced as interiority in the culture she lives in subverts the internal limits—in others—through which the culture marks out what it is possible to do, think, and feel. And this discovery, that it is possible to go further than what is possible in the culture, leads the people around her to futures that are different than what the past would have dictated, and which in turn have consequences for themselves and others. Her ex-husband quits his job and opens a nightclub; her mother realizes she has given up on her dreams to serve her husband and moves to Paris to be an artist; her father realizes he has abandoned the political and social engagements that motivated him when he was young and quits his job as a professor of math at Columbia to be a theater critic at the *Village Voice*.

Each subject suffers from the effects of the censorship of the feminine in isolation, as if the insistence of energies that are censored by the culture were the trace of a defect in the person. From the perspective of the culture, the feminine is selfish and destructive. What is out-of-language is something to be controlled. But the human in each subject suffers from the way that the address is controlled, suffers from the censorship of the feminine. In both the documentary about Finkelstein and in *The Marvelous Mrs. Maisel*, it is through a grand act, on a stage, that a person discovers a space of freedom of expression beyond how the address is structured in the cultural *montage* of the sexual. The problematic of a double life—of the discovery that it is possible to live otherwise, but that there would be consequences to taking responsibility for this new life—is given an especially clear expression. Regardless of how one discovers that it is possible to live otherwise, to want more than is allowed in the culture and authorized by the civilization, the question of how, and whether, a person is going to act on the basis of what he or she knows poses itself. And the consequences of acting on what one knows plays out in the most intimate relationships, in the fabric of the lives we live with others. In this moment when different cultures and civilizations exist in the same spaces, the rules that govern what is receivable have lost their credibility. The symbolic castration that is imposed by the culture to cut off access to the creative energy of the drive no longer functions, and even neurotics are confronted by the fact that there is something active in their bodies that is censored by the culture. This historical moment calls for a psychoanalysis that can accompany a person in the exploration of, and responsibility for, a dimension of experience that goes beyond what is structured by cultural models and made credible by a certain interpretation of the human.

In his novel *Whatever*, Michel Houellebecq's narrator describes his disdain for women who have entered into a psychoanalysis: "A woman fallen into the hands of the psychoanalysts becomes absolutely unfit for use, as I've discovered time and again." Houellebecq continues, "This phenomenon should not be taken as a secondary effect of psychoanalysis, but rather as its principal goal" (102). A person who finds a space of speech in a psychoanalysis, who enters into the transference and discovers that the body, censored by the cultural *montage* of the sexual, is the site of creative energies, is confronted by the question of how far they will go in taking responsibility for the consequences of what they know. If the person acts on what they have discovered, this will have consequences that must be managed. The human in Houellebecq's narrator, whose violent refusal of the feminine is easily recognizable across cultures and civilizations, is also suffering from the violence of the cultural *montage* of the sexual. And the fact of domestic violence, as well as the economic consequences of divorce for women, only underline that the consequences of the feminine go beyond what a person can manage alone. The discovery of the aesthetic opens to a collective responsibility for the future of the human, for a future where each person can discover that they are not only "absolutely unfit for use," but also free to act on a desire that brings something new to humanity, beyond the limits of receivability maintained by the culture. If psychoanalysis does not take the side of the human, beyond the limits of culture and civilization, then it can only function to keep the subject within an interiority traced in language.

## Notes

1. See N. Sullivan, "The Matter of Gender," *Fuckology: Critical Essays on John Money's Diagnostic Concepts.*

2. This chapter approaches the cultural *montage* of the sexual from the perspective of neurosis—that is, from the perspective of the person who has entered into the cultural *montage* of the sexual. The psychoanalysis that Apollon

and his colleagues in Quebec have developed to offer a psychoanalytic treatment of psychosis—an offer for people who never entered into the cultural *montage* of the sexual—necessarily sustains desire beyond the objectives of the culture and civilization. This equally means that Apollon's psychoanalysis offers, to those who entered into the cultural *montage* of the sexual, that it is possible to leave the cultural *montage* of the sexual.

3. See Sigmund Freud and Ilse Grubrich-Simitis, A *Phylogenetic Fantasy: Overview of the Transference Neuroses*, Belknap Press of Harvard University Press, 1987.

# Works Cited

Apollon, Willy. "Citoyen du monde . . . mais de quelle nationalité." *Mondialisation, défis pour l'humain*, GIFRIC, 2016.

———. "L'événement ou l'avènement de l'Autre." *L'Universel, perspectives psychanalytiques Conférences et écrits*, Éditions du Gifric, 1997.

———. "The Human in Question." Unpublished manuscript.

———. "Métapsychologie." Unpublished seminar, 26 Feb. 2021.

———. "Mondialisation." Unpublished seminar, 8 June 2022.

———. "Psychanalyse et mondialisation." Unpublished seminar, 10 June 2020.

———. Séminaire clinique du Gifric. Unpublished seminar, 19 May 2020.

———. Séminaire clinique du Gifric. Unpublished seminar, 6 Oct. 2020.

———. Séminaire clinique du Gifric. Unpublished seminar, 23 Feb. 2021.

———. Séminaire clinique du Gifric. Unpublished seminar, 21 Dec. 2021.

———. Séminaire de Montréal. Unpublished seminar, 11 Nov. 2021.

———. Sessions de Formation: "La clinique du fantasme." Unpublished seminar, 24 Apr. 2020.

———. Sessions de Formation: "La chose." Unpublished seminar, 8 May 2020.

———. "The Subject of the Quest." Translated by Daniel Wilson, *Penumbr(a)*, vol. 2, 2022, pp. 1–14.

———. "Unpublished Diagram on the Address." 7 Mar. 2019.

———. "The Untreatable." Translated by Steven Miller, *Umbr(a): Incurable*, no. 1, 2006, pp. 23–39.

———. "La vie humaine ouvre sur un abîme." *L'universel, perspectives psychanalytiques: Conférences et écrits*, GIFRIC, 1997.

Bergson, Henri. *Mind-Energy: Lectures and Essays*. Translated by H. Wildon Carr, Greenwood Press, 1975.

Butler, Judith. *Gender Trouble: Feminism and the Subversion of Identity*. Routledge, 2006.

Condran, Ed. "'A Jew Walks Into a Bar' Is More Than a Funny Joke." *The Spokesman-Review*, 17 Feb. 2022, www.spokesman.com/stories/2022/feb/17/a-jew-walks-into-a-bar-is-more-than-a-funny-joke.

Deneen, Patrick, *Why Liberalism Failed*. Yale UP, 2018.

Fader, Ayala. "Ultra-Orthodox Jewish Interiority, the Internet, and the Crisis of Faith." *Hau: The Journal of Ethnographic Theory*, vol. 7, no. 1, Mar. 2017, pp. 185–206, https://doi.org/10.14318/hau7.1.016.

Foucault, Michel. *The History of Sexuality. 1: An Introduction*. Translated by Robert Hurley, Vintage Books, 1990.

Freud, Sigmund. *The Ego and the Id. The Standard Edition of the Complete Psychological Works of Sigmund Freud*, vol. XIX, translated and edited by James Strachey, Hogarth Press, pp. 3–66.

———. *Totem and Taboo. The Standard Edition*, vol. XIII, translated and edited by James Strachey, Hogarth Press, pp. ix–162.

———. *Civilization and Its Discontents. The Standard Edition*, vol. XXI, translated and edited by James Strachey, Hogarth Press, pp. 57–146.

Freud, Sigmund, and Ilse Grubrich-Simitis. *A Phylogenetic Fantasy: Overview of the Transference Neuroses*. Belknap Press of Harvard UP, 1987.

George Washington's Mount Vernon. "Cherry Tree Myth." *George Washington's Mount Vernon*, www.mountvernon.org/library/digitalhistory/digital-encyclopedia/article/cherry-tree-myth/#_edn1.

Houellebecq, Michel. *Whatever: A Novel*. Serpent's Tail Classics, 2011.

Jude, Radu, director. *Bad Luck Banging or Loony Porn*. MicroFILM, 2021. 106 min.

Kaufman, James C., et al. "Evolutionary Approaches to Creativity." *The Cambridge Handbook of Creativity*, edited by James C. Kaufman and Robert J. Sternberg, Cambridge UP, 2010, p. 283.

Lacan, Jacques. *Television: A Challenge to the Psychoanalytic Establishment*. Edited by Joan Copjec, translated by Denis Hollier, Norton, 1990.

———. *The Seminar of Jacques Lacan: Book I: Freud's Papers on Technique*. Translated by John Forrester, Norton, 1991

———. *The Seminar of Jacques Lacan: Book VII: The Ethics of Psychoanalysis*. Translated by Dennis Porter, Norton, 1992.

———. *The Seminar of Jacques Lacan: Book XVII: The Other Side of Psychoanalysis*. Translated by Russell Grigg, Norton, 2006.

Miller, Jonathan, director. "A Jew Walks Into a Bar." Aeon Video, 2017, psyche.co/films/an-orthodox-jew-struggles-to-balance-his-two-callings-religion-and-comedy.

Mithen, Steven J. *The Singing Neanderthals: The Origins of Music, Language, Mind, and Body*. Harvard UP, 2006.

Moore, Tracy. "Does Your Kid Want to Change Her Pronouns? Read This." *Washington Post*, 4 Oct. 2021, https://www.washingtonpost.com/opinions/2021/10/04/does-your-kid-want-to-change-her-pronouns-read-this/.

Puar, Jasbir K. *Terrorist Assemblages: Homonationalism in Queer Times*. 2nd ed., Duke UP, 2017

Savage, Dan, host. "Episode 846." *Savage Lovecast*. 10 Jan. 2023, https://savage.love/lovecast/.

Srinivasan, Amia. *The Right to Sex*. Bloomsbury Publishing, 2022.
Sullivan, N. "The Matter of Gender." *Fuckology: Critical Essays on John Money's Diagnostic Concepts*, edited by L. Downing et al., U of Chicago P, 2015.
Wray, Alison. "Protolanguage as a Holistic System for Social Interaction." *Language & Communication* 18, 1998, pp. 47–67.

# Clinical Concepts and
# Their Application

6

# From Address to Transference

Jeffrey S. Librett

I have thought while I was awakening
That I might address them
And then I thought not at all
Not while I am feeling that I will give it to them
For them
Not at all only in collision not at all only in mistaken
But which will not at all.
I thought that I would welcome
And so I could be seen.
I then thought would I think one and welcome
Or would I not.
I then concluded that I might be deceived.

—Gertrude Stein, Stanzas in Meditation[1]

Qui n'a plus qu'un moment à vivre
N'a plus rien à dissimuler.
[One who has but a moment left to live
Has nothing more to dissimulate.]

—Philippe Quinault, Atys, cited as
epigraph to Edgar Allan Poe, "MS Found in a Bottle"[2]

227

To address oneself to another does not go without saying. Nor is it ever even possible to know the correct address of the addressee, that is, where they actually "live," the place of their experience, beyond one's own hypotheses, which in turn always remain in large part beyond one's own awareness and control. In this sense, a letter certainly does not always arrive at its destination.[3] In fact, it never quite does, if the destination is where it is aimed, which does not render insignificant the act of addressing oneself to another. Indeed, far from it: the significance of such an act begins with the impossibility of any closed hermeneutic dialogue with the other. The reason why the address to the other is a pressing concern is precisely that language prevents us from understanding each other in the dimension of our experience that exceeds language itself.

I begin by recalling the obvious point that the situation in which one subject addresses another is *the very core of the analytic situation*. In analysis, one subject attempts to speak to another virtually absent one about radically intimate experiences, those so intimately the subject's own that they elude conscious awareness. Freud proposed the "talking cure" on the basis of such an address; Lacan elaborated and displaced the Freudian discourse by exploring in detail—inspired first by surrealism, then by structuralist linguistics, and later still by mathematical logic—the importance of speech and language in the analytic situation and process. From the Rome Discourse of 1953 through the leitmotif of "L'étourdit" ("That one says remains forgotten behind what is said in what is heard/ understood"), passing by way of the notion that the unconscious is nothing other than the effects of speech upon the subject (*Seminar XI*), Lacan pushed as far he could the explication of the entanglement of the unconscious in language—with which the unconscious nonetheless remains at odds—and ultimately stressed also the importance of speech, by naming the human being "parlêtre."[4]

The clinically based reflections of the Quebec School, and of Apollon in particular, develop this attention to the dynamics of speech and language further. They do so while emphasizing strongly, as we saw in Apollon's introductory essay on "The Human in Question," the sense in which language determines the limits of ego-consciousness to ensure the solidity of the social order by actually effacing the singularity of solitary experience. This erasure occurs regardless of any ideology of individualism that might be in play, since any individualism is necessarily defined by the very language of the socius. Language excludes singular lived experience and thereby constitutes the unconscious as outside of language.[5]

Today, many representatives and practitioners of non-analytic therapeutic discourses dismiss the power of speech and language to enable the human being to achieve meaningful change. Hence, they dismiss psychoanalysis, for example as excessively intellectual and distant from the body, or as lost in hermeneutics and alienated from the referent. These dismissals constitute, however, unfortunate oversimplifications. They are predicated on the failure to think through the implications of both the influence of language on the experience of the subject (who always remains also a subject of/in language), and the limitations of this influence. The provision of a clinically attentive theoretical account of the act of the address is crucial to such a thinking-through.

But we are not just talking about the analytic situation here. The situation of analytic address obviously resembles a *fundamentally human situation* in which the very same act is undertaken. One person paradoxically—quasi-impossibly—attempts to express or represent for another person, in a movement that implies some form of intimacy (friendship, love, hope for mutual concern and attentiveness), what no one other than the speaker can ever possibly have access to. The object or content of the address here is a kind of immediacy that is at once elusive, inchoate, and infinitely specific to the (temporally complex) moment, as well as the multiple ontological modality (neither merely possible nor merely real and yet somehow both) and singular texture of its appearance precisely as subjective experience.

The distance between such an act and the everyday practical communications by means of which we negotiate our paths through social reality is, on one level, quite vast. On another level, however, the more or less constant, immanent (self)disruption of communicative processes—for example, as social dissonance or communicative breakdown—appears to be at least in part due to the insistent, indirect presence of some subjective experience that unsettles the common sense (or meaning) in terms of which the society attempts to function and to reproduce itself in every new moment. In short, people act out (in the everyday sense)—*a lot*. That is, they enact and perform acts of speech and gesture that are unattached to the reality of the situation and that remain enigmatic. They express themselves unwittingly, in accordance with what Freud called the psychopathology of everyday life. Consequently, language (understood as the semiological concretization—or synecdoche—of the social network, system, or structure) is constantly being asked to accommodate what it excludes, and it is always trying to say "no": what it excludes can only be accommodated by an alteration of the socio-semiological apparatus, the disruption of its present mode of functioning. Thus, despite their mutual distance, the attempts at intimate communication and practical reality are not *entirely* separate spheres of existence. The former impinges on the latter, and the latter both blocks and necessitates the former.

Before coming back to the function of the address (and the pathway of its call to the Other) in the *analytic situation*, we need to develop a description of the main elements and trajectory of the address *in general*, and then to situate the address (both phylogenetically and ontogenetically) in the history of the human subject. (We will see that, in its emphatic sense, the address begins prior to the installation of language and recurs—differently—at the limits of civilization both ontogenetically and phylogenetically.) After situating the address in the history of the subject, I go on to consider the modification that the trajectory of the address undergoes in the analytic situation, where we will see both its repetitive character and its sense as synecdoche for the entire analytic process. At this point in the exposition, we will examine the close yet paradoxical relationship between address and transference, according to the specific sense of "transference" developed by Gifric. Finally, I discuss as a literary illustration Edgar Allan Poe's "MS Found in a Bottle."

## Trajectory of the Address in General

To address oneself to another does not go without saying because it is obvious neither that one will manage to convey something of one's own singular experience through the (always generalizing) terms of language, nor that, even if one does so, the addressee will manage to hear—nor even that he, she, or they will make an effort to listen for—what is singular in one's experience. For the addressee's consciousness, too, is constitutively shaped by the—always-generalizing—languages of social and cultural convention. This situation, which essentially blocks the reception of the evocation of the unconscious, is what Apollon calls "the structure of the address." The Other (i.e., the person addressed) functions socioculturally and civilizationally as the "guardian of the receivable," nolens volens policing the limits of what may (or even can) be said. "How do you really feel about that?"—this everyday utterance meant to suppress the expression of strong feelings or opinions can function as a paradigmatic illustration. Skepticism concerning the possibility of successful communication in the address appears in many avatars—from social anxiety and shyness, to cynicism, to idealization of the emotive sphere, to brutal aggressiveness, and so on. In light of the realism of such skepticism, all hesitation to reach out and address another person—like the hesitation expressed in the epigram above from Gertrude Stein's poetry—is understandable. This does not mean, however, that the address is an entirely vain undertaking (in either sense of "vain"). Nothing succeeds, after all, like failure.[6]

Before describing any further the communicative intentionality and the experiential trajectory of the address in the psychoanalytic sense to be developed here, it will be useful to consider Roman Jakobson's linguistic description of the address in his far-reaching essay "Linguistics and Poetics" to *contrast* with it the psychoanalytic description.[7] For Jakobson, any given message involves six constitutive factors. It must have, in addition to the utterance or *message* itself, an *addresser* (the one emitting the message), an *addressee*, a *contact* ("physical channel and psychological connection") between them, a *code* common to both, and a *context* to which the message refers. Each of these factors, Jakobson argues, determines a function of language. Any given message will involve six functions, while the variety of kinds of messages will be determined by the relative priorities the messages give to the different functions. In these priorities, it's a question of what the message is essentially *about*. Thus, if the message is stressing the perspective of the *addresser*, it focuses on the "emotive" function; if it means to influence rhetorically the *addressee*, it privileges the "conative" function; if it aims at objectivity or *context*, it concerns itself with the "referential" function; if it refers to the *code*, it functions "metalinguistically"; if it primarily tries to maintain *contact* with the Other, it privileges the "phatic" function; and if it refers to *itself*, then it is functioning "poetically."

With reference to this admirably comprehensive and suggestive model: what function of language would be privileged in an address—to a radically *exterior* human being—of an intimate *interiority* outside of language? And how would the other functions be involved? It would seem initially as if we were speaking of a focus on the "emotive" function here, with subordinate emphases on the phatic and conative functions (which would certainly come into play in any ego-seduction or narcissistic play for the Other's attention). The poetic and metalinguistic functions would then apparently play roles subordinate to these. However—and this is where the reference to Jakobson becomes useful—the transmission of an experience of a subjective real that is outside of language would necessarily scramble and exceed the very categories that determine these functions. When the emotive is equally referential, when the code can't be separated from either reality or feeling (or the reverse), when self and other are neither clearly distinguished nor clearly unified, when touch can coincide with absence or numbing, and when the message can differ from itself: how should we determine the type of message mobilized by the address, or its primary generic or discursive affinities? The sense of this rhetorical question will determine the place of analytic listening—outside of cultural and civilizational categories, on the edge of language—to which we will return below.

Given this radically ex-centric status of the psychoanalytic address, speech in the direction of another—speech aiming to convey the character of one's experience—is always a risk, a wager. The Other cannot only fail to understand, but even more disruptively they can reject us, judge us negatively, and so on. We can never know in advance what the Other will do. Nonetheless, in addressing some intimate experience to the Other, we *hope*—not necessarily very explicitly or consciously—for some specific type of response, a response of understanding, affirmation, approval, empathy, and so on—but what we *expect* may be something else, and what the Other seems to *deliver* yet a third thing. At any rate, the Other's response will be difficult—read: impossible—for us to consider as coming from outside the social and cultural conventions within which we live our social lives. This is because all (social) egos are primarily constructed so as to confirm and reproduce the sociocultural status quo (even when it is a future-directed one). Again, the Other is always the "guardian of the receivable": a sociocultural and civilizational policeman of one sort or another. Moreover, the Other's lived response can only be expressed in some kind of semiological coding. This response will consequently fall short of what we hope for, since what we hope for is that our singularity will be recognized for and as what it is, outside of all social and cultural rules, and beyond all civilizationally determined modalities of value and belief. In the case of any given, concrete response, we cannot *not* appear to ourselves as having been falsified and caricatured in the response of the Other—who thus cannot fail to have failed to understand. Hermeneutics finds its limit in the unconscious, as what is beyond the imaginary instance of meaning per se.

What happens within us, then, when we encounter this failure of the communicative gesture? It's disturbing and disappointing not to be understood or accepted as one is, to find no place for one's own contribution in the social world. This social world appears through the Other as incapable of receiving the gift contained in the address. So now the subject is confronted not just with its own singularity but with the experience of its unbridgeable *solitude* with this singularity: one is struck by the fact that one is *alone* with this Thing. There is some anxiety in such a situation, to which there are an infinite variety of possible responses.

Because the truth will out—unconscious desire insists—every response to any gesture of address will occasion in the subject of the address a resurgence of the intimate experience of the subject, that is, *the reactivation of drive components* linked to erotogenic zones, or what Apollon calls "the letter of the body," scars in the organism from which symptoms emanate like fresh blood from an old wound, albeit sometimes a wound of delight. Confronted with an experience that it now knows anew to be "inappropriable by the other and inaccessible to the collective," the subject is forced either to *repress* this experience anew (and lend strength to symptoms) or to lend it some kind of *expression* in relation to some (present or absent, specific or general, internal or external) Other.[8] Such an expressive *act* of the unconscious in general does not necessarily take the form of verbal language, nor does it even necessarily appear outside the body of the subject. It can appear as a dream, a symptom, a lapsus, an accident, an acting out in the technical sense, a creative contribution or innovation, and it does not necessarily involve trusting or entrusting something to an explicit Other per se. It may well lack the conscious, linguistic dimension that affects all speech.

If the process of address per se is then to continue, to be renewed and repeated, such an act, arising as a result of a certain failure in an iteration of address, will have to be verbally processed and renewed in relation to some definite Other, even if its intimate content can only be "intimated"—suggestively evoked—by means of displacements of the elements of the social "language." Thus, another *act—an act of address*—follows upon the act in response to the limits encountered in the previous attempt at address. The address resumes in a new form, and the cycle of address repeats itself, if the subject is willing to risk making another attempt to rearticulate its own new act in the form of speech. Having thus far sketched the trajectory of the address, it remains to clarify at this point the sense in which, while not every act of the unconscious is an address to the Other, the address is nonetheless its own kind of act.

In what sense, then, is the act of the address itself also an *act*? In what consists its "act" character, and how should that be understood? Although it is an act of speech, the address is an act marginally outside of language, in that it is not just a matter of talk, or discourse, in the sense of a pragmatic or theoretical use of language that intends to remain within what the contextual society, culture, and civilization sanction as acceptable usage. Despite the fact that its medium is language, the act here attempts to bend language to its own purposes. Nor is it, in this act of speech, just a matter of the *performativity* of speech as envisioned by speech-act theory, since such performativity—"felicitous" performance—occurs only according to the rules of the social-conventional game, and is conceptualized without regard to subjectivity or at most in terms of a conscious intention. Beyond this speech-act character of the act of address—its illocutionary and perlocutionary dimensions as described by speech-act theory—the address is understood as an act here in the sense that it involves an (un)conscious undertaking on the part of the subject that precisely crosses the line between unconscious and conscious. It involves a risk, a wager—it's a "pari," in Pascal's terms, although a leap of human, rather than religious, faith is involved, a leap of decision. While emerging into consciousness, it is not an act of the self-mastering or sovereign ego, for there is a *driven* dimension that makes it pulsating—perhaps impulsive, repulsive, propulsive, compulsive, or expulsive—in that it is linked to the energies of jouissance at work in the body. This is what makes it compelling.[9] It follows that the term "act" is potentially misleading. For the *act* here is also *passive*, involving the *pathos* and *passio* of passion and compassion. One might consider the address, indeed, as *middle-voiced*—neither active nor passive and both. In this sense, it is an act that is experienced also as an *event*, an event of the exposure and vulnerability to the subject one is addressing (but also to one's own emergent speech). And yet in its active and expressive dimension, it *brings something new* into the world. It affects therefore not only the subject of the utterance, but also the reality of language (and the language of reality), as well as—crucially—the subjectivity, which means also the erotogenic body, of the recipient. Finally, in temporal-ontological terms, the "act" of the address is "actual," in the sense of placing something *now* into reality, the ontological zone of *presence*.

## When Does the Improbable Possibility of the Address Begin?

Given this general structure of the address, the question immediately arises as to its temporal-historical conditions, and on two levels: Do all human beings at all developmental stages and at all moments in history have recourse to the function of the address in the same manner? Let us consider the ontogenetic question of developmental stages first. Manifestly, we don't speak to others in the same way across our lifetimes. From the psychoanalytic point of view being articulated here, not only does it not go without saying, but it cannot be said that the human address as such, in the emphatic and not simply phatic sense, can be fully possible until a certain point has been reached in the development, genesis, or individual evolution of the human being—the point of adolescence. To circumscribe this moment when the address in the emphatic sense becomes possible, it will be useful to consider the four phases in the coming-into-being of the subject: first childhood, second childhood, puberty, and adolescence. Of course, these are historically and culturally-civilizationally conditioned and variable in a way to which we cannot do justice here, although we will touch upon the historicity of adolescence below. A certain degree of abstraction will therefore have to granted here as unavoidable.

In the *first phase of childhood*, approximately from birth to age five, the child is not yet fully or firmly inscribed in language in the sense of the social order. Little children are allowed, after all, a certain amount of *Narrenfreiheit* (the "freedom of the mad"), and they are not responsible for the social order and cultural rules. The parents assume responsibility (or don't). Young children have innumerable experiences that remain outside of language, and for which the question of how they might be addressed to another does not quite emerge as such. The children may speak of these experiences as if out of a dream, as exemplified by the sublime surrealism of the toddler. Of course, here already cultural notions of gender roles are being established, through dolls and toys that begin to instill the language of social rules and norms, including gender norms. But this is the age of speech prior to the mastery of language qua social order, such that speech still remains to a great extent outside of language.

When the child comes to consciousness and begins to realize that its inner experience is imperceptible to the parental or other caregivers, and that large segments of its experience are also unwelcome to the caregivers and surrounding adults, it passes into *second childhood*. It learns to repress what doesn't fit into what the parents are capable of recognizing, as it works to gain approval. What cannot be addressed to the other, the child keeps to itself. In this way the child discovers in a much more conscious way an "unaddressable" dimension of its experience, putting one of the conditions of (im)possibility of the address into place, necessary but insufficient. Apollon characterizes this point of passage from the first to the second childhood phase (this latter corresponding in time roughly to Freudian "latency") in terms of the first successful lie the child tells. When the child tells a lie that goes unperceived, it realizes both a certain freedom and a certain loneliness based on the separation of its interiority from the exterior world of the others, and it enters into negotiation with the social world (in neurosis, at least), in the attempt to obtain sufficient approval to survive and thrive there. Second childhood corresponds roughly to the years of grammar school, from around age six to age eleven, when the child learns the three R's and tends to appear most "reasonable"—it's the age of Enlightenment within individual development. (We return to Enlightenment in its historical sense below.) Here, the child is no longer involved in the infantile proto-address—which, at the limit, is the pure cry or cooing prior to language. Nor is the child yet again involved in the address in its developed form (as will occur in adolescence), because this latter address presupposes a sense of the radical inadequacy of the social language, a sense that the repression of the nonreceivable has constituted an insufficient strategy.

When *puberty* arrives—the physical, biological maturation of the reproductive system roughly between the ages of ten to fourteen, and the cultural response to this—this phase presents itself quite differently to boys and girls: the boy has the experience of ejaculative orgasm, phallic jouissance, whereas the girl has the experience of menstruation. This nascent adulthood and independence of the children threatens the society, culture, and civilization with the danger that the children will diverge from the parental and societal expectations. The result of such a divergence would be that the society, along with its concentric cultural and civilizational frameworks, would not manage to reproduce itself. Censorship is redoubled at this point—the woman, who is biologically coming into being, must now be generated and shaped as object of the man's desire, and as mother of the children to come. (Of course, this is the culmination of processes that began even prior to the birth of the female child.) The man must now be constructed symmetrically as the one who seeks to assert himself by choosing a female object of desire, and by developing himself into an instrument of the preservation of the collective status quo, through military or quasi-military activities (such as sport), and subsequently through entry into the pre-given professional pathways. What imposes itself with particular force on the pubescent young—the set of expectations that organize gender identity and sexual and pairing behavior, within the larger context of rules about how to be a proper human being in the given civilizational space (which determines what to believe and what not to believe, as grounding of the more specific cultural regimes)—is what Apollon has called *"the cultural montage of the sexual."* One of the main emphases of his work in the recent decade has been on the development of the claim that in all civilizations of which we have any knowledge, the cultural montage of the sexual has always involved the *censorship of the feminine*, that is, of feminine jouissance, in both men and women, and even principally in men. Think of the caricatural expectations of masculinity and proto-maternity that we still largely impose on our young, but with especial force on the pubescent young. To be sure, in Occidental liberal circles, the expression of "feminine" traits (however defined) in the male has become explicitly acceptable or receivable, for example, as homosexuality and more recently as gender fluidity or as trans female identity, and even as non-toxic masculinity. But this expression of the feminine in the male remains, even in these circles, mostly without rigorous conceptualization, and it stands politically under grave threat outside of these circles, in large portions of the United States, Europe, and so on. Moreover, it is often isolated in specific identity categories rather than being regarded as universally expressible. Likewise, the conflation of the feminine with the maternal is still widely pervasive in our world and strongly present in our thought, supported by the scientistic biologism of our age. The implications for the address in puberty are that it is quasi-impossible for young people to speak with one another, outside conventional forms, about what they are going through. Their physical maturation brings them into contact with new modes of sensation and inner experience (experience of their erotically developing bodies, and of their social experiences with others) that are excluded from the language of the cultural montage, entangled as these new forms of sensation and experience are, moreover, with infantile memories, childhood fantasies, and so on. How should they—middle schoolers—speak precisely of such things on the scene of social role reality?

The distinction between puberty and *adolescence* is almost entirely disregarded in our culture, which tends to reduce adolescence to puberty (i.e., to biological maturation and the direct causal consequences thereof), and this generally still in Freud's work. The passage from puberty to adolescence involves the collapse of the plausibility of the cultural montage of the sexual (i.e., the experience of its radical insufficiency as a model for singular inner experience) and the loss of confidence in the sociocultural semiosis in general, as well as in the civilizational belief systems that back it up.[10] This is not a result of the natural mechanisms of homeostasis (which culture and civilization attempt to replace with a "second nature"), but of what disrupts them in the human spirit. In Apollon's formulation, the adolescent (somewhere roughly between the ages of fifteen and twenty-five) rediscovers within the self a dimension—beyond the pleasure principle—that exceeds all cultures and civilizations. This dimension is at once radically singular and—precisely by virtue of this trait—universally human. The adolescent is, as it were, a "natural" primitivist (I return to the connection with modernist "primitivism" below). The adolescent can accordingly seem at times infantile, and they indeed rediscover in their singularity a connection with early childhood experiences of what is outside of language and unaddressable as such—real castration. This sensed singularity implies the potential to make a new contribution to the evolution of the human, the contribution of a new voice and new vision, however small: a new "spirit." In the sense Apollon gives to this term, "spirit," it refers to the capacity to represent to oneself what doesn't exist, to desire it, and to bring it into existence. Such a notion revives and displaces what one can encounter in more traditional terms, for example, as productive (rather than reproductive) imagination and the capacity for *poiesis*.[11] With the upsurging of the drives—as distinct from natural instincts (a point Freud underlines by using "Trieb" rather than "Instinkt")—that occur at this time, the adolescent reencounters an internal difference from the others. The event of this radically renewed encounter coincides with the collapse of the belief in the authority of those who hitherto seemed to be legitimately in charge (and of all that they stood for). The collapse of the belief and the encounter with internal difference, indeed, reinforce each other reciprocally. At this juncture, the address in the emphatic sense appears. The hope of speaking with another about intimate experiences, and of obtaining a hearing that goes beyond the obscurantism of all socially given languages—the hope of encountering an Other who would not function as the "guardian of the receivable"—pushes the human being to address in this fuller sense someone else, despite the fact that the adolescent is rightly uncertain at this point that anyone could have the patience and openness to hear what he, she, or they are searching for the means to express. The adolescent search for singular expression—as distinct from the pubescent divergences from conventional parental expectations (which are more easily susceptible to cooptation by the discourse of the peers, that is, little more than the nascent next form of the oppressive social order)—is so crucial to the newfound eroticism of the human being at this point that Apollon has formulated the connection as an identity: *"the address is sex."* And this is the case not only during adolescence but also thereafter. To *receive* the address of the other—that is, to occupy the position of the Other of the address while refusing to function as the guardian of the receivable—is to accompany the subject of the address in their search for the object and end of their endless jouissance. The liberation of unbound drive activity, pervading the erotic *body* of the young person (as distinct from the *organism*), leads the (speaking) human being to seek *expression* of these intensities in some *aesthetic-rhetorical* manner in relation to the body of the other. The being seeks this expression in acts in (and on) the language of social reality, through which the "sexual" dimension makes itself felt as a desire to have one's singular existence heard and registered, and a desire to receive the unreceivable desire of the Other in turn. This aesthetic-rhetorical space is necessary to the address itself, because beyond culture and civilization judgment must proceed without a law. Regarded in terms of nonessentialist gender determinations, furthermore, the representation of the unrepresentable in such a space emerges (from beneath its censorship) as the *feminine* (within a man or a woman), related to a jouissance that has no determinate beginning or end. In this sense, the risk one assumes in undertaking the address is the risk of the feminine as such. The reception of the address, again whether in a man or a woman, accordingly may be regarded as appearing in a *masculine* light, albeit as the passivity more passive than passivity, since it concerns the assumption of an ethical position in response to the Other, along with its responsibilities.[12]

## Historical Excursus: Adolescence in the Age of *Mondialisation*

Following Apollon, we have said that (ontogenetically) the address enters the human horizon with particular force and explicitness in adolescence. Now, because both adolescence and psychoanalysis exist in history, we need—resisting the ahistorical tendencies of some forms of psychoanalysis—to consider the *historical situation* of adolescence today, in connection with that of psychoanalysis. How do we understand the situation of *adolescence* in *history* both as to its origins and today? I recall here just several points of reference concerning this large and complex question.

First, adolescence does not appear explicitly in (Western) history until the *modernist* moment. For example, Philippe Ariès, the great historian of childhood, tells us that the first adolescent in history was Richard Wagner's Siegfried, and calls the twentieth century "the century of adolescence."[13] Further, adolescence does not enter psychological discourse as an interesting and nameable phase-entity until G. Stanley Hall's book on *Adolescence* (1904). This was a time when the "youth" movements in Europe were developing, and when the arts and letters were strongly emphasizing "youth," for example not only in *Jugendstil* (the "Young style" of the turn of the century), but also before that in "das junge Wien" ("Young Vienna," a post-naturalist writers group, which in turn was preceded by "das junge Deutschland" ["Young Germany"] in the 1830s–1850s), and somewhat later in the formative rhetoric of expressionism. Literary texts in diverse genres and national traditions were thematizing the problems of "youth" and especially young sexuality in a repressive society.[14] This is also the time when modern art (starting with some post-impressionists and continuing in cubism and expressionism) pursued a certain "primitivism," whose desire to escape civilization was masked (literally), impoverished, and limited by the fact that it was still formulated within Western civilizational notions of the a- or pre-civilizational "primitive."[15] Adolescence thus emerged in the broad sense in the modernist period, albeit—a point on which Apollon insists—most frequently as conflated with puberty.

But—although this is a much more complicated question than can be dealt with here—modernism itself harkened back in some of its key manifestations to the irrationalist tendencies in the Counterenlightenment and Romanticism. Not inappropriately, G. Stanley Hall defines adolescence as the "Sturm und Drang"—or (according to the conventional but inadequate translation) "Storm and Stress"—period in a person's life. Here, he refers, through the expression "Sturm und Drang," to the Counterenlightenment period in German literature during the late eighteenth century (which of course was accompanied by parallel movements in other national traditions in the West), when the rationalism of the Enlightenment, which had been meant to provide a lingua franca for all religious cultures in Europe (like what schooling accomplishes in second childhood), was placed in question. The specific reference—as is rarely recognized in the psychological literature—is to

Friedrich Maximilian von Klinger, whose play *Sturm und Drang* (1777) gave its name to the movement and the sensibility represented by people like Friedrich Heinrich Jacobi, Johann Georg Hamann, Johann Gottfried Herder, the young Johann Wolfgang Goethe and Friedrich Schiller, and Jakob Michael Reinhold Lenz, all of whom criticized the Enlightenment as failing to do justice to individual subjectivity in its irrational and passionate character.[16] From this perspective, adolescence seems to have announced itself already in a particularly poignant form with the first (anti)modern turn against the first properly modern sociocultural norms. These norms had been defined by the Enlightenment discourse of "reason," with its attempted separation of public rationality from what was to have been henceforth private belief and feeling. This earliest, in some respects still preliminary emergence of adolescence as a modern phenomenon consisted, then, in the first rebellion against the felt nihilism of modern reason and, in a sense, against language itself. This became particularly explicit, for example, in Friedrich Heinrich Jacobi's critique of Spinoza as a "nihilist," and in his subsequent leveling of the same claim against the German Idealists.[17]

The resurgence of certain Counterenlightenment tendencies (primarily on the right) in the early twentieth century must then be understood as a reaction against later versions of reason: the discourses of positivism, realism, and literary naturalism in particular (with its ostensibly scientific foundations). However, in the resurgence of "youth" culture and the rejection of "reality" by aesthetic modernists, for example, it is by no means as if all were simply well with the adolescent sensibility, nor as if the address to the other appeared as nonproblematic. Indeed, with the avant-gardes as World War I approached, and especially after 1914, the capacity of the young to imagine a seamless articulation with the social order became more troubled than ever. Adolescent (anti) modernism was primarily at odds with the society around it. Of course, this is a topic for a book of its own. Suffice it therefore briefly to recall further—in terms of *literary-historical* points of reference, which I mention because of their *sociohistorical* and psychoanalytic significance—the fact that all three major literary genres in modernism were affected by a certain critical condition of adolescence and, along with it, precisely the problematization of the function of address.

The first of these genres, the novel, has thematized "youth" in a particularly important subgenre, the *Bildungsroman* (the "novel of formation" or coming-of-age story), which always traces precisely the passage from childhood to adulthood, and the integration of the protagonist into the social order. This form first became particularly important in the late eighteenth century as a neoclassical reaction *against* the disruptive form of adolescence the Counterenlightenment had formulated as "Sturm und Drang." But the novel of formation had already become extremely problematic by the middle of the nineteenth century (as indexed by Gustave Flaubert's *A Sentimental Education*), and then diverged into formal experimentation in the twentieth century, when such an integration was no longer dimly imaginable, not even on the level of novelistic form.[18] This disruption extended, for example, into Sartre's *Nausea*, the existentialist novel in general, and beyond. At the same time, *drama* tended to lose or challenge in modernism its dialogical and interpersonal core or coherence, as address and response become increasingly disjointed and nonsequential.[19] Finally, in *lyric (poetry)*, the address to the Other, especially as apostrophe, became increasingly suspect, contrived, and difficult.[20] The poem became increasingly hermetic and withdrawn in order not to be absorbed into the bad status quo by the socially functional language of the given cultural collective.[21] In short, first of all, modernist literature highlighted the importance of *"youth" and young adulthood as a period of crisis* in which it seems impossible to enter the social order without losing one's authenticity. Second, at the same time, this literature highlighted a more general *impossibility of addressing another person* in a coherent way, and the pressing need to find some way of doing so.[22]

And what now? If both adolescence and the entailed pressing need for the expression of intimate experiences—experiences that exceed language and consciousness—exploded onto the scene in the modernist period, how much more strongly must they assert themselves in our *own* age? Apollon usefully characterizes this age, under the heading of *"mondialisation,"* as an age in which the conflict between not just cultures but also civilizations has become so broadly pervasive—especially in the urban centers—that we can less and less manage to uphold the separate and "substantial" identities of these various foundations of the civilizationally determined beliefs and promises that are called upon to ground cultural norms.[23] Just as adolescence in general, regarded *ontogenetically*, recalls and reconnects with the spirit of infantility that appeared well prior to the educative inscription of the young child in culture and civilization in second childhood, so adolescence in the age of mondialisation recalls *phylogenetically*—and reconnects with—the origin and universality of the human in speech before language by pushing beyond all given forms of civilization as they collide with each other.[24]

This juncture contains both positive and negative potential. The contemporary responses to the nihilism resulting from civilizational conflict are taking new forms different from the late eighteenth- and late nineteenth- (and early twentieth-century) forms. The context has changed drastically. The civilizational reference points today radically relativize and suspend each other by interpenetrating in the urban spaces, the minds, the marriages, the aesthetic sensibilities, and the ethical discourses of the current globalizing subjects. In this context, the adolescent discovery of an inner dimension that exceeds any given culture or civilization is more *generalizable* than ever before (extending plausibly into adulthood) because the cultures and civilizations are starting to dissolve: the inner dimension is more undeniable and inescapable than in the past. The discovery of this inner, singular dimension is also, however, more *problematic* than ever before, because as the grounds of the norms (and the norms themselves) start to dissolve, the possibility of any shared language that would enable the *expression* of an inner experience becomes more and more doubtful. This situation makes it seem as if it must be both *more* and *less* possible to communicate inner experience than hitherto, insofar as inner experience can only be communicated simultaneously *through* language and *against* language. If "civility" (for example) fades, inner experience seems to emerge in immediate expression. But if language evades one's grasp—social and cultural norms are fluid and unclear—how can one use it and displace it in order to speak? No doubt, the emergence of this problem—this impossibility or aporia—accounts for much of the global backlash we are currently experiencing against *mondialisation* itself. But—to stay with our topic—where is the place of the *analyst* in this historical situation of quasi-universalized adolescence (which nonetheless remains under the censorship of the feminine in the society at large) in the face of a crumbling language, a social order widely felt to be in fundamental disarray? And how is this place of the analyst determined with respect to the address the analyst is called upon to receive beyond the realm of the socially receivable or acceptable?

## The Analyst as Absent Other: From Address to Transference

How does an analysis begin? When the communicative connection between the subject and the social network is not working out so well—when the ego's self-narrative (i.e., its ongoing autobiographical discourse) is faltering, and the mutual seductions of world and self are issuing in a seemingly unnecessary degree of conflict and/or dissatisfaction—the individual may find his, her, or their way into the office of an analyst. Here, the patient's ego will attempt, at first, to rectify that link; it will work to achieve a more successful mode of communication with others. And the ego will work to harmonize the different parts of itself. While Freud says at one point that the neurotic suffers from "reminiscences," one might with equal plausibility say that the neurotic suffers from the failure of the address. Even more broadly—including perversion and psychosis—the subject confronts the failure to create harmony between world and ego by excluding the undeniable and pressing intensities and pulsations within that subject, the forbidden or simply inarticulable elements that are thus already present, albeit veiled, in both self and world. The person who seeks treatment is encountering some difficulty in managing the effects of this failure and in accepting a kind of responsibility for these effects.

But it is not the analyst's aim to fix the functioning of the address. The analyst does not attempt to return the subject's acts (of speech or self-expression) into the culturally and civilizationally constituted and sanctioned space of the norms, that is, into the "structure of the address." To fix the address is precisely not the *analyst's* aim, although it *would* be the aim of the *therapist*, who works to reestablish the smooth integration of the ego within the social network. Such integration can be facilitated, but never perfected. Instead, analysis works with the necessary limits of the address, given that language—the signifier—can never fully access, convey, or comprehend the unconscious per se.

How, then, does the analyst respond to the act in which a subject of the unconscious addresses itself to the Other, attempting to insert its own spirit (i.e., the lived experience of its own ultimately hallucinatory jouissance) into the social space of the others? The analytic situation distinguishes itself from the non-analytic one in that the analyst *withdraws* from the scene of the cultural montage of the sexual. That is, the analyst takes an inner distance from the conventions about what forms of communicative behavior are acceptable, recognizable, acknowledgeable—again, "receivable," in Apollon's language—within the bounds of the society (as overdetermined by its cultural and civilizational dimensions). The social interlocutor gives the *wrong* answer; the analyst gives *none* at all, so to speak, in order to say nothing but: keep going toward *that* singular Thing. The analyst says this "nothing" primarily by underlining intermittently any (indirect) manifestations of the unconscious in the analysand's speech, actions, and reported experiences. This self-withdrawal of the analyst from the scene of social interaction on the one hand has the effect of clarifying that no Other can receive the subject's address in a direct manner, that there is no mirror in the Other, no one there to save (or condemn) the analysand. On the other hand, the analyst's relative silence indicates the absence of any (sociocultural) ego inserting itself there to block the analysand's creative transmission of their truth. The reduction of responsive expression to a minimum indicates the presence of a listening not circumscribed by the socially acceptable (or unacceptable), a listening that is directed toward the apprehension of the plangent silence that resonates around the words of the address itself, in the midst of which they appear and fade away. In its most thoroughgoing preparation, such listening arises out of the identification with the object (a), with which the analyst enters into the position of analyst through the procedure of the passe. Such identification renders this listening possible, because the object delineates a site radically outside of the sociocultural as well as civilizational surround and constraint, a zone outside the given. (As we will see below, for the sake of an analysis with a neurotic or a pervert, the stakes of which concern the sociocultural Other, or symbolic castration, but do not extend to the civilizational limits—the limits of a world per se—attainment of the penultimate stage in the clinician's own analysis may be sufficient for the constitution and sustenance of the transference.) The notion of the analyst's silence refers, therefore, not primarily to an absence of any verbal response, but to the silencing *within the analyst* of the voices of the social order, of the norms, imperatives, and proscriptions of the cultural contexts, and of the delimitations of the believable in the civilizational grounds of cultures. The usual reference to being "nonjudgmental" is given a more rigorous formulation here; it cannot come about simply as an assertion of goodwill.

The condition for the possibility of an analytic process in the analysand is thus the transformation of the singular address into a series of addresses without a specific addressee that sustain a transference, and one condition of this transformation is the falling silent of the voices of society, culture, and civilization within the analyst. The analyst must have become maximally emptied, through an analysis, of the sociocultural-civilizational Other. The way in which these voices can be induced to fade into the background, however, concerning the sociocultural level, is through the traversal of symbolic castration, whereas, concerning the civilizational level, it is through the passage through the fundamental fantasy to the object. I'll restrict myself to the former in this context. Where is such a traversal of symbolic castration situated in the trajectory of an analysis, and what does it concern?

In the perspective of Gifric and the *École freudienne du Québec*, an analysis involves four principal (temporally interpenetrating) stages or levels, which I present in excessively schematized form here. Each stage corresponds to a stage of development, concerns a particular level of the unconscious, and relates in some way to the modalities of castration.[25] Thus, the first stage of analysis (which can follow a shorter or longer preliminary period of ego-resistance), involving the engagement of the *transference*, concerns the reawakening of *early childhood* memories and drives and the renewed mobilization of the letters of the erotogenic body. These elements of the body begin to resonate with the resurgence of the human spirit in the face of the absent Other as the subject tries to speak about its experience. The analysand experiences, in anxiety, the beginning of the repetition or reliving of the effraction of the psyche by an *unaddressable* inner real, a solitary singularity—implying the partial exile from the natural organism into the erotogenic body—which the analysis will sustain across its subsequent phases. The analysand begins to have an encounter with the unconscious in the sense of the *real castration* of psyche by spirit.

In the second phase or on the second level, the analysand *traverses seduction* toward the fall of the Other. That is, they revisit and deconstruct the effects of *second childhood*, in which the subject attempted to address and seduce the parental and societal Other, an attempt that was attended by the *repression* of that part of its interiority that the child imagined would not be receivable by the social Other. How did one lie by omission, to oneself and the Other, to survive in the world of the family and its social-contextual language, and how has this survival strategy affected one's subsequent trajectory? What has one left out? Here, the analysand works through the *imaginary castration*, whereby the construction of the self in the image of the proximate Other was once achieved, always at the cost of losing track of what did not appear in the mirroring eyes of the Other. The clinic of the *dream* is particularly crucial here, as the dream contests palpably the ego-narrative that was built up substantially during this phase of life.

In the third stage, the work of analysis involves primarily the remembering, enacting, and working-through of *symbolic castration*: the manner in which the subject lived and still lives the imposition of the *cultural montage of the sexual* during the phase of *puberty* (which may never have ended, since the passage into adolescence is not a mere question of biology). The reconsideration and (dis)articulation of the effects of this imposition on the subject of a "cultural identity" and all that such an identity entails (prescriptions and proscriptions of roles in socio-sexual reproduction) requires that the analysand begin to undo the *censorship of the feminine* within themselves and in their responses to others. This undoing will pass largely by way of the analysis of the *symptoms* that here both resisted and acquiesced to the impositions of culture. This analytic movement issues in the emergence of an aesthetic dimension in terms of which the subject's act will orient itself in the space beyond the *cultural* law.

Finally, in the fourth stage, an analysand will work to return to (or experience for the first time) the *adolescent* experience of an inner dimension that exceeds any *civilization* whatsoever. This even more radical process will involve the experience of an ethics (of the sublime) that will supplement the aesthetics (of the beautiful) previously (re) discovered. Self-responsibility shifts and expands here in the direction of a concern for the human whose future is always in the process of unfolding, and to which the subject finds itself called to contribute, precisely in terms of the spirit—the real of jouissance—that has been disrupting its organic wholeness since the prenatal moment when it found itself struck by the voice of the father in the mother's body. Transformation of the originary (or primal scene) fantasy into the *fundamental fantasy* is worked out here. At this point, beyond the culturally censored, what is at stake is that which the given *civilization* renders *unsayable*, as the object of unconscious desire.

While this schematization risks in its extreme brevity the emptiness of all formalizations, it has been unavoidable here in order to sketch and situate briefly, and still in an introductory manner, the sense of the claim that only the traversal of symbolic castration in the analyst can enable the analyst to respond to the analysand's address in such a way as—at least with regard to the structures of neurosis and perversion—to create the space in which transference can be possible. Again, the analyst does so by responding from outside the culturally given structure of the address, which is organized in consistency with the cultural montage of the sexual. To answer from within this structure of address would, of course, also prevent the possibility of an analysis of a woman by a man, or the reverse, and indeed it would equally deeply compromise the analysis of a man by a man, or of a woman by a woman. For—as Apollon argues in various places—the culture always creates the "man" and the "woman" that it needs for its own reproduction, thus closing out whatever escapes the language that the given culture speaks. None of the four levels of the unconscious, and none of its still living history, can be welcomed in the analysand's speech if the analyst is not able to avoid the position of social conversation. For social relationality perpetuates the exclusion of infantile experiences, childhood silences, and the (nonessentialist) feminine and masculine dimensions. Instead of these, it favors the constructs of the *woman* as mother and object, of the *man* as the one who uses this object for orgasmic pleasure and reproductive respectability, and of the exemplary *human* as the one who upholds what the civilization determines as worthy of belief. Indeed, concerning civilization, which is—again—a crucial stake in the treatment of psychosis, the analyst must have completed the fourth stage of their analysis in order not to refuse on some level the psychotic position, insofar as it is beyond the limits of any given civilization. In sum, the beginning of the process—engagement of the transference—can only occur if the address of the analysand confronts the silence of an absent Other who has, minimally, worked through their own inscription in the cultural symbolic order.

But what exactly *is* transference? How is it conceived here? Precisely not in the sense that has become standard in psychoanalysis in general, namely as the transfer of an affective and cognitive relationship with a primal "object"—such as father or mother or sibling—onto a new "object"—for example, a lover or friend or, in the classical case, the analyst himself. This form of transference as resistance, the explicit analysis of which drives and organizes much in a classical psychoanalytic therapy, is characterized from the standpoint of the analytic theory developed at Gifric, in the wake of Lacan, as an "imaginary" transference.[26] It makes up one dimension of the structure of address as socioculturally established. Nor is transference conceived here as a "symbolic" one, according to the middle-period Lacanian notion of the analyst as a symbolic rather than an imaginary Other, to whom would be addressed the deconstruction of the imaginary ego, in favor of the disenchantments of the signifier. Rather, the transference envisioned here could be characterized as a "real" transference: the "transfer" of the unconscious qua extra-linguistic experience—the real of jouissance—into the aesthetic space that has been opened up by the analyst's voiding of the imaginary-symbolic position.[27] While the Lacanian notion of the analyst as identified with the object (a) is still relevant here, the notion of such an identification has been displaced in Apollon's thought to the degree that the object (a) cause of (the analyst's) desire is now understood as the concern for the human as such in its open future.

The transference consists, then, in the transfer of what was previously outside of language into the analysand's consciousness. This can only happen when, under the effect of the analyst's silence, the analysand stops addressing the analyst as a sociocultural(-civilizational) Other. The beginning of the transference can be glimpsed, for example, when the analysand speaks of something of which they have never spoken before, perhaps even says: "I never knew I knew this," or "I didn't realize I was going to say that," or something of the sort. By withdrawing from the position of the Other whom the analysand would address, the analyst opens up an *alternative* to the socioculturally constructed and constrained "structure of the address" and provides the space in which the analysand may find a different way of addressing the Thing to an absent or barred and nonidentified Other. The act of the analyst must be to *maneuver* in such a way as to avoid supporting the limits defined by culture and civilization, and instead to intervene only to re-mark or underline the emergences of that which has hitherto never been said by the analysand, in order to support the analysand's work to give expression to what still remains outside of language. What the analyst then needs to await in subsequent sessions is the analysand's acts and experiences outside of (and/or within) the session—dreams, symptoms, enactments, speech-acts, fantasies—that will extend the transference—that is, the ongoing transfer or transferal—of unconscious contents into the space of consciousness determined by language. The analysand's response to what they have said will be to do and say more, if the said has not been deflected by interpretation, but has been received and welcomed, given space as such to the maximum achievable degree. In this way, the address to the Other is transformed into address without address (no longer seeking validation by a symbolico-imaginary social Other), that is, transference, which also involves a love of the knowledge of the unconscious, and the analysis can proceed. Here, the analysand doesn't speak to be recognized by an Other. (In this crucial trait, we can see how the notion of transference developed by Apollon and the other analysts at Gifric and the École freudienne du Québec is consistent with the treatment of *psychosis*, which in traditional Freudian theory was deemed incapable of forming a "transference" in the sense of an imaginary investment in the person of the analyst as social Other.) Thus begins the movement toward an ever more decisive ethical assumption of responsibility. The unconscious will act repeatedly now to contest the illusions of the ego-narrative and move the analysand from one phase of the analysis to the next, for as long as the analyst maintains the position of sociocultural(-civilizational) abstinence, and for as long as the analysand's ethics enables them to sustain the effort of this work, including the disruptions it entails for the ego's functioning on the social stage.

Finally, we can see that the altered cycle of the paradoxical address-without-address that characterizes the elementary movement of analysis as such (under transference) constitutes a *synecdochic summary*, with each turn, of the analytic treatment as a whole. 1) The movement begins with the insistence or upsurging of some unaddressable unconscious impulse, which, as in early childhood, finds initially no language in which to speak. But the analysand nonetheless attempts to speak of this, as in the engagement of the transference. 2) They pursue the knowledge *of* the unconscious and encounter—as in second childhood, or in the struggle with imaginary castration in general—the obstacles of (parentally mediated) language, as socially given names for things. 3) In confronting the silence of an absent Other, the subject is necessarily thrown back upon its own experience, which mobilizes drives in the anxiety of solitude. The analysand here is like a pubescent young person encountering the alienation of the cultural montage of the sexual and beginning to struggle with it. But in this mobilization the subject is also confronted with the eroticism of the body and the aesthetic experience it evokes beyond the pleasure principle. Like the third stage in analysis, in which the cultural montage is worked through and exceeded with joy, sorrow, and exuberance, this moment structurally leads to the next. 4) Some internal act manifests itself then—as symptom, dream, lapsus, enactment, creative gesture, or social intervention. This is the adolescent and a-civilizational moment, as it were, of the cycle of address-without-address that leads to the next session of importance and corresponds to the last phase of analysis. In turn, the next significant session corresponds, on the one hand, to the act of termination in the passe and, on the other hand, to the beginning of analysis anew. From the act between the sessions to the distinct act of its being spoken as an address-without-address in the next session, the movement is—in miniature—that of the sublime passage from aesthetics to ethics, since here the movement of speech is a movement toward an assumption of responsibility for a contribution to the human as the space of the paradoxical sharing of an un-shareable singular experience. Thus, the modified movement of the address-without-address under transference carries the analysis from one session to the next and embodies the movement of the entire analysis synecdochically in each cycle.

## Postscript: Address-without-Address from a Subject at Sea

Edgar Allan Poe's story "MS Found in a Bottle" is well suited to concretize certain aspects of the act of address-without-specific-address I have sketched above under the notion of the transference.[28] Not only is Poe already deeply involved in the twentieth-century history of psychoanalytic discussions, from Marie Bonaparte's earlier large study of author and work to the later debate about the relationship between the signifier and the letter in the exchange between Lacan and Derrida. But, more importantly for our purposes, Poe is a late romantic proto-modernist, something of an outsider in American literary history, and a writer whose purple prose and affective and imaginative excesses make it hard not to see in him an exemplary instance of adolescence. I do not provide anything like an exhaustive reading of this small text here, but merely suggest a way of receiving the text as an aesthetic work that points to an experience that is outside of language and thus beyond socioculturally sanctioned reality in the sense invoked above. Further, I underline that this fictional text attempts to communicate that experience not for the sake of the *ego* (the anonymous fictional author of the manuscript-report, who is in any case literally and figurally lost, out of control, and at sea) but for the sake of what it can contribute to future *humanity*, its readers, by opening them up to an experience that is singular in the extreme, and cannot be anticipated by an Other. Of course, Poe himself achieved early recognition with this story and earned $100 for its publication in 1833, but we can assume that, being an exemplary *poète maudit* (gloriously celebrated in Charles Baudelaire's distorted account, which established Poe's international reputation), he writes out of a desire for something more and other than mere success on the social scene.[29]

The fictional author and narrator of the manuscript tells us at the outset on the one hand that he is estranged from family and country. Thus, it appears as if he had already in some degree dealt with both imaginary and symbolic castration. (We will see below how this reckoning—if it was one—will turn out to have been child's play compared with the more radical traversal he will experience when he is lost at sea—a journey without return, like analysis, as Apollon stresses.) In addition and on the other hand, the narrator assures us also from the start that he is a rational ego, given to physicalistic explanations, a "mind to which the reveries of fancy have been a dead letter and a nullity" (2). Hence, we are supposed to know and believe that the experiences of which he is telling us are not the "raving of a crude imagination" (2)—in short, what he is presenting is supposed to be a *reality* of some kind. However, what ensues will be difficult to connect with any reality our own rational egos can sanction. The "incredible tale" (2) reads like the description of a purely *subjective* interior journey, or some sort of allegory. The "dead letter" will be awakening here with a vengeance. The upshot is that the story this narrator tells, and within which he exists, is posited at once as subjective and as real, as a *subjective real*.

If we return, as we read Poe's narrator's message, to Roman Jakobson's analysis of the functions of language in speech in "Linguistics and Poetics" discussed above, we will readily see that this message conflates, first of all, the emotive and the referential functions of verbal communication (expressing the narrator's feelings, describing his situation), the lyrical and the epic literary modes. It also places in question, moreover, the codes of rational discourse and reality (employing the metalinguistic function). Further, it reaches out to an absent and extremely implausible reader (thereby both emphatically stressing and questioning the phatic function). And it evidently tries to persuade the reader of the reality of these impossible events (the conative function), even while it ironizes their plausibility. Finally, it highlights its own use of language through a hyperbolic, elevated, but also purple rhetoric (the poetic function). The evocative singularity of this act of address (which pushes beyond and against the "structure of the address" in its socially normative form, including the socially normative form of the literary conventions of its day) asserts itself in a reading experience in which *one cannot quite discern* which of these functions is being emphasized and where it is being emphasized. In trying to determine what sort of message this is, one is, like the narrator, "at sea": the experience of the form is thus very much like the experience of which it is the strange "vehicle" or "vessel." Something not quite linguistically graspable is being communicated here indirectly, suggestively evoked, by virtue of the force of the author—the drives—exercised both in and against language.

The simple story refers to this inner Thing outside language indirectly but compellingly, through the vintage Poe aestheticism that always borders—deliciously—on tastelessness: the narrator has set sail as a passenger on a ship from Java "having no other inducement than a kind of nervous restlessness which haunted me as a fiend" (2). A demonic haunting drives him from the start: death-drive seeking appeasement beyond the pleasure principle. Without delay, the ship is suddenly overwhelmed by a storm-wave that drowns everyone on board except the narrator and one "old Swede," and the ship is driven head-long southward for five days by an uncontrollable wind. In the form of this wind, the inner fiend appears without: some kind of alien spirit at once natural, supernatural, and unnatural is driving them along, like a figure for the unconscious itself, the real of the spirit that breaks into the organic psyche and drives it in ways it cannot control. The storm, then, figures the unconscious, and according to traditional conventions, the sea figures its feminine dimension, a feminine dimension that is situated within the subject, yet quite real.

This spirit not only disturbs the seafarers' existence in space but disrupts the continuity of time in a way that points to both an *escape* from the human and an *anticipation* of the human, prior to the imaginary. Strikingly, the sixth day never arrives, and for the remainder of the text the ship is "enshrouded in pitchy darkness": "eternal night continued to envelope us" and "all around were horror, and thick gloom, and a black sweltering desert of ebony" (7). Of course, the fifth day of creation in the Old Testament—a civilizational founding text—features the creation of the creatures of the sea and the air, whereas on the sixth day the creatures of the earth, including humans, are created. Thus, in the inner experience figured by the narrator's story, the subject finds himself in a moment prior to the creation of all those who live on solid ground or in air, and most especially the human beings. Marie Bonaparte is probably not entirely wrong to see in this text a fantasy of the return to the womb, but with a bit more hermeneutic modesty or reticence we might say merely that the ego is going into a space of experience that is outside and prior to its own emergence as ego, prior to the imaginary.[30] In this preternatural darkness the characters lose track of time and space entirely—they are outside the civilizational and cultural constructions of temporal and spatial existence—and the language comes to resemble increasingly a language of metaphors for purely inner experience.

Having outlined this much, and given limitations of space, let me focus on the way in which the social Other appears here, and on the significance of this appearance for the subject of the address-without-address. First of all, the narrator moves from a dyadic situation in which there is almost no communication to a situation in which—after the old Swede gets killed when their ship is crushed by a larger ship that falls from a great height—the narrator finds himself among a ghostly crew of ancient mariners who speak a "language which I could not understand" (10) and who are unable to perceive him at all: "Concealment is utter folly on my part, for the people *will not* see" (11). This sequence reads like the passage from a hopeless imaginary dyad to a situation of inscription in society and the symbolic order of culture. In the company of this very strange crew, however, the narrator finds himself in a society, culture, and civilization to which he radically does not belong and where he is literally not seen. In our context, we can read this as a figuration of a moment in the traversal of castration, a more profound experience of alienation from "my country and my family" than he had known before this dream-journey, because there the alienation was contingent and voluntary, based on "ill usage and length of years" (1), whereas here it is necessary and compulsory. The figures surrounding him are ghostly and unreal, and he is entirely on his own, in an unimaginably extreme and deadly storm. He is cut off from the others and exposed directly to death, to fantasy, and to the very real drives concretized by the storm, with which he must manage on his own.

In this situation, however, the narrator has an aesthetic response to his situation, and one that takes him in some respects ethically—this is the sublime experience—beyond the fear for himself. At the moment when they are "at the bottom of one of these abysses"—a deep depression in the waves—and the huge ship mentioned above is about to fall upon their smaller ship, he describes the event in aesthetic terms: "For a moment of intense terror she paused upon the giddy pinnacle as if in contemplation of her own sublimity, then trembled, and tottered, and came down" (9). The rhetoric and the subjective experience of the sublime enter explicitly here. In a similar vein, the narrator also describes somewhat later, for example, his response to the ghostly captain—who would not fall under traditional definitions of the beautiful—as "a feeling of irrepressible reverence and awe" mingled "with the sensation of wonder." He says that "it is the singularity of the expression which reigns upon the face, it is the intense, the wonderful, the thrilling evidence of old age so utter, so extreme, which excites within my spirit a sense, a sentiment ineffable" (15). Again, the narrator foregrounds his aesthetic experience of something insusceptible of articulation in language, something unrepresentable. Even more interestingly, here it has to do with the appreciation of the singularity of another *human* with whom he cannot communicate and who does not even perceive his presence. We are outside the social link here, but not outside humanity. Finally, near the end of the text, the narrator describes a positive dimension of this extreme experience of exposure to the imminence of death: "To conceive the horror of my sensations is, I presume, utterly impossible; yet a curiosity to penetrate the mysteries of these awful regions predominates even over my despair, and will reconcile me to the most hideous aspect of death. It is evident that we are hurrying onward to some exciting knowledge, some never-to-be-imparted secret, whose attainment is destruction" (16). Likewise, on the crew members' faces he perceives towards the end "an expression more of the eagerness of hope than of the apathy of despair" (17). The "curiosity" expressed by the narrator here recalls, in our context, perhaps somewhat hyperbolically, not only the analysand's desire to know, whose awakening constitutes transference-love of something—the unconscious—that will mortify the ego in every sense, but also more generally a sublime pleasure taken in the ethical orientation that carries one beyond the ego's self-interest.

And then the address-without-address concludes: "we are whirling dizzily, in immense concentric circles . . . the circles rapidly grow small, we are plunging madly within the grasp of the whirlpool, and amid a roaring, and bellowing, and thundering of ocean and tempest the ship is quivering—oh God! and—going down!" (17). Whether this signals the disappearance of the ego in feminine jouissance, or anxiety in the face of the (always coming) literal death of the human being, in any case Poe's text ends with the disappearance of its fictional author and narrator, the subject of the act of address-without-addressee of which the text is the "vessel," like the ship, as well as the bottle.

What are we to make of this disappearance? What have we discovered here? In a sense—the process of discovery itself, as the discovery *of* the Other (objective and subjective genitive). Which we discover more specifically in the following way. The narrator previously painted random flecks of tar—"while musing on the singularity of my fate"—on "a neatly folded studdingsail" (12). When it was hoisted, the sail turned out to read, by a surrealistic chance: "DISCOVERY" (12). In this we discover that the address-without-address here figures the unwitting discovery of unconscious experience, outside of the languages sanctioned by and sanctioning the social order. Like all such discoveries, it also covers over what it uncovers, revealing it only beneath the veil of language itself. As a manuscript *found* in a bottle, it has in turn been discovered, and covered up again, when we read and interpret it. This covering aspect reminds us why, for an analyst, interpretation is a dangerous thing. The subject here—not accessible to the reading Other—will have sent it in an act of address-without-address to an indeterminate, absent but hoped-for, addressee and recipient. This kind of address, an anonymous sharing of an unnamable unconscious experience, is the kind that is facilitated by the movement of analysis. It goes without saying that not everyone analyzed becomes an Edgar Allan Poe (or wants to), and Edgar Allan Poe had no need of an analysis to become the writer he was. But the message in the bottle that he sends us in "MS Found in a Bottle" still perhaps helps us—in its own rigorously adolescent way—to see how an ethics committed to the opening up of aesthetic spaces for the expression of unconscious experience—for the sake of the human—can orient itself toward the speech of the subject of address.

## Notes

1. Gertrude Stein, "Stanzas in Meditation," *A Stein Reader*, 581.

2. Edgar Allan Poe, "MS Found in a Bottle," 1.

3. This question was at the center of the exchange between Jacques Lacan and Jacques Derrida. See John P. Muller and Willian J. Richardson, *The Purloined Poe*.

4. For Lacan's Rome Discourse, see "Fonction et champ de la parole et du langage en psychanalyse"; for "L'étourdit," published originally in 1973, see *Autres écrits*; for Seminar XI, held in 1964, see *Les quatre concepts fondamentaux de la psychanalyse*.

5. There is a notable continuity with Freud's notion of the unconscious as outside of language here, although in Apollon's work, following upon Lacan's, significant displacements have been introduced.

6. See David Martyn, *Sublime Failures*.

7. Roman Jakobson, "Linguistics and Poetics."

8. Willy Apollon, Unpublished schema from 8 Nov. 2019.

9. I am alluding here to the French translation of Freud's *Trieb* for "drive" as "pulsion." The French "pulsion" as translation of "drive" diverges from the sense of the German "Trieb" as "drive," yet it usefully carries the various connotations of "pulsation," which are relevant to the psychoanalytic concept of the "drive."

10. See Peter Blos, *On Adolescence*, an ego-psychologically oriented standard work, which views adolescence as "the psychological processes of adaptation to the condition of pubescence" (2), and understands it as straining toward harmony between ego and social norms, as did the older novel of formation.

11. For a late Enlightenment account of "productive" vs. merely "reproductive" imagination, see Immanuel Kant, *Anthropologie in pragmatischer Hinsicht abgefaßt*. On *poiesis*, see Martin Heidegger, "Die Frage nach der Technik." And on "spirit" in the analytic tradition, see the complex motif of the "progress in spirit" [*Fortschritt in der Geistigkeit*] in Sigmund Freud, "Der Mann Moses und die monotheistische Tradition."

12. I invoke here a motif from the ethics of Emmanuel Levinas, *Autrement qu'être ou au-delà de l'essence*. For essays on his relation to Lacan, see Sarah Harasym, ed., *Levinas and Lacan*.

13. Philippe Ariès, *Centuries of Childhood*, 30.

14. Key authors in the German/Austrian world from the late nineteenth and the early twentieth centuries include Frank Wedekind, Arthur Schnitzler, Robert Musil, Thomas Mann, Franz Kafka, Gottfried Benn, and the other expressionist poets, just to get started. For a brief summary of the youth movements in the German-language sphere, see the chapter on "Benjamin and the Idea of Youth" in John McCole, *Walter Benjamin and the Antinomies of Tradition*, 35–70.

15. This primitivism is prominent in works by painters as diverse as Pierre Gauguin, Pablo Picasso, Henri Rousseau, Emile Nolde and the German expressionists, and many others. Freud's *Totem and Taboo: Some Points of Agreement between the Mental Lives of Savages and Neurotics* both participates in and resists this primitivism. Through the "points of agreement," he does not just primitivize neurotics, showing them to be "primitive," but also neurotizes and modernizes primitives (and children), showing how they participate in the problematics of repression and so on. Still, his interest in the manner in which the beginning and the end of civilization, so to speak, coincide in certain respects is relevant to Apollon's understanding of the effects of *mondialisation* on the subject.

16. The term "Drang" (mistranslated as "stress") is what is known from the Strachey translations as the "pressure" aspect of the "drive" in Freud (which consists also of "aim," "object," and "source"), and it is present obviously in the term for "repression"—"Verdrängung"—an impulse against drive. Cassell's dictionary gives as the senses of "Drang": "throng, crowd; pressure; oppression; urgency, stress; hurry; violence; craving, impulse; distress."

17. The famous Spinoza debates of the day begin with Jacobi's attack on Spinoza in *Über die Lehre des Spinoza in Briefen an den Herrn Moses Mendelssohn*.

18. See the fabulously useful and insightful book by Franco Moretti, *The Way of the World: the Bildungsroman in European Culture*.

19. Cf. Peter Szondi, *The Theory of the Modern Drama*. From this perspective, the analytic situation might appear as a form of modernist or avant-garde drama: a drama where, for the most part, only one character speaks, and the stage has gone private, but the off-stage (obscene) is on-stage.

20. One can date this turn perhaps above all from Charles Baudelaire's *Fleurs du mal* [*Flowers of Evil*] (1857), whose opening poem "To the Reader" famously apostrophizes its reader as "—Hypocritical reader,—my semblable,—my brother!" The gesture problematizes both the addressee and the subject of the address as figures who say something other than what they mean, or whose actions do not coincide with their enunciated principles or words—and who cannot be trusted. The hypocritical (self)accusation turns around "boredom" as the worst "evil"—but also the most aesthetically productive—when the social order of use has lost its meaning, and pleasure goes beyond the pleasure principle, death drive emerges as the center of the aesthetic, and beauty merges with the grotesque. From here to the adolescent poet Arthur Rimbaud's "I is an Other" (1871) is just a short step, and the lyric as a form of intimate self-expression will never be able to return persuasively to the illusions of immediacy or simplicity articulated in language.

21. Cf. Theodor Adorno, "Rede über Lyrik und Gesellschaft," and consider also the figure of the adolescent in Stefan George (in German modernism), and of the ephebe in Wallace Stevens, in Anglo-American modernism, not to mention the problematic figure of the young man in T. S. Eliot's "Love Song of J. Alfred Prufrock."

22. One of the main prooftexts of this development in Western letters is the Austrian Hugo von Hofmannsthal's prose text "Letter of Lord Chandos to Francis Bacon," in which the protagonist explains that he can no longer think or use language coherently. Another crucial example would be Gertrude Stein's experimental poetry. Symptoms of the emergence of the address in modernism as a problematic possibility would include emphatic doctrines of dialogue as well, such as Martin Buber's *I-Thou*.

23. See his "Citoyen du monde, . . . mais de quelle nationalité?" See Jeffrey S. Librett, "The Subject in the Age of World-formation (mondialisation): Advances in Lacanian Theory from the Québec Group." One can see the recent rise of the notion of "Civilizational States" as indicating a backlash against, or a disavowal of, the fading credibility of the given civilizations, a backlash that, as Apollon acknowledges, could last for some time.

24. Drawing on anthropological discussions, Apollon understands *speech* as coinciding with the beginnings of Homo sapiens, not more than 300,000 years ago, whereas *language* only would have arrived around 50,000 years ago. This

distinction associates speech with smaller groupings of humans, whereas it links language with the shift to the formation of larger collectives.

25. Willy Apollon, unpublished lecture—Intercircle Days of the Freudian School of Quebec, 12 Feb. 2022.

26. Cf. Bruce Fink on the question of the imaginary transference in *Fundamentals of Psychoanalytic Technique*, 186ff.

27. Freud himself does, on occasion, speak of "transference" in a closely related manner as a "transfer" of the unconscious representation into the linguistically conditioned space of the pre-conscious, even though he primarily and increasingly came to use the term "transference" to refer, as I've suggested, to the superimposition of an earlier object-relation onto a later one, including the object-relation with the analyst himself. For the former usage, see the section of the *Interpretation of Dreams* on "Wish-fulfillment" (*Traumdeutung*, in *Studienausgabe*, vol. 2, p. 536).

28. The importance of this text for modernist aesthetics is indicated, for example, by the fact that Theodor Adorno repeatedly invokes the image of the message in a bottle as a model for the modern work of art, as is already suggested when, for the epigram of his *Kierkegaard: Construction of the Aesthetic*, he excerpts the moment when the enormous ship is about to crash down upon the infinitely smaller ship in which the protagonist is situated (which I discuss below). In addition, it is significant that Paul Celan, a somewhat "hermetic" German poet and certainly the single most important German-language poet who comes out of the Holocaust experience, alludes, not without awareness of the Poe story, to its main figure in his characterization of the poem in general in his day: "Since the poem is a form of appearance of language and therewith essentially dialogical, it can be a message in a bottle [*Flaschenpost*], given up in the belief (which is not always strong in hope) that it might be washed onto land somewhere and someday, onto the land of the heart. Poems are also on-the-way in this sense: they're going somewhere. / Where are they going? To something that stands open, something they could occupy, perhaps to an addressable [*ansprechbares*] 'you,' to an addressable [*ansprechbare*] reality. The poem is concerned about such realities, I think." (My translation: "Address [*Ansprache*] on the occasion of the reception of the Literatur-Prize of the Free Hanseatic City Bremen," 186.)

29. A convenient English-language edition is Charles Baudelaire, *Fatal Destinies: The Edgar Poe Essays*.

30. Marie Bonaparte, *The Life and Works of Edgar Allan Poe*, p. 352ff.

# Works Cited

Adorno, Theodor. *Kierkegaard: Construction of the Aesthetic*. Translated by Robert Hullot-Kentore, U of Minnesota P, 1989.

———. "Rede über Lyrik und Gesellschaft." *Noten zur Literatur*, Suhrkamp, 1974, pp. 46–68.

Apollon, Willy. "Citoyen du monde . . . mais de quelle nationalité?" *Mondialisation, défis pour l'humain*, Gifric, 2016, pp. 205–74.

———. Unpublished schema. 8 Nov. 2019.

———. Unpublished lecture—Intercircle Days of the Freudian School of Quebec, 12 Feb. 2022.

Ariès, Philippe. *Centuries of Childhood: a Social History of Family Life*. Translated by Robert Baldick, Vintage, 1962.

Baudelaire, Charles. *Fatal Destinies: The Edgar Poe Essays*. Translated by Joan Fiedler Mele, Cross Country Press, 1981.

Blos, Peter. *On Adolescence: A Psychoanalytic Interpretation*. The Free Press, 1962.

Bonaparte, Marie. *The Life and Works of Edgar Allan Poe: a Psycho-Analytic Interpretation*. Imago Publishing Company, 1949.

Celan, Paul. "Address [*Ansprache*] on the Occasion of the Reception of the Literatur-Prize of the Free Hanseatic City Bremen." *Gesammelte Werke*, edited by Beda Allemann and Stefan Reichert, vol. 3, Suhrkamp, 2000, p. 186.

Fink, Bruce. *Fundamentals of Psychoanalytic Technique: a Lacanian Approach for Practitioners*. W. W. Norton and Company, 2007.

Freud, Sigmund. "Der Mann Moses und die monotheistische Tradition," *Studienausgabe*, vol. IX, edited by Alexander Mitscherlich et al., Fischer Verlag, 1974.

Harasym, Sarah. Ed. *Levinas and Lacan: The Missed Encounter*. State U of New York P, 1998.

Heidegger, Martin. "Die Frage nach der Technik," *Vorträge und Aufsätze*, Neske Verlag, 1954.

Jacobi, Friedrich Heinrich. *Über die Lehre des Spinoza in Briefen an den Herrn Moses Mendelssohn* (1985). Felix Meiner Verlag, 2000.

Jakobson, Roman. "Linguistics and Poetics." *Language and Literature*, edited by Krystyna Pomorska and Stephen Rudy, Harvard UP, 1987, pp. 62–94.

Kant, Immanuel. *Anthropologie in pragmatischer Hinsicht abgefaßt*. *Werkausgabe*, vol. XII, edited by Wilhelm Weischedel, Suhrkamp, 1964, § 25, "Von der Einbildungskraft," pp. 466ff.

Lacan, Jacques. "Fonction et champ de la parole et du langage en psychanalyse." *Écrits*, Seuil, 1966.

———. *Les quatre concepts fondamentaux de la psychanalyse*. Seuil, 1973.

———. "L'étourdit." *Autres écrits*, Seuil, 2001.

Levinas, Emmanuel. *Autrement qu'être ou au-delà de l'essence*. Martinus Nijhoff, 1994.

Librett, Jeffrey S. "The Subject in the Age of World-formation (mondialisation): Advances in Lacanian Theory from the Québec Group." *Innovations In*

*Psychoanalysis:Originality, Development, Progress*, edited by Aner Govrin and Jon Mills, Routledge, 2020, pp. 75–99.

Martyn, David. *Sublime Failures: The Ethics of Kant and Sade*. Wayne State UP, 2003.

McCole, John. *Walter Benjamin and the Antinomies of Tradition*. Cornell UP, 1993.

Moretti, Franco. *The Way of the World: the Bildungsroman in European Culture*. Translated by Albert Sbragia, Verso, 2000.

Muller, John P., and Willian J. Richardson. *The Purloined Poe: Lacan, Derrida, and Psychoanalytic Reading*. Johns Hopkins UP, 1988.

Edgar Allan Poe, "MS Found in a Bottle." *The Complete Works of Edgar Allan Poe*, G.P. Putnam's Sons, 1902.

Stein, Gertrude. "Stanzas in Meditation." *A Stein Reader*, edited by Ulla E. Dydo, Northwestern UP, 1993, p. 581.

Szondi, Peter. *The Theory of the Modern Drama*. Translated by Michael Hays, U of Minnesota P, 1987.

7

# The Insistence of the Untreatable in the Social Link

## The Symptom

Danielle Bergeron

Translated by Steven Miller

"The unconscious is not a concept; it is what's lived in an experience. The unconscious is the part of the human spirit that inhabits and acts in each of us without our culture or civilization being able to do anything about it" (Apollon, *The Unconscious*). In the present text, I address the major stakes of the psychoanalysis of the symptom such as Willy Apollon developed them in his teaching and his writing. Apollon is witness to the ways in which the psychoanalytic clinic of the symptom has been modified after Freud and Lacan. He has sustained the clinical work of the psychoanalyst with his teaching and the dynamic schemas that illuminate it, with his innovative concepts fully inscribed within the movement of *"mondialisation,"* and with his abiding concern to transmit the clinical results of psychoanalytic action. Accordingly, within the framework of the psychoanalysis of the symptom, I address a number of the concepts central to clinical practice.

# From the Organism to the Erogenous Body: The Rupture of Mental Representation

"Mental representation is primary; it defines the letter of the body, the origin of the drive that searches for an object not in social space but in the time of the subject, the time of desire." We begin with this assertion from Willy Apollon's teachings to address the question of the human and what characterizes it: namely, the impact of the spirit, which constitutes the human as human, upon the meaning that a life assumes in relation to others.

## THE CATHEXIS OF PURE MENTAL REPRESENTATION

Thirty-two thousand years ago, in the Ariège region of France, a man, so we think—who might as well have been a woman!—designed a fascinating creature on the wall of a cavern, "half-human, half-animal with a bird's face, a stag's antlers, a horse's body, a striped beard and a penis jutting out backwards" (Cleyet-Merle 8).[1] This human creation of a nonexistent being was dubbed "The Sorcerer" when scientists catalogued it as a parietal paleolithic artwork, thereby assigning it to a "stage" in human history. This inspiring parietal artwork wasn't the first. Indeed, we now know that graphic expression appeared late, 82,000 years ago, in South Africa, well after music and the earliest signs of humanity (American Museum of Natural History), such as funeral practices in which the dead are buried along with gifts, everyday objects, and victuals (Cleyet-Merle 3). Such practices already suppose the acquisition of a representation of life after death, which we recognize as a pure representation of the spirit because it is marked by an impossibility that, even today, hasn't been superseded, that of representing in reality the aftermath of death. Religions continue to develop ways of giving a space of meaning to such representations, Apollon suggests, to lend credibility to the values of civilization and the norms of culture.

Scientists concur that modern man is characterized by the practice of funeral rites and graphic expression. In fact, one constant that connects us to our immemorial ancestors is the capacity of the human spirit, on the one hand, to produce "impossible" representations, with no link to reality, such as that of life after death, and, on the other hand, to cathect these representations for the benefit of human survival on planet earth, but also often at the expense of the individual imperative of survival.

When our prehistoric artist from Ariège set about drawing the mental representation of a fantasmatic half-human, half-beast that haunted him to give it visibility on the walls of a grotto, he was by definition not out hunting to feed his family. Likewise, if he set out to hunt and capture this "animal," he would be unlikely to bring home anything of use for the survival of his group! But it remains possible that his act of creation might set life drives free outside of himself for use among the group of his close relatives. The human being has a tendency to cathect hope-bearing thoughts much more than "reality" with its multiple constraints. Only thousands of years hence, when the trace of his act of creation has been revealed for all to see, does the artist of the "Sorcerer" assume his full importance. His act reveals the existence of the human spirit, which Apollon defines as "the capacity to think what does not exist, to will it and to actualize it, in other words the capacity to think heretofore unseen and unheard-of things, to wish for their existence and to succeed in creating them, for better and for worse" (Apollon, Psychanalyse et mondialisation: *L'humain en question*). Indeed, spirit is what makes us human, a member and participant in a history that comes before us and leads us elsewhere—but where and for what, better or worse?

The cave drawing turns us toward an essential element of being, a quest that is already at work in the small child and that drives the human to cathect the objects of his mental representations. However, when he confronts the reality principle upheld and exploited by culture and civilization against unconscious desire, the subject keeps silent about the inner space that contains his most intimate ambitions, his secret garden. Confronted repeatedly with the impossibility of expressing his mental representations, these representations colonize his organism, giving rise to symptoms and disruptive acts.

The psychoanalytic clinic is entirely centered on this otherwise inaccessible domain of the human. In an analytic cure, the analysand will work on his dreams. More specifically, he will examine the navel of these dreams, their blind spot. He will devote time to "deciphering" (Lacan, *Télévision* 21, 35) the path that the drive opens in the organism when, instilled with mental representations, it retraces the letters of the erotogenic body and the symptom. In other words, the analysand will take the risk of speech, a "naked speech," stripped of narcissistic resistances and worries about rejection or abandonment, often stemming from the time of life when the child was still wholly dependent on the parent. Everything new and unheard-of that surges up in the analysand's life, everything that returns from the past and derives from these registers, everything unknown that brutally imposes itself becomes the source of the analysand's work. And this work is full of risk.

## The Body is Not the Organism: The Insistence of the Quest in the Letter of the Body

To clarify the difference between the organism as the scientist defines it and the body as lived by the subject, I have chosen to focus on a public figure, Aimee Mullins. She is an elegant woman, an aesthete, born in 1975. After she gained recognition as an athlete, Aimee pursued a career as a fashion model and an actress after Alexander McQueen invited her to walk for him in his 1999 London runway show. To convince her, he offered her a pair of magnificent legs hand sculpted in ash wood, which she can be seen wearing in the catwalk photos.[2] This might well be the first time that a woman, eschewing the cultural norms of beauty, took part in a runway show that highlighted an unusual form of artistic production—the prosthetics that replaced her legs, whereby she herself became a work of art.

This American woman was born with a serious illness, fibular hemimelia, and at age one both her legs were amputated below the knee. She might have been limited to a future as a poor, handicapped, mutilated child. But this did not happen. At a very early age, since she couldn't be "normal," she chose to become extraordinary; she would make her difference into a motivating force (Girard). We all have an organism endowed with a finite number of systems, organs, and limbs. There is nothing original about that. On the level of our organism, we are all ordinary in that we are all alike, and thus replaceable. For the psychoanalyst, what is original in each of us is our manner of creating our body as impacted by the unbound drive—unbound from the requirements of the particular culture and civilization that we inhabit. Nothing is as extraordinary and original as the body that we each construct on the basis of the mental representations that emerge from our spirit. The body is what makes us irreplaceable. For Aimee, the singularity of her difference would seem to have become the mainspring of her life.

Early in life, Aimee wore "standard issue" prostheses; she played sports with the "normal" kids and later became a para-athlete. At this period, she also began to consult with avant-garde fabricators who could devise prostheses that would combine "science, function and aesthetics" (Girard). As an actress in science-fiction films, her costumes came with intriguing futuristic prostheses; as a TED lecturer, she had fun expounding on the features of her twelve unique pairs of legs. One might suppose that she was a child of privilege, born to a rich family. But this wasn't the case. Our respect for this woman is based on her ability to seize and create opportunities to build her life rather than resign herself to the parameters of a disabled organism. Moreover, Aimee affirmed that "her prosthetics are not a handicap, that beauty has nothing to do with normality, and that everyone, when confronted with reality, must reinvent themselves." Aesthetics, Apollon proposes, expresses and governs the space that transcends the norm.

In an interview with Mullins, the journalist Mehdi Atmani writes that "she metamorphoses her body as she wishes" and that she makes "her disability into a space of experimentation" (Atmani). This is exactly right, and Aimee does not contest it. When Medhi asks about her body and its technological hybridity, she acknowledges wanting this hybridization and enhancing it with the help of specialists in technological innovation. Following Apollon, we hold that the body is essentially born of experience, a lived experience that remains inaccessible to the Other, even using scientific methods. Mullins evokes this lived experience when she speaks of forming "an intimate relationship" with her wooden sculpted legs because they are not merely shoes but legs. She states further: "when I saw them for the first time, I truly felt that I was looking at a part of my own body. I would have to impregnate myself with this object and give it life with my movements. It is a very intimate relationship with the object" (Atmani). Indeed, it was not technology that dispossessed her being, but she, the subject of the unconscious in her, who appropriated the wooden legs and feet, giving them a share of her life drive. The object of her quest, the extraordinary thing that she wanted to achieve, had nothing to do with the functioning of her organism. Whence her feeling about the impact that "this object" would have upon her. What she designates as the impact of the artwork on her as a subject corresponds to the intimate relationship between an artist and the aesthetic dimension of her work. To give life to a work means that it must first be made one's own, that the artist is able to integrate it into the intimacy of her desiring body.

In his article in *Le Temps*, Atmani speaks of Mullins as an "augmented" woman and then wonders: "In your case, 30% of your body is technologically enhanced. At what point does a body become so inextricably bound up with technology that it can no longer be qualified as human?" Does this question negate Aimee's humanity and her subjectivity, turn her into a mere curiosity, or impose on her—to emphasize her nonconformity—the parameters of the "cultural montage of the sexual"? Apollon, who proposed this formulation, indicates how, when adolescents experience an upsurge of unbound drive that pushes toward a jouissance—this "something that is beyond any biological mechanics"—culture will censor this quest, in men as well as in women, promoting the orgasm in place of jouissance. This is, in fact, the objective of the cultural montage of the sexual (Apollon, "Homme, femme, masculin, féminin"). Does Atmani suggest that, for him, technologists have the ability to modify a defective organism to such a degree that it could no longer be qualified as human? There is no better testimony to the censorship of femininity that such a cultural montage of the sexual tries to express!

Aimee Mullins skillfully parries this suggestion with subtle words on the soul that recall that the human does not reside in the organism. "Humanity is something intangible that certain people call the soul," she says. "If you think about it, a non-negligible portion of my body—specifically, my legs—is already dead. But they could be replaced. Everything is replaceable, except the soul" (Atmani). She thus articulates an unavoidable truth: in each being there is something that the ancients called the soul, which we designate, following Apollon, as the *"effect of the effraction of the psyche by the spirit."* This is what makes the being into a human and, no matter the changes or supplements to its envelope, the soul, the spirit always sustain the quest for a beyond of the materiality of things.

In her further reflection on the human, Mullins, who "travels with several pairs of legs in her suitcase," adds: "my entire relationship with the ground is imaginary. I have never known the feeling of walking on concrete, sand, gravel or wet soil. I must constantly adapt my stride based on nothing but my idea of each type of ground. I am thus in perpetual negotiation with the ground" (Atmani). We understand her well: her body is an imaginary, a purely temporal experience in which she must perpetually negotiate with the space where the ground is located. She cannot know anything in advance about the experience that will make her live. We are no longer in the domain of the observable: the beautiful example of Mullins illustrates the power of the spirit and the action whereby it constructs the body. Her interviews are an inspiration for others who, like her, must rely on prosthetics to survive or to live as far as possible with others. She shows them a way: it is imperative to create a creative intimacy with their prosthetics. Therein resides beauty. Beauty has nothing to do with normality. It transcends normality; it is beyond. Faced with their own reality, everyone must reinvent themselves.

Spirit is a source of hope because it has the capacity to make something new exist. Only the spirit in the human, according to the specific way it makes the unconscious exist in a subject, can extract the being from repetition, imitation, and despair. This is verified by the push-to-act that constitutes the subject's signature. For an act to qualify as an act, it must be original, like that of Aimee Mullins. The clinic creates the conditions for the spirit in the patient to create the solutions that she needs in order to take full advantage of the humanity within her. This is what Aimee evokes: she seeks to take full advantage of the dimensions of humanity and the aesthetic in her.

Let us invite François Cheng to speak of "beauty": "We might imagine a universe that would only be *true* without the least beauty entering into it. This would be an entirely functional universe deploying undifferentiated, uniform elements that would move in an absolutely interchangeable manner. This would be an order of 'robots' and not that of life . . . In order for there to be life, there must be differentiation among elements" (Cheng 20).

## From the Symptom as the Resistance of the Unconscious Faced with the Ideals and Imperatives that Delineate the Ego to the Psychoanalytic Symptom as the Writing of the "Untreatable," the Insistence of the Quest in the Letter of the Body

"Psychoanalysis would allow you, of course, the hope of refining and clarifying the unconscious of which you are the subject. But everyone knows that I don't encourage anyone into it, anyone whose desire is not resolute" (Lacan, *Télévision* 47). In such direct terms, Lacan in *Télévision* warns anyone who wishes to enter into psychoanalysis that its unfolding requires a resolute desire on the part of the analysand. This vigorous warning evoked for me a passage from Rilke's *Letters to a Young Poet* in which he counsels an attitude comparable with the position that one must adopt when entering into a psychoanalysis.

After trying his luck with a number of publishers, the young man asks Rilke to judge whether his poetry is any good. The writer begins his response with a warning: "you are looking outward," he writes, "and that above all you should not do now" (Rilke 18). He then adds: "nobody can counsel and help you, nobody. There is only one single way. Go into yourself. Search for the reason that bids you to write: find out whether it spreads out its roots in the deepest places of your heart." And finally, he asks: "Would you have to die if it were denied you to write?" (Rilke 18)

When a person says she wishes to enter analysis, is it a matter of life and death for her? When an analysand is committed, she is fully aware that her entire life will be modified by analytic work, that her relationships with others will change, that analysis will suffuse her life from the highest moments to the hollowest, just as Rilke writes about the budding poet: "Your life even into its most indifferent and slightest hour must be a sign of this urge and a testimony to it" (Rilke 18). It requires heart . . . courage to bring an analysis to its logical conclusion. And that supposes a "resolute desire," as Lacan would say, because everything will be called into question . . .

In his teaching at the Clinical Training Seminar in Psychoanalysis and the Clinical Cases Seminar, Willy Apollon clarified Lacan's discourse, establishing that "psychoanalysis is not a form of psychotherapy; it is an ethical practice that sinks its roots into the deepest recesses of the being." Not only does it suppose a recognition of the subject's responsibility in relation to the obstacles and impasses unto which his unconscious pushes him, but it also calls upon the subject to act with regard to his symptoms and their consequences for himself and for others. Where psychotherapy revolves around interpretations based on the therapist's knowledge and the therapist's responsibility to offer treatments designed to achieve "outward facing" results, psychoanalysis calls upon the analysand's ethics and the knowledge she gains from experience as the basis for decisions about what her life should be. The unconscious cannot be "therapized" in order to adjust it to the norms and criteria of social life or the demands of other people. In any event, this is an impossible mission. When success appears to be at hand, the symptom will return with a vengeance; it is waiting around the corner.

## THE SYMPTOM AND THE CONTESTATION OF THE EGO, THE RESISTANCE OF THE UNCONSCIOUS TO CONTAINMENT WITHIN THE EGO

Once again, we begin with a citation from Apollon: "When there is something for which the quest does not manage to find expression in the space opened up within culture by civilization, it attacks the organism and the social bond, investing the letter of the body under the sway of the drive" (Apollon, "Sessions de formation clinique en psychanalyse").

To understand better what is at stake in the symptom, we will address the exemplary and yet tragic story of David Servan-Schreiber, who died at an early age and in the books he wrote—*Anticancer* (2007) and *Not the Last Goodbye* (2011)—had the courage to share the results of his research together with autobiographical accounts of his path in life.

Servan-Schreiber discovered his symptom in a manner that was as unpredictable as it was catastrophic. At the age of thirty, he was living in Pittsburgh and committed body and soul to research in neuropsychiatry, building momentum for what "promised to be a long race . . . and meaningful achievements." He held a prestigious position as the co-director of a laboratory of functional brain imaging funded by the National Institutes of Health. His research focus was a small, infrequently explored area of the brain, the prefrontal cortex. In order for this area to reveal itself in MRI images, it must be goaded to react through specially designed, complex exercises. It is the area that links the past and the future; it is the basis for decision-making processes. With the naive ambition of a young researcher, Servan-Schreiber hoped to one day understand the mechanisms of thought itself by observing what happens to the brain when this area is stimulated (Servan-Schreiber 24). Impossible, says the psychoanalyst!

One evening, at the lab with his colleagues, a volunteer test subject failed to show up. In order not to lose precious lab time, Servan-Schreiber offered to put himself into the scanner. He began the exercises, but there was something wrong with the readout. His colleagues restarted the machine but then stopped again to inform him: "We can't do the experiment. There's something in your brain." The brain image showed "a ball the size of a walnut" (28) on the right side of his prefrontal cortex.

Twenty-five years later, the shock of this discovery remains acute. He writes: "I could never have imagined what this research would reveal—my own disease" (24). On the screen, what he saw was a glioblastoma, an aggressive form of cancer with a very poor prognosis at that time, a survival rate of two weeks to six months. He was both devastated and stupefied to realize that the cancer had developed in the exact area of the brain that was the object of his research. After enduring two relapses, he would die twenty years later.

At the moment that he learned about his tumor, Servan-Schreiber says, he was "living life to the fullest" (25). But was he really? Which life does he mean? To respond to this question, let us proceed as we would in the clinic with an analysand, by examining the aspects of his narrative and his behavior that make it possible to delineate what we call the "ego square." The elements of the ego define what is receivable within the cultural framework that regulates the social link in which the individual lives, in which the ego aspires to success and recognition by others. The ego adapts to the social link within the specific culture and civilization to which the individual belongs and is constituted within her kinship group. The construction of the ego is thus intimately bound up with seduction as the modality of being that ensures the individual's survival.

In "The Subversion of the Subject and the Dialectic of Desire" (*Écrits*), Lacan elaborates the different instances of the ego across the graph of desire. He furthers the propositions of linguistics, situating language as the human subject's point of departure. Language, he writes, is a "treasury of signifiers" whose action transforms the living being into a being of desire. For Lacan, language is what creates the human subject, the subject of desire. Apollon, relying on the scientific discoveries of human evolutionary history, asserts that the action of language moves in the opposite direction; it "organizes and guarantees the social link." He distinguishes speech from language, and with reference to new data about human history, shows that access to speech preexists language. In fact, language comes to limit the spirit's effervescence and the push to act that, since the rise of Homo sapiens, can be found in every new human being. The children of homo sapiens have a powerful, inborn creative force that is destined to be shackled by the process of acculturation. Nonetheless, the human spirit, through its acts, resists containment and combats the ideals and injunctions upheld by the repression and censorship of cultures and civilizations.

## THE EGO SQUARE

For Apollon, the "ego square" consists of the four principal elements of the ego that are installed during the individual's childhood and adolescence, setting traps for the adult to come. They are oriented by the stakes of seduction.

*First element. The ego: a narrative recounted by the being on the social scene,* **"that which I must aim for within the framework where I am placed."**

At the moment when his cancer was revealed, what does David Servan-Schreiber have to say about himself? He describes himself as ambitious, precocious, hungry for success, a rising star in psychiatry, a brilliant young scientist with mastery of cutting-edge technologies, at the dawn of a great career and already proud of his achievements. He had just published an article in a venerable journal, *Science*, and had been invited by the respected professor Daniel Widlöcher to offer two days of lectures in Paris on his current research: the use of computer simulation of neural networks to "understand psychological and pathological mechanisms." He also calls himself a bit arrogant, not really interested in the patients and their suffering, his main goal being to advance big ideas.

Such is the manner in which the young researcher presented his ego, which we define as the story that a person recounts about himself on the social scene, how he presents himself to others, what he wishes them to remember about him, how he wishes to be perceived with the objective of being loved.

*Second element. The ego-ideal: the response to cultural demands,* **"what I aim for."**

The ego of an individual is constructed within an ideal founded on the cultural demands that define what a man or a woman must aspire to and attain in order to be accepted in a group and to actualize the objectives of the sociocultural ensemble to which he belongs. This ideal that establishes the criteria of the receivable is the ego ideal, an agency of the ego aligned with the norms and values imposed by civilization and "normalized" by culture, incorporated into the norms that underlie each culture's specific rules and prohibitions. As for Servan-Schreiber's ego-ideal, what he aspired to attain, in accordance with the demands that discourse clearly articulates for a young man of his social class in a specific Francophone civilization, comes down to success, prestige, mastery, and performance, with the hope of "meaningful achievements." He sought to gain notoriety, to become a star in the scientific firmament. To this end, he had heavily invested in his future. Nonetheless, as he recognized, his emotional life was unstable. We might already wonder: For whom are these achievements supposedly meaningful?

*Third element. The superego: cultural exigencies transmitted through impossible parental expectations, **"the impossible to satisfy."***

The superego has a major and complex impact within every human subject. Indeed, the superego is formed and imposed in early childhood on the basis of the cultural exigencies that become charged when parents articulate them, no matter their intentions, with the burden of their personal dissatisfactions. Cultural dictates, moral values, and rules of conduct thus acquire an arbitrary dimension suffused with the unsaid. Through the superego, the parents demand achievements from their children that will rectify the disappointments they suffered in their own lives beginning in childhood—which is what makes the superego an agency with a potentially "cruel and ferocious" dimension, as Lacan would say.

Born the "eldest son of the eldest son," Servan-Schreiber tells how he was taken at birth from his twenty-two-year-old mother by his paternal grandmother, who had judged his mother incompetent, and handed over to nursing assistants and then a nanny (Servan-Schreiber 2007, 183). His grandmother thus monitored the fate of this "treasure" who was "going to carry on the family line" (183). Her eldest son, young David's father, an influential man at the time, ran the "country's most prominent news magazine" (183). And for the paternal grandmother, her first grandson would have to honorably carry on this lineage. Taken from his mother at birth, then, Servan-Schreiber describes how his relationship to his mother was marked by distress and absence. Of his mother, he writes: "My body preserves the memory of the painful void I experienced as an infant" (183). Separated from his mother, he developed a strong relationship with his eighteen-year-old nanny whose love for him was constant and sincere, albeit clumsy. Nonetheless, she often threatened to leave if he didn't behave, if he didn't obey. Overwhelmed by "a terrible state of powerlessness and despair," he chose to stifle his emotions to keep his nanny and to rise to his grandmother's superegoic expectations. "Quickly, I learned to give what was expected of me and of a firstborn. No temper tantrums, no outbursts. Instead, discipline and an attention to appearances" (194).

On the one hand, the expectation that each generation will uphold the social prestige of the family has no regard for the affective impact of this task; on the other hand, this impact is exacerbated by the arbitrariness of the superegoic exigencies that the father transmits by leaving unsaid. Servan-Schreiber speaks beautifully of these exigencies at the moment in his story when he tells how much he dreaded having to tell his father about his cancer. "My heart sank [when my father picked up the phone]," he writes. "It was as if I was about to plant a dagger in his chest" (79). A young man should be able to expect compassion from his father upon hearing that his son's life is in peril, but instead he felt responsible, guilty, and frightened to witness the impact of the bad news. He goes on to explain why: "I had long been tortured by the fear of betraying the huge hopes that my father had placed in me" (80). His cancer removed him from scene where he should have shined; it dismantled the pedestal that the paternal superego forced him to climb: "Even though he never said it so clearly, I knew he was disappointed that I was 'only a doctor.' He would have liked me to go into politics as he had done, and perhaps succeed where he had not fully lived up to his own ambitions" (80). This is a particularly clear description of the arbitrariness of the superego, the way in which it insidiously compels the child to shoulder his parent's disappointments with respect to their own unrealized adolescent hopes and dreams.

The most cunning aspect of the superego is transmitted by what is left unsaid by the parents: attitudes, gestures, looks, mimicry, or sighs—all of these are inscribed, like a knowledge of the body, in the child and remain open to multiple interpretations with potentially catastrophic consequences. In the case of Servan-Schreiber, his father could probably be reconciled with the idea that his eldest son was "only a doctor" as long as he gained recognition as a scientist. "Even though he never said it so clearly, I knew . . . ," he says. Such recognition is what made his "betrayal" tolerable. But the prospect of completely disregarding the injunctions of the paternal superego made his "heart sink": to abandon everything in death was psychically the same as planting a dagger in his father's chest.

Considering the role of the superego for Servan-Schreiber, we consider why, at least according to his own account, his body was led to produce a symptom that presented as a metaphor of his own impasse. Let us recall that the function of the prefrontal cortex, where the tumor developed, is to link the past and the future and thus to make decisions possible. Very young, he found himself immobilized by something "unaddressable" locked in his body while he sought in vain to achieve the impossible, that is, to repair his mother's suffering, to satisfy his grandmother's expectations, to escape his nanny's threats, and to become worthy of his father's disappointed aspirations. He thereby lived in the grip of unsurpassable contradictions. His principal symptom presented as the writing of these contradictions; the tumor inscribed within his body the impossible reconciliation of the past and the future. We can conclude that the desire within him, his own quest, caused this contradiction to be engraved in the very area that became the object of his research.

*Fourth element. The ideal ego: "What I believe I must be for the other"*

"I'll worry about happiness later," Servan-Schreiber writes, "When we put off till tomorrow the quest for the essential, we may find life slipping through our fingers without ever having savored it" (40–41). This reflection is a good introduction to the fourth element of the ego square: the ideal ego. With the "mirror stage," Lacan established the centrality of the infant's choice, while still an entirely dependent nursling, to apprehend himself as the object of his mother's smile in the mirror (cf. Lacan, "The Mirror Stage" and "Aggressivity in Psychoanalysis"), to identify with this object, which he believes that he must become in order to satisfy her, at least as far as he understands at such a young age. This identification saves him from the disordered and disorganizing work of the quest of desire in him. Nonetheless, this "total form of the body," Lacan says, is only given to him as a Gestalt. Accordingly, this external form remains alienating with respect to the "turbulence of the movements that he feels animating him" (Lacan 2006, 76). "It is in this erotic relationship, in which the human individual fixates on an image that alienates him from himself, that we find the energy and the form from which the organization of the passions that he will call his ego originates" (Lacan 1966, 113).

For the neurotic, the ideal ego is built up first in relation to the mother in the mirror. In the mother's smile, he finds what he believes that he must be for the Other. He is ready to renounce his subjectivity in order for the turbulence in his being to cease. In his book, Servan-Schreiber suggests that he can never fully understand, not "in his flesh," when others get emotional about their mothers. Let us recall that this period of his life, defined by suffering and lack, left behind a single memory—that of the void. The alleged incompetence of his mother, she who would have fashioned an ideal "self-image" for him in the mirror, instead produced something unstable and censored in the space where the subject of the unconscious could have been mobilized and recognized. What stuck with him as an adult, however, was the chasm of the void in his relationship to his mother. We appreciate the distress into which these "non-memories" must thrust him: there was nothing—no space either for the ideal (i) or for the subject of the unconscious (a)—nothing but a void, as if the child's only role was to mend the suffering and lack of his mother. These early years would thus be determinative for his future life.

One can only conclude that it was precisely in this void, precociously inscribed in his flesh, that the tumor developed, while his quest for the essential was diverted by an amalgam of family issues that didn't regard him as a subject.

From our time spent as an analyst with autistics and psychotics, and sensitive to the stakes of perversion, we note that these subjects refuse to give up on "the quest for the essential," the human quest within them. They—the subjects in them—refuse to adopt the image that their parents expect of them, an image already distorted by the values of their culture and the beliefs imposed by their civilization; they refuse, in other words, the alienation or even the eradication of their spirit. We know from experience that the psychotic does not construct an ego; that he isn't even remotely interested in this ego that the neurotic is so proud of and clings to, at the expense of the subject in him. It is as if the neurotic wished to remain within the limits of culture and civilization, recoiling from the unknown, while the psychotic, on the contrary, wants to delve into the unknown that he, like the neurotic, was at some point allowed to glimpse. To circulate within the "ego square," between the ideals and the superego, is not the psychotic's goal in life. "Look how sad my eyes are," says a young psychotic man whom I had asked to bring childhood memories to his next session. He had just placed a photo of himself on the little table. "I wasn't even two years old!" The psychotic child is sad because he is misaligned with the other's gaze, which bears a request in which he doesn't recognize himself, a request that totally effaces him.

## THE SYMPTOM: THE WRITING OF THE *UNADDRESSABLE*, A WARNING FROM THE UNCONSCIOUS ABOUT THE RAVAGES OF *REPRESSION*, *CENSORSHIP*, AND *THE UNSAYABLE*

### *The Voice of the Subject*

When the young researcher returned home thinking he would die of cancer at the age of thirty-one, what he called an "extraordinary" event took him by surprise. While he despondently repeated to himself that it was impossible that such a thing should happen to him just as his life was about to yield "meaningful achievements," he heard a voice in his head speaking very softly, his own, which said with self-assurance: "You know what, David, it's perfectly possible, and it's all okay." From then on, he writes, the paralysis that had overtaken him was lifted: his voice had spoken from inside his being and it reminded him that what he was going through was a human experience and that it is fine to be "simply human" (Servan-Schreiber 2007, 29). If we connect this moment to David's stupefied realization that "his" cancer emerged in exactly the area of the cortex that was the focus of his research, and that this zone functions to connect the past and the present, then it becomes clear that his symptom was an act of his unconscious, which had inscribed something in his body that couldn't pass through language but that he had to confront. It was something of which he never became conscious because it was unaddressable, impossible to say, but which now the voice of the subject in him could evoke. The unconscious subjective quest, which was his alone and gave rise to this inner voice, had remained outside of language and made no sense to the brilliant ego of the researcher who repeated to himself, "that could never happen to me!" "The letter," Apollon posits, "institutes the body as the site of a 'voice' where speech tears open the limits of the collective by marking the agency of the subject" (Apollon, seminar for analysts, 2021–2022). Accordingly, the voice represents a subject that transcends the cultural exigencies and the promises of civilization with something closer to the human.

On this night of great distress for the young researcher, the voice of the subject of the unconscious—his true voice, in fact—arose to force him to consider the human in him, while his symptom inscribed in "the letter of his body" what he couldn't verbalize. Wishing to repair his mother and to respond to familial ideals through the cultural exigencies of the superego, he took upon himself a duty that, we can say, required him to function as the prefrontal cortex for the family: to make the decisions necessary to forge a bond between past failures and ambitions for the future. In the final instance, however, the cancerous mass in his prefrontal lobe signed the impossibility of linking the past and the future on the basis of the plan mapped out by the diverse instances of his ego, inseparable from the objectives of culture and civilization. As if something beyond civilization and culture was at play on the level of the brain, his cancer revealed to him how the subject of the unconscious was blocked from expressing itself, especially during his early childhood. The "unaddressable" that had tormented him in his body during early childhood, the void experienced in his relation to his mother that had been calligraphed in his being, now outlined a salvational space for the "*tu meurs*" [you are dying].[3] It was necessary for "everything to fall apart" in order for the unaddressable of the subject of the unconscious to find an escape hatch elsewhere than in a subversion of the logic of the organism by the letter of the body.

The symptom, then, is a writing, we can say with Apollon. It writes in the organism or in the social link what is at play within the body of the subject: an unaddressable, a lived experience of the body that is inaccessible to others and that cannot be said. In response to the montage that represses and censors the subject's quest, the symptom is the insistence and the resistance of the unconscious quest, which finds recognition in an act that pitilessly deranges both the smooth functioning of the organism and the trajectory of the individual throughout his life.

This painful story of Servan-Schreiber's early years clearly leads us to the definition of the symptom as the "*insistence of the human quest in the letter of the body.*" "That which the quest cannot manage to express in the space opened in culture by civilization ends up attacking the organism and the social link by cathecting the letter under the sway of the unbound drive" (Apollon, Clinical training seminar in psychoanalysis, The Symptom, October 15, 2021).

## The Symptom, "Untreatable" by Medicine

If the unconscious is the portion of the being that has been excluded from the social link and that remains active in the body, then it is through his body during an analytic cure, in the symptom, that the subject will be revealed to himself. Following Apollon, we define *the body* as "the inscription of a subjective experience that is lived but not accessible to the Other." Only the subject can gain access to his body. For the symptom to become a source of revelation about the subject's quest in the analytic cure, it is imperative that the symptom that cathected the organism be made to speak. This is how the subject will identify what he had to renounce in order to be loved, admired, and recognized—the "ego square." He will thus become capable of naming the true stakes of human life along with the distortions occasioned by the goals of the Ego in culture. Finally, he will manage to accept the exclusion from his social group that results from adopting a different position in relation to sociocultural dictates.

For Apollon the psychoanalytic symptom is, by definition, an *"untreatable"* (Apollon "The Untreatable" 2006 and Sessions de formation Clinique 2018. Medicine loses itself in conjectures and hypotheses when it attempts to pinpoint organic causes. Why? Because the lived dimension of the human doesn't pertain to the domain of the observable. Psycho-analysis, however, seeks to calculate the non-observable. The subject's lived experience, perhaps, belongs to the same order as what physicists call the "quantum" (Guillemant): what is not manifest or measurable but is, to a certain extent, calculable. In fact, the quantum for the physicist is the calculation of the non-manifest. We can advance, then, that an analysand is someone who lends himself to the work of the non-observable within himself, the non-manifest, the "quantum" that is his inner life, made up of ordeals, aesthetic emotions, irrational fears, mortal terrors, feelings of emptiness or evanescence, and all of the instants inspired by the intangible, beyond experience. These are events in the life of a subject that circulate outside of language and that the body allegorizes by engendering dreams, acts, and symptoms. As Apollon underscores, "this outside-language is foreign to the space-time of collective consciousness that language structures in the social bond in order to control what manifests itself to observation." Through the signs of the action of the subject of the unconscious—dreams, acts, symptoms—psychoanalysis will attempt to calculate the desire that manifests itself in them, on the condition that the analysand finds in the analyst an address for It. The desire of the subject will thus become manifest through the calculation of this inaccessible thing, this quantum, in a psychoanalysis.

*No Address for the* Untreatable

In 2011, twenty years after the shock of the tumor and shortly before dying of a relapse, David Servan-Schreiber published *Not the Last*

*Goodbye.* In this book, he notes that the MRI images taken during his second relapse showed "a gigantic, vein-filled mass occupying the cavity in my frontal lobe, the site of two previous operations many years earlier" (Servan-Schreiber 12). He relates: "At the time, I was constantly on the move; following the publication of my book *Anticancer*, I was taking part in conferences and appearing on radio and TV, especially in the United States, where the book was generating widespread interest. So I attributed my fatigue to frequent air travel, jet lag, and the stress of public speaking" (15). "The thing I'd been dreading all these years had finally happened" (17). Then he makes the following statement: "Perhaps that is what happened to me: I was so fulfilled and absorbed by my work that I neglected my body's needs" (40). He observes that the "epic battles" to gain recognition for his new approach to cancer had literally "charged my life with meaning." "I was driven by such an intense sense of purpose," he writes, "that it was impossible for me to let go" (48). Regretfully, he recognizes that he has not been "the ideal embodiment of the anticancer lifestyle" (34). Along with him, we must deplore that his life was only saturated with the type of meaning conferred by the round of lectures and honors he received for his publications, the meaning that civilization imposes upon the ego as the signification of things. "The ego," Lacan reminds us, "represents the center of all the resistances to the cure of symptoms" (Lacan 1966, 118).

The subject of the unconscious and its quest for the realization of the human has nothing to do with honors and the stakes of social success. If David Servan-Schreiber had gone down a psychoanalytic path to discover the true meaning of his life, that borne by his unconscious, all of these egoic "extras" and the narcissistic reinforcements enacted in the address to the Other would have fallen by the wayside to make room for creation without a demand for recognition, without any satisfaction other than having contributed to the future of humanity thanks to his insubordinate spirit brimming with creativity.

We must recognize that Servan-Schreiber achieved remarkable things in the field of medicine to transform the approach to cancer treatment. Nonetheless, from a psychoanalytic perspective, what led him to a premature death was the fact that he never found an address for the untreatable in him and thus could not reach a "construction" able to account for his symptom and why it appeared. Although he wrote and published, it wasn't enough because he had no one to whom he could speak of it; he never encountered, with his avowals and confessions, any resistance from the unconscious of a psychoanalyst as an address for the untreatable, which would extract him from the dramatic relationship to his organism and open him to the tragic dimension of a life marked by the unaddressable of what never stops insisting and writing itself.

Without analytic experience, without an Other for an *improbable address*, Servan-Schreiber remained within the purview of the ego. No place for the thing in him, the unbound drive, the mental representation, the subject. Consequently, as he recognized himself, all that remained for him was the glory and hustle of performances filled with the stress of public speaking, the demand for success drilled into him by the paternal superego, and the emotional wasteland that his grandmother created, all of this playing out within the limits of his civilization. Accordingly, a void was re-created within him under the pressure and insistence of the subject of the unconscious. But we must still recognize that he did seek to contribute something to the human and did so with great elegance through the impressive work of his book *Anticancer*.

## The Great Dictates of Puberty and the Censorship of the Cultural Montage

Now we turn our attention to a young woman, Sylvia, who, after an adolescence rife with disorganized sexual behavior and frequent risk taking over several years, "settled down" when she met a man who refused to treat her as "a piece of meat," despite her best efforts to push him away. He wanted to start a family and have children. Her highly devout in-laws expected the new couple to have a big family. They would have to compensate for the grandchildren that their other son, being gay, would never have; and their youngest daughter had absolutely decided against having children. Sylvia was not opposed to children, and she felt "so good together" with this man. At the same time, she was not thrilled at the idea of becoming the mother of a family. She never went to college and worked a low-paying job that just allowed her to pay the bills. This is the context in which she "got pregnant" and then had a "miscarriage." Afterward, her progesterone levels remained high and she underwent a curettage, in order, she was told, to remove the bits of placenta that must be responsible for her elevated pregnancy hormones. Even after this intervention, however, nothing changed: her progesterone remained high and she was thus in the hormonal state of pregnancy. She couldn't get pregnant again, she lamented. A further series of gynecological tests and interventions also yielded no results.

Not until eighteen months later did a gynecologist discover a minuscule bit of placenta from her ectopic pregnancy, which, all along, had been producing the state of fictive pregnancy.

During this period, fortified with the teaching of this resistant and novel symptom that she worked on in analysis, Sylvia decided to enroll in a vocational college (CEGEP, Collège d'enseignement général et professionnel) that stimulated her spirit and favored the development of satisfying and productive relationships with others. Her "untreatable" symptom had helped her to decide on her own life goals, whereas she had previously remained subservient to the wishes of her mother and the dictates of her in-laws.

At puberty, a young girl is liable to grasp the devastating scope of what the "cultural montage of the sexual" holds in store for her as she looks forward to participating as a subject in the history of humanity, which, although it has existed since time immemorial, now opens the door and invites her to contribute to a better future. "The spirit," noted the sociologist Edgar Morin on the eve of his 100th birthday, "must confront crises in order to master and move beyond them. Otherwise, we will become its victims" ("Entrevue").

The human spirit invents solutions. Anouk, for example, at thirteen years old wanted to become a sociologist to contribute to the resolution of the great problems that lead to the starvation of whole populations while others luxuriated in overabundance and squandered resources. She had no interest in repeating the destiny of the women she saw get caught up in motherhood and consigned to a second-class future. She couldn't handle the weight of her family's expectations of her. She wished to remain a little girl. During a party, she asked one of her favorite aunts: "can a woman have her breasts removed?" This is now more than fifteen years ago, at a time when such surgeries were not yet the latest thing! Still young, it occurred to her that if a woman couldn't breastfeed then she wouldn't be made to have children, and she would thus be left alone to pursue her studies. On that day, her aunt's face told her this was not a welcome idea, that mutilation wouldn't be the solution to her position as a victim of sexuation. She was already confronted with the violence directed against women, a violence that censors a dimension of their being, with regard to their choice of a future life. She learned without understanding it, Apollon would say, that an essential portion of her of life as a woman in her civilization was "unsayable."

## The Body:
## The Erotic Memory of the Subject

With Willy Apollon, we posit that "the body is the subjective consciousness of a lived experience; and what the psychoanalyst offers is access to what does not become conscious in this experience but acts through the symptom upon the organism" (Clinical Training Seminar in Psychoanalysis, The Clinic of the Symptom).

Contrary to the examples of Sylvia and Anouk, grappling with the censorship of their being as women, other cultures, other civilizations have found their own solutions without need for censorship. We are thinking, in particular, of the Luba people from central Africa. They have two modalities of official memory. One pertains to collective memory, while the other pays homage to what I would call the erotic memory of the subject. The first is traditionally conserved by lukasas (Nooter Roberts and Roberts), which are wooden tablets decorated with pearls, shells and metal objects, engraved with symbols that represent personages, places, and events in the history of the people. Central to the social structuration of the people, lukasas are known to members of the group and spoken aloud by the historians of the royal court, who use them as a point of reference. The tablets thus constitute the people's consciousness of a lived experience that defines them. The bodies of young, pubescent women are also, in a certain respect, treated as lukasas when the elder women transform their bodies into veritable sexual objects for men by scarifying their bellies, lower backs, and vaginas with culturally significant figures. Thus modified, offered up for motherhood, they also serve to reinforce the structuration of Luba society.

Until she becomes a mother, the body of a Luba woman is treated largely as a reproductive organism, a cultural property. After the rite of passage of maternity, however, a Luba woman may participate in the modification of her "body" in order to constitute it as a subjective erotic memory. Once she fulfills her duty to perpetuate the Luba people, the woman is permitted to engrave whenever she wishes, and in accordance with her own aesthetic considerations, the jouissance and terror, suffering and jubilation that the human quest of desire has inscribed in her. From such mute traces of the drive that remain at work in the organism once it becomes a body, the psychoanalyst waits for speech. This body is the erotic memory of the subject.

## "It Is Written into My Skin": The Psychoanalytic Symptom and the Unaddressable

We have previously considered the appearance of cancer, a deadly physical symptom that arose when a young researcher full of ambition and passion, David Servan-Schreiber, was in his early thirties. Thanks to his copious publications, we have been able to follow the installation of a symptom charged with a particular suffering that the ego, identified with the parameters of culture and civilization, couldn't recognize. Let us clarify that his glioblastoma, medically diagnosed, was a symptom delineated by science whose personal basis and stakes we could only deduce from his writings. This was not a symptom that we would qualify as psychoanalytic. "In a psychoanalytic symptom," Apollon specifies, "the unconscious mobilizes the letter of the body to open beyond the limits of the organism and the conditions of the relation to the other in the social link. What is perceptible in common space is ruptured by a lived experience in subjective time" (Apollon, Clinical Training Seminar, The Clinic of the Symptom). In an analytic cure, in the space created by the unconscious of the analyst, impermeable to the egoic stakes of culture and civilization, David Servan-Schreiber would have been called to find speech to express this unknown portion of his being, constituted of lived experiences excluded from the social link, inaccessible to the Other, and yet active in his body and in his relationships with others. On the basis of unmotivated acts and symptoms developed during his analysis, he would have explored, from his early childhood to his adolescence, what was inscribed in him as unaddressable, repressed, censored, and unsayable.

These four dimensions of the subject of the unconscious are traversed in a psychoanalysis under the impact of the singular space-time created by the analyst's desire to know, which, in turn, calls upon the ethics of the analysand to take responsibility both for his acts and their consequences, even if they were initiated in the field of the unconscious. This investigation of the bases for his life necessarily leaves unexplored other unrecognized zones where the human spirit in him continues to act. But he has the capacity to resolve the enigma with knowledge from his own unconscious, knowledge acquired about this "portion of his being outside the social link that remains active in the letter of his body" (Apollon, Enseignement et formation, Réunion clinique du Centre de traitement psychanalytique pour psychotiques, le 388). What the analysand discovers in his analytic work is the impact of this letter in his life as "the inscription of a lived experience outside of language, an unaddressable constitutive of his body, the source of repetitive acts substitute for the unsaid" (Apollon, *Le symptôme*). By virtue of tracing his acts and their repetition, the subject in analysis will establish a knowledge about his singular relationship to the outside of language, to the real that "does not cease not to write itself" (Lacan), and will be able to unravel the effects of this real in his life.

To assemble knowledge of the body, the subject in analysis must be welcomed by the unconscious of the analyst, which is what makes possible the transference whereby this Thing without words is elaborated, a real that couldn't be named until then, in the space created by his unconscious. In this space of transference, the analyst is unmoved by pleas from the analysand's ego for recognition, often expressed through various "fashionable" symptoms: loss of self-esteem, anxiety, panic attacks. What he hopes for is an unmotivated act driven by the Thing that espouses a rupture with the structure of the address. With this maneuver in the address, he provokes the opening of a space for the unconscious.

Let us take an example. Still very young, Doreen became a mother. She has been monitored by "child protective services" ever since the police found her on top of a viaduct with her little boy in her arms, prepared to jump. She is unhappy; she has lost control of her life. "It happens," she says, "that I have compulsions; it's not the first time I went out to the viaduct." The analyst offers a nonjudgmental listening, a listening devoid of cultural censorship or the values of civilization. A few sessions later, she begins to speak: "My father, when we were bothering him, would kick us to the ground, speaking angrily. My father was aggressive; you had to fall down!" And then, stunned, she added: "it's as if I myself wanted to repeat that! As if my body wanted to. When my little one acts up, I have the urge to kick him. It's as if it were written in my skin, like an automatism. It's scary!" Devoid of norms and demands, the analyst's listening called upon an unnamable Thing that slipped into Doreen's unmotivated act, an act that her "woman's body sought to commit" with nameless violence, a source of terror for the mother in her.

The analyst's opening of a space for the nameless gave Doreen access to a speech initiated by an unmotivated act. And then further analytic work on this act triggered a dream whose ending revealed even more about what, with an uncommon violence, had been "written in her skin." In the dream, she ends up killing a little boy who bullied her child. This dream flabbergasted her; it shook her profoundly. Even under the sway of truth, however, Doreen gave voice to her distress. "Thoughts or drives like this mustn't be spoken of . . . It's unforgivable, just not possible, but only here could I speak of it. My child, he was knocked down by another child at daycare . . . I could have killed that kid, like in the dream! But it can't be done. Thoughts like this might lead someone to kill themselves!"

Confronted by the "unsayable" in the dream occasioned by the withheld act that pushed her to attack her own child, Doreen could both recognize her own murderous drives and take a distance from the violence that preoccupied her as "written" (unbeknownst to her) in her skin. Although violent, the dream that arrived in the space created by the unconscious of the analyst, the space of transference, became presentable in speech as the product of her imagination. This conjuncture made it possible for her to link the five decisive elements in her life: the compulsion to jump to her death from a viaduct with her child, her past with a father capable of killing his own children, her dream of child murder, her own impulse to kill, and her suicidal gestures. What had previously been expressed in acts now passed through consciousness in the field of true speech, thereby reducing the intensity of her murderous impulses and bringing to an end the suicidal passages to the act that used to completely seize hold of her. What had been inscribed in her skin in early childhood and had remained unaddressable now found a salutary space for speech addressed to an Other who, in the framework of analysis, occupied the place of the Other of the Address. This salutary space for the subject in distress is that of transference, which Apollon defines as "the space opened by the unconscious of the analyst to allow the work of the analysand's unconscious to manifest itself . . . a space in which there is no room for repression and its strategies. It was established in the analyst's own analysis by his overcoming of repression, his traversal of symbolic castration which offered a site for the expression of femininity, and his confrontation with the unsayable where his ethics is founded, his concern for the human carried forth in the unconscious" (Apollon, *Le Transfert*).

Doreen now understood the basis, deciphered in her speech, for what was written in her body and pushing her to violent acts. No matter the intensity of the force that pushed her to protect her child from all external aggression, she knows that neither murder nor suicide is an option.

The unaddressable of early childhood is, for Apollon, witness to the upsurge of spirit in the small being. Because the small child has not yet entered language, the *unsayable* conditioned by the unaddressable will return to haunt the adolescence of the subject. Whereas the child might think about and wish for something unaddressable, the adolescent has the capacity to make it exist, to create it: although, at this point in her life, she will have to negotiate the impulse to act linked to the unsayable and the consequences of the act with regard to the rules of culture and civilization. For Apollon, adolescence is characterized by the experience of wishes, ambitions, and also forms of violence that go beyond what culture permits and what civilization can promise.

## The Psychoanalytic Symptom and the Analyst's Maneuver

To address the theme of the maneuver with respect to the psycho-analytic symptom, we first cite Apollon's most recent claims from his teaching in spring 2022. "The letter, constitutive of the body, refers to the (un)consciousness of an unaddressable lived experience outside of language, wherein is inscribed and repeated, as circumstances dictate, the impossibility of speaking either about the repressed, the censored, or the unsayable, sustaining and orienting the act that substitutes for the non-said" (Apollon, *Le symptôme*).

"The symptom is constituted right at the letter of the body. It is the result of a series of events, acts by the other or by the subject himself, and speech out-of-bounds on one of the four dimensions of the unconscious: the unaddressable, the repressed, the censored or the unsayable. These situations significantly modified the smooth functioning of a part of the organism; the subject expresses them in the form of a destabilizing, intimate feeling, an experience inaccessible to the other, something unobservable, his body. The letter constitutive of the body thus defines the consciousness of a lived experience outside language, a feeling produced by modifications that the unconscious introduced into the functioning of the organism. The letter is the source of the symptom" (Apollon, *Le symptôme*).

Supported by a clinical example, we will now consider how these different dimensions of the unconscious that Apollon has established arise within the psychoanalysis of a person with a neurotic structure. Let us mention up front that these dimensions are not elaborated in chronological order but rather in terms of the being's relation to them and what they present or evoke as stakes.

## Part One: "The Repressed" and the Satisfaction of the Other in Children Ages Five to Ten

With a weak, faint voice, Karine begins to speak: "I no longer have a voice, I am extinguished, exhausted, in pain, at the limit of my defenses. My mother thinks that I have fibromyalgia. My doctors can no longer help me; they no longer know what's going on with me. I want to change this."

At the second session, she refuses to lie on the couch: "no, you won't be able to hear me, my voice is too weak, there's no point in talking . . . Before, I used to have a voice, I killed my voice."

Then, one day, after about twelve sessions, Karine enters the office and goes to lie on the couch. There is a long and agitated silence before she begins to speak. She says:

> lying here is like entering a coffin. At the age of three, I broke my leg, I couldn't move, I was lying in my bed. I heard someone yell, "fire!" I heard the sound of steps as people left the house. Then, nothing. I cried out . . . I had been forgotten in my bed, as if I were nothing. I could have died. It's this memory that comes back to me when I lie down on this couch: will I be forgotten here? What will happen to me if I'm no longer in your field of view? If I speak, will you abandon me?

From the outset of her analysis, the couch episode brings up a painful memory from her early childhood, that period of life when the child must enter language and when a relation to the "Other of the Address" is constructed as the structure of the social link. First, she verbalized the fear of not being heard; then there was the return of the repressed when she moved from the chair to the couch while her body recalled, in session, the episode that made manifest for her the failure of seduction, the failure to satisfy the other: so unsatisfying was she for the other, so little did she count for her father, with whom she sought to have a privileged relation in the absence of any love from her mother, that he forgot her like everyone else—him too! Now it was her exhausted body, her barely audible voice, that reminded her she was "extinguished" . . . in the eyes of others.

## In Analysis: The Return of the Repressed in Response to the Analyst's Maneuver

What had remained repressed since Karine was nine in order to satisfy the Other, and had remained at work in her body, could finally be liberated through her speech. The analyst's maneuver discerned a blind spot in her refusal to lie on the couch; there was something impossible to say that had taken hold in her body, and it had to be respected in order for the repressed to arise in time and space. Without this maneuver, the beginning of the analysis would have stalled out. As early as the first meeting with the analysand, the analyst waits for manifestations of the unconscious and maneuvers to give a space to them. The act of the analyst in this maneuver opens a space for something that cannot pass through language. It calls for the aesthetic expression of what violently killed the being's spirit. The aesthetic, Apollon says, goes beyond the limits of the receivable, welcoming in the Other what cannot be said. Accordingly, the aesthetic subverts the structure of the address.

Karine's demand for analysis—in the form of a statement ("I am extinguished"), a question ("if I speak, will you abandon me . . . forget me?"), and in the assumption of her failed relationship with her father—was bodily transposed, we might say, into her relational life. Everything was set up in order to allow her to forget! Her weak voice, the rupture of the social link caused by extreme fatigue, lack of interest in almost everything, general dissatisfaction with her life, frequent and inconclusive visits to the doctor, something akin to death looming in her compromised immune defenses, and so forth. In analysis, the repressed is manifest in symptoms that hamper social life, perturb relations with others, in problems linked to an ego that has become fragile and unstable and to the disorganization of an organism beset by the work of the death drive in the letter of the body.

## Part Two: The "Censored" in Puberty, a Barrage against the Feminine. Puberty, in Which the "Cultural Montage of the Sexual" Censors Femininity, Ages Ten to Fifteen

After exploring the repressed, this young woman was able to approach another aspect of the constitution of the body, which occurs at puberty, the time of life when the impact of the censored hinders, for many young women, the constitution of their women's bodies. For the majority of girls, at the onset of their period, their parents hasten to consign them to a future of motherhood, which has a deleterious effect on the development of their femininity. Following Apollon, we note that the fantasy of seduction is what governs the symptoms linked to repression in early childhood, while for both boys and girls, the fantasy of castration is what governs the symptoms linked to the censorship of femininity in puberty.

In Karine's case, the devastating effects of the censorship of her femininity were due to the total absence of recognition of the fact that girls and women have a spirit and that they can create; which is to say, they can create more than babies in the cycle of social reproduction wherein cultures and civilizations tend to delimit the status of women. She remembered that each time she mentioned some little discomfort, her father, unemployed at the time, would encourage her to stay at home with him, saying, "stay with me, kitty cat, you will feel better, you don't have to go to school today." As a little girl, he had forgotten her, and she could have died. As a pubescent girl, however, he invited her to become daddy's truant kitty cat, which not only barred her femininity but also failed even to recognize the spirit in her that made her a human subject. Indeed, when she began to speak in analysis about the extremity of life with her father, it became apparent that he didn't actually love the subject that she was; that he not only censored her femininity, this motor of creation in her, but everything that made her human. She arrived in analysis without a voice, her power of speech dried up.

There are several angles from which the censored can be approached in an analysis. For another analysand, Aurelia, who arrived in analysis to finally consider in depth her repetitive relationships defined by the brutality of her partners toward her, one thing quickly became clear: when she gained weight on antidepressants, it wasn't the effect of the drugs on her organism, since plenty of women take them and don't get heavier. Although she didn't realize it, the best thing for her at the time was to "look fat," to no longer be the beautiful girl who systematically fell for the violent men who hit on her. She, too, was battling against the censorship of the feminine inherent to the cultural montage of the sexual. Gaining weight was a measure of protection: it allowed her to defect from the sexual marketplace central to a culture in which the woman is offered up as an object of satisfaction for a man in order to ensure the renewal of the collective.

## Part Three: The "Unaddressable" of Early Childhood, Birth to Five Years

After Karine reconsidered what had constituted the repressed and the censored within her, she delved into her early childhood and only then could envisage what had been unaddressable. There were two key memories, one highlighting what she perceived as her mother's hatred for her and her vindictive response to it, the other bringing to speech her own experience of hatred toward her mother.

First memory: still very little, she hopped onto her mother's knees, which didn't happen often. Her mother looked at her and brusquely pushed her away, calling her a "moron." At this precise moment, she added, "I wanted to kill my mother." A strong feeling of being rejected coupled with a murderous hatred toward her mother came to possess her and to be inscribed in her body as a lived experience.

Second memory: "We were at my uncle's cabin when I got diarrhea, which had spilled all over the floor, and everyone was looking at me. Then there was a loud noise. My mother had just fallen down and my father was running to her. It was a big drama for him. I would have liked her to die! I was just left there . . . dumped. From then on, I began to reject my mother, I thought she smelled bad." This event would produce for her a new bodily inscription associating odors, noises, and feelings of abandonment.

## Part Four: "The Unsayable" in Adolescence, Ages Fifteen to Twenty-five

The approach to these two events that were, on the one hand, unaddressable, because at an early age she wasn't yet in language, didn't yet have words, and on the other hand, unsayable, because a child cannot say she hates her mother to the point of wanting to kill her, presided over the identification of the psychoanalytic symptom. Lingering in the shadows until this moment, a symptom that "didn't bother her," and that first arose as a problem of constipation during her rebellious adolescence, could now be approached to reveal the scope of its restrictive impact on her life. It was accompanied by outbursts of uncontrollable rage infused with hatred that harmed her relations with others.

Under the effects of the analyst's maneuver, Karine was invited to discover, the further she examined her memories and described her symptoms in minute detail, how she spent years gaining control over her digestive tract, subjugating it, so that she could retain her stool for days on end in order to determine when the appropriate moment had come, depending on her schedule, to go to the bathroom, which became a ceremonial. It was the inverse of her humiliation and the death wish against her mother during the diarrhea episode from her early childhood.

At this point in her analysis, Karine began her session by saying that she'd had enough of speaking, of her verbal diarrhea, that she had said everything and had no more to say.

The analyst thus had to renew her maneuver by urging her, with a funny play on words that recalled a pivotal memory from her childhood, and thereby addressing herself to the human subject and her capacity for humor, to return to the experiences and memories from her childhood starting from precisely this "famous diarrhea," in light of what she had learned about her efforts to subjugate her intestine. Intervening with the assertion—"I won't tear words from your mouth, but are you content with this verbal diarrhea that won't ever create anything new in your life?"—the analyst urged the subject analysand to take an ethical position. The fantasy from which her symptom stemmed would have to come to speech in order to unveil and disable the unconscious motivation of the symptom that spoiled her life. Let us recall: the work on the unaddressable relies on the analysand's desire to traverse the ambushes that marked her life, whereas her psychoanalytic symptom arises from what couldn't be said at any previous moment, even as it remained active, outside language, unbeknownst to the Other and to the ego.

THE *UNSAYABLE* AND THE ETHICS IT DEMANDS WITH RESPECT TO THE CONSEQUENCES OF THE UNSAID IN THE SOCIAL LINK

Upon reflection, Karine clearly states that she has made the decision to live. And she begins to speak. Sometimes experiences of humiliation overwhelm her, or the stink of her feelings of hatred overcomes her. Armed with her firm ethical position, she can make a connection between the hatred of her mother from early childhood, her constipation, the control over her intestines, and the work of the symptom that transforms her digestive tract into a factory of fecal boluses, which, unbeknownst to her until then, served to wage merciless, fantasmatic war on this mother from her early years: her body served as a battlefield. In fact, each time that she went to the bathroom, she avenged herself on this mother by killing her metaphorically, in fantasy, with fecal boluses. To kill the mother: this is something unsayable in her civilization, as impossible as it was unaddressable for a child who felt brutally rejected when her mother dismissed her with a terrifying gesture and epithet.

"My body knows things that I do not!" Karine marvels: things she never even suspected, in fact. The purpose of the analyst's maneuver, here, is to allow the analysand to make connections between what she brings forth as the repressed, the censored, the unaddressable, and the unsayable, all the elements that formed what Apollon identifies as "the body of the letter." The maneuver also spurs her to take responsibility for the consequences of what she called the intestinal war waged against her mother. From now on the desire in her, the subject's desire, will supplant the imaginary, with the symptom and fantasy that it fomented inside of her, as the axis of her acts in life.

The maneuver is the modality through which the analyst constantly upholds care for the human as the ethical rule at the heart of her intervention, in support of the analysand's ethics. With her ethics, her refusal to renounce the expression of the human spirit and the desire that founds it, the analyst supports the ethics of the analysand in exploring what is happening in her body, including what escaped her knowledge, so that the fantasy can be revealed and its deadly bonds to the symptom dissolved. Only the ethics of the analysand with respect to the consequences in cultural space of what's at stake in her fantasy can liberate her from the symptom.

One day, Karine sent me a card with some very touching words. It was a few years after her analysis had reached its end. She began to create, she wrote, for the joy that comes with the act of creation but also to respond to the exigency that gripped her to account for the distress and despair that is dissimulated behind the impasse of faces. She also evoked the power of experiences lived in childhood, that fateful site where our way of being in the world is traced out. She mentioned that at the end of her analysis, which she experienced as the painful quest of the desire to live, she decided to change life, to change *her* life: her experience of analysis had thrust her into a journey motived by the exploration of the desire for desire.

# In Conclusion

We have elaborated the clinic of the symptom as it has been developed by Willy Apollon and its application in the analysis of persons with a neurotic structure. We have clarified the difference between two types of symptoms, that which appears in the social link as an appeal to the Other for help, which the doctor will name in his diagnosis, and that which has its source in what cannot be said and remains active outside of language, the psychoanalytic symptom. What allows this symptom to enter the analytical apparatus is the space created by the unconscious of the analyst when the stakes of the ego in the social link have become obsolete. At this point, the act of the analyst, through her maneuver, calls upon the ethics of the analysand to open a space in her life for the Thing outside language and to assume its consequences.

Apollon's advances, founded on a metapsychology that centers the becoming of the human both in the individual and in the collective on the human's capacity to create solutions, have also made possible the analysis of persons with a psychotic structure. A fundamental difference in the analysis of the psychotic is that the primary emphasis does not fall upon the interrogation of the ego square, because the ego is not really constructed in psychosis. In the initial phase of working with a psychotic analysand, the emphasis is placed on the delusion and its deconstruction through the analysis of the acts that it provokes and through the analysis of the dreams that the desire of the analyst triggers, opening a space for the unconscious. In the second phase, the ethics of the subject will be called upon to reconsider the mission and to restore objectives to the subject that can be actualized by a human "like any other" with others.

The new metapsychology for the psychoanalysis of the human that is upheld by Apollon's advances also facilitates the psychoanalysis of the human subject who is inscribed in the structure of perversion. For this subject too, ethics in relation to others is placed at the heart of analytic work after the stakes of the relation to the mother's jouissance have been named and reconsidered.

## Notes

1. The reader may consult the photographs of the Sorcerer of the Cave of the Trois-Frères that are widely available on the internet.

2. See the many fascinating photographs, available on the internet, of the legs alone and of Mullins wearing them.

3. In French, the word "tumeur" (tumor) is the homonym of the declarative phrase "tu meurs" (you die or you are dying).

## Works Cited

American Museum of Natural History, Permanent exhibition, *Anne and Bernard Spitzer Hall of Human Origins*, New York, 2017.

Apollon, Willy. Séminaires cliniques du Gifric. Québec City, 1980–present. Unpublished.

———. Enseignement et formation aux Réunions cliniques hebdomadaires du Centre de traitement psychanalytique pour psychotiques, le 388. Québec City, 1982–present. Unpublished.

———. Sessions de formation clinique en psychanalyse. Québec City, 1985–present. Unpublished.

———. Training Seminar. Québec City, 1996–present. Unpublished.

———. Clinical Seminar. Québec City, 2002–present. Unpublished.

———. "The Untreatable." *Umbr(a) A Journal of the Unconscious*, 2006, pp. 23–41.

———. Conférences Psychanalyse et mondialisation: "Un devenir pour la Chose Humaine dans la mondialisation." 2017–2018. Unpublished.

———. "Homme, femme, masculin, féminin." Teaching, Québec City, Feb.–June 2020. Unpublished.

———. Conférences Psychanalyse et mondialisation: "L'humain en question." 2021–2022. Unpublished.

———. *Journées annuelles de l'École freudienne du Québec*. Teachings. 2021ff. Unpublished.

———. "Sessions de formation clinique en psychanalyse." *Le symptôme*, Québec City, 1 Dec. 2018. Unpublished.

———. Clinical Training Seminar in Psychoanalysis. The Clinic of the Symptom. 15 Oct. 2021. Unpublished.

———. *The Unconscious, Penumbr(a)cast: The Other Scene*, hosted by Fernanda Negrete, Interviews on Contemporary Lacanian Psychoanalysis, Buffalo, 2021. Online.

———. Seminar for Analysts, 2021–2022. Unpublished.

———. *Le Transfert*. Text distributed to the analysts and clinicians of Gifric, 20 Apr. 2022. Unpublished.

———. *Le symptôme*. Text distributed to the analysts and clinicians of l'École Freudienne du Québec, 17 Mar. 2022. Unpublished.

Atmani, Mehdi. "L'athlète et mannequin amputée Aimée Mullins métamorphose son corps comme elle le veut." *Le Temps*, 27 Dec. 2017.

Bergeron, Danielle. "Éthique et symptôme." *L'Éthique et le symptôme, Correspondances, courrier de l'École freudienne du Québec*, vol. 18, no. 1, 2017, pp. 7–21.

———. "L'écoute du corps parlant." *Correspondances, courrier de l'École freudienne du Québec*, vol. 21, no. 1, 2020, pp. 7–21.

———. "The Symptom." *Penumbr(a) A Journal of Psychoanalysis and Modernity*, vol. 1, 2021, pp. 79–95.

Cheng, François. *Cinq méditations sur la beauté*. Le livre de poche, 2020.

Cleyet-Merle, Jean-Jacques. "La vie des hommes de la préhistoire." *Le Figaro: Beaux-arts magazine*, special issue, 2008.

Freud, Sigmund. "Instincts and Their Vicissitudes." *General Psychological Theory*, edited by Philip Rieff, Touchstone, 1963.

———. *The Ego and the Id*. Edited and translated by James Strachey, W. W. Norton & Co., 1990.

Girard, Isabelle. "La beauté n'a rien à voir avec la normalité." *Madame Figaro*, 29 Jan. 2011.

Guillemant, Philippe. *Le physicien Henri Guillemant. conscience, intelligence artificielle, questions existentielles*, 26 Mar. 2020, https://youtu.be/sMj289moVNs.

Lacan, Jacques. *Écrits*. Seuil, 1966.

———. *Télévision*. Édition du Seuil, 1974.

———. *The Seminar of Jacques Lacan: On The Limits of Love and Knowledge, Book XX*, translated by Bruce Fink, W. W. Norton & Co., 1999.

———. "Subversion of the Subject and the Dialectic of Desire." *Écrits: The First Complete Edition in English*, translated by Bruce Fink, W. W. Norton & Co., 2006, pp. 671–702.

———. "The Mirror Stage as Formative of the *I*-Function as Revealed in Psychoanalytic Experience." *Écrits: The First Complete Edition in English*, translated by Bruce Fink, W. W. Norton & Co., 2006, pp. 75–81.

———. "Aggressivity in Psychoanalysis." *Écrits: The First Complete Edition in English*, translated by Bruce Fink, W. W. Norton & Co., 2006, 82–101.

Morin, Edgar. "Entrevue." *La Revue pour l'intelligence du monde*, 26 Jan. 2021.

Nooter Roberts, Mary, and Allen F. Roberts. *Memory, Luba Art and the Making of History*. The Museum for African Art, 1996.

Rilke, Rainer Maria. *Letters to a Young Poet*. Translated by Charlie Louth, Penguin, 2011.

Servan-Schreiber, David. *Anticancer: A New Way of Life*. Viking Books, 2009.

———. *Not the Last Goodbye: On Life, Death, Healing and Cancer*. Viking Books, 2011.

8

# The Fantasy

## Its Function and Modalities, Traversal, and Clinic

Lucie Cantin

Translated by Alexander Miller

This text is part of the renewal of the fundamental concepts of psychoanalysis, such as they have been rethought and developed by Willy Apollon. We designate this as a new metapsychology, which we understand to be required by the radical changes we are living through as human beings in our era of *mondialisation*, and which entails a new psychoanalysis: a psychoanalysis that intends to return to its own origins and to what it has instituted as revolutionary knowledge about the human being, but with the added concern that it should be relevant for all human beings, whatever their cultural or civilizational origins, and whatever their psychic structure. This revision and evolution of the central concepts of psychoanalysis is characterized by being articulated as close as possible to the clinic, where they open a new field for the treatment not only of the neurotic but also of the pervert and the psychotic, making such treatment both possible and effective.

## The Unconscious Is Not in the Space Created by Language

The question of fantasy, which is the subject of our work here, presupposes a distinction between two concepts that are often confused: repression and the unconscious. Repression is situated within a cultural space, in which it finds its essential raison d'être. Repression concerns what cannot be said because of the prohibitions imposed by culture through the ideals, norms, and laws it promotes, and which define the field of the receivable in a given culture. Something is repressed by the individual, for whom the other's assent and recognition, conditions for inclusion in the collective, take precedence over his position as a subject bearing a singular desire. Freud's definition of "repression proper" applies only to the neurotic. The pervert and the psychotic, each for their own specific reasons, do not invest the givens of Culture and therefore are not subject to this concern for conformity to ideals and acceptance by the other.

Furthermore, the repressed is distinct from the censored, which concerns what can be neither said nor thought, because it is not named in the culture and civilization in which an individual finds themself. So, for example, certain words or formulas will have no possible equivalent from one language to another, as if the thing they name and designate in one culture didn't exist—or rather, shouldn't exist—in the other. "*Jouissance*" is not named in English; no word exists to describe this experience of stepping outside oneself (*sortie de soi*), this loss of limits, in an overwhelming joy, an ex-stasis that is neither reducible nor assimilable to pleasure, which, to the contrary, remains within the boundaries of the ego. The word "spirit" discussed in this book is another eloquent illustration of the censorship deriving from language. What it evokes in a series of idiomatic expressions in French—*le mot d'esprit, l'esprit d'entreprise, avoir de l'esprit, l'esprit de la Loi, l'esprit du temps, les grands esprits, l'état d'esprit, perdre l'esprit*, etc.—is diluted in the various translations to which it gives rise in English. The meaning of the word "*esprit*," which in all these French expressions always and unequivocally refers to that immaterial, elusive thing that is the seat of human thought and the place of origin of the human subject's creativity, has no equivalent in English. We move from "mind," which can be used alongside "brain," to "spirit," often associated with the religious sphere, as there is no single equivalent that would designate what is meant by the word "*esprit*" in French. The novelist Karine Tuil (Tuil, *La décision* 54) rightly points out that, while we have the word *orphelin* (Eng. orphan) to designate a child who has lost a parent and the word *veuf* or *veuve* (Eng. widower, widow) for the loss of a spouse, no word exists in French (or English, for that matter) to designate a parent who has lost a child. It's as if there were something unspeakable and unnameable here, something that does not accord with the way things are supposed to be. These fundamental differences, which concern the possible ways of expressing subjectivity, and not the naming of observable things in reality, reveal a censorship that passes through language and determines what is posited by a given culture as "outside meaning": what one must neither think nor live nor say.

Censorship thus testifies not only to the power of cultural discourse, but above all to the force of the lines of thought, the beliefs and the interpretations that a civilization imposes on the intimate experience of a being. Something can thus be censored in one culture or civilization that is not necessarily censored in another cultural or civilizational space. It is perhaps from this perspective that we need to understand Freud's "primary repression," which marks the human being from the moment he or she enters the world, in a universe structured by language that strands and censors this "thing" that remains unknown, because it does not exist in language, but which the subject experiences in the silence of his or her flesh.

In the case of both repression and censorship, then, we are similarly in the relationship of the subject to the Other, whether it's the other as companion of the social bond or the symbolic Other that is represented by Culture and the values and beliefs that guarantee its foundations. Repression and censorship remain anchored in the space constructed and conditioned by language to structure and organize a social bond without regard for the subject of the Unconscious.

But the unconscious is not part of the space created by language. The unconscious is that real, that lived experience that has never been represented, which is inaccessible both to the other and to the subject himself, and which therefore escapes any hold, any influence by Culture and Civilization. The unconscious is neither reducible to repression and censorship nor dominated by the *"unsayable"* (*l'impropre-au-dire*) that is determined and defined by language. Rather, the unconscious is outside language, and thus cannot be treated by what has already been represented. The clinic of the symptom presents a radical illustration of this: symptoms resist interpretation, which can only come from what already has been named or can be named. In this respect, interpretation serves as an attempt to reinforce and restore repression. Freud himself noted the failure of treating the symptom through interpretation when he came up against the rock of repetition. He discovered that what is at work in the symptom remains hermetically sealed from any grasp by the signifier of language, untouched by the meaning that interpretation provides.

This lived experience, inaccessible to the other and unbeknownst to the subject himself, which is the very stuff of the unconscious, can only be "ex-pressed" through the writing of what has never been named: the writing of the symptom or the act. The tool of this writing is the *"letter of the body,"* that which is inscribed or imprinted in the body, at the most intimate level of being, and which is reactivated, revived, remobilized at the whim of life's experiences. Here, we are in the field of the subject, beyond the Mirror, in what has instituted and established the body as a set of inscriptions of silent, unheard-of experiences, traumatic experiences insofar as they are unassimilable and unmanageable by what is available to the being, both internally, by its psyche, and externally, by what comes from the other: lived experiences of things seen, heard, felt, hallucinated, outside the field of perception-consciousness, which trigger singular "responses" in the being, neither dictated nor regulated by the pleasure principle. This marking, which alters and affects the functioning of the organism in a singular way, eroticizing certain functions or systems, gives rise to a body that is not only no longer governed by neuro-physiological logic and the pleasure principle, but is invested with energy mobilized by another logic, a quest whose object remains unknown. This birth of the body detached from the organism, a body that is eroticized and is traversed by something other than the quest for equilibrium, pleasure, and homeostasis, marks the birth of the subject: what Apollon once referred to as the *"constitutive trauma of the subject,"* and which has come to be referred to more precisely as *"the effraction of the psyche by the human spirit, by the human capacity to represent what does not exist."*

This new energy of the drive of desire, born of the original history of the subject and indelibly inscribed in the flesh, remains active, working in the body and never ceasing but by finding an outlet, a way of expression. This work in the shadows, which ignores language and is inaccessible to the subject himself, can only lodge itself in an act, a symptom, a "passage to the act" (*passage à l'acte*), or a "crisis" in psychosis—in short, in a writing in space. Such a writing makes visible what cannot be perceived, offering to the gaze of the other the encrypted expression of that unknowable Thing that works on being. The failure of a modality of expression relaunches the repetition of the act. Symptoms and passages to the act appear in apparently varied forms, but their repetition reveals a structure, a logic at work: the logic of an active fantasy.

## The Fantasy

Freud first approached fantasy in relation to the symptom, looking for the repressed representations that are active in the patient's unconscious and that give the symptom its symbolic form. As early as his *Studies on Hysteria*, but then more clearly in *The Rat Man and The Wolf Man*, Freud grasped the symptoms present as symbolic expressions of something that, because of repression, could only be said through its bodily expression. Lacan would later translate this, speaking of the symptom as a "bodily metaphor of fantasy." In these clinical cases, Freud notes that the body speaks and responds to the analyst's act without the patient being aware of it. The very form of the symptom, then, is controlled by a logic that remains unsaid.

Freud continued to advance with respect to the question of fantasy by highlighting two important aspects. On the one hand, in "A Child is Being Beaten," fantasy is reduced to a formula whose final version is the result of a series of transformations, during which the subject moves further and further away from a truth and a jouissance that must remain repressed. Thus, the formula "a child is being beaten," in which the subject of the drive and the object remain indeterminate, overlaps with repressed formulations that would reveal the subject's position and the object of his jouissance: "the father beats the child I hate," "I am beaten by the father." Not only is fantasy defined as a formula, but its logic can be subjected to a work of transformation.

At the same time, Freud recognized that there are common fantasies encountered in a large number of people. In the course of his work, he would take up this idea by establishing common types of fantasy, which he identified as fantasies of the primal scene (the originary fantasy), of castration, and of seduction (Freud, *Three Essays* 187).

Lacan's rereading of Freud marked a definitive break with the post-Freudian approach to fantasy, which had evacuated its unconscious dimension by reducing it to scenarios, more or less conscious imaginary stagings that, as such, are in fact part of a dimension of repression that Apollon summarizes as "what the other must never know." In other words, far from being unconscious, it's something the subject "knows," a sine qua non for wanting to and for being able to hide it. With Lacan, then, we move from fantasies approached as imaginary scenarios to fantasies thought of as axioms of meaning, a formula that accounts for an unknown logic at work in the unconscious, determining and structuring both the form of the symptom and the paths taken by the subject's acts, decisions, and choices in life. Lacan formulated this "fundamental" fantasy in a matheme: S ◊ (a), that is, the subject's relationship to the object as cause of desire.

Although Freud and Lacan addressed the fantasy, psychoanalytic literature on the clinic of fantasy remains particularly poor. Apollon reminds us that if the unconscious is at the heart of psychoanalysis, then fantasy is at the heart of the psychoanalytic clinic. Central and inescapable questions arise when we no longer reserve psychoanalytic treatment for neurotics alone but rethink this treatment and make it possible for perverts and psychotics. We then need to recognize the type of fantasy that is principally at play in the clinic of each of these three psychic structures, and that constitutes the central obstacle to be removed and overcome. Which fantasy fixes the repetition of the symptom in neurosis? What logic organizes the staging of the pervert? What aim traps the psychotic's enterprise? In each case, a free and assumed access to the quest of the subject of the unconscious is hindered. Does the analysand remain stuck in the fall of the seduction fantasy, resisting the traversal of castration and the lifting of censorship? Does he remain locked in a relation to the Other of an originary fantasy in order to avoid a direct confrontation with what is outside language and hence its management? It is no longer enough to say that the cure ends with the traversal of the fantasy without considering the modality of the fantasy in question, the stage of the cure in which it takes place, and, above all, the opening and therefore the new subjective position that this crossing creates, obliging the analysand to take ethical positions.

## "The Stuff of Fantasy is the Out-of-Language" (Apollon, Training Seminar)

The approach to fantasy is intrinsically linked to the conception of the unconscious as *outside language*. A number of characteristics follow from this. First, fantasy is a logic, hence the idea that it can be reduced to a formula. Fantasy circumscribes the logic that structures the expression of what cannot find its way into language and is written in the body with the symptom, the logic that organizes the aim of the drive in the passage to the act, and structures the repetition, aims, and consequences of the act in the relation to the other and in the social link. The act or the symptom thus expresses what has never been able to pass through language, either because of the repression initiated by the individual or because of the censorship and the unsayable of culture and civilization, or again, because it cannot be treated by words and is thus unaddressable.

Despite these barriers, the energy of the free drive, reactivated in the course of life's circumstances whenever they remobilize a lived experience that has been inscribed in the body and has remained unresolved, will find its way of expression in a symptom or an uncontrolled act whose consequences are unpredictable and rupture the social link. Failing to create a form of expression that is satisfying for the subject and aesthetic for the other, what is seeking its way out can only find "treatment" in these acts, which are repeated for as long as the stakes they conceal remain locked in the silence of the body. "The logic that supports the repetition of symptoms and/or acts reveals to the analyst the insistence and resistance of an untreatable" (Apollon, Training Seminar). These passages to the act or symptoms thus become what makes it possible to calculate what has been inscribed but never named, and the representations that structure them.

Unlike the symptom and the passage to the act, which offer themselves to be seen in space, fantasy remains outside the realm of the observable. Unfathomable by science, it escapes any instrumentalized measurement, any psychiatric or psychological "mental examination." Fantasy arises in the defect of the signifier, in the defect of language, constructed so as to manage the unmanageable, to treat the untreatable. If it can only be deduced from the symptom, the act, and the structure of repetition, then fantasy is not a given. It cannot be spoken by the patient; it can only be calculated and constructed in the course of analysis, as the logic that structures the acts and symptoms appears and is extracted from them. It then delivers a formula that "says well" that which, in the field of what is outside language for this particular subject, is at the root of the repetition of the act he performs, of what never ceases to return in the writing of the symptom, or again, of what calculates the contours of the object of the irrepressible quest of desire, which expresses itself in an incessantly relaunched and renewed, an always unfinished creation.

Fantasy, a pure creation of the human spirit, is without doubt the best evidence of the human subject's ability to create mental representations that have no echo in language, no connection with what exists and can be perceived, no relation to "reality" and no regard for the limits of the organism and the pleasure principle. *Jouissance*, desire, and the quest for something other than what has been or already is—these are structured by a fantasy, an unconscious representation that acts beyond what is agreed upon and organized within language. While the term "symptom" can still be used in medicine or even animal biology to designate an organism's dysfunction, the fantasy is irrecoverable in the discourse of science, from which it escapes absolutely. It presupposes an unsurpassable break in the regime of the living, which makes the human subject a being inhabited by an immaterial thing, elusive except in what it produces as effects and creations.

## For a Clinic of Fantasy: Modalities of Fantasy

With Apollon, we take up four modalities of fantasy: the originary fantasy, the fantasy of seduction, the fantasy of castration, and the fundamental fantasy, articulating their logical transformations at key moments in the constitution of the human subject.

The clinics of neurosis, psychosis, and perversion have also led us to consider the way in which each of these three psychic structures is organized around one of these modalities of fantasy: the originary fantasy in psychosis, the fantasy of castration in perversion, and the fantasy of seduction in neurosis. While the clinic of fantasy always aims to remove the obstacle posed by the repetition of the symptom and of acts that invest in the repair or management of a past, thus blocking the way to the free expression of what desire can create that is new and is yet to come, particular stumbling blocks will be encountered in traversing the principal fantasy at the heart of the structures of neurosis, perversion, and psychosis.

### The Originary Fantasy

"A fantasy that bears the mark of a deep-seated trauma in which the origin of the body is allied to the first manifestations of the spirit. What takes this form is an untreatable that links the being to the destiny of the human." (Apollon, Training Seminar)

The originary fantasy is rooted in the earliest intimate experience of a being, long before the use of speech and, of course, before the entry into language, which, for Apollon, is the "*structure of the social link*."[1]

The unborn child lives in the body of an other. It lives in the body of a woman who is herself constituted as a subject by a series of significant experiences that have remained unmanageable, inscribed in her and censored, out of language. These inscriptions are both solicited by the mental representations that the energy of the drive invests in its own fantasies and reactivated by what is experienced on the occasion of this real—this human being inside her—who takes possession of her body and of whom she cannot speak except in the words and formulas that culture and language authorize. The child is exposed to this censored Thing, which acts upon and traverses the body of the woman who is the mother, and he or she experiences its effects. These effects disturb the proper functioning of the child's bioneurophysiological logic, introducing disturbances that are even potentially fatal to the organism, to which the body "responds" in turn, generating new upheavals that are also inscribed. These experiences, which every human subject has necessarily undergone and which have remained deeply unconscious and forever inaccessible directly to consciousness, are written into us, in what Apollon defines as *"letters of the body."*

What thus began for the child even before he or she came into the world will continue throughout early childhood, in this period of life when, having no access to speech and no freedom to act, the child is both delivered over and subjected to the Other and confronted alone with what acts within him or her. The being of the child is thus sub-jected to things experienced in their being that cannot be named by the other, who has no access to them, and that are unmanageable by speech, of which the child does not yet have use. Likewise, they are unassimilable to any possible action of adaptation to the environment. The being is thus faced with something intractable and untreatable. Only the child's spirit—their ability to create a representation, their creative strategies—can be mobilized to cope with this experience, which the child must live alone and for which each child must find their own solution.

It is in analysis, by following the trace of what returns—which is written in the symptom or the act in neurosis, in the staging in per-version, in the crisis or through Voices in psychosis—that the logic of the fantasy that structures these manifestations of an out-of-language that works on the being can be reconstructed. The originary fantasy bears the mark of this untreatable at the origin of one's human destiny. It traces and represents the child's confrontation with the Thing that is censored in the body of the mother as a woman and is encountered from before birth, but also as it became lodged during early childhood in the depths of the Other's unformulated but no less effective demands. These demands, the object of which remained unbeknownst to the child, will have introduced questions and the search for answers, which were also unmanageable in language, and thus further mobilized the energy of the drive in representations and responses to what may have become a more or less powerful and inescapable super-egoic injunction for the subject. For example, as a fantasy of aggression by the Other, as a fantasy of devoration or of the annihilation of the being, the originary fantasy reduces, in a way, the creative freedom of the spirit by tying down the energy of the drive in a defense against this Thing introduced by the Other, this jouissance of which the child would be the object.

It is surely the psychotic who, in the progress of his or her speech in analysis, most directly illustrates what's at stake in the originary fantasy: those "visions," says Freud, "according to which the child imagines that, sojourning in the mother's womb, he or she has passed through all sorts of vicissitudes" (Freud, *Three Essays* 187). A psychotic woman undergoing analysis will say: "My mother was diabolical. When I was in her womb, she was able to put things into my brain. She could program me by implanting things to harm me. At the start of my schizophrenia I thought I had a chip in my head that she had programmed, and she refused to tell me how it worked." This fantasy, which speech liberated in analysis through a series of dreams during treatment, had been at the root of an aggressive act against her mother, which led to a long stay in hospital before she began treatment at the Centre.[2]

On the side of the woman who is the mother, what has not found expression of her femininity and of the quest of desire will come to trap her relationship with her child. Motherhood in such circumstances remains caught up in an "address" to the child, a tacit demand for love, for reparation and recognition, in which something is expected of the child through a series of unconscious expectations, acts, affective reactions, gestures—in short, a series of unspoken things that the child feels and responds to reluctantly (*à son corps défendant*). The child is confronted with an excess, with a nameless Demand, and experiences it in the body as a danger, as an anguish or a jouissance, in any case, as something unmanageable and with respect to which nothing in what is said makes it possible to cope. This is precisely what a young autistic woman recoils from, refusing to be a prisoner of this relationship with the Other, a prisoner of this power that the address confers on the other: "to speak," she would say, "is to be annihilated by the Other."

Another psychotic is invaded by terrorizing Voices. The Voice tells her to kill a baby, and so she's paralyzed by the fear of carrying out the act. The originary fantasy to which the content of the Voice had given us access, and which the analyst had grasped as a possible opening for speech on a never-named real, could finally be formulated as "a baby is being killed." This work had brought to the surface the events that had marked this patient's birth, which she now spoke of for the first time. She herself had been the baby who had almost died when she was in her mother's womb following a suicide attempt. But above all, the patient interpreted this suicide attempt, from which her mother nearly died, as a refusal to give birth to a daughter: the first daughter of the family, awaited by the invasive grandmother, detested and hated by the mother, who anticipated the child with the fixed idea of what the future of this daughter "who was hers" was to be. From the mother's speech, which our patient questioned with the desire to know more, she learned that she had been an extremely difficult baby, insomniac, always crying, refusing to breastfeed and then also to eat. These behaviors had provoked sometimes violent reactions from her depressive mother.

During early childhood, a series of accidents that the patient considered "voluntary," a kind of "suicide in disguise," also corresponded to this acted-out logic, structured by the fantasy that she was "the baby who should have died." On two occasions, she had thrown herself off a swing, or had "amused herself" by crossing the street with her eyes closed, without first checking for cars. Similarly, "forgetting" to feed the animals in her care had even more explicitly "realized" this fantasy: the baby animals were eaten by their starving mother. These accidents, acts, and forgetfulness that marked her childhood repeated the same logic, more clearly formulated as "a baby is killed by its mother."

But in psychosis the Voice brought back the injunction in an inverted mode: the actor of the murder was no longer the Other, but herself. And, literally paralyzed by the fear of carrying out the act, by becoming deeply prostrate and reclusive, by refusing all contact with others and with the outside world, the "baby," the object of the injunction, could live. This reversal was a clear indication of the strategy she had adopted in dealing with the original fantasy to escape the Other, as evidenced by the symptoms of her psychosis: she escaped death by playing dead.

In the absence of the Mirror, which, by producing the figure of a loving Other, would have tempered and distanced this censored Thing encountered in the Other, the psychotic remains captive to an originary fantasy in which the effraction of the psyche by the spirit is experienced in the mode of a mortifying relationship to an Other of which she would be the object. Such a fantasy evokes the very origin of every human subject, insofar as it is created as such by the subjection of the being to something foreign to the logic of the life of the individual and the species. Subjected to the effects of events that mark one's being and institute one's now eroticized body, and thus triggering singular drive "responses," the subject is born of *the "effraction of the psyche,"* this capacity of the human mind to represent what acts outside language. The originary fantasy concerns this effraction, this founding trauma of the subject, which it manages by producing a representation of the origin of the effraction, giving this intrusion of an ungraspable, unnameable real the imaginary consistency of a "figure." To explain what was taking over her body in the moments of panic she was experiencing, the patient said, "it's as if I'm trapped in my mother's womb and I can't get out, I might die."

In analysis, *"the analyst sticks to the logic of what insists in repetition, until the analysand discovers the series in which his life is suspended. The formula then undoes the imaginary that obscured an exigency"* (Apollon, Training Seminar). Working on the repetitive form taken by the acts and accidents of early childhood and their consequences revealed the logic of the fantasy that structured them: "a baby is killed by its mother." The responses of the body, which staged its own disappearance in the psychosis, revealed the subject's confrontation with the Thing, but within herself. To this call of the free drive at puberty, she had responded by "disappearing" as a subject, shutting herself away in silence and reclusion. The work of analysis revealed that this mortifying jouissance imputed to the maternal Other had been discovered in her at puberty. She was terrorized by it, and from then on everything had to be constructed to subdue this intractable Thing that was taking possession of her body. She identified this drive as "violence mixed with sexuality," she "refused" it, and she tried to control it by erasing herself as a subject and refusing any relationship with the other. Progress in analysis allowed for a gradual disinvestment in the devouring figure of the Other in the fantasy, which now crumbled, making it possible for the subject to take responsibility both for what had been inscribed in her, in her body, as traumas, and for the way she had managed them in the fantasy. This dismantling of the Other of the fantasy enabled her to lift the symptoms with which she was "defending" herself from the Other, and freed up the energy of the drive that could be invested in a study project that had been the object of her passion since childhood. Her journey through the originary fantasy thus led her to the ethical imperative of creating new solutions for the future, linked to the desire that carried her as a subject.

The originary fantasy takes shape in the child's unconscious as a mental representation of *"the effraction of the psyche by the spirit."* What the child's spirit constructs as a fantasmatic representation from what he or she experiences and what has been inscribed in the body is fundamentally singular. Clinical experience provides an irrefutable insight into this. We cannot but see the fundamental freedom and boundless creativity of the human spirit at work here. All that a child experiences before entering the world of language and the social link, and therefore before anything that constrains this freedom to create the unprecedented, is the subject of a very special and unique, intimate form of management.

Artificial intelligence researchers are studying what they call "deep intelligence" by observing babies. They emphasize the great "intelligence" of babies, who, they say, have no "cognitive limitations" when it comes to grasping the world around them, no preconceived patterns that limit their exploration and interpretation of the world. In fact, the baby's spirit, its capacity to imagine and create solutions, is not yet constrained, formatted, and marked out by the reality that will be produced by its entry into language, the thought patterns, interpretations, and Meaning imposed on it by Culture. Luc Langevin, an illusionist whose job is precisely to create the illusion that deceives the spectator's mind, points out that such work consists of getting the spectator to perceive, grasp and interpret on the basis of what he calls "cognitive automatisms." Deception works because the ability to grasp and represent the cause of what is happening is locked into frames of meaning produced by what can be thought. He notes that children and autistic people are the bystanders who most often guess the trick. They don't let themselves be led down the most common paths of "logical" explanation, as adults do. Autistic people, like very young children, have not entered the world of language, of the formatting imposed by culture. So their attention is not locked into what is determined by what must be perceived, or by an obligation of verisimilitude dictated by "reality."

Transformations of the Original Fantasy in Neurosis: Seduction and Castration: Four Poles for the Installation of Repression and Censorship

How is the originary fantasy transformed? How is it that the way in which one manages the effects of the invasion of one's being by these lived experiences, untreatable by the psyche, left outside language and unaddressable, comes to be modified? In neurosis, the entry into language initiates the detour of drive energy in favor of issues imposed by the collective.

As a first sketch of this mutation, the baby, by identifying with the self-image produced and invested by the Other in the Mirror, initiates the first stage of distancing from and repression/censorship of the experiences that are lived outside language and that constitute the singularity of his or her being. The discourse held about the baby by the maternal and parental Other will support and consolidate the image during the first years of childhood. At the same time, the production of reality, which is structured and constrained by the naming of the things in the environment, restricts what can be represented by linking representation to what is perceptible and observable by all. In this way, "reality" amounts to what is appropriate to see and to know. As a result, not only does the gap widen between what is said about the baby and what he or she experiences, but the production of a consensual "reality" blocks the unconscious mental representations linked to their intimate life. Psychiatry could hardly be more precise when it states that those who continue to act on the basis of what they imagine and represent subjectively have "lost touch with reality." In fact, such an individual is indeed delirious: they do not perceive what they are supposed to perceive, they do not interpret reality in the manner that others think they should. The child will quickly be taken to a psychologist if, with socialization in second childhood, they do not enter into the reality in which others live. The child will only recognize this division between intimate experience and the Other's discourse when he or she becomes aware that the Other has no access to this intimacy. The progress of the treatment with the psychotic sometimes makes it possible to see clearly for the first time this experience that the subject was unable to have in childhood. Invaded to that point by the certainty that their thoughts can be read, the analysand now experiences in the cure that the Other, in this case the analyst, has no access to their intimacy, and can know nothing other than what they are willing to say, or what they try to evoke through speech.

And so the stakes of this first step in the transformation of the originary fantasy are in fact double. On the one hand, the self-image, the first milestone in the production of the ego, represses the eroticization of the being by the set of experiences inscribed in the letter of the body, thus covering the subject of the unconscious, which remains outside language. On the other hand, the "reality" produced by consensual representations stands in the way of the singular and novel mental representations that the child's mind can create, and whose expression will be more or less suppressed, even if they will of course remain active in the unconscious, as evidenced by symptomatic manifestations and eventual acts, as well as by the success of creative acts that the child may produce.

A second major transformation of the originary fantasy takes place through the change in status of the Other. The real entry into the social bond as structured by language takes place at the moment of socialization,

Figure 8.1. "The First Moment of Transformation: The Rejection out-of-language of the Intimate Experience of the Subject." *Source*: Lucie Cantin.

**The First Moment of Transformation:**
**The Rejection out-of-language of the Intimate Experience of the Subject**

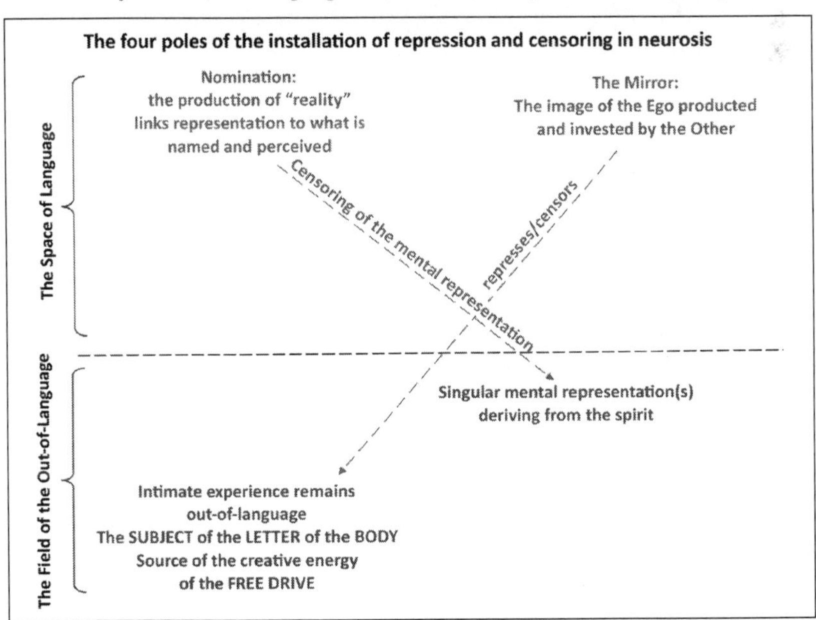

which schooling, among other things, obliges. The child encounters here the Other of Culture: an Other who represents the social and cultural requirements to which he must submit, and which define what he must be and do to be in companionship with others and to be part of the group. But the child is unaware that these laws, norms, ideals, and prohibitions are imposed by the need to live together in a human collective; and so, in passing through the demands of parents or other authority figures, they are experienced as demands for satisfaction from the Other. On this satisfaction depend the love, recognition, acceptance and assent that the Other may or may not grant, as well as the rejection, abandonment, and punishment to which the child may be subjected.

This entry into the social link forms the foundation on which the concomitant construction of castration and seduction fantasies can occur. It's not a question here of symbolic castration, the inevitable loss for every human being that is linked to his or her inclusion in a culture and civilization, but rather an imaginary castration linked precisely to what is experienced as a demand for satisfaction from the Other, on whom the ego depends as a more or less adequate object. Castration and seduction become two sides of the same coin, built on the basis of the same experience. On the one hand, there is an anticipated, imagined lack, an experience linked to the reprobation or rejection of the Other: imaginary castration. And on the other hand, there is the Ego's search for adequacy with the object imagined as the object of love and therefore of the satisfaction of the Other: seduction.

But above all, in this adherence to the demands and constraints of the social link, what is put in place, for the neurotic alone, limits the free drive by monopolizing part of the subject's creative energy, which is now constrained by the work required to consolidate the ego as dependent on the satisfaction of the Other. Responding to the cultural and civiliza-tional demands that nourish the neurotic ego diverts the free drive from its unconscious quest. Puberty is the last stage of repression before the onset of adolescence. At this point, culture takes over the installation of censorship by promoting a *"cultural montage of the sexual,"* for which the fantasy of seduction will have opened and prepared the terrain. The aim of the montage of the sexual is to censor the unconscious quest by promoting a conception of "desire" linked to and inscribed within the relationship with the Other as defined and regulated by Culture.

The impact of this second movement of transformation of the status of the Other of the originary fantasy is also double. On the one hand, the creative energy of free drive, which is diverted and subjugated to the service of an Other to be satisfied, covers over *the absence of the Other* and the *Defect of language*, sparing the subject direct confrontation with the unsurpassable solitude of being. On the other hand, adherence to the cultural montage of the sexual diverts the free drive from its quest, enclosing the subject's desire in a formatting defined by the ideals required for the survival and reproduction of the Collective. Henceforth, castration comes from the symbolic, from Culture, though it clings to the fertile ground prepared by imaginary castration, where lack is attributed to the ego's inadequacy in responding to the demands and requirements of an Other.

Symbolic castration is thus linked to what language, in its function of structuring the social link, introduces as an obstacle to the free expression of unconscious desire, through the promotion of cultural ideals, norms, and prohibitions that are supported by myths and beliefs that underpin their credibility in each civilization. In this way, symbolic castration diverts and limits the force of the drives in search of something other than what has been imposed on the subject since its entry into the relationship with the Other. Apollon describes the stakes and effects of symbolic castration by emphasizing its two dimensions. On the one hand, there is the "*censoring of the feminine*," the censoring of that real in being that has remained outside language, which escapes the grasp and control of culture and civilization, and which is the source and the terrain of the free and limitless creative activity of what the human spirit can produce. On the other hand, there is the establishment of the "*cultural montage of the sexual*," where culture censors eroticism, feminine jouissance, and desire, confining and framing them within a sexuality whose modalities, objects, and forms remain within the relationship with the other in the social link. The montage attempts to control the unknowable object, the cause of an ever-unfulfilled quest of desire, by substituting for it an other who would be promoted within reality and elevated to the status of object of desire. The establishment of the "*censoring of the feminine*" and the cultural montage of the sexual become the very means by which the collective keeps a tight rein on the limitlessness of the quest of desire that runs through every human being, beyond what any culture or civilization can attempt to subdue.

Censorship, to restrict the movement of desire, takes on its full force at puberty, the moment when the work of the drive awakens in the body, and when the young person is most sensitive to the ideologies,

Figure 8.2. "The Second Moment of Transformation: Production and Investment of the Other of Culture." *Source*: Lucie Cantin.

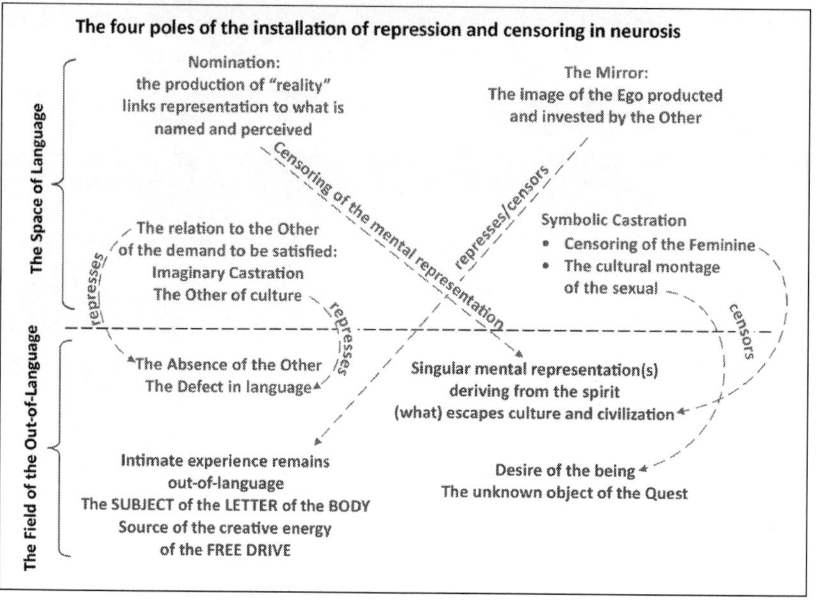


ideals, and objects of identification that Culture produces to anchor the energy of the drive to the objects and objectives of the collective. It is with the fantasy of seduction and the montage of the sexual that Culture roots the production of an "*Other of the address as guardian of the receivable*" who defines what can be said and what must be kept silent. A discourse adjusted to what the Other wants and can hear delimits the boundaries of what can and cannot be evoked in speech.

In spite of everything, adolescence will lift the obstacle imposed on desire, as the subject will experience, in the entirety of their being, that they are inhabited by something that escapes all possible control by Culture and Civilization. What adolescence profoundly calls into question is not what Culture imposes, but far more radically the very foundations on which the construction of Culture and the structure of the social link rest. In this respect, the adolescent, like the psychotic, experiences the defect of language. They experience in their bodies what Apollon once described as "*the unfoundedness of the symbolic*," thereby releasing the energy of the drive of desire, just as the cracks and subsequent collapse of a dam release the flow of water that it had previously imprisoned and contained. With this new experience and awareness, the adolescent rediscovers the creative freedom and the limitlessness of what they carry as a quest for something other than what is already there. The adolescent's desire is directed toward the future, in a quest now unshackled from the past. What will they do with it? What will the adolescent do with this chaos? What will they create in this moment of opening for desire, when they are disarticulated from the expectations and demands that organized the conditions for "succeeding in life" as defined by the Other of superego and culture? And what responsibility will they assume for what their quest produces in the social link?

These questions lie at the heart of the objectives and destiny of an analytic cure. We will come back to them as we elaborate on what Apollon's metapsychology offers in the way of new insights into the stakes of the end of an analysis.

## PERVERSION AND PSYCHOSIS IN RELATION TO CASTRATION AND THE ORIGINARY FANTASY

The transformation of the originary fantasy by castration and seduction concerns only the neurotic. The traversal of these latter will bring the neurotic back to what constituted him or her as a subject, to the experiences inscribed in the body that have determined their particular sensitivities, their singular eroticism, the modalities of jouissance, and the unknown quest of desire that runs through their life, for which they will now have to take responsibility in the social link.

Very early on in childhood, the pervert experienced a division between what was experienced in the body and what was named by the Other. So the pervert "knew" relatively early on that the Other could have no access to what they experience internally. This experience of the inviolability of one's intimacy gives rise to two particular features of this subjective position. First, a resolute refusal of what is imposed by Culture: ideals, norms, prohibitions, laws that one knows from experience to be arbitrary and to have no hold on one's inalienable freedom as a subject. This refusal, which proves to be the consequence of lived experience, logically entails the absence of a fantasy of seduction and therefore the scope of *the Other of address* produced by culture. So at a time when the child is called upon to enter the structure of the social link and faces the challenges of a relationship with Demand and with the satisfaction of the Other in order to be recognized and loved, the experience and position of the perverse child enable him or her to escape the grip of the Other that is experienced by the neurotic. The position of the pervert is thus neither constructed nor determined by a response to the demands of the Other of Culture.

Freud spoke of perversion as the denial of the mother's castration. Apollon's concept of *"censoring of the feminine"* sheds light on Freud's intuition, but above all, it takes perversion out of the cultural montage of the sexual. The perverse child, by the very fact of this "refusal" of the castration imposed by language in Culture, remains as close as possible to the real that inhabits the body and escapes the control of Culture. He or she remains interpellated, intrigued, solicited by this Thing that haunts the body of the woman who is the mother, the dissatisfactions, frustrations, and deprivations at the source of a never-formulated demand to which the perverse child will be devoted. This attentive recognition of the feminine that inhabits the maternal Other enables the pervert, unlike the psychotic, to avoid a paranoid, anguished position in relation to the Other of the originary fantasy.

At puberty, with the emergence of a drive energy in the body, the pervert rediscovers the action of the out-of-language, that is, of the feminine. But this time it is experienced within one's own being. This raises the question of how to manage this thing that one lives, with the newfound awareness and profound knowledge that the jouissance that one has already experienced can neither be subdued by the laws and prohibitions laid down by Culture nor assimilated to the orgasm-centered sexuality that Culture promotes.

In place of the *"cultural montage of the sexual,"* which, in neurosis, installs the censorship of the feminine dimension, that outside-language that inhabits being, claiming to assimilate desire and jouissance to a sexuality defined and controlled by Culture, the perverse subject will have to put in place an entirely different strategy to manage both the feminine within their own being, which they are no longer willing or able to keep at arm's length, and the relationship to the other in social space.

If the experience of adolescence, marked by the discovery of a dimension of being that goes beyond what Culture and Civilization can control, vindicates the pervert, the social requirement that the young adult must now assume responsibility for his or her acts and manage their consequences in the collective poses a new challenge. How, in public space, are we to take responsibility for the consequences of acts that, by definition, cannot fit into the cultural montage they fundamentally challenge? Several solutions are possible. Certain perverts, precisely by virtue of this position of returning to the truth that constitutes us as human subjects and resists censorship, can create and inscribe in Culture profound changes that irreversibly modify and advance one of its dimensions, whether artistic, philosophical, social, or legal. These advances presuppose a subjective ethic, stemming from and articulated to a quest: a desire that informs what the subject produces, introduces, and reveals in the face of what is receivable or already thought in the cultural space. The example of Sade, but also many of the great perverts who have left their mark on our cultures by assuming responsibility for their acts and managing their consequences in the social space, illustrate the ethics that their desiring positions have required.

Others will stick to a private solution, designed to treat and control jouissance through the development of scenarios created and staged in reality. Apollon has described the structure of these scenarios in which, on the one hand, the establishment by the pervert of a tacit or explicit contract with another, whoever he may be, provided he accepts the conditions, makes it possible to avoid the Address to the Other, which would open onto the incalculable and the unforeseeable. On the other hand, a controlled staging of the conditions that create and ensure the emergence and framing of a jouissance outside norms maintains both the denial of the castration imposed by Culture and the refusal of censorship of the feminine.

The perverse subject finds themself at an impasse when they remain captive, locked in the repetition of these "private" stagings that replay the childhood experience of being able to escape from the Other, who can do nothing against what is experienced in the intimacy of one's being. The strategy of a division between private life, where scenarios and stagings are played out, and public life, where they respond perfectly to social demands, is a good illustration of this division, which the perverse subject decides to maintain without necessarily being "sick." The challenge of the analytic cure for the person involved is logically defined by the confrontation with the feminine in their own being as a source of creativity, which requires an exit from the repetition of scenarios and the crossing of this "private-public" division, through which they have avoided assuming in the social link the effects of what can be created from the singularity of a subjective position and a management of the consequences in the relationship with others.

The experience of the psychotic subject meanwhile gives us the most direct access to the effects of the effraction of the psyche by an experience and by mental representations that are outside language and beyond the pleasure principle. The psychotic has never entered into the relationship with the Other of seduction or into the cultural montage of the sexual. Escaping the grip of the Other of seduction, and thus the construction of an ego that depends on the recognition and assent of the Other, the psychotic has no experience of imaginary castration. There is no Other of address for what the psychotic experiences as unaddressable. Although psychotics are confronted with the language that structures the social link, unlike neurotics, they have not adhered to what culture promotes. In fact, the psychotic has never entered into the social link and so doesn't call it into question the way the pervert does.

As we learn in the analysis, it is from early childhood on that, without being aware of it, the psychotic lives, in an absolute solitude, intimate experiences that have remained unassimilable, senseless, and unaddressable, and that are accompanied by the certainty that he or she is the only one who can manage them. The psychotic best illustrates not only what is experienced as an effraction of the psyche by the spirit, but also what gives form to this experience, representing it, even explaining or justifying it in the elaboration of an originary fantasy that would account for what has constituted him or her as an object sculpted by these invasions to which he is subjected. What we call a delusion takes shape at puberty, with the emergence of the free drive in the body, which revivifies the experience of aggression by the Other. The structure and objects of the elaboration of the delusion are determined by the singular logic of the originary fantasy, which expresses the experience of the effraction. In it, the psychotic accounts for an unidentified Other, a faceless Voice, a "they" that assaults him or her in their body, uses them, manipulates them, and makes them act; an Other that has introduced things into their organs and takes possession of them—in short, an Other of which one is the object and which alters one's very being. So many explanations and representations of the aggressions one has had to deal with, without the tempering that would have been provided by the relationship to the Other of the address and the repression that would have been established by symbolic castration.

But it's during adolescence that these unmanageable, hitherto unconscious experiences of early childhood, when the psychotic was too soon confronted without mediation with the Defect of language, are revived, mobilizing the energy of the free drive in the solitary quest for a solution to implement. This is when the renewed encounter with a flaw in the structure of the social link and, above all, in the values and beliefs on which this social organization is based, triggers what we have termed the psychotic enterprise. An enterprise in which the psychotic will invest themself with the idea of creating a new language to structure new social bonds, or that will initiate a sacrificial withdrawal of their being onto this Evil to be eradicated, an Evil that they bear and for which they are responsible.

The stakes of the psychotic's "work," which will always touch on a central problem facing the whole of mankind, reveal the extent to which the psychotic is situated beyond culture, as if he or she were aiming to create a new "civilization" that would transcend all cultures and social organizations to found the universality of what constitutes the human: whether through the attempt to solve the problem of hunger on earth, to eliminate the flagrant injustices that everyone knows and seems to accept, to overcome the hierarchization that makes some second-class humans, to establish peace and sharing between peoples, to build a universal social link through art, to eradicate violence against women, to denounce and to attempt to rebuild a language that would be able to say all—in short, an enterprise that concerns the human and eliminates whatever stands in the way of human advancement. Of course, the specificity of this undertaking is articulated by and responds to the singularity of what is inscribed as fundamental subjective experiences in each individual. It is linked to what has constituted his body and monopolized his mind, mobilized by the representation of an object to come in a quest that both inhabits the being from its origin and goes beyond it to reach the human in each of us. The enterprise thus gives specific form to the logic of a fundamental fantasy that links the subject to the object of a quest that traverses him.

The psychotic is sick from the failure of this enterprise. Not because it's crazy or far-fetched, since each of us can recognize how right the psychotic is to denounce the defect in language that leads to the rejection of an essential part of humanity, and not because they are wrong to want what they want for humanity, but rather because the commitment of their entire being to what we have called their "work" is underpinned by the certainty of being invested with the ethical responsibility of solving alone what they consider to be an impasse in humanity's future. The real objections and obstacles that a psychotic encounters along the way are experienced as hindrances imposed by others or by the Other, and therefore as aggressions. It is thus the failure of this "work" that makes the psychotic "sick": he or she reacts to what makes the project impossible by acts (*passages-à-l'acte*) that would remove the obstacles, or by an inner collapse that is caused by their failure. It is also at this point that the so-called delusion takes definitive shape. The content of the delusion is nourished by mental representations from childhood and structured by the original fantasy, but its elaboration at the time of the onset of psychosis will henceforth be nourished and supported, bolstered and enriched by explanations and theories, by conceptions of the universe, by religious or spiritual beliefs that are those of his time and of the world in which the individual lives.

The cure will therefore aim to deconstruct this original fantasy and bring down the Other that the delusional explanation identifies as the cause of the effraction, so that the true stakes of the quest conveyed by the enterprise and the ethics it commands become apparent. The aim, then, will be to transform the enterprise by eliminating its narcissistic or paranoid dimension, while preserving the object at its heart, for which the subject will have to find a new means of expression, articulated with some others in a collective.

## From Fantasy to Its Traversal for Access to Desire

### The Necessary Deconstruction of the Other, Endpoint of the Traversal of the Fantasy

The decisive stages in an analytic treatment from the point of view of the clinic of the fantasy are linked to the particular strategies favored in each psychic structure.

The neurotic's choice is essentially based on the investment of cultural requirements that ensure their insertion into the collective. The neurotic's position, based on repression and censorship, which necessarily fail, is at the mercy of the manifestations of the unconscious, through symptoms and acts that convey a truth that remains encrypted, allowing the individual to avoid the responsibility that neurosis leaves to the Other who inhabits the fantasy.

From then on, the clinic of the neurotic will encounter two main pitfalls, both linked to this unassumed responsibility, guaranteed by the relationship to the Other that lies at the heart of neurosis. The first, present in the first stage of the treatment, concerns the obstacle to speech constituted by the "Other of the address" as instituted by culture, the representative and guarantor of the receivable, which the neurotic brings to the field of analysis. More or less subtly, the neurotic addresses the analyst in a strategy of seduction whose roots go back to the Mirror. So doing, he or she flees the risk of a true speech, outside the norm, of which he anticipates the distressing effects, dreading the inadmissibility of the consequences it would entail.

The second major stumbling block for the neurotic in their analytical work concerns the fall of the "responsible Other," whether it's the figure of the Other resulting from the never-formulated, censored Demand, the exigencies of which seduction will have attempted to temper by working to "respond" to them, or the Other of Culture anchored in the cultural montage of the sexual. So we need to distinguish between, on the one hand, the fall of seduction, after which the neurotic faces up to what acts within him or her, without being able to imagine that the love or recognition of an Other in reality can shield or even manage it; and, on the other hand, the deconstruction of the Other of the originary fantasy, a figure that obliterates and covers up the Absence of the Other, and whose fall confronts the subject with the responsibility of the free drive that haunts his body. This confrontation with the "No Other" would liberate the subject from super-egoic and cultural exigencies, making the subject fully accountable for their actions and for managing the consequences for others.

Such is the case for an analysand who, at the age of two or three, was plagued for months by a recurring nightmare in which "a witch was cutting into pieces all the children in the house." This nightmare expressed the strength of an originary fantasy in which the child was the object of an abusive Other who threatened his physical integrity and his life. During early childhood, an "accident," a kind of passage-to-the-act, had reproduced the scene evoked in the nightmare, producing a major bodily injury, a deep cut. In second childhood, through to puberty and adolescence, several other accidents and symptoms, which repeatedly either physically mutilated him or destroyed his image in the eyes of others, drew their logic from this same fantasy. Analysis had revealed the precise moments when these symptoms or acts occurred, demonstrating the failure of the transformation of the originary fantasy through castration and seduction. These manifestations of the unconscious expressed the strength of the anxiety inscribed in him by the confrontation of his being with the excess encountered in the body of the mother. Until well into adulthood, the "excessive demands" made on him by the women he chose reproduced what he had experienced from early childhood as the impossible-to-satisfy demands of women: a grandmother whom he had to "protect from the ghost of the dead grandfather," a mother who had become deeply frustrated and bitter as a result of injustices for which she blamed men and who had "treated him like a girl" until he started school. At that point, the appearance of pimples on his penis that had necessitated a call to the doctor plunged him into a panic attack. The anticipated medical intervention concretized in reality the imaginary fear of being castrated, "cut into pieces" by the Other.

The entry into the social link, which is regulated by prohibitions, norms, and cultural requirements linked to the necessities of companionship and life in society, and which should have set a symbolic limit to the Other of which he was the object in fantasy, had failed. Instead, a symptom once again inscribed a real limit with a "mutilation" on his body, clearly visible to others. In the same way, a series of acts were repeated, all in the same form, in which the aim was to provoke a physical intervention by the Other. The patient provoked and called for a physical limit, which at once came in the absence of a symbolic limit and, at the same time, never ceased to inscribe the real threat to his physical integrity. He remained caught up in an originary fantasy and in a castration imposed by a real or imaginary Other from which he was unable to escape. The failure encountered in the social scene was progressively compensated for within the family by his attempt to respond to his mother's complaint as a woman, and to satisfy her where his father had failed. He invested himself as the man capable of consoling her and repairing the wrongs that men had inflicted on her.

The imaginary "success" of this impossible task, which served as a fantasy of seduction in which he was the object of "desire" of the woman who was his mother, had been a strategy that, until early adulthood, entrenched him in a solution that made the Other, the father as well as the mother, responsible for all his happiness and misfortune. In the end, it was the failure of this solution with the experience of adolescence, a time of both inevitable inscription in the social link and the first relationships with women, that led him to analysis. The "choice" of excessive women for whom he was to be the "savior," the "gallant knight-servant," and the manic episodes in which he would "sell" himself, successfully moreover, to businessmen proposing a project that he was then unable to realize and had to abandon, reproduced both the attempt and the failure of seduction. The ego proposed itself as capable and then deflated. Here again, the intervention of a third party, an external limit, police or psychiatrist, was "called in" by what was being acted out in each of these episodes. The reproduction of this cycle of attempted seduction, followed by physical castration imposed by an Other, remained firmly anchored in the relationship with the impossible satisfaction of the Other. The figure of the Other responsible for the Thing that had worked on him since childhood remained untouched, undiminished. As he put it at a key moment in the treatment, "I'm being asked to do something I can't do, and I can't get away from it."

By following the writing of the symptom and unmotivated acts, what they mobilize as letters of the body, the precise circumstances in which they occurred, and their consequences in the relationship to the Other, a structure of repetition gradually emerged, the logic of which was given by a fantasy. The fall of the Other of the originary fantasy, with which the patient had struggled since childhood, went through stages of deconstruction that the patient was able to formulate. The ego, "the image I was building up in front of others" collapsed "like a deflating balloon." The analysand "couldn't believe in it anymore." He traversed seduction, recognizing that with his mother and women, he had "always acted as if I could be what they wanted me to be." From then on, the entry into castration—no longer the imaginary castration resulting from his failure to satisfy the Other, but the castration that came to bar the Other—could complete the deconstruction of the originary fantasy and lead to the fall of the responsibility imputed to the Other. Not only could no other do anything for him, but above all he was faced with the inescapable fact that he could do nothing for the Other, which was for him the real source of anxiety. "Thinking that I can't do anything for others is like falling into a void." A dream marked this passage: "In a boat on fire, everyone is running to save an object in a safe. Everyone is in danger of burning, so I jump in to save them and go to get the object. When I get out of the boat, I realize that the object in question is a ring that's worthless, and I realize that I risked my life for it."

The void created by the fall of the Other left him solely responsible for what had been inscribed in him, for his mental representations, his choices, decisions and actions, all of which had consequences that he alone had to deal with. "I always had the idea somewhere in my head that I was being used. There was always a search for an excuse. Why was it so difficult to admit that I'm responsible for my life and that I have to accept the consequences of my actions, whatever the reasons and motivations?" Here again, a dream aptly described the fall of the Other: "There is a marionette, and I realize that it has no string, no one is manipulating it." With this traversal, which lifted the demands of the Other of fantasy and deconstructed the cultural montage of the sexual, the creation of a space for a subjective quest, on foundations other than those of the past and the lost, could be begun.

## The Mourning of an Other Who Guarantees a Possible Address, a Stumbling Block in the Cure of Women

The analytic cure of the neurotic woman deserves our attention insofar as it is traversed by specific, profoundly interrelated stumbling blocks that relate in a particular way to the traversal of symbolic castration and the management of the out-of-language. Or more precisely, it concerns a more or less subtle resistance to breaking out of the cultural montage of the sexual and the difficult lifting of the censorship of the feminine, with all that this implies in terms of responsibility for the consequences and upheavals to be managed. The source of these obstacles, which shield the individual from an assumed access to a subjective quest, is implanted very early in a girl's first childhood and is nurtured in her second childhood so that it can be exploited from the dawn of puberty.

The first of these difficulties concerns the pervasiveness of the cultural montage of the sexual, which is unfolded and takes on its full weight at the moment of puberty. The fantasy of seduction that, from childhood and in the path traced by the Mirror, alienates and subjugates the subject to the satisfaction of the Other is confirmed and reinforced in its foundation by the montage of the sexual in culture, which places a woman in the position of object of "desire" of an Other: a being in a position of passive expectation, whose value lies in the fact that she is chosen, the object of covetousness, the painter's and poet's muse, and who falls into this trap by imagining herself the chosen one, the cause of another's desire. The traversal of this montage of the sexual in culture, which confronts a woman with the fact that she is neither the object of a man's desire, nor the object of *any* other's desire, leads to a loss that first plunges her into a state of depression. It's as if the experience profoundly affects her whole being, and not just the image of "woman" produced by a given culture. Deborah Levy, in her book *The Cost of Living*, expresses this moment of disarray, as experienced by her newly divorced heroine: "You'd think she was ashamed of living alone. If she had reluctantly left the societal narrative that offered her symbolic protection, how would she protect herself?" (Levy 61). When the montage, the "societal narrative" that makes her a "woman" insofar as she has a man and/or children in her life, collapses, this "symbolic protection" that maintained the subject in an imaginary position of infantile incapacity breaks down.

The second and more radical stumbling block concerns a woman's relationship to the *defect of the Other*, that is, the Defect of the *Other of the address*, this Other that is the guardian of the receivable produced by Culture and that is necessarily lacking in relation to an Other who is "awaited," always in vain. This latter is the Other who would hear the unaddressable and who would be able to welcome, unconditionally, and to support the out-of-language in the woman, beyond its unreceivability. The strength of this attachment to a hope that has locked itself into a more or less passive expectation will have been established very early in her life, in the experience a woman has from infancy in which her destiny as the "object of another's desire" alienates her position as a subject of speech, the author of a possible address to the other. This confinement in the position of object, which exiles her not only from the field of addressed speech but also, and consequently, from the act of creation, will often be interpreted by the girl as a lack, a defect in her being. Such interpretation remains within the very cultural montage of the sexual that nurtures a tenacious, even inextricable confusion between what she is as a human subject and the image of "woman" produced by the cultural formatting to which she has more or less deeply assimilated and alienated herself. Clinical experience shows us the extent to which women, and not only neurotic women, have adhered to this belief, which they have drunk with their mother's milk, that they carry within them something bad or at fault, responsible for a lack, a disorder, a defect or an illness. The cure will often have to unravel this belief, which has particular consequences in neurosis and psychosis. The young schizophrenic, for example, finds in this belief the soil in which the idea that she is responsible for an Evil that affects humanity, and for which she must sacrifice her very being, takes root.

In adolescence, by the time the young girl can experience that the quest she has been living since childhood has no possible address, the censorship of jouissance and the montage of the sexual have already mortgaged her future as a subject and proposed the mirage of an Other of the address for this Thing she could not bear alone: an Other that would spare the subject the "celibacy" of her relationship to a quest that has always mobilized her; an Other that would spare her the full responsibility for the destiny of her life.

It's as if, by renouncing the "presence" of the Other, she risks being plunged back into the painful experience, encountered too early in childhood, of an essential part of her being that was left out or left behind. This difficult *"mourning of the Other,"* which confronts her with the need to assume this part of herself, becomes a veritable bedrock in the treatment, a kind of last bulwark against the solitude so abhorred and feared by women. The confrontation with this mourning of the Other is sometimes marked by a symptom that is without address, characterized in its very form by the inescapable solitude to which it refers the analysand for the management of this out-of-language at work in the symptom and seeking its way outside the montage.

## THE CENSORSHIP OF THE FEMININE IN A WOMAN

The importance and strength of the censorship of the feminine in the little girl, which begins before puberty, are supported by cultural practices that justify them. Rana Ahmad, in her autobiography, *Here, Woman Do Not Dream*, recounts her escape from Saudi Arabia. She recounts a defining memory of her childhood, when she discovered and enjoyed a newfound freedom as she rode the bicycle her father had just given her as a present for her tenth birthday. "I can hardly contain the joy. I feel the wind blowing in my face and, through my hair, the smell of summer wafting through the air . . . I'm happy, quite simply . . . my spirit has never been so light. This is one of the most important moments of my life" (Ahmad 34). This experience of joy and of jouissance, however, marks for the grandfather who witnessed it a threshold not to be exceeded. He ordered the father to take the bicycle away from his daughter to give it to her brother, forcing her henceforth to wear the abaya over her body, the tarha over her head and shoulders, the niqab over her face. The same is true of little Hasidic girls, for whom their first menstrual period marks the moment when they can no longer ride their bicycles and play freely as they used to, reduced henceforth to the domestic sphere where they must learn the role they will have to play as wives and mothers.

These caricatural examples of the influence of culture and civilization on the destiny of girls cannot erase the discourses and practices that, in our "free" Western societies, confine girls to ideologies that are all the more effective for their deviousness. Insidiously disguised as individual "freedom," these nonetheless cannot escape the conformism of the ideas conveyed by the discourses and images that pollute the cultural space. It suffices to observe the influence of social networks and media of all kinds on the production of body images that young girls continue to invest in to gain recognition. This violence is falsely "embellished," under the guise of a freedom that is moreover being undermined by the religious right in our Western societies, who, with the return of the ban on contraception and abortion, intend to regain possession of women's bodies and the destiny of the lives of women, which must not escape the Collective's control.

Lifting the censorship of the feminine opens the being to that part of itself that remains outside language and that can only be expressed through acts that necessarily go beyond what is acceptable, and thus require a management of their effects and their consequences for others. For a woman, such possible management of the feminine within her may be supported by the decisive experience she has had as a child of an Other who was for her the *"guardian of jouissance."* It is in these terms that Apollon designates the true function of a Father, an Other who is the attentive guardian of the destiny of that precious part of herself that makes her a subject beyond any identification imposed by the cultural montage of the sexual. An Other who, at the very moment when the little girl can't cope with what remains unaddressable, unmanageable, and unreceivable within her, opens a space for her to speak, and supports for her and with her the exploration and expression of what drives her as a subject, outside and beyond all that Culture and the Mirror expect of her.

Rana Ahmad bears witness to this experience, which undoubtedly played a decisive role in the highly risky choice she was able to make and assume, not only by fleeing her country but also by denying the culture and religious beliefs that had "educated" her. Two years after fleeing, she finally dared to open the two hundred emails she had received from her father. "My father has written to me almost every day since I ran away.

I look for phrases like 'You're not my daughter anymore," but I can't find anything like that." "What I've done is the worst thing a daughter can inflict on her father in our culture. I have sullied the honor of the family. I've brought shame on my father. And yet he doesn't hate me or write me even one resentful message. I feel that he sees me as a person, not just as a girl to be married off and who should cause his family as few problems as possible" (321–22).

> He asks me if I'm in good health and is delighted that I've gone back to school. And one day, finally, he wrote in an e-mail an answer to a question I could never have asked him, that I would never have had the courage to bring up: "I know you're different now. I don't mind that you believe in different things than I do. You're still my daughter in spite of everything." . . . What I've always secretly wished for, but never really dared to express, has come true: my father continues to support me, even though I've abandoned him, buried in shame and drowning in worry. (337–38)

This encounter with an Other who represents an Elsewhere, another space, that transcends the "reality" produced by language and escapes what civilization defines as believable, constitutes a fundamental, foundational experience for a woman in her relation to the feminine, that part of her being that escapes all possible coercion and has no other place than the one she can create for its expression. For the little girl, it opens the way to traversing the Mirror, to recourse to a place within herself where the desire for something else, creativity and the freedom of the subject, cannot be normalized or sequestered in the montage of culture.

The recuperation and instrumentalization of maternity and the pro-duction of women as "objects of desire" by culture, in order to reproduce its values, are based on this censorship of the feminine, which concerns men, as Apollon clarifies, just as well as women. But the beliefs and the conceptions of the human created by each civilization have for the most part identified this Thing to be censored, because it is considered dangerous to the collective, in the bodies of women.

Through the ages and across civilizations, these bodies have been burned, exorcised, searched, and repudiated; they have been veiled and hidden or, alternatively, exhibited, cut into selected, coveted pieces, for the "desire" of the other. These bodies have been punished or magnified; they have had violence done to them, have been violated, raped, and transformed into the spoils of war. These objectified bodies reduce the being to what it must be and what purpose it must serve for the other; a being whose freedom to act as a subject, on the basis of a quest that transcends what the Collective imposes on it, has thus for such a long time been historically constrained and denied, all too often by women themselves.

Furthermore, the censorship of the feminine in a woman is not only based on the myths and beliefs of her own civilization, but is also deeply rooted, anchored, and justified in its foundation by a History of humanity that transcends civilizations. It's as if, at a deeper level, women are inhabited, unknowingly traversed by the vestiges of History, where a muted conviction lies inscribed in their bodies, assigning them to a state of being that justifies not only their exclusion from social space, but their inability to manage alone the out-of-language within themselves, to make it the source of a creativity that is free and assumed in both its risks and its exigencies. This subterranean experience, deeply inscribed in a woman's unconscious, comes to "validate" in a way a position of reclusion that acts as a mute and inhibits a position as desiring subject, author of her life. Fear of freedom, fear of losing the other, resistance to breaking out of the montage of the sexual, often find their support in this deep-seated conviction of the "inability" of their being to face up to desire and responsibility for its future.

Beyond the lifting of the censoring of the feminine, which gives access to the drive freed from its shackles, a new difficulty is thus raised: that of the responsibility of assuming the effects of acts resulting from this freedom of the subject, necessarily outside the norm, and therefore of managing their effects and consequences in the relationship with the other and in the social link. The clinic of women encounters a decisive point here: the need to not back down in the face of the consequences of the lifting of censorship, which raises the question of both an aesthetic of the act and an ethic for its management in the social link. The part of the self that Apollon refers to as the "masculine," which assumes full responsibility for the consequences of acts and manages them within the social bond, is a decisive stage in a woman's treatment. For many, this is precisely the point at which they retreat, deciding to close in on a subjective position liberated by the work of the cure, but which does not transcend the experience of the body and its expression.

# Beyond the Fundamental Fantasy: What End for the Cure?

## THE SAME CHALLENGE: MANAGING THE FEMININE AND MASCULINE DIMENSIONS OF ONE'S BEING

The object of the fundamental fantasy, as it appears and reveals itself in the work of the cure, is necessarily beyond what culture and civilization propose and frame. It refers to the subject's fundamental relationship with the singularity of a quest that runs through his or her life: a quest born of the work of the human spirit, stemming from the events that have created an effraction and from their unconscious representations, weaving the original fiber of one's being. This unknown quest, the contours and shape of which analytic work has been able to calculate, leaves the question of its becoming unanswered. And the fundamental fantasy, this relationship between the subject of the unconscious and the drive of desire that inhabits the being, raises a new issue: that of the destiny of this desire, which remains the ethical responsibility of the subject. What use will this boundless creativity of the mind serve? What legacy, what mark, what signature will it leave?

The revision and evolution of the fundamental concepts of psychoanalysis as articulated in the metapsychology developed by Apollon has not only opened up a new field for the treatment of the neurotic, the psychotic, and the pervert, but has also brought to light a logical endpoint of treatment that is similar in all three structures. The return to the specificity of the human subject, beyond the cultural and civilizational framework in which one finds oneself, and the consideration of two fundamental dimensions in each being, designated as the feminine and the masculine, are linked to the two axes of the aim of a cure. On the one hand, there is the lifting of the censorship of the feminine, that left behind, out-of-language dimension that until then had no other destiny than that of the symptom and the act, and that confronts the subject with the free drive and its future, opening up a new space. Henceforth, the creativity of the human subject is freed from the shackles that diverted it from its quest to find its own way. And on the other hand, this lifting of the censorship of the feminine introduces a new and inescapable challenge. What will be its mode of expression? What path, what destiny for the free drive? What will its effects be for the other? What will its effects be on the future of humanity? The history of mankind is there to remind us that human beings are capable of both the best and the worst, that in either of these directions, imagination and creativity know no bounds. The end of a treatment cannot be the liberation of the drive of desire without the subject being confronted with the question of its becoming.

Apollon defines the feminine and the masculine by linking them to aesthetics and ethics, respectively. The act of the subject of the unconscious, which therefore originates outside language, produces effects and consequences in the Other and in social space that may or may not be foreseeable or calculable, and for which the subject must nevertheless assume responsibility. The constraints and limits imposed on the free energy of the drive, assured to that point by the Other, by Culture, by Civilization and the structure of the social bond, are replaced by aesthetics and ethics, which become the new signposts, to be created and assumed by the subject henceforth.

Neurosis, psychosis, and perversion—each of these psychic structures is challenged in a particular manner by these two dimensions. In neurosis, the lifting of the censorship of the feminine, with the traversal of symbolic castration and the responsibility of desire and its effects and consequences for the other, constitute the axes of the cure. In perversion, where the feminine is not censored but rather held at a distance within the subject thanks to the staging that controls its occurrence in the other, the central point becomes the "masculine" dimension, that is, responsibility in the social space of the out-of-language that the perverse subject has experienced since childhood: this Thing that had no place either in language or in the relationship with the other. How can the subject leave this private space and assume responsibility in social space for the effects of what he may create from his desiring position? How to articulate the object of one's quest in the collective space, by bringing it into a form that can be negotiated with some others? As for the psychotic, for whom there is no censorship of the feminine, and who continues to grapple with the effects of the defect of language in the body and throughout his or her being, it is both the form taken by the quest and the responsibility for what it produces that are raised by this position. In the course of the analysis, the psychotic is confronted with the impossibility of resolving the defect of language, and therefore with the need to deal with the out-of-language in a different way. Then he or she has to create a form for the object of his quest, which became the object of the enterprise, a form for which responsibility can be borne collectively, with a few others.

The opening created by the conception and consideration of these two dimensions of being, the feminine and the masculine, orients the end of analysis in a completely different way. It radically displaces the very objective of psychoanalysis, taking it away from the issues of understanding, interpretation, and insight, on which many have sought to focus it, but which confines it to a more or less detailed explication of the history of the past. Instead, the focus is on what is to come, engaging the subject's responsibility in managing his or her life, whatever the past may be. With the necessity to create "*a space in the social bond, and therefore in the relationship with others, for that part of being that goes beyond the limits and the issues of civilization, in which the collective ensures its own existence*" (Apollon, Sessions de formation clinique en psychanalyse: "Le Fantasme"), the subject finds himself or herself confronted with the effects of his act in the other, the only one who can feel its either aesthetic or violent dimension. Likewise, with the requirement to take responsibility for one's actions, wherever they may come from, and to manage their consequences for the other, the subject finds himself on a path where only his ethics can serve as a guide. With such a goal, the end of an analysis is truly a beyond of the fantasy, a beyond the logic internal to the subject, in order to find oneself centered on what this being creates, which can only be measured by the effects and results of one's actions for others. These others are the only ones who can recognize the action of a quest that bears the signature, however discreet, of what lies at the heart of the human, and which either does or does not advance humanity, in the best it has to offer.


# Notes

1. Apollon distinguishes between speech, an act of the individual, and language, a necessity of the collective, drawing on data established by specialists in human evolution. He links speech to the emergence of the human spirit in Homo sapiens, whose artefacts testify to the ability to represent things that do not exist in the environment, notably representations of death and of a beyond, and the production of aesthetic and artistic objects that are useless for the survival of the species. Addressing the Other, speech, thus precedes the appearance of language, which is conceived as the structure of the social link, or again, as what provides the organization of companionship, which became necessary to ensure the survival and reproduction of the group when, thousands of years later, collectives began to exceed hundreds and thousands of members.

2. The Center for the Psychoanalytic Treatment of Psychosis in Quebec City.

# Works Cited

Ahmad, Rana. *Ici les femmes ne rêvent pas: Récit d'une evasion.* Éditions Globe, 2018

Apollon, W. "L'intraitable." *La cure psychanalytique du psychotique: Enjeux et stratégies,* Collection Nœud, Éditions du Gifric, 2008, pp. 326–52.

———. Training Seminar. Unpublished, June 2018.

———. Sessions de formation clinique en psychanalyse: "Le Fantasme." Québec, 2022.

———. Sessions de formation clinique en psychanalyse: "Le Symptôme, Fantasme." Québec, 2019–2020.

———. "The Unconscious." *Penumbr(a)cast: The Other Scene,* hosted by Fernanda Negrete, Interviews on Contemporary Lacanian Psychoanalysis, Buffalo, 2021. Online.

Bergeron, Danielle. "The Symptom." *Penumbr(a),* vol. 1, 2021, pp. 79–95. Online.

Brousse, Marie-Hélène. "La formule du fantasme? S ◊ (a)." *Lacan,* edited by Gérard Miller, Éditions Bordas, 1987, pp. 105–22.

Cantin, Lucie. "L'absence de l'Autre, le sujet de la pulsion libre et sa quête intraitable." *Correspondances Courrier de l'École freudienne du Québec,* Numéro spécial *Enseignements des analystes de l' École,* vol. 17, no. 2, June 2017, pp. 23–29.

———. "L'emprise du 'montage de la culture,' une hypothèque pour l'avenir du désir." *Correspondances, Courrier de l'École freudienne du Québec,* vol. 17, no. 2, June 2017, pp. 99–106.

———. "The Drive, the Untreatable Quest of Desire." Translated by Tracy McNulty, *differences,* vol. 28, no. 2, 2017, pp. 24–45.

———. "Castration." *Penumbr(a)cast: The Other Scene,* hosted by Fernanda Negrete, Interviews on Contemporary Lacanian Psychoanalysis, Buffalo, 2022. Online.

Freud, Sigmund. "Un enfant est battu. Contribution à la connaissance de la genèse des perversions sexuelles." *Névrose, psychose et perversion,* PUF, 1981, pp. 219–43.

———. *Three Essays on the Theory of Sexuality.* Gallimard, 1962.

———. *Métapsychologie.* Champs Classiques, 2012.

———. "From the Story of an Infantile Neurosis: L'homme aux loups." *Cinq psychanalyses,* PUF, 1984, pp. 325–420.

———. "Remarques sur un cas de névrose obsessionnelle: L'homme aux rats." *Cinq psychanalyses,* PUF, 1984, pp. 199–261.

Lacan, Jacques. "Le stade du miroir comme formateur de la fonction du Je." *Écrits,* 1966, pp. 93–100.

———. *Le Séminaire, livre XX: Encore.* Seuil, 1975.

Levy, Deborah. *Le coût de la vie.* Éditions du Seuil sous la marque Éditions du sous-sol, 2020.

Tuil, Karine. *La decision.* Éditions Gallimard, 2022.

9

# On the Metapsychology

## Interview with Willy Apollon

TRANSLATED BY JEFFREY S. LIBRETT

DANIELLE BERGERON, LUCIE CANTIN, JEFFREY S. LIBRETT,
ALEXANDER MILLER, TRACY McNULTY,
FERNANDA NEGRETE, DANIEL WILSON

Dec. 8, 2023

*Lucie Cantin:* In preparation for this interview, each of you wrote a number of questions. Most of you introduced your questions with an explanation to establish their context. This set of questions was sent to Willy Apollon beforehand. During today's interview, your questions will be addressed in an order determined by both their theme and the logical development of the concepts they concern. It was necessary for certain questions to take precedence over others in order to facilitate the comprehensibility of the foreseeably resultant conversation.

*Willy Apollon:* Hello everyone. I'd like this interview to be a real exchange. I've also written a text, which constitutes not an extended response, but the core of the response that I would make to the questions you sent me from the viewpoint of the metapsychology. Also, I conceived it not so much for you, but for the reader, a reader who might be, for example, somebody in analysis, or a faculty member in physics, philosophy, psychology, or neurology. I had such people in mind because in general these are the kinds of people one sees in analysis or encounters as an interlocutor on the subject of metapsychology.

Thus, there are four themes or concepts that are decisive, because I give them definitions that diverge from the habitual ones.[1] If you consult a dictionary of philosophy or the *Encyclopédie universelle* or the *Britannica* or *Wikipedia*, what you'll find as a definition will not correspond to the definition I give these terms, and this has important consequences, for example, for my conception of adolescence from the metapsychological perspective. And as I indicate in introduction to my responses—because what I say there is a kind of introduction—all of it is bound up with what we are experiencing today: *mondialisation*. When I defined the concept of *mondialisation* in the years 1999–2000, it was at a time when the concept, such as I developed it, did not yet exist. Everyone spoke of *globalization*. But what I meant by *mondialisation* was conflicts between cultures, which were already placing in question the believable [*croyable*], and what I foresaw and announced at that time: the war between civilizations. Today, we find ourselves in the midst of the conflict between cultures and the war between civilizations. We're currently undergoing four inter-civilizational wars, and our countries are being ravaged, I would say, by cultural conflict. This context obliges the metapsychology to exit from its Freudian and Lacanian versions. Because what we're dealing with—Freud could not imagine it, and Lacan did not experience it. We ourselves, however, are in the process of experiencing it. We're living through cultural conflicts. Right here, we're a group of people who come from three or four completely different cultures and civilizations. Thus, we must leave behind the requirements and concerns of culture as Freud conceives it, as well as those of civilization as Lacan conceives it, which turn around the establishment and maintenance of the believable, for these things no longer apply to our world.

To leave this behind is first of all to come back to the concept of spirit [*l'esprit*]. Beginning with the seventeenth century, the West progressively disentangles itself from the concept of spirit, for the sake of an atheism that will enable the construction of the ideologies that support the believable in the form that the West will impose on other civilizations. The Western world needed this in order to colonize Africa, the Middle East, Latin America, America in general, and Asia. From this perspective, therefore, I wanted to come back to the concept of the *spirit, which I define as this subjectively lived experience that is the capacity to represent to oneself things that do not exist, to want them, and then to create them.* This is what humanity has done. The human is, in a certain sense, the manifestation of spirit. It suffices to look around us. There is nothing around us that hasn't been thought, wanted or willed [*voulu*], and created by the human. Outside of nature, everything comes from human creation. In other words, spirit as such—in any case, in this region of the galaxy in which we find ourselves, in what we know of this galaxy—spirit as such manifests itself for the first time in the human. I remarked recently in another context that this manifestation of the spirit in the human occurs in two fundamental aspects, on which I consider the stakes of human consciousness to depend. And when spirit manifests itself, it does so by way of what these two dimensions—number and address—enable the human to construct as consciousness. Note that I define the human for the moment as manifestation of the spirit by the capacity to want and to create what it represents to itself that does not exist. But this introduces into the human the notion, which I have reconceptualized in a specific way, of a quest. What does the human seek? What does the human want, what is it looking for? Everything around us has been created by the human, but for what? It's here that I introduce this question of *the quest whose object remains unknown to us.* We do not know what the human is searching for. Simply: the human creates; the human advances. It's not what it was in 1980 at the moment of Lacan's death. It's not what it was in 1938 at the moment of Freud's death. It's not what it was in 1715.

*This notion of consciousness, moreover, is fundamental within the frame of a psychoanalysis.* The human is self-conscious. Humans know perfectly well that it is they who have created what is all around them. We have no idea how the spirit would manifest itself in another galaxy. And even in the galaxy in which we find ourselves, how the spirit would manifest itself in other beings—we know nothing about it. Yet the human is not without representing to itself this possibility that spirit manifests itself in the galaxy elsewhere than in the zone where we are. But the evocation of this notion of consciousness is important to the extent that, in the metapsychology, I am led to give consciousness a definition. There, too, if you look up a definition of "consciousness" in the dictionaries, in *Britannica,* in the *Encyclopédie universelle,* in *Wikipedia,* you will be struck by the fact that more and more what is said is that, at bottom, one doesn't really know what consciousness is. Today, the quantum physicist turns toward the philosophers to ask them: Help us, what is consciousness? The quantum physicist but also the mathematician. The quantum physicist turns to the mathematician on the question of time, to resolve the question of time by way of number, hence by mathematics, and the mathematician realizes that it's not possible. Does time come from number like space apparently, or does it rather come from the address, hence in some way from the Other? Doesn't consciousness tells us something else about this? Thus, this notion of consciousness is a problem today.

But if the notion of consciousness is problematic, psychoanalysis speaks of the unconscious. So it's there that consciousness, as the third concept, becomes very important for the metapsychology—because we have to ask ourselves the question: What do we mean by consciousness? Thus, I propose in the metapsychology that consciousness is the structuration and the management [*gestion*] of space-time. This notion of space-time troubles mathematicians and physicists to the point where they realize that, beyond their consciousness of it, there is neither space nor time. The last Nobel prize in physics was for work on quantum entanglement, which properly places in question both space and time such as we have conceived them up until recently, and maybe still conceive them.

I'll stop for a minute. Let's exchange a bit.

*Fernanda Negrete*: Your distinction between psyche and spirit implies or opens up a different perspective on the possible articulation of the subject with the social link. This articulation of the individual with the social link is not equivalent to what is at stake for the subject of the quest in your view, where the care or concern [*souci*] for the human has a central place. The question is thus: How should one see the difference between making greater or lesser concessions in order to coexist, on the one hand, and on the other hand, acting in the world on the basis of the quest within us?

*Willy Apollon*: The metapsychology is a metapsychology for the clinical domain. So the response I will make presupposes the clinic. You can see that from our perspective, the human appeared 300,000 years ago, and what manifests itself with the appearance of the human is spirit. The question about the psyche arises in the eighteenth century, when the West wants to disentangle itself from the notion of spirit for the sake of what's going on in the civilization. At that moment, one replaces spirit with psyche [*psyché*] and one evokes a psychic operation [*psychisme*], and progressively one considers this to be a product of the brain. It's important to see this key moment in the history of the West, the moment when it's necessary to efface the notion of spirit with that of the psyche. This becomes necessary to the extent that, across the seventeenth, eighteenth, and nineteenth centuries, what will be at stake is the importance of the cultures made credible by Western civilization, which will be considered superior to other cultures. One will measure the skull of the Negroes, one will measure the space between the bones of the face compared to those of the White, etc., in order to justify slavery because it's not certain that these are humans. At the moment when the West represses spirit to the point of censoring it from all debate, in order to put the psyche in its place, there's an operation of the colonization of Africa, America, and Asia where the colonist must be perceived by the colonized as superior. Thus, one cannot separate the difference between the spirit and psyche from the history of the stakes of civilization that have fabricated this difference. Evidently, in the eighteenth century, the question of cosmic consciousness was not raised, nor the question of a humanity beyond the line that, from Egypt, crosses Greece and the Middle East in order to give rise to Christianity. But at the end of the sixteenth and beginning of the seventeenth century, we are in the middle of the war of religions, in other words, of civilizations. Islam has already occupied a part of the South of Europe, and Protestantism is attempting to build a civilization against the Catholicism of the Latins, a civilization moreover that will win this first phase in the war.

Thus, I would say that in the clinic, in the psychoanalytic clinic that is born under this censorship of the spirit by the psyche, there is in this psychoanalysis a radical distinction to be made between the psyche and what is spirit: the capacity to represent—this is why one does not have this definition, which is the simplest one, the one easiest to experience—the capacity that the child of three or four years old possesses, to represent to itself things that do not exist. Such a child is not yet old enough to create them, but begins to want them. In second childhood, when the children begin to accede, as they are required, to language, the adult world will take it upon itself to make them give up certain of their representations. The psyche is part of the history of psychoanalysis, of the history of psychology, but one must not forget: there isn't just censorship of the feminine. The censorship of the feminine concerns this censorship of the spirit, of which it is one dimension.

*Fernanda Negrete*: Great. So why does one call that the feminine? Can you say something further about that?

*Willy Apollon*: It's very important. One must note that I define the feminine as the acting-out [*passage-à-l'acte*] of something that is outside of language [*un hors-langage*]. However, precisely what has been placed outside of language in this adventure of the psyche is spirit. One must not forget the witch, the woman possessed by a demon, Joan of Arc, and the borderline, and one must not confuse the feminine with the woman [*le féminin et la femme*]. The feminine is a dimension maintained out-of-language for specific reasons linked to cultural concerns that are in turn credibilized by beliefs and values of a civilization. In other words, the feminine exists long before the human creates language. The human created language about 50,000 years ago, but the human has been there for 300,000 years, and the feminine is a dimension of the human, as is the masculine. But when I say a dimension of the human, I mean it's a dimension of every human being, like the masculine. When the collectivities are going to create language in order to survive, they will produce the woman and the man. The masculine—that has nothing to do with the man. The feminine—that has nothing to do with the woman. To say the masculine and feminine as dimensions of the human, this is long before the collectivities create woman and man. A given collectivity with forty members that needs to associate itself with another collectivity of sixty members, in order to protect itself or to create agriculture or for whatever reason, needs then to give itself rules and prohibitions concerning the association of its women with men of other collectivities. It's a question of survival. The moment the collectivities need to associate with each other, they have a problem. If just any man can associate himself with whatever woman, the collectivity will not survive. It's necessary to realize that. From the moment when they are 200, 4000, or 6000, etc., the freedom of association between men and women is over. They must produce the woman now as property of the collectivity such that a man coming from another collectivity cannot take a woman from this collectivity. It's a matter of the survival of the collectivity. Hence, the creation of the woman and the man must be accomplished for the sake of the survival of the collectivity. But then one is no longer in the masculine and the feminine as before the creation of language qua structure of the social link, that is, this set of rules, prohibitions, and norms that define the relations between members of the collectivity. Masculinity is a subjective dimension that appears when spirit manifests itself in the human with this characteristic of number that makes possible the thought of space. Femininity, for its part, refers to this subjective dimension that appears when spirit surges forth in the human with this other characteristic of the address, which posits the Other as condition of the quest. But man and woman, of which we can speak only after the creation of language, are cultural products that are supposed to assure the survival of the collectivity. The Oedipus in Freudian psychoanalysis is supposed to articulate for the collective consciousness the man and the woman as cultural products. As you may have noticed, I never speak of Oedipus.

*Alexander Miller*: My question concerns the manner in which psychoanalysis and psychoanalytic experience in particular have informed your reflection on temporality. How is it that psychoanalysis enables a unique perspective on the question of time, a question that no doubt should be approached in different manners by different disciplines?

*Willy Apollon*: Well, precisely, the feminine in the human is time, in other words a subjective lived experience where the perspective introduced by the Other becomes a question. How to articulate this subjective lived experience in the space of collective consciousness? Time is a product of consciousness. We must distinguish between the time produced by collective consciousness and the lived experience we call our time, which is in an individual consciousness. But at the same time we're humans. That is, there is within us the manifestation of the spirit. There is within us a quest that the collective cannot control, a quest that was there long before the collectives, long before cultures, long before civilizations. Cultures pass away, civilizations pass away, but this quest within us, which preceded them, will not pass away. Thus, there is the dimension of a human consciousness that is there long before the collectivities—since 200,000 or 300,000 years ago—and then there is a collective consciousness that has been there for 40,000 or 50,000 years. In the interior of the individual, in the individual consciousness, these two dimensions of consciousness—the subjective dimension linked to human consciousness and the dimension of the ego or the "me" [*de l'ego ou du moi*], linked to collective consciousness—in the interior of the individual these two dimensions of consciousness are in conflict. How does each individual manage within themselves this conflict in their subjective consciousness? In other words, in the interior of each individual there is the time that is produced by human consciousness, and there is the time that is produced by the collective consciousness, and the question becomes: How will the individual manage the conflict between these two times? At the start, before the collectivities, human consciousness produced a time and a space. Beginning with the large collectivities, culture produces a time. Jewish time has nothing to do with Muslim time. Shinto time has nothing to do with Pentecostal time. The time of the practitioner of Voodoo in the Antilles has nothing to do with time of the Californian. And when two people say they love each other, this means that each one has created a singular space different from their own and different from the collective space for the subjective time of the other, because time is first of all the intimate lived experience of the being, which has nothing to do with the time determined in the collective consciousness by the cultural montage of the sexual. But does the collective consciousness make possible such a creation? Is there a space in the collective consciousness in which one can create in one's life a space for the intimate lived experience of the other? When, in addition, *mondialisation* puts all of these collective consciousnesses, all of these cultures, into conflict, one sees—with the disappearance of the believable that *mondialisation* entails—the multiplication of the results of the sexual montage in terms of characteristics and models—with which the new generations are confronted today, in a total absence of points of reference.

*Alexander Miller*: Yes. So I have posed a question on time precisely in connection with this question, a question on the "concern," or "care" [*souci*] for the human, because it seems they are inseparable.[2] The question of the concern for the human involves the question of time in a precise and interesting manner. Above all, in the way in which you define the concern for the human, it always implies something that is to come, something that remains in the future. This is the first aspect of the question, which deals with time and the concern for the human. The other aspect, which is also linked to this one, deals with two dimensions of this question of concern. In a sense, the question of concern can be interpreted or translated in two different ways. On the one hand, "souci"—in English for example—can mean "concern," which posits a sort of disquiet, and this jibes with the etymology of "souci," which is from the Latin "sollicitare," something that calls. On the other hand, "souci" is also "care"—which suggests rather a practice that must be developed. Thus with the "souci de l'humain"—the "care, or concern, for the human"—one has a privileged relation with the question of time and one has also a sort of question—I don't know—the possibility of assuming the care for the human and of making it progress from being a disquieting call to the becoming of a practice. So my question is about that.

*Willy Apollon*: First of all, a remark. What is currently the primary concern [*souci*] of the Secretary General of the UN? We have four intercivilizational wars in progress. There seems to be no common point of reference acceptable by all nations concerning what is a line not to be crossed, if not the immediate perspective of the use of arms of mass destruction, which only some nations possess. So is this, for the new generations, the future of humanity, the destruction of the Other put into play by this dimension of the address where, we said, the spirit manifests itself in the human? This dimension is, in a sense, at the foundation of the question of time. The Other introduced by the address plays a determining role in the constitution of time in human consciousness. For with time, what is in play is the subjective consciousness of lived experience, which is properly speaking incalculable. The wars of civilizations endanger the very possibility of a time for the Other. This effacement of the time of the Other is an effacement of the Other, a fundamental dimension of the manifestation of spirit in the human. If one is in North America, one feels safe, one is provisionally protected—I say "provisionally protected" advisedly. But if one is European, if one lives in the Middle East, if one lives in a certain number of countries in Africa, in Brazil, or Ukraine or Taiwan, and if one is between eighteen and twenty-three years old: Is one principally concerned for the success of the ego in the social link as defined by the culture in North America, or is one principally concerned for the future, a future one would like to be finally human?

For the new generations born in *mondialisation*, the time to come finds itself thus linked to the human, to a concern for the human experience in adolescence as a dimension of the self that transcends cultures and civilizations. Hence, what happened between the 1980s and 2010s unsettled the notion of time, both on the level of subjective time, and above all on the level of the time constituted by collective consciousness. For the first time a certain dimension of human time is imposing itself. Human time is imposing itself for the new generations as more important than the future of their civilization and more important than their existence itself. In this sense, we are in the process of living through something more important still than what the West lived through during the Renaissance. The Renaissance was a European drama. What we are in the process of living through today would be rather a Tragedy that risks involving the whole world. We're not there yet. I want to suggest by this that this human time is making a place for itself, and along with this human time comes a whole set of things that are outside of language. For these young men and women from seventeen to twenty-four years of age, a whole number of lived experiences are unaddressable, outside of language, outside of the time of the collective consciousness. This unaddressable articulates their human time; a time in which there is no future without the Other nor without this quest of the human in them that the address supports.

This time will seek for itself paths of expression with an anxious desire to save the human from what the civilizations make of it during *mondialisation*. One sees this also with the psychotic.

*Lucie Cantin:* I'd like to jump in here with Daniel Wilson's question. (Daniel Wilson was not able to join us today.) He posed the question of the believable. It seems that's connected to what you were just saying.

*Willy Apollon:* The totality of cultures and civilizations are maintaining their position while the new generations are increasingly having the experience of adolescence, the experience that there is, within them, an intimate dimension that wants more than a civilization can offer. They want more than their culture makes possible. Their intimate lived experience—in other words, their time—the intimate lived experience of what they expect from life no longer has anything to do with what their civilization supports as credible. The problem today for those between the ages of eighteen and twenty-eight is that there is no longer anything believable. There can no longer be for them a signifier of the Name-of-the-Father that would support the believable in their civilization as a substitute for the defect of language in the structure of the social link. The signifier of the Name-of-the-Father functioned in civilization to make values and norms believable, despite the defect of language with regard to the censorship of femininity in the sexual montage, effacing thus in a way this witness to a dimension of the spirit's manifestation in the human. And what is it to make believable the stakes of culture? What is it that would confer credibility, for the new generations, upon this sexual montage under the aegis of the Oedipal Father? What was at stake, however, was to ensure that the new generations would continue what was begun by the preceding ones, assuring a future that would make up part of the same time produced by the collective consciousness, a future that would be a future for the present time. This was the function of civilization, providing a foundation for meaning, that is, what is receivable according to the cultural conditions of membership in the collective. This is what all the right wing and extreme right wings movements promise, in order to exorcise from the collective any fear of the disappearance of civilization: the Return to the Name of the Father, return to the sources.

*Fernanda Negrete:* I see that Daniel has also posed the question about violence or aesthetics, of which you often speak. He posed it in relation to this question of the believable.

*Willy Apollon:* Well, by means of the believable, the civilization was able, in a cultural montage, to reduce the aesthetic to art in its attempt to control the function of the Other in the address. The acting-out of what cannot make a space for itself in language creates in the Other a profound reaction, mobilizing precisely an intimate manifestation of the spirit in the human that totally escapes the control of the collectivity. This is the very source of the aesthetic, when the Other discovers a new time, outside of collective consciousness: an intimate lived experience they under no circumstances would want to lose. It is on this subject that I proposed that the acting-out of what is outside of language provokes in the Other a response that is either aesthetic or violent, for it could be also something of which the Other wants to know absolutely nothing. To modify in depth the address that reveals the fundamental importance of the Other, the cultural montage of the sexual in the structure of the social link must modify this function of the Other. Have you noticed the difficulty that the large civilizations—American, European, in various Western countries—have had over the past thirty years in attempting to classify works of art? Some have even made reference to an aesthetics of violence. What the new generations are encountering in the experience of adolescence as a field of the aesthetic does not have much of a relationship with what their cultures and civilizations still consider to be aesthetic, which is only the manner in which the collectivity establishes a controllable space for a part of what is outside of language. You see, the problem of psychoanalysis—and it is for this reason that one must take the time to reconsider the metapsychology—the problem of psychoanalysis is that its functioning in terms of the Oedipus within the context of the cultural montage of the sexual has nothing to do with the adolescent experiences of the new generations within the context of *mondialisation.*

*Lucie Cantin:* Can I come back to this question of the believable? At bottom, if I have understood correctly, you say that in *mondialisation* the civilizations are no longer capable of making their cultural frameworks believable. And therefore that the question of the believable can no longer be raised from within cultures and civilizations. But would you say that the question of the believable has changed and will become henceforth the concern for the human?

*Willy Apollon*: No, it hasn't changed. This question of the believable has precisely nothing to do with the concern for the human. The concern for the human is not of the order of the believable. The concern for the human is something that one experiences. It's a lived experience. It's not about what one can believe. The believable made one believe in something that will come, made one believe in the justice of something, and made one believe, by this very fact, that there is a future in continuing to do the best of what we are currently doing. The concern for the human is something else. The concern for the human does not believe in a future. The concern for the human is responsibility for the future. The new generations are discovering that they are responsible for the future of humanity. And they don't understand why the values of our society and the projects of our civilization should be more important than the human future endangered by the wars that have been provoked by these values and projects. They are discovering that the future of the human will be for the best or for the worst. We are no longer in the universe of the believable created by atheism and the materialist ideologies since the end of the seventeenth century. We are no longer in this universe. The concern for the human in us, the concern for the human around us, the act of coming together to save the human—this is the possibility, the perspective that the new generations are discovering. What the young psychotic discovers is that henceforth they cannot be alone in imagining it, but that they need the Other's welcome. But what's still unimaginable for these generations is the implication and the engagement of immense groups formed by all cultures and civilizations to assume together such responsibilities. It's not a question of believing in this, but rather of applying oneself to the task and making it happen, which many cultures and civilizations will oppose, and are already opposing.

*Lucie Cantin*: This is something that Alexander defined, I would say, in his question on the concern of the human.

*Alexander Miller*: Yes, I ask myself if psychosis in particular cannot help us in thinking this through. In a way, it seems one could say that the subject in psychosis is perhaps absorbed in concern, the acute experience and consciousness of a danger or a problem, a solicitation, but without having necessarily developed the dimension of the practices or techniques of care that enable them to respond to this solicitation, being submerged by it and therefore having recourse only to delusion.

*Willy Apollon*: Exactly. But what is delusional for and within the collective consciousness takes a completely different form in the subjective consciousness of the psychotic.

*Lucie Cantin*: In connection with what you said of the Name-of-the-Father, Danielle Bergeron had a question.

*Danielle Bergeron*: My questions were based principally on the clinical dimension, and I had begun by posing the question of the Freudian Oedipus, since now the Oedipus appears obsolete, given the entire development of our societies in a direction completely opposed to a relation to the father and the mother. But with respect to Lacan, who developed the notion of the foreclosure of the Name-of-the-Father with, as its consequence, the recrudescence or development of hallucinatory symptoms and difficulties of articulation with language, I asked myself if you could tell us more about this: How do you treat the question of the Father in psychosis, and what are the implications of these new modalities, the implications in the clinic, in the treatment of psychotics?

*Willy Apollon*: I'm tempted to say: let's try to imagine this question of the Father 100,000 years ago. There would not have been the Oedipal structure because there would not have been, at this time, a cultural montage of the sexual, which the collectivity creates with language to censor a part of what in the human subject the collective can neither access nor control. One must not separate the Freudian father from the censorship of the feminine in the Oedipus that the sexual montage puts to work. A good example is the patient diagnosed as perverse because he puts into question the sexual montage when he discovers in puberty that his mother is a woman. He puts into question precisely this Father of the Freudian Oedipus, and this yields him his diagnosis.

*Danielle Bergeron*: This enables me to connect up with the other question. In your text, you spoke of the role of the Father—or rather, the function of the Father—for the girl as guardian of jouissance, which is a very strong notion. I would like it if you could speak to us further about this, and then, in contrast, about the case of the boy, since the text does not contain anything equally precise concerning the role of the Father for the boy.

*Willy Apollon*: If you will, I will start at the beginning. I'm attempting to lead you all onto a certain path, because what I call the Father probably has nothing to do with what Lacan means by the signifier of the Name-of-the-Father nor with what Freud calls the Father. Concerning this Father in psychoanalysis today, there would be the function and the signifier. But what I evoke by the concept of Father is neither on the side of the function nor—even less—on the side of the signifier, because for me, this Father is a moment in the lived experience of the adolescent where subjective consciousness opposes the collective consciousness in which the Oedipal Father functions. As a result of the sexual montage that functions in puberty within the collective consciousness, the Oedipal Father maintains for the pubescent individual the censorship of the feminine. In puberty, if the girl does not exit this montage she has a serious problem, because when she's thirteen or fourteen years old and her classmates are fourteen, fifteen, sixteen years old, she's an object of satisfaction or not in the sexual models and behaviors that the culture puts to work during this period of their lives. She is satisfying, satisfiable, or not. For the guy, at fourteen or fifteen, he's there because Mom satisfied Dad. This leads us today, in *mondialisation*, to the girl who wants to change her gender, because the cultural practices make that possible. But as the cultural practices make gender alteration possible for her or for him—for him, because his fantasies that are considered perverse by the culture incite him to, and for her, because she cannot imagine existing in order to serve this idiot who doesn't even reach up to her ankles in mathematics—culture, i.e., the collectivity, in the frame of *mondialisation* offers them a multiplicity in the choice of gender. And precisely there arises the question of the repression or censorship of adolescence, whose aspirations transcend culture and civilization in a quest of the human. One remains in the montage or else one decides to find a way to get out of it to live the relation to the Other on foundations other than those of the cultural offering. In other words, in the frame of *mondialisation*—which undermines the censorship of the feminine by promoting the subjective experience of adolescence that was repressed in puberty by the collective consciousness—the function of the Father no longer produces a signifier. The signifier of the Name-of-the-Father supports the believable as a substitute for the defect of language with regard to the feminine in the sexual montage. There is an incapacity in language to assume and give a place, a space for an eventual lived experience of the feminine as such in adolescence. According to culture, the signifier, in ensuring the believable, tempers the defect of language. But precisely, the believable is no longer possible, nor would it even be useful in the space opened up to adolescence in *mondialisation*, which is breaking into the collective consciousness. The signifier goes by the board along with the believable.

What I've introduced in the metapsychology is something different concerning this position of the Father. For the Father is first of all a position that makes possible an experience, that of the human, which transcends or opens a breach in the collective consciousness. Thus, concerning this position of the Father I have suggested that the father for the girl is the guardian of jouissance, i.e., of this exit from the montage that breaks open collective consciousness to make something else possible, beyond the believable. But quite precisely the montage makes it impossible for there to be a question of feminine jouissance—because if at the moment of the creation of the collectivities women would have retained access to jouissance, why would they waste their time making babies? This remark was suggested to me by Aristotle's remark in the *Politics*. The man has little interest in this waste of time that consists in making babies, says Aristotle. But I think that this is equally true for the woman, except if there is a sexual montage, for then the woman as such does not exist—she's only a product of culture. Simone de Beauvoir said it well: "One is not born a woman, one becomes a woman." Today, we recognize that Simone de Beauvoir was right: the woman does not exist. "One is not born a woman, but one dies for being one," according to signs carried by participants at a recent demonstration in Paris, denouncing the vertiginous augmentation in the number of feminicides in the world. It would have been nice if, during the 1970s, when Lacanianism was at the height of its success, the status of the Father could have been something other than the signifier that assures the believable with regard to the defect of language. The censorship of femininity in the sexual montage, which suppresses a dimension of the human, is the defect in this structure of the social link, i.e., the link that ties the member into the collectivity to which they belong, in the effectuation of the collective consciousness. You will recall that I consider it necessary to take my distance from the field of linguistics when I have to define language. I insist on the fact that it was necessary for humans, 50,000 years ago, to create language to survive in large numbers under the conditions in which they found themselves. What was at stake was the organization of the links of companionship for the creation of a collectivity united by a collective consciousness: the set of rules, norms, and prohibitions that were necessary to enable 50,000 people or more to live together, in the same space-time, where the believable becomes what a civilization, a certain vision and conception of what it is to be human, creates in order for the new generations to ensure continuity in the survival of the collectivity. A survival that includes evidently this defect of language, which is however fatal for one dimension of this humanity—femininity.

It's important to see clearly that when I characterize adolescence as the internal discovery of a human dimension that says "no" to this montage that the culture makes, and that says "no" equally to the believable that the civilization creates to make this montage credible, I am attempting to circumscribe what is literally making these new generations sick.

*Jeffrey Librett*: So, to come back to Danielle's question, what is a Father for the boy?

*Willy Apollon*: I'm getting to that. The girl of fifteen or sixteen years of age discovers in the father's look something whose stakes and consequences she will not grasp until she is twenty-six to thirty. There is in this look of the father—if there is, for the girl, what I call a Father—there is in this look of the father an expectation, at the limit a disquiet. What the girl discovers in the look of the father is an expectation, let's say, the expectation of the witch. This look of the father, when it exists, enables the girl to leave behind the sexual montage and to confront the discourse of the others who will henceforth see in her the witch, a woman possessed by a demon, the borderline, the madwoman, the hysteric, etc., i.e., a being who has needs that one cannot satisfy. But we'll come back to this.

As for the boy, when he discovers that his mother is a woman—because this is his drama, that around fifteen, sixteen, or seventeen years of age, he discovers that his mother was a woman, and therefore he refuses this position where his mother would be an object for the satisfaction of another, whether this other would be the one called his father or anyone else. This discovery creates in him a void that cuts him off from the montage of the collective consciousness. This void sends him back to a perspective where the woman could be the girlfriend to whom an address would be possible, and not the object of a dissatisfaction who would translate as an enemy. For the first time he has a question for which the response is perhaps on the side of an attitude of the father that can be perceived at once as an expectation and a demand—or more precisely as an expectation that he, the youth, will take to be a demand. But there, like the girl faced with the father's look, the boy faced with this attitude of the father, which he takes to be an exigency, is projected beyond the collective consciousness. Both the boy and the girl are then beyond what the sexual montage expects of them; this is doubtless what makes them accessible to the experience of adolescence. In this experience, there is for him as for her something that goes elsewhere and further than what the collective consciousness proposes to them in the sexual montage. Suddenly, and for a moment that they cannot manage, the father's look sends them into a dimension of their existence they have not known before. At the same time, the boy, in the attitude of the father—which he takes to be a demand—feels this dimension of his being that is, in a way, in accord with this exigency because at the same time is born within him a will to go beyond what his culture or civilization proposes. It is there that one sees both of them, but above all the boy, being drawn to the idea of plunging themselves into excesses of all sorts, not knowing where this strange quest might lead them, which the expectation in the look of the father, perceived as an exigency, will have aroused. This excess sometimes leads to drug use. Because drugs are an easy way to leave behind collective consciousness, the youth tries in this way to go as far as possible in a subjective consciousness whose power he is barely beginning to discover—the power to leave behind the space-time of the collective consciousness and experience something else. There, the psychotic prefers the hallucination.

The father is in a way the guardian of the very possibility of these excesses. His look supports for subjective consciousness an elsewhere; it is the symbol that these excesses could become something else. That they could become the occasion of effective creation, collective creation, if the conditions for this were realized. The limits of collective consciousness are there, prejudices are there, ideologies are there, the cultural montage is still there, with the multiplication of genders. Yet none of these manage to account for these excesses that this Father in a certain way protects, on the outside of language and absent from the collective consciousness.

*Lucie Cantin:* Because of the hour, I'd like us to move onto two or three questions that seem to me important. Jeffrey had precisely a question on adolescence.

*Jeffrey Librett:* Yes, it seemed to me that, given this new conceptualization of adolescence, one could ask oneself what "to be adult" means now in relation to adolescence. Is there a passage beyond adolescence that is not repression and censorship of adolescence once again?

*Willy Apollon:* The notion of being an adult was situated within the framework of collective consciousness as produced by the culture and supported by the civilization for the coming generations. Adulthood was supposed to assume the defect of language and to find a personal way of dealing with it. The new generations will be elsewhere. It's culture, and above all civilization, that need the young adolescent male and female to become adults, i.e., to accept life within the stakes and conditions of culture and civilization. We are already elsewhere. Adolescence is going elsewhere. Once again, in the adolescence of the new generations, it's the responsibility for the becoming of the human that will henceforth be the fundamental concern. They're beginning to realize already that it's more important than their very existence.

*Danielle Bergeron:* In order for a properly analytic process to take place—whether for the neurotic, the pervert, or the psychotic—one must be able to establish a transference. You've redefined transference and demonstrated that it is also possible in psychosis. Tell us, from a clinical point of view, the general principles in the establishment of the transference.

*Willy Apollon:* As you see, as we envision it, the transference should support and make possible the passage from puberty to adolescence, in other words access to human consciousness. The transference should be a subversion of the very structure of collective consciousness, such that the cultural montage of the sexual comes to an end. In fact, there is no adolescence without the exit from this symbolic castration that is the sexual montage, i.e., that encloses the young pubescent within the limits of the collectivity's culture values. The sexual montage is what's at stake for the collectivity; it's the collectivity that censors the feminine to control reproduction and assure its own survival. All the extreme right wing movements feed upon this, even when they don't dare admit it to themselves. Without an exit from this symbolic castration, i.e., without an exit from the sexual montage, there is no access to femininity. Hence, the two statuses I have defined. First, there is the clinician analyst, the one who has exited from the cultural montage of the sexual and traversed symbolic castration. In doing so, they've broken with an important dimension of collective consciousness, and this fact gives them the possibility of provoking the transference that opens onto human consciousness. And then there is the analyst, who goes further, assuming responsibility for the management of the consequences, for subjective consciousness, of a concern for the human. Their unconscious, that within them which is unaddressable within the collective consciousness, has exited from the unsayable [*l'impropre-au-dire*]. They know a lot about what is not manageable within the limits of the collective consciousness and that will have to be enacted.

Thus, when someone encounters an analyst, they encounter a subject who is beyond language—hence, the silence. The analyst's silence does not emerge because the analyst does not want to speak. Rather, this silence evokes the position in the address of a subject who is outside of language. Hence, the person who encounters an analyst does not know what they will encounter in the addressee. What's at stake in the subjective consciousness of the analyst is outside of language, and subverts the function of the Other in the address as defined within the collective consciousness. This outside-of-language justifies the analyst's silence. But it is a silence that introduces into the address the concern and the responsibility for the human. Thus, the silence that defines this position expects the person who encounters the analyst to want to exit from the montage in order to accede to something else, to accede to this human dimension that adolescence has revealed. This is why, very often, the analysand in turn is brought to silence. It's not that they do not want or do not dare to speak. They do not know what to say, at first, nor how to manage the consequences of what they would say. Then what they have as a point of reference is what, for them, does not function in the collective consciousness. But they will be confronted by a reaction of the analyst, which does not come from the collective consciousness, hence by a silence of the analyst, just where they expected some help returning to the collective consciousness. This situation in the address created by the analyst's unconscious is what I call transference.

*Jeffrey Librett*: If we can come back to the question of the feminine and the masculine, perhaps also in the context of the transference, you said that the feminine and the masculine come long before language—which I find illuminating. Thus, apparently there is a particular relation between the feminine and the masculine, on the one hand, and speech, on the other hand. That's the question. Can one say that femininity and masculinity would be modalities of speech, or aspects of speech?

*Willy Apollon*: Everything that does not come either from the masculine or from the feminine within us is just discourse. It's an attempt at mutual understanding, if you like, within the limits of the collective consciousness. But speech always concerns something that comes from subjective consciousness. Speech is a risk taken in the space-time of subjectivity; it gives the Other access to something which the Other would in no way have been able to access, and without knowing what the Other will do with this. There is no speech in the space-time defined by collective consciousness, where that which is "unsayable" [*impropre au dire*] defines the limits of the possible. Speech occurs in the space-time defined by human consciousness. Before creating language, humans spoke to each other. Once language is there, they have to take into account all the other persons whenever they address themselves to one person. They are obliged to take into account what is acceptable in the space-time of the collectivity when they address themselves to one individual. But when humans were in groups of nine, ten, eleven, even fifteen, they did not have to take into account a space-time defined by the collectivity in order to address themselves to the companion who was there. Speech defines a space-time that articulates masculine to feminine. One could suggest thus that the dimension of the masculine is tied to the structure of human space, while that of the feminine is linked to the structure of human time in the intimate lived experience of each human consciousness. Everyone counts on a space for the time that measures its most intimate experience, whatever the limits of the Other in the space-time of the collective. I'm aware that I'm proposing something complicated here.

*Alexander Miller:* What you just said poses also the question of the aesthetic. I haven't heard before this idea that the space-time posited by speech is the masculine and the feminine.

*Willy Apollon:* It's conditioned by the masculine and the feminine.

*Alexander Miller:* Yes, and defining thus a space proper to speech enables us to approach the question of the aesthetic.

*Willy Apollon:* The space-time proper to speech is precisely the field of the aesthetic. The aesthetic consists in enacting something that cannot pass by way of language and that—as a result of the act—will not be without an effect in the Other. This is very important. In a picture, a dance, a musical piece, what expresses itself cannot pass through language, whose limits culture and civilization have defined. The artist would not know how to say precisely what it is that mobilizes them to this point, for it is something fundamentally unaddressable, which reveals to us something of the human that would be inaccessible to us otherwise.

*Lucie Cantin:* May I pose a last question? An apparently simple question: what is that—the human—but above all, in what way does this conception of the human radically modify the logical termination of an analytic process whatever be the psychic structure involved? That is, in what way does it enable us to go beyond the differences in psychic structure in the question of the logical completion of an analysis?

*Willy Apollon:* The term "logic of an analysis" up to now bore witness to what permitted a subject to function in their culture and their civilization with a certain result, one could say with a certain success. That supported what I formulate sometimes by saying: to assure the success of the ego in the social link. What we have entered into since the period from 1990 to 2010 is something else, and what the new generations will find themselves in soon is something else again. This other thing is the becoming of humanity. That's the point. It's not just a problem for the Secretary General of the UN. The totality of cultures and civilizations have put the human into a situation in which the fate of women, social inequality, poverty, the destiny of humanity in the environment, incessant wars whose end is nowhere in sight, in short an entire set of problems cannot be resolved by one nation, however powerful it may be, nor can they be resolved by a group of nations. A set of problems where all the collectivities, all the nations have to apply themselves in order for the beginning of a possible solution to appear. But this totality of nations—what is it? Well, that's what the human is, a dimension of existence that transcends all the cultures and civilizations and that will outlive them. And this is what the new generations are experiencing in their adolescence, as the suffering of a certain impotence that nourishes their revolt. The way in which this will increasingly present itself for them is that the human begins in oneself. There are radical changes that have to be made in the interior of the person. One cannot imagine humanity in the next sixty years without changes in the young individuals of all nations—because what is happening is modifying the very structures of space-time for all the collectivities.

*Lucie Cantin:* Since we have gone beyond our two hours, we'll stop here, thanking Willy Apollon very much for all of this new, truly clarifying work, whose depth would necessitate multiple further questions. This interview will certainly raise as many questions in the reader of the present work.

*Willy Apollon:* It's I who thank you for having pushed me. If you hadn't pushed me, I might not have done this work. Thank you.


## Notes

1. The four concepts are: "mondialisation"; "the spirit"; "the quest without determinate object"; and "consciousness."

2. The term "souci de l'humain" ["concern" or "care" for the human] is a recurrent terminological phrase in Apollon's recent work, and the question here turns around the ambiguity of "souci" as "concern" and as "care."

# Appendix

## General Bibliography of
## Willy Apollon's Teachings and Seminars

Apollon, W., Séminaires cliniques du Gifric, Québec, since 1980.

Apollon, W., Enseignement et Formation aux Réunions cliniques au *Centre de traitement psychanalytique pour psychotiques*, le 388, Québec, weekly, since 1982.

Apollon, W., Clinical Training Sessions in Psychoanalysis, 8 days/year, since 1985, Québec.

Apollon, W., Training Seminar and Clinical Seminar, Teaching Americans, Quebec, 5 days/year, since 1996.

Apollon, W., Teaching at the Journées annuelles de l'École freudienne du Québec, Quebec, since 2000.

Apollon, W., "Homme, femme, masculin, féminin," Enseignements à Québec, February–June 2020.

Apollon, W., Public Lecture Series, 5 lectures/year, Quebec City and Montreal, since 1999.


## On the Theme: Psychoanalysis and Mondialisation

"L'adresse improbable," 2021–2022.
"L'humain en question," 2020–2021.
"A new ethics? De l'humain au politique/L'humain en question," 2019–2020.
"Lost Femininity," 2018–2019.
"Un devenir pour la Chose humaine dans la mondialisation," 2017–2018.
"This Thing in Search of a Clean Place!," 2016–2017.
"Aesthetics, a Space for What Is Unfit to Be Said," 2015–2016.
"This Human Thing That Speaks!," 2014–2015.

"Pour ce qu'il en reste de l'humain . . . en revenir aux fondamentales," 2013–2014.
"The Subversion of the Foundations of the Social Bond and Its Consequences for the Individual," 2012–2013.
"Autrement . . . c'est quoi? for the Survivors That We Are," 2011–2012.
"Modalités de jouissance et mondialisation," 2010–2011.

## On the Theme: Psychoanalysis and Society

"Human Collectives, Science and Psychoanalysis Facing the Impasse," 2009–2010.
"Capitalism, Science and Psychoanalysis: The Ethical Stakes of the Impasse Created by Globalization," 2008–2009.
"Psychoanalysis and Human Madness," 2008
"An Unpresentable Cause," 2006–2007.
"L'Im-Passe: L'horreur du vide à peine aperçu . . . du ciel étoilé au-dessus de nos têtes," 2005–2006.
"L'impasse," 2004–2005.

## On the Theme of Psychoanalysis and Aesthetics: The Unheard-of, the Breaking-Through of the Visible

"Transcendance, un espace autre pour l'imprésentable," 2003–2004.
"De la beauté au mal, le deuil de l'Autre, une esthétique du pire," 2002–2003.
"From Pictorial to Musical," 2001–2002.

## Psychoanalytical Evenings

"From Eroticism to Aesthetics: The Freudian Break," 2000–2001.
"The Freudian Break on the Question of Sexuality," 1999–2000.

# Contributors

**Willy Apollon**, PhD, is a senior psychoanalyst at Gifric and a philosopher (Paris, Sorbonne). He is a supervising analyst and consultant analyst at the Psychoanalytic Treatment Center for Psychotics Adults, the "388"; past president and founder of Gifric, director of the Psychoanalytic Center for the Family; and director of a control seminar for the training of analysts and of a seminar on *mondialisation* and psychoanalysis in Montreal and Quebec City. He has published widely on topics including psychosis, the formation of analysts, the psychoanalytic clinic, perversion, aesthetics, family, and the analysis of cultural, social, and political practices. He is the author of *Le Vaudou, un espace pour les Voix* (Editions Galilée, Paris); *Psychoses: l'offre de l'analyste*; *La différence sexuelle au risque de la parenté*; and *L'Universel, perspectives psychanalytiques*, published by Gifric. Together with Bergeron and Cantin, he founded the Psychoanalytic Treatment Centre for Adults Psychotics, the "388." They are coauthors of three books in French: *On the Treatment of Psychosis* (*Traiter la psychose* [1990]; Spanish translation, *Tratar la psicosis*); *On the Stakes and Strategies for the Psychoanalysis of Psychotics* (*La Cure analytique du psychotique: enjeux et stratégies* [2008]; and *A Future for the Psychotic: The Structure of a Psychoanalytic Treatment* (*Un avenir pour le psychotique: Le dispositif du traitement psychanalytique* [2013], published by Gifric). In English they have published the volume *After Lacan: Clinical Practice and the Subject of the Unconscious* (State U of New York P, 2002); "The Treatment of Psychotics" in *The Subject of Lacan, a Lacanian Reader for Psychologists*, edited by Kareen Ror Malone and Stephen R. Friedlander (State U of New York P, 2000, pp. 209–27); and "Problems of Femininity in the Psychoanalytical Treatment of Psychotic Women" in *Lacan on Psychosis: From Theory to Praxis*, edited by Jon Mills and David L. Downing (Routledge, 2018, pp. 132–57).

**Danielle Bergeron**, MD, is a senior psychoanalyst and psychiatrist. She is medical chief for the Psychoanalytic Treatment Center for Psychotics Adults, the "388." At Gifric, she is supervising analyst and responsible for training; she also conducts a control seminar of the analytic act with clinician analysts and teaches a seminar in short-term analytic treatment. She is an associate professor for psychiatry at Laval University, where she teaches psychoanalytic concepts, and is supervisor of a fellowship program for psychiatrists at the 388. She is a distinguished life fellow of the American Psychiatric Association and has published on the psychoanalytic treatment of psychosis and neuroses, ethical questions, aesthetics and the Thing as psychoanalytically conceived, and femininity, as well as science in relation to psychoanalysis.

**Lucie Cantin**, MPs, is a senior psychoanalyst. She is a psychoanalyst at the Psychoanalytic Treatment Center for Psychotics Adults, the "388"; supervising analyst and co-responsible for teaching at Gifric; and responsible for a control seminar for the training of analysts. She also conducts a seminar on psychoanalysis and clinical psychology and is vice president of Gifric, where she is also responsible for publication; editor of *Savoir, a Journal of Psychoanalysis and Cultural Analysis*; professor of clinic at the School of Psychology at Laval University; supervisor in the master's program in psychology at the University of Gand (Belgium) and at the Université Libre of Bruxelles; and responsible for the Orientation Council of the Freudian School of Quebec. She has published on the psychoanalytic treatment of psychosis, the clinic of neurosis, mysticism, femininity, masculinity, and perversion.

**Jeffrey S. Librett** is a professor of German in the Department of German and Scandinavian at the University of Oregon and an analyst of the Freudian School of Quebec. He is the author of *The Rhetoric of Cultural Dialogue: Jews and German from Moses Mendelssohn to Richard Wagner and Beyond* (Stanford, 2000), *Orientalism and the Figure of the Jew* (Fordham UP, 2015), and numerous essays on psychoanalysis, philosophy, and literature. He is the translator of Jean-Luc Nancy, *The Sense of the World* (Minnesota UP, 1997) and Jean-François Courtine et al., *Of the Sublime: Presence in Question* (State U of New York P, 1993).

**Tracy McNulty** is a professor of French and comparative literature at Cornell University. She is a practicing analyst, a member of Gifric and an analyst of the Freudian School of Quebec, and author of *The Hostess: Hospitality, Femininity, and the Expropriation of Identity* (U of Minnesota P, 2007) and *Wrestling with the Angel: Experiments in Symbolic Life* (Columbia University Press, 2014). Currently she is completing two new books: *Libertine Mathematics: Perversions of the Linguistic Turn; and* a fourth book project on the role of the body in relaying an unconscious transmission from one person, or one people, to another.

**Alexander Miller** has a PhD in psychoanalysis and clinical consulting from Ghent University and is completing a PhD in comparative literature at NYU. He has been the recipient of a Fulbright Fellowship, is a visiting researcher at Humboldt University Berlin, and is a member of Gifric and the EFQ.

**Fernanda Negrete** is the author of *The Aesthetic Clinic: Feminine Sublimation in Contemporary Writing, Psychoanalysis, & Art* (State U of NY P, 2020), and of several essays engaging modern literature in French and Portuguese, contemporary art, aesthetics, and psychoanalysis. Her work has been published in various scholarly journals and volumes. She is the editor of *Angelaki*'s special issue and the book *Philosophy with Clarice Lispector*, and coeditor of *Beckett beyond Words*, a special issue of *Samuel Beckett Today/aujourd'hui*. She is an associate professor of French at the University at Buffalo, where she also directs the Center for the Study for Psychoanalysis and Culture. For the Center she hosts *Penumbr(a) cast—The Other Scene*, a podcast on psychoanalysis today, and coedits the online open-access journal *Penumbr(a): A Journal of Psychoanalysis & Modernity* (penumbrajournal.org).

**Daniel Wilson** is an independent scholar who lives in Montreal. He has a PhD in English literature from Cornell University. He has published articles on topics including the Freudian Thing, the role of nineteenth-century energetics in Freud's metapsychology, and Freud's Lamarckism. He is a member of Gifric and of the École freudienne du Québec. He works in private practice with autistic children and children with language delays.

# Index